Tamaki Nozomu Presents Dance In The Vampire Bund 7

ダンス イン ザ ヴァンパイアバンド

7

環 望

Der Mensch ist gegen sich selbst,

gegen Auskundschaftung und Belagerung durch sich

selber sehr gut verteidigt,

er vermag gewöhnlich nicht mehr von sich

als seine Außenwerk wahzunehmen.

Die eigentliche Festung ist ihm unzugänglich,

selbst unsichtbar es sei denn, daß Freunde

und Feinde die Verräter machen und ihn selber auf geheimem Weg hineinführen.

Mankind is a species which surrounds its innermost self with high, strong walls. Should he ever attempt to seek out and overcome this barrier himself, he is repulsed almost immediately. Thus it is impossible for him to see aught but those towering walls which surround him. The castle hidden within lies not only unapproachable, but all but invisible.

However, should a friend —or perhaps an enemy— play the role of traitor and lead him through secret passageways to the castle beyond, then the story may be different.

Nietzsche, Menschliches Allzumenschliche

Dance In The Vampire Bund 7

Contents

Chapter 38: Demon Seed
3

Chapter 39: Crest of the Wolf
27

Chapter 40: Hour of the Wolf
57

Chapter 41: An Afternoon with Wolves
91

Chapter 42: Elegy for a Wolf
121

Chapter 43: Wolf, Never Cry
153

Appendix: Dances with Wolves
195

Chapter 38: Demon Seed

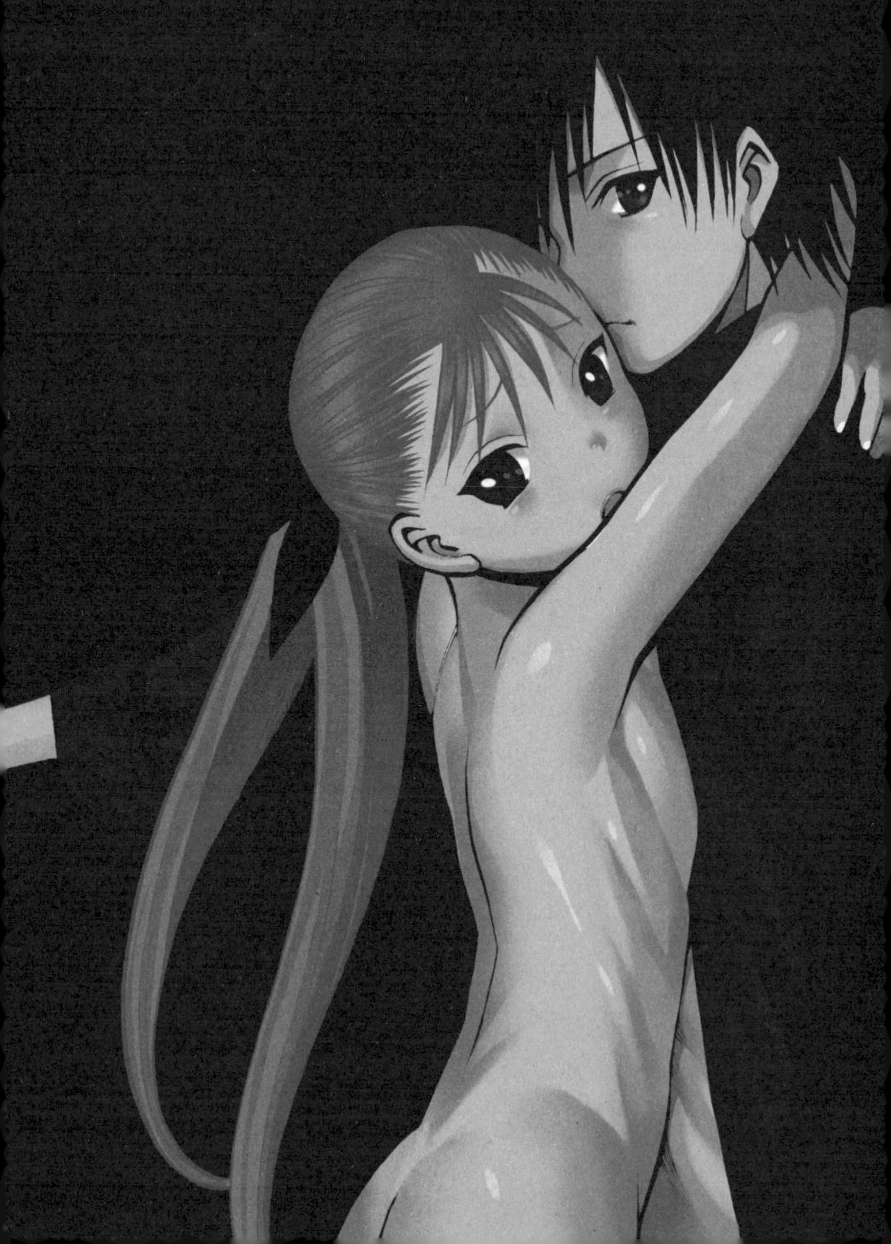

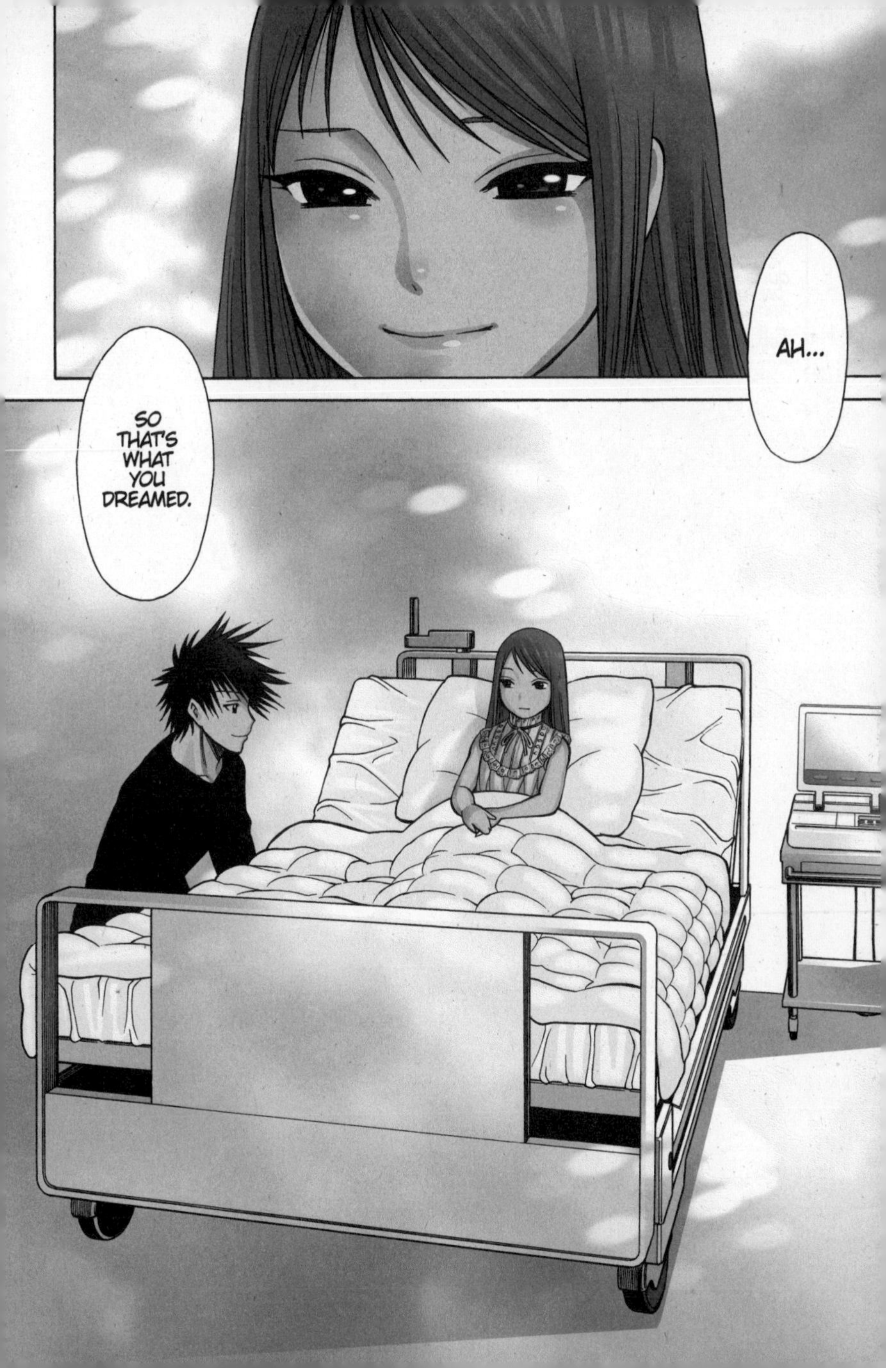
AH...
SO THAT'S WHAT YOU DREAMED.

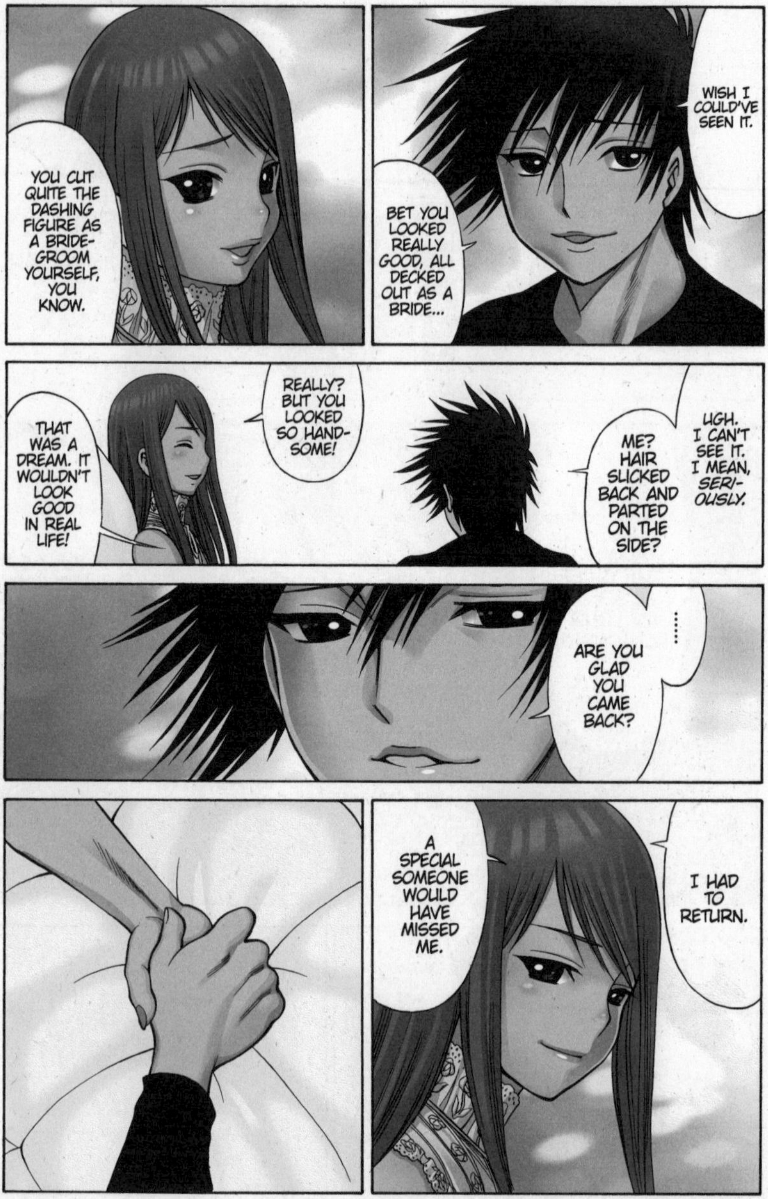
WISH I COULD'VE SEEN IT.
BET YOU LOOKED REALLY GOOD, ALL DECKED OUT AS A BRIDE...
YOU CUT QUITE THE DASHING FIGURE AS A BRIDE-GROOM YOURSELF, YOU KNOW.
UGH. I CAN'T SEE IT. I MEAN, *SERI-OUSLY.*
ME? HAIR SLICKED BACK AND PARTED ON THE SIDE?
REALLY? BUT YOU LOOKED SO HAND-SOME!
THAT WAS A DREAM. IT WOULDN'T LOOK GOOD IN REAL LIFE!
......
ARE YOU GLAD YOU CAME BACK?
I HAD TO RETURN.
A SPECIAL SOMEONE WOULD HAVE MISSED ME.

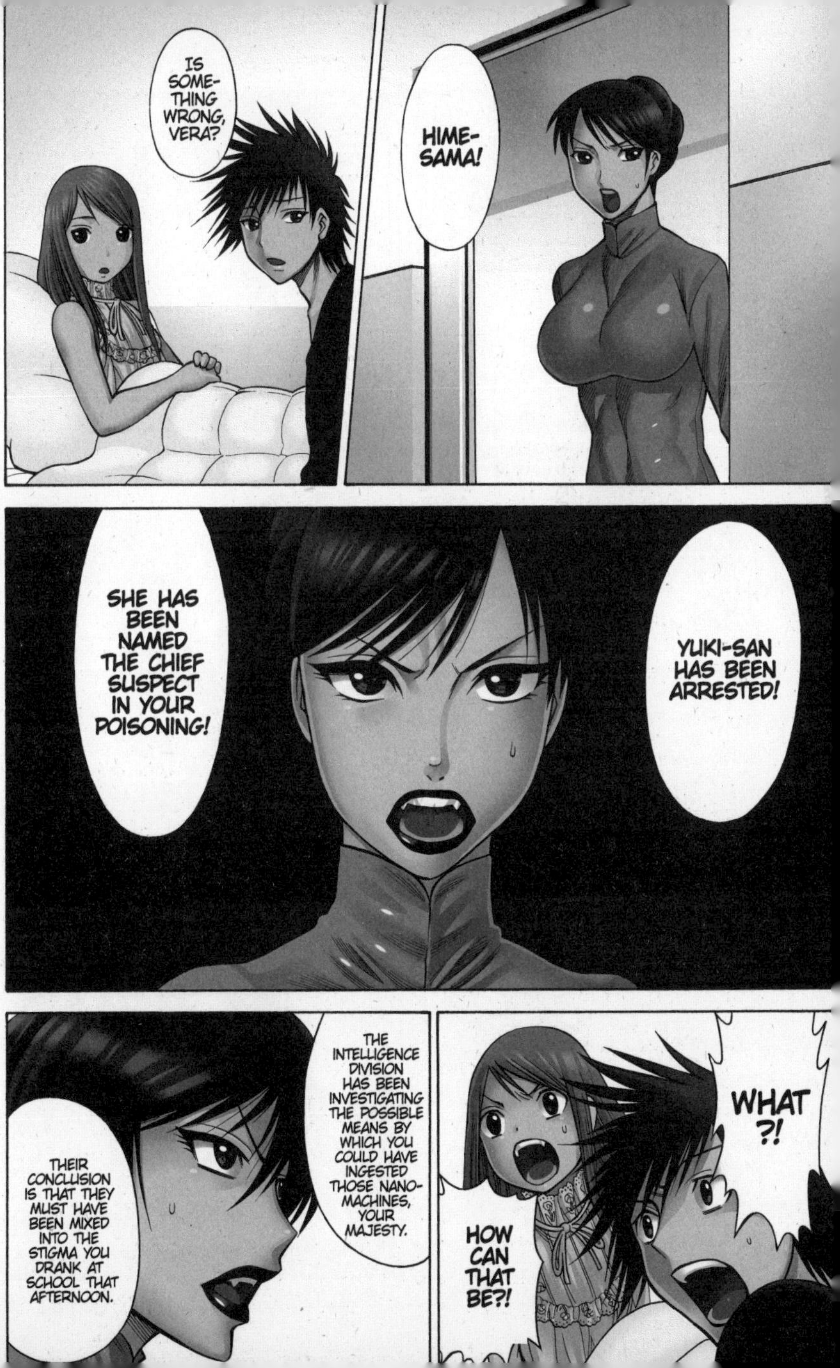
HIME-SAMA!
IS SOMETHING WRONG, VERA?
YUKI-SAN HAS BEEN ARRESTED!
SHE HAS BEEN NAMED THE CHIEF SUSPECT IN YOUR POISONING!
WHAT ?!
HOW CAN THAT BE?!
THE INTELLIGENCE DIVISION HAS BEEN INVESTIGATING THE POSSIBLE MEANS BY WHICH YOU COULD HAVE INGESTED THOSE NANO-MACHINES, YOUR MAJESTY.
THEIR CONCLUSION IS THAT THEY MUST HAVE BEEN MIXED INTO THE STIGMA YOU DRANK AT SCHOOL THAT AFTERNOON.

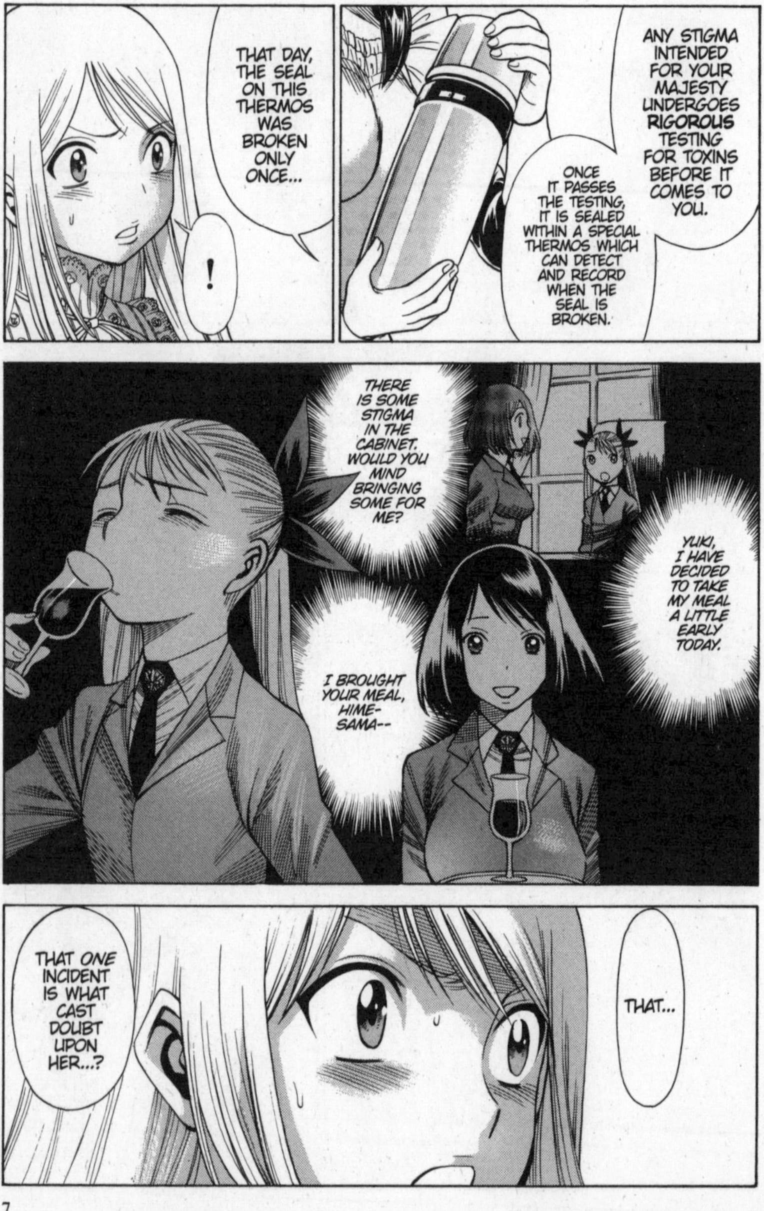
ANY STIGMA INTENDED FOR YOUR MAJESTY UNDERGOES **RIGOROUS** TESTING FOR TOXINS BEFORE IT COMES TO YOU.
ONCE IT PASSES THE TESTING, IT IS SEALED WITHIN A SPECIAL THERMOS WHICH CAN DETECT AND RECORD WHEN THE SEAL IS BROKEN.
THAT DAY, THE SEAL ON THIS THERMOS WAS BROKEN ONLY ONCE...
!
YUKI, I HAVE DECIDED TO TAKE MY MEAL A LITTLE EARLY TODAY.
THERE IS SOME STIGMA IN THE CABINET. WOULD YOU MIND BRINGING SOME FOR ME?
I BROUGHT YOUR MEAL, HIME-SAMA--
THAT...
THAT *ONE* INCIDENT IS WHAT CAST DOUBT UPON HER...?

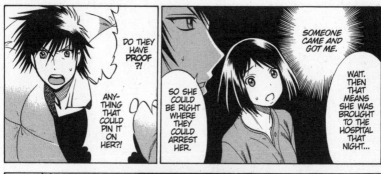

SOMEONE CAME AND GOT ME.
WAIT. THEN THAT MEANS SHE WAS BROUGHT TO THE HOSPITAL THAT NIGHT...
SO SHE COULD BE RIGHT WHERE THEY COULD ARREST HER.
DO THEY HAVE PROOF?!
ANYTHING THAT COULD PIN IT ON HER?!
NO TRACES OF THE NANOMACHINES WERE FOUND WITHIN THE THERMOS.
HOWEVER, ONCE THE NANOMACHINES WITHIN YOUR MAJESTY WERE DISABLED, THEY SELF-DESTRUCTED AND DISSOLVED. THE INTELLIGENCE DIVISION INSISTS SOMETHING SIMILAR MUST HAVE HAPPENED TO THE NANOMACHINES WITHIN THE THERMOS.
IT IS, OBVIOUSLY, A VERY FAR-FETCHED CONCLUSION.
WHERE IS YUKI NOW?
SHE IS CURRENTLY BEING HELD IN THE INTERROGATION ROOM AT THE STATION.
I TRUST THAT NO ONE HAS YET QUESTIONED HER?
OF COURSE NOT.
I TOOK THE LIBERTY OF ASSIGNING BEOWULF TO PROTECT HER, UNDER THE PRETENSE OF GUARDING AGAINST HER ESCAPE.
I BELIEVE SHE IS QUITE SAFE FOR THE MOMENT. HOWEVER...

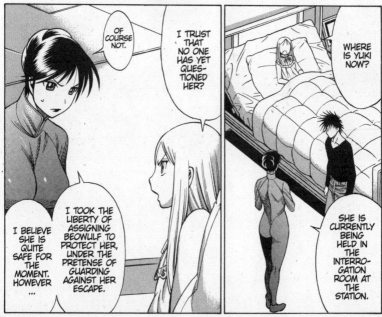

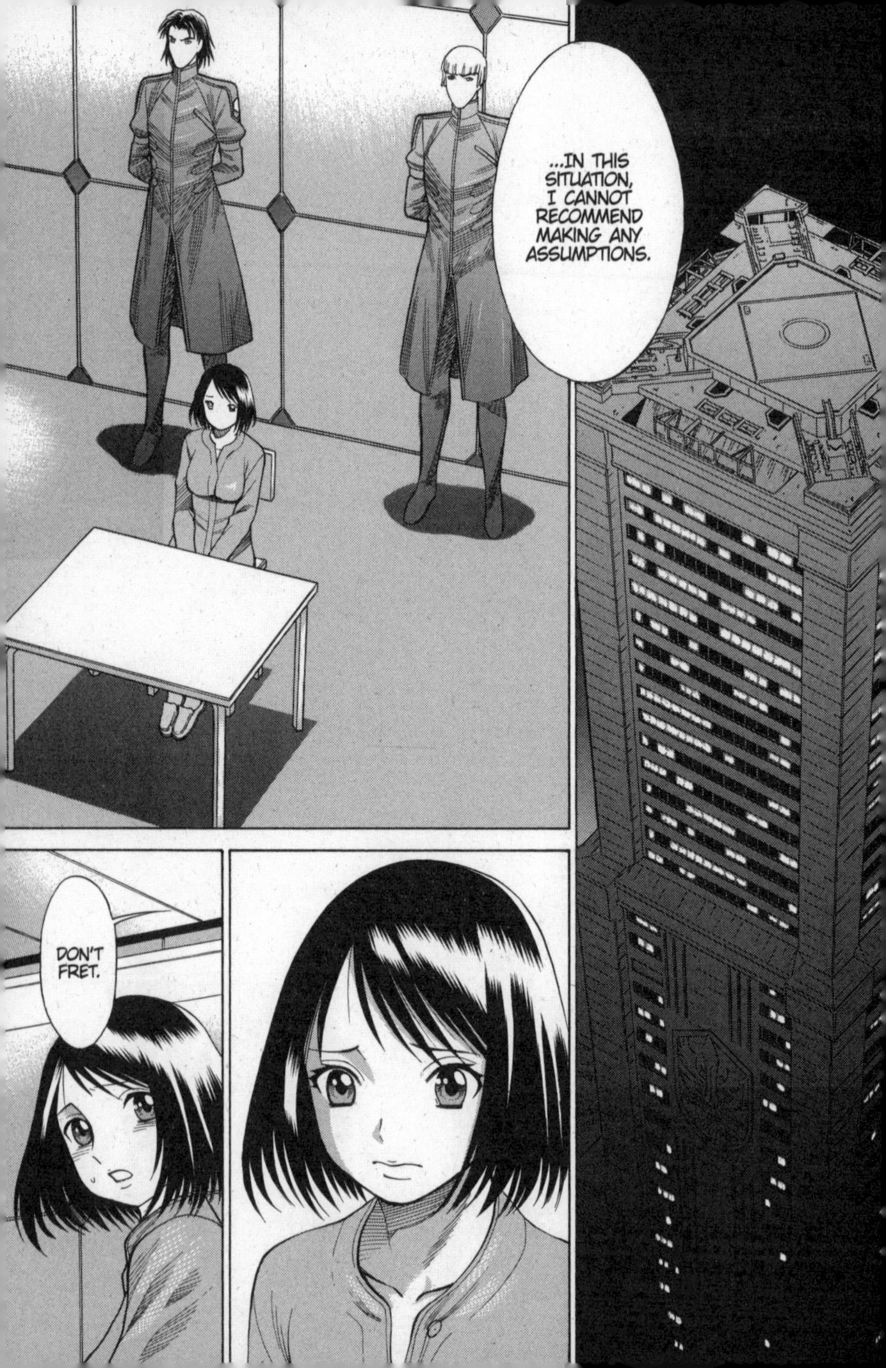
...IN THIS SITUATION, I CANNOT RECOMMEND MAKING ANY ASSUMPTIONS.
DON'T FRET.

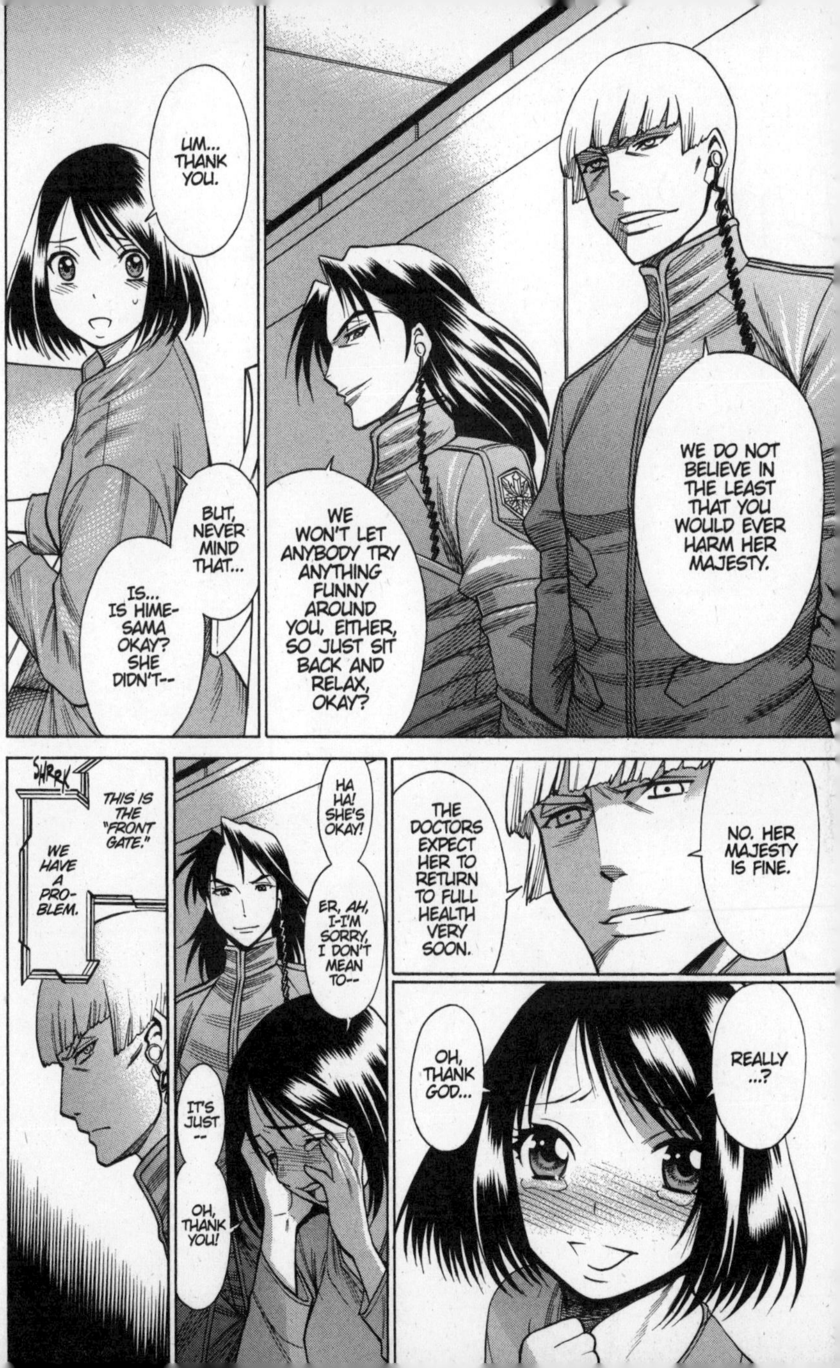
WE DO NOT BELIEVE IN THE LEAST THAT YOU WOULD EVER HARM HER MAJESTY.
WE WON'T LET ANYBODY TRY ANYTHING FUNNY AROUND YOU, EITHER, SO JUST SIT BACK AND RELAX, OKAY?
UM... THANK YOU.
BUT, NEVER MIND THAT...
IS... IS HIME-SAMA OKAY? SHE DIDN'T--
NO. HER MAJESTY IS FINE.
THE DOCTORS EXPECT HER TO RETURN TO FULL HEALTH VERY SOON.
REALLY ...?
OH, THANK GOD...
HA HA! SHE'S OKAY!
ER, AH, I-I'M SORRY, I DON'T MEAN TO--
IT'S JUST --
OH, THANK YOU!
SHRRK
THIS IS THE "FRONT GATE."
WE HAVE A PRO-BLEM.

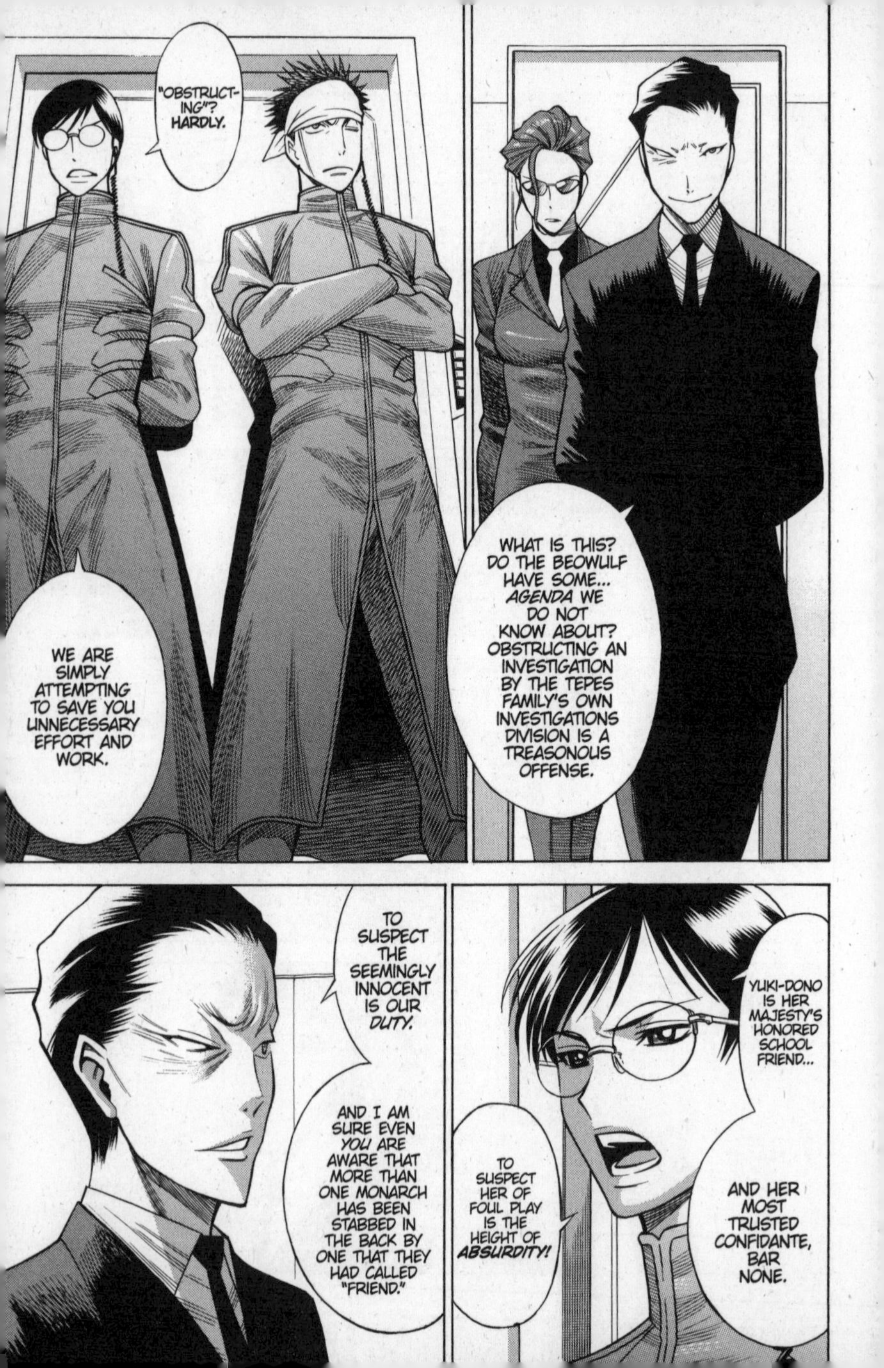
WHAT IS THIS? DO THE BEOWULF HAVE SOME... *AGENDA* WE DO NOT KNOW ABOUT? OBSTRUCTING AN INVESTIGATION BY THE TEPES FAMILY'S OWN INVESTIGATIONS DIVISION IS A TREASONOUS OFFENSE.
"OBSTRUCTING"? HARDLY.
WE ARE SIMPLY ATTEMPTING TO SAVE YOU UNNECESSARY EFFORT AND WORK.
YUKI-DONO IS HER MAJESTY'S HONORED SCHOOL FRIEND...
AND HER MOST TRUSTED CONFIDANTE, BAR NONE.
TO SUSPECT HER OF FOUL PLAY IS THE HEIGHT OF ***ABSURDITY!***
TO SUSPECT THE SEEMINGLY INNOCENT IS OUR *DUTY.*
AND I AM SURE EVEN *YOU* ARE AWARE THAT MORE THAN ONE MONARCH HAS BEEN STABBED IN THE BACK BY ONE THAT THEY HAD CALLED "FRIEND."

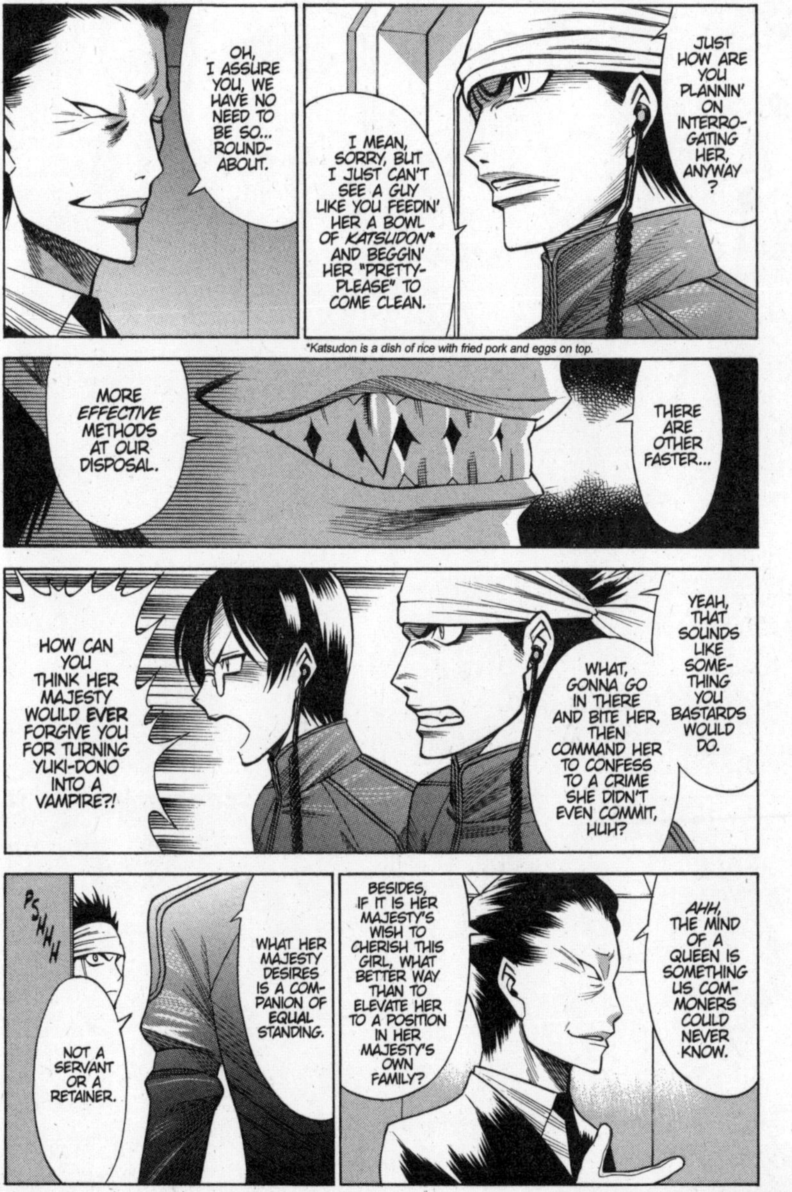
JUST HOW ARE YOU PLANNIN' ON INTERRO-GATING HER, ANYWAY?
I MEAN, SORRY, BUT I JUST CAN'T SEE A GUY LIKE YOU FEEDIN' HER A BOWL OF *KATSUDON** AND BEGGIN' HER "PRETTY-PLEASE" TO COME CLEAN.
OH, I ASSURE YOU, WE HAVE NO NEED TO BE SO... ROUND-ABOUT.
THERE ARE OTHER FASTER...
MORE *EFFECTIVE* METHODS AT OUR DISPOSAL.
YEAH, THAT SOUNDS LIKE SOME-THING YOU BASTARDS WOULD DO.
WHAT, GONNA GO IN THERE AND BITE HER, THEN COMMAND HER TO CONFESS TO A CRIME SHE DIDN'T EVEN COMMIT, HUH?
HOW CAN YOU THINK HER MAJESTY WOULD EVER FORGIVE YOU FOR TURNING YUKI-DONO INTO A VAMPIRE?!
AHH, THE MIND OF A QUEEN IS SOMETHING US COM-MONERS COULD NEVER KNOW.
BESIDES, IF IT IS HER MAJESTY'S WISH TO CHERISH THIS GIRL, WHAT BETTER WAY THAN TO ELEVATE HER TO A POSITION IN HER MAJESTY'S OWN FAMILY?
WHAT HER MAJESTY DESIRES IS A COM-PANION OF EQUAL STANDING.
NOT A SERVANT OR A RETAINER.
PSHHH

**Katsudon is a dish of rice with fried pork and eggs on top.*

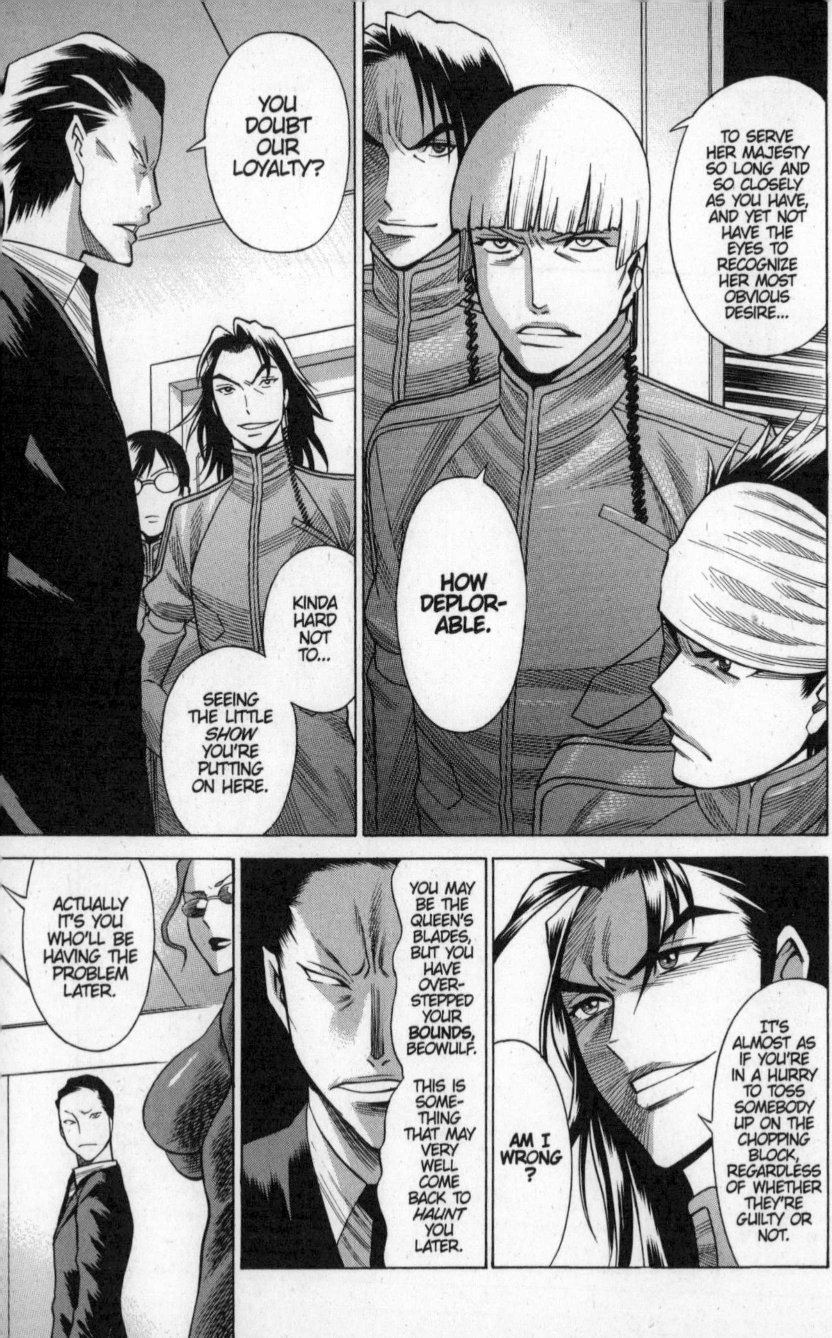
TO SERVE HER MAJESTY SO LONG AND SO CLOSELY AS YOU HAVE, AND YET NOT HAVE THE EYES TO RECOGNIZE HER MOST OBVIOUS DESIRE...
HOW DEPLOR-ABLE.
YOU DOUBT OUR LOYALTY?
KINDA HARD NOT TO...
SEEING THE LITTLE *SHOW* YOU'RE PUTTING ON HERE.
IT'S ALMOST AS IF YOU'RE IN A HURRY TO TOSS SOMEBODY UP ON THE CHOPPING BLOCK, REGARDLESS OF WHETHER THEY'RE GUILTY OR NOT.
AM I WRONG?
YOU MAY BE THE QUEEN'S BLADES, BUT YOU HAVE OVER-STEPPED YOUR BOUNDS, BEOWULF.
THIS IS SOME-THING THAT MAY VERY WELL COME BACK TO *HAUNT* YOU LATER.
ACTUALLY IT'S YOU WHO'LL BE HAVING THE PROBLEM LATER.

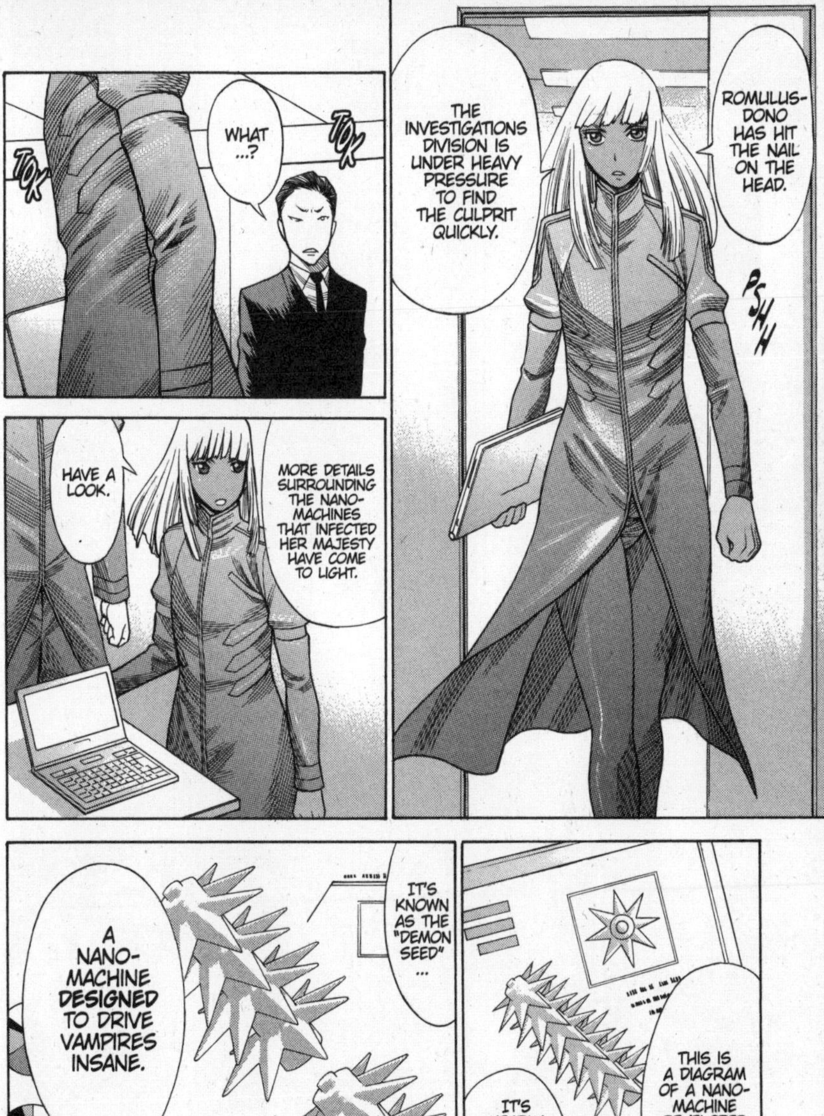
ROMULUS-DONO HAS HIT THE NAIL ON THE HEAD.
THE INVESTIGATIONS DIVISION IS UNDER HEAVY PRESSURE TO FIND THE CULPRIT QUICKLY.
PSHH
TOK
WHAT ...?
TOK
MORE DETAILS SURROUNDING THE NANO-MACHINES THAT INFECTED HER MAJESTY HAVE COME TO LIGHT.
HAVE A LOOK.
THIS IS A DIAGRAM OF A NANO-MACHINE DEVELOPED ONLY A FEW YEARS AGO.
IT'S NEARLY IDENTICAL TO THE SPECIMEN USED ON HER MAJESTY.
IT'S KNOWN AS THE "DEMON SEED" ...
A NANO-MACHINE DESIGNED TO DRIVE VAMPIRES INSANE.

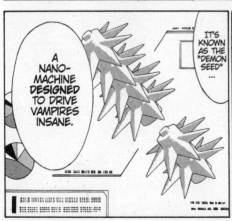

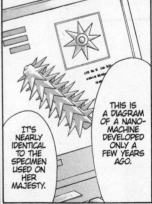

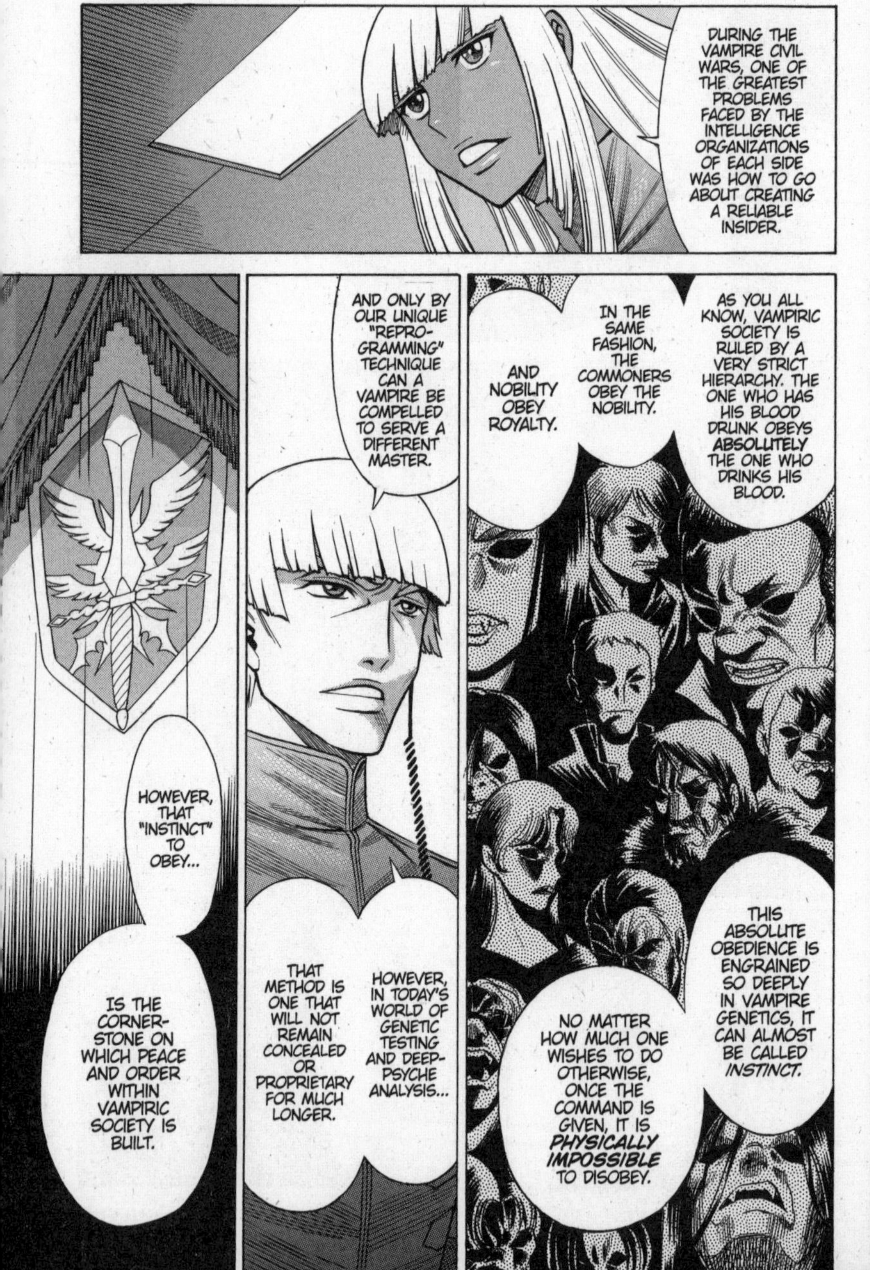
DURING THE VAMPIRE CIVIL WARS, ONE OF THE GREATEST PROBLEMS FACED BY THE INTELLIGENCE ORGANIZATIONS OF EACH SIDE WAS HOW TO GO ABOUT CREATING A RELIABLE INSIDER.
AS YOU ALL KNOW, VAMPIRIC SOCIETY IS RULED BY A VERY STRICT HIERARCHY. THE ONE WHO HAS HIS BLOOD DRUNK OBEYS ABSOLUTELY THE ONE WHO DRINKS HIS BLOOD.
IN THE SAME FASHION, THE COMMONERS OBEY THE NOBILITY.
AND NOBILITY OBEY ROYALTY.
THIS ABSOLUTE OBEDIENCE IS ENGRAINED SO DEEPLY IN VAMPIRE GENETICS, IT CAN ALMOST BE CALLED *INSTINCT.*
NO MATTER HOW MUCH ONE WISHES TO DO OTHERWISE, ONCE THE COMMAND IS GIVEN, IT IS ***PHYSICALLY IMPOSSIBLE*** TO DISOBEY.
AND ONLY BY OUR UNIQUE "REPROGRAMMING" TECHNIQUE CAN A VAMPIRE BE COMPELLED TO SERVE A DIFFERENT MASTER.
HOWEVER, IN TODAY'S WORLD OF GENETIC TESTING AND DEEP-PSYCHE ANALYSIS...
THAT METHOD IS ONE THAT WILL NOT REMAIN CONCEALED OR PROPRIETARY FOR MUCH LONGER.
HOWEVER, THAT "INSTINCT" TO OBEY...
IS THE CORNERSTONE ON WHICH PEACE AND ORDER WITHIN VAMPIRIC SOCIETY IS BUILT.

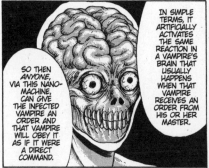

AND IT'S FOR PRECISELY THAT REASON THIS NANO-MACHINE WAS DEVEL-OPED.
IT IS DESIGNED TO LODGE ITSELF IN THE HOST VAMPIRE'S BRAIN AND EMIT A VERY PRECISE TYPE OF SIGNAL TO A VERY **SPECIFIC** PORTION OF THE BRAIN.
IN SIMPLE TERMS, IT ARTIFICIALLY ACTIVATES THE SAME REACTION IN A VAMPIRE'S BRAIN THAT USUALLY HAPPENS WHEN THAT VAMPIRE RECEIVES AN ORDER FROM HIS OR HER MASTER.
SO THEN *ANYONE*, VIA THIS NANO-MACHINE, CAN GIVE THE INFECTED VAMPIRE AN ORDER AND THAT VAMPIRE WILL OBEY IT AS IF IT WERE A DIRECT COMMAND.
THE VAMPIRE WILL EVEN PERCEIVE THE ORDER AS ONE COMING *FROM* THEIR MASTER, AND HENCE THEY DON'T EVEN REALIZE THAT THEIR ACTS ARE ACTUALLY ONES OF BETRAYAL AND SABOTAGE.
EVEN WORSE, THE INFECTED VAMPIRES ARE NOT TRULY "REPROGRAMMED," PER SE, SO ALL OF OUR CHECKS ESTABLISHED TO DETECT REPROGRAMMED VAMPIRES WILL MISS THE NANOMACHINES.
IN SHORT, THIS DEVICE TRULY IS THE ULTIMATE WEAPON THAT CAN **DESTROY** VAMPIRE SOCIETY AS WE KNOW IT.
THE ONES THAT INFECTED HER MAJESTY, HOWEVER, WERE NOT PRECISELY THAT VERSION. THEY WERE A CUSTOMIZED *VARIANT* DESIGNED ONLY TO SCAN HER SUBCONSCIOUS.
THE QUESTION IS... WHO WOULD DARE CREATE SUCH A DEVICE?

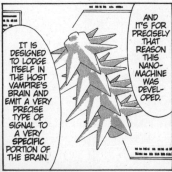

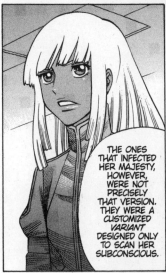

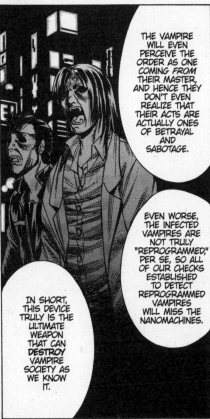

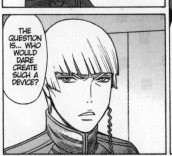

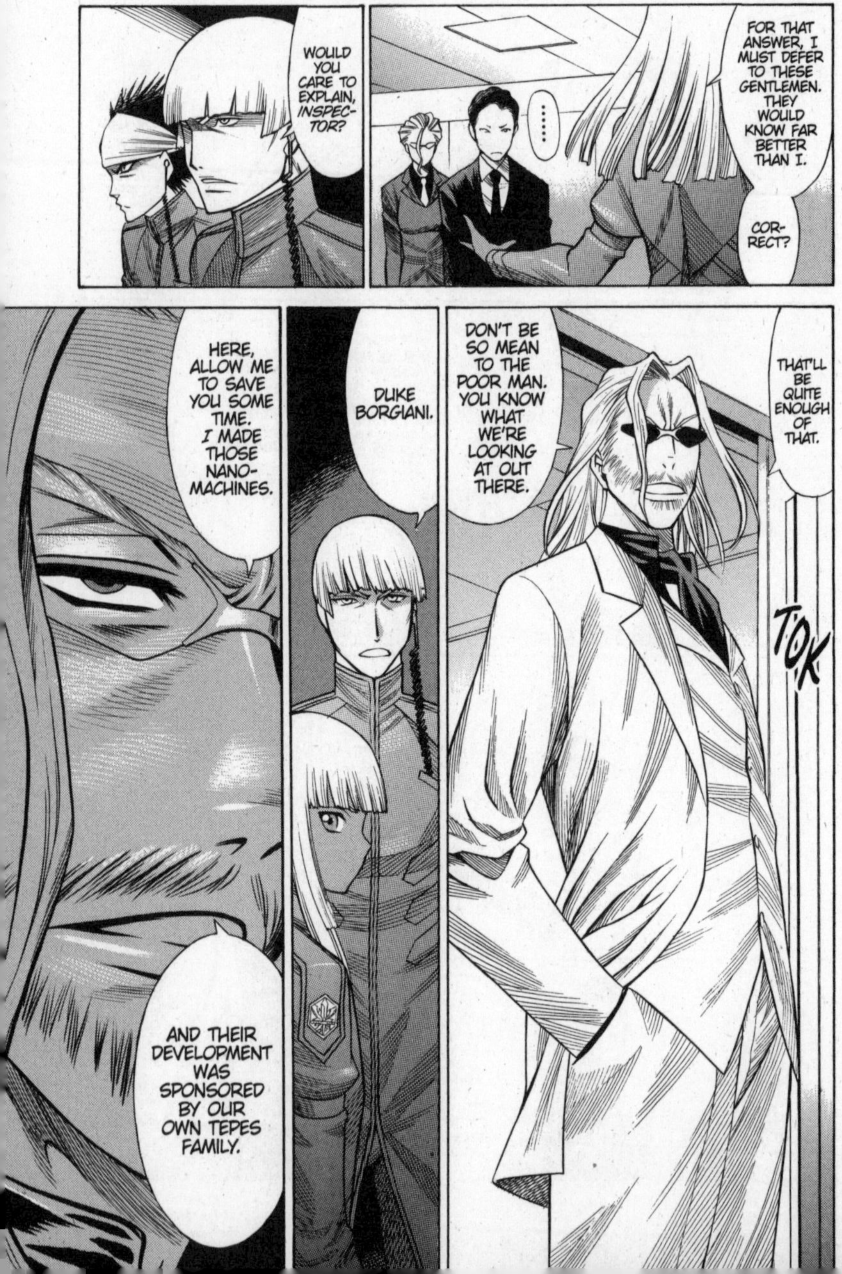
FOR THAT ANSWER, I MUST DEFER TO THESE GENTLEMEN. THEY WOULD KNOW FAR BETTER THAN I.
CORRECT?
......
WOULD YOU CARE TO EXPLAIN, *INSPECTOR?*
THAT'LL BE QUITE ENOUGH OF THAT.
TOK
DON'T BE SO MEAN TO THE POOR MAN. YOU KNOW WHAT WE'RE LOOKING AT OUT THERE.
DUKE BORGIANI.
HERE, ALLOW ME TO SAVE YOU SOME TIME. *I* MADE THOSE NANO-MACHINES.
AND THEIR DEVELOPMENT WAS SPONSORED BY OUR OWN TEPES FAMILY.

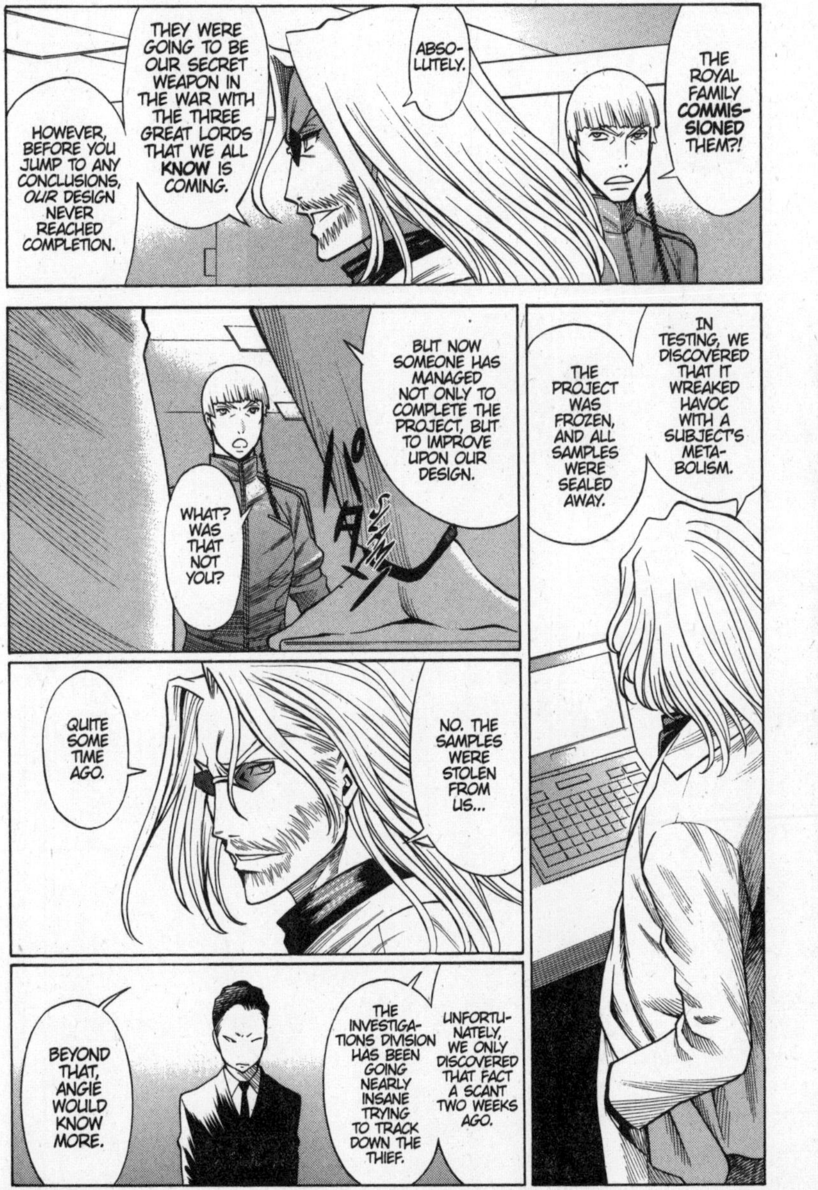
THE ROYAL FAMILY COMMISSIONED THEM?!
ABSOLUTELY.
THEY WERE GOING TO BE OUR SECRET WEAPON IN THE WAR WITH THE THREE GREAT LORDS THAT WE ALL **KNOW** IS COMING.
HOWEVER, BEFORE YOU JUMP TO ANY CONCLUSIONS, *OUR* DESIGN NEVER REACHED COMPLETION.
IN TESTING, WE DISCOVERED THAT IT WREAKED HAVOC WITH A SUBJECT'S METABOLISM.
THE PROJECT WAS FROZEN, AND ALL SAMPLES WERE SEALED AWAY.
BUT NOW SOMEONE HAS MANAGED NOT ONLY TO COMPLETE THE PROJECT, BUT TO IMPROVE UPON OUR DESIGN.
SLAM
WHAT? WAS THAT NOT YOU?
NO. THE SAMPLES WERE STOLEN FROM US...
QUITE SOME TIME AGO.
UNFORTUNATELY, WE ONLY DISCOVERED THAT FACT A SCANT TWO WEEKS AGO.
THE INVESTIGATIONS DIVISION HAS BEEN GOING NEARLY INSANE TRYING TO TRACK DOWN THE THIEF.
BEYOND THAT, ANGIE WOULD KNOW MORE.

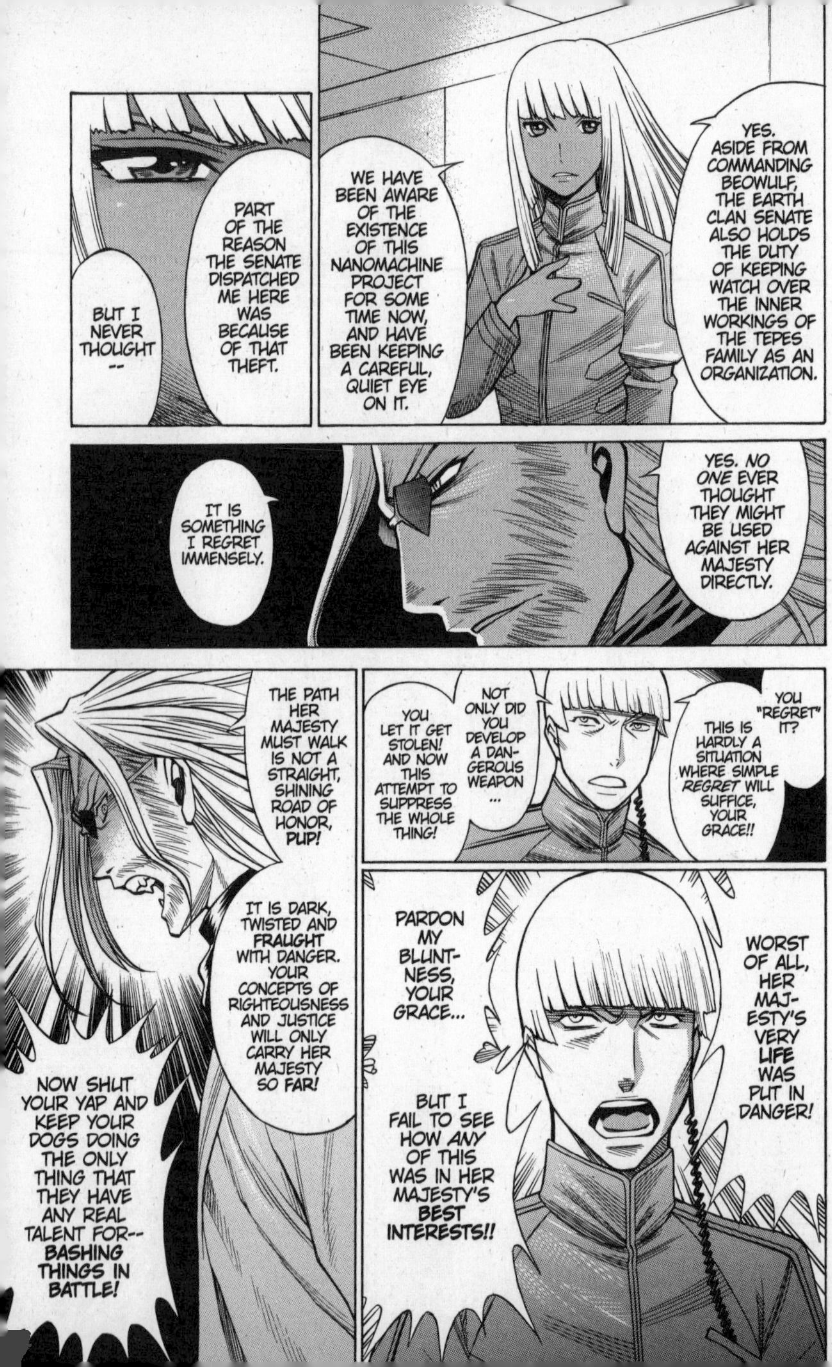
YES. ASIDE FROM COMMANDING BEOWULF, THE EARTH CLAN SENATE ALSO HOLDS THE DUTY OF KEEPING WATCH OVER THE INNER WORKINGS OF THE TEPES FAMILY AS AN ORGANIZATION.
WE HAVE BEEN AWARE OF THE EXISTENCE OF THIS NANOMACHINE PROJECT FOR SOME TIME NOW, AND HAVE BEEN KEEPING A CAREFUL, QUIET EYE ON IT.
PART OF THE REASON THE SENATE DISPATCHED ME HERE WAS BECAUSE OF THAT THEFT.
BUT I NEVER THOUGHT --
YES. *NO ONE* EVER THOUGHT THEY MIGHT BE USED AGAINST HER MAJESTY DIRECTLY.
IT IS SOMETHING I REGRET IMMENSELY.
YOU "REGRET" IT? THIS IS HARDLY A SITUATION WHERE SIMPLE *REGRET* WILL SUFFICE, YOUR GRACE!!
NOT ONLY DID YOU DEVELOP A DANGEROUS WEAPON...
YOU LET IT GET STOLEN! AND NOW THIS ATTEMPT TO SUPPRESS THE WHOLE THING!
WORST OF ALL, HER MAJESTY'S VERY **LIFE** WAS PUT IN DANGER!
PARDON MY BLUNTNESS, YOUR GRACE...
BUT I FAIL TO SEE HOW *ANY* OF THIS WAS IN HER MAJESTY'S **BEST INTERESTS!!**
THE PATH HER MAJESTY MUST WALK IS NOT A STRAIGHT, SHINING ROAD OF HONOR, **PUP!**
IT IS DARK, TWISTED AND **FRAUGHT** WITH DANGER. YOUR CONCEPTS OF RIGHTEOUSNESS AND JUSTICE WILL ONLY CARRY HER MAJESTY SO **FAR!**
NOW SHUT YOUR YAP AND KEEP YOUR DOGS DOING THE ONLY THING THAT THEY HAVE ANY REAL TALENT FOR-- **BASHING THINGS IN BATTLE!**

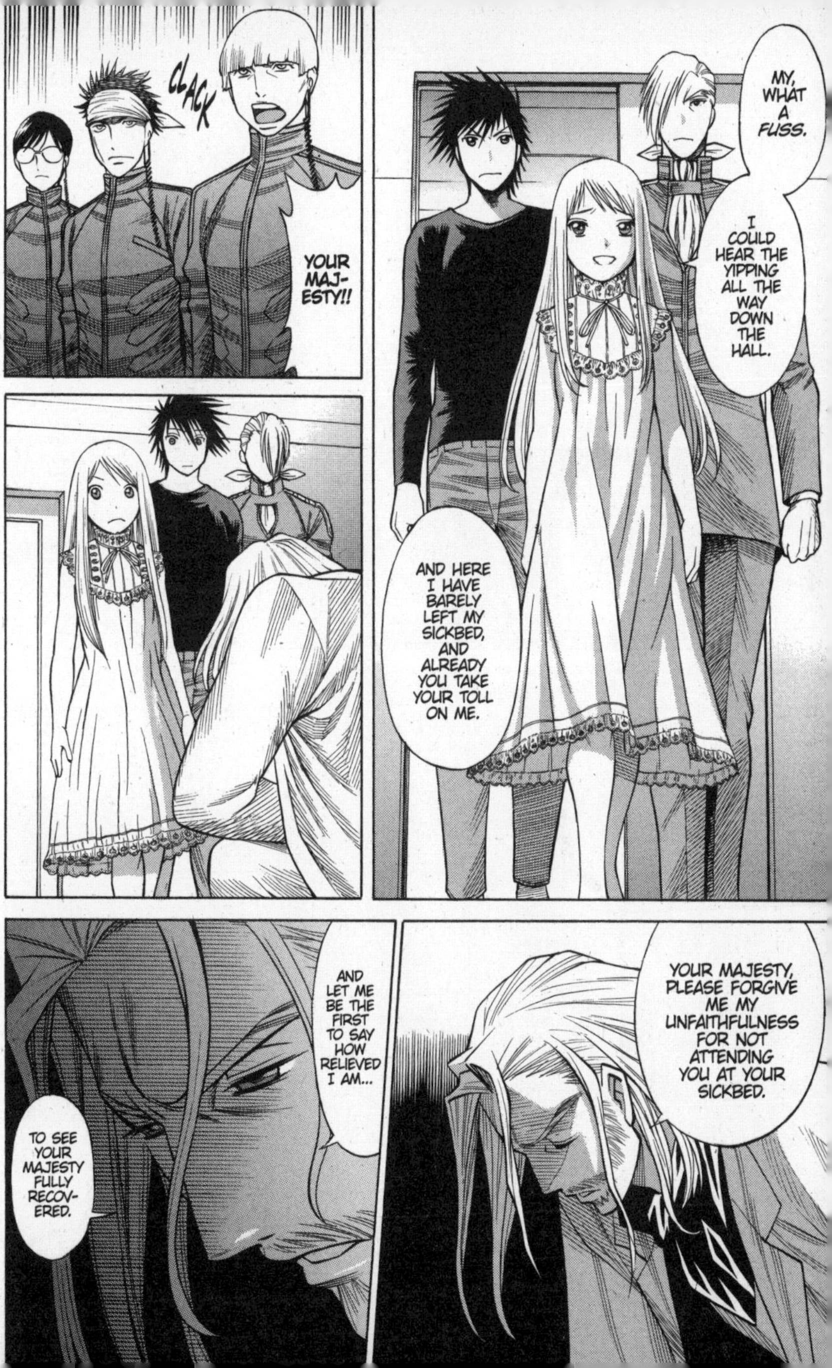
MY, WHAT A FUSS.
I COULD HEAR THE YIPPING ALL THE WAY DOWN THE HALL.
AND HERE I HAVE BARELY LEFT MY SICKBED, AND ALREADY YOU TAKE YOUR TOLL ON ME.
CLACK
YOUR MAJ-ESTY!!
YOUR MAJESTY, PLEASE FORGIVE ME MY UNFAITHFULNESS FOR NOT ATTENDING YOU AT YOUR SICKBED.
AND LET ME BE THE FIRST TO SAY HOW RELIEVED I AM...
TO SEE YOUR MAJESTY FULLY RECOV-ERED.

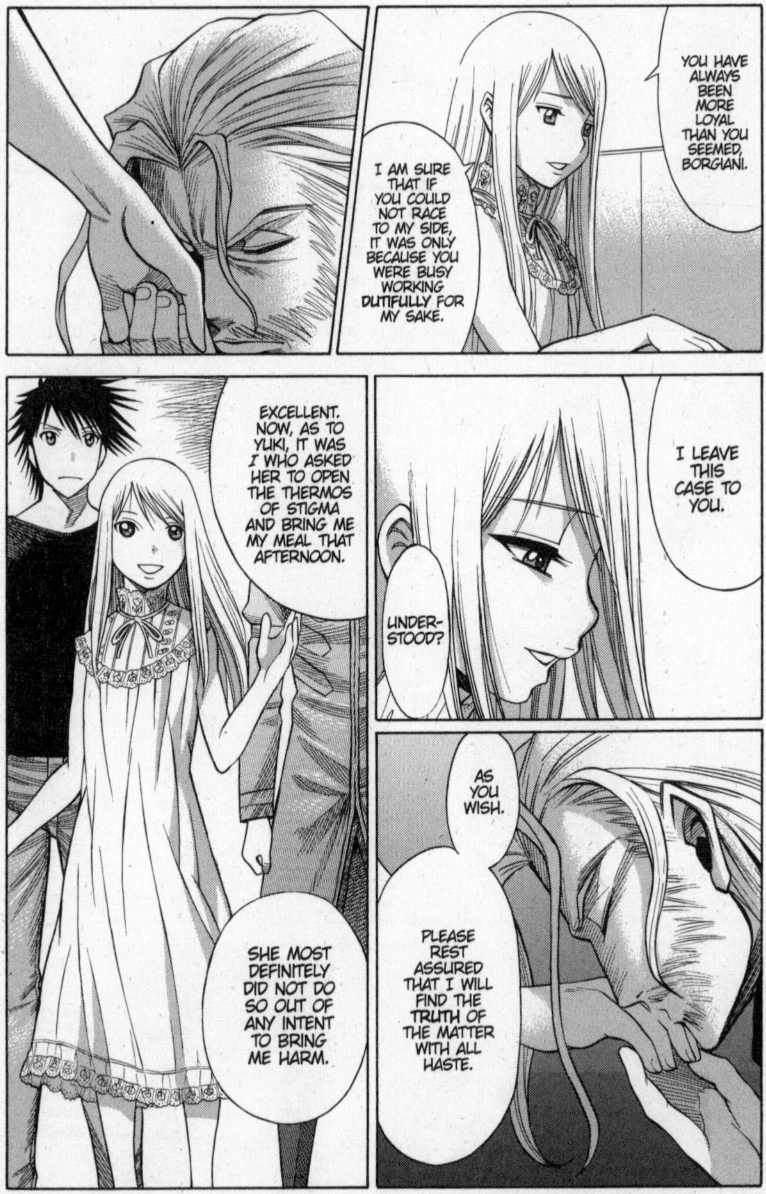
YOU HAVE ALWAYS BEEN MORE LOYAL THAN YOU SEEMED, BORGIANI.
I AM SURE THAT IF YOU COULD NOT RACE TO MY SIDE, IT WAS ONLY BECAUSE YOU WERE BUSY WORKING **DUTIFULLY** FOR MY SAKE.
I LEAVE THIS CASE TO YOU.
UNDER-STOOD?
AS YOU WISH.
PLEASE REST ASSURED THAT I WILL FIND THE **TRUTH** OF THE MATTER WITH ALL HASTE.
EXCELLENT. NOW, AS TO YUKI, IT WAS *I* WHO ASKED HER TO OPEN THE THERMOS OF STIGMA AND BRING ME MY MEAL THAT AFTERNOON.
SHE MOST DEFINITELY DID NOT DO SO OUT OF ANY INTENT TO BRING ME HARM.

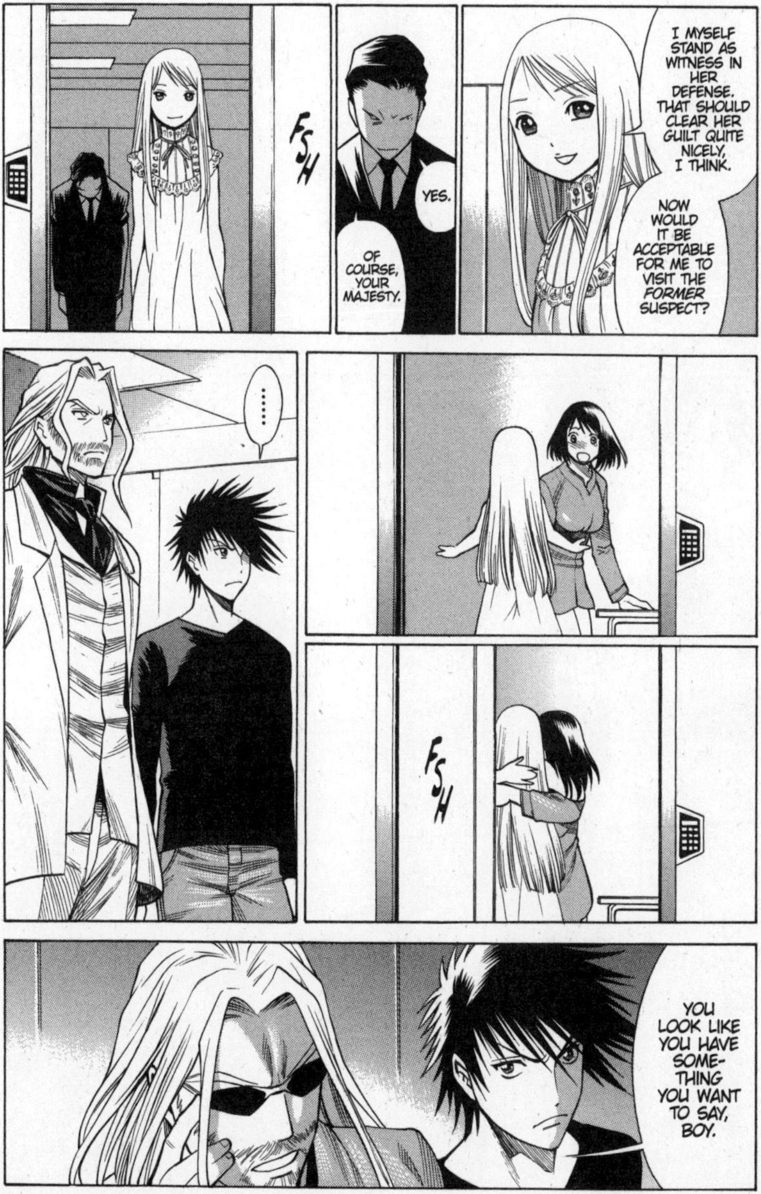
I MYSELF STAND AS WITNESS IN HER DEFENSE. THAT SHOULD CLEAR HER GUILT QUITE NICELY, I THINK.
NOW WOULD IT BE ACCEPTABLE FOR ME TO VISIT THE *FORMER* SUSPECT?
YES.
OF COURSE, YOUR MAJESTY.
FSH
FSH
......
YOU LOOK LIKE YOU HAVE SOME-THING YOU WANT TO SAY, BOY.

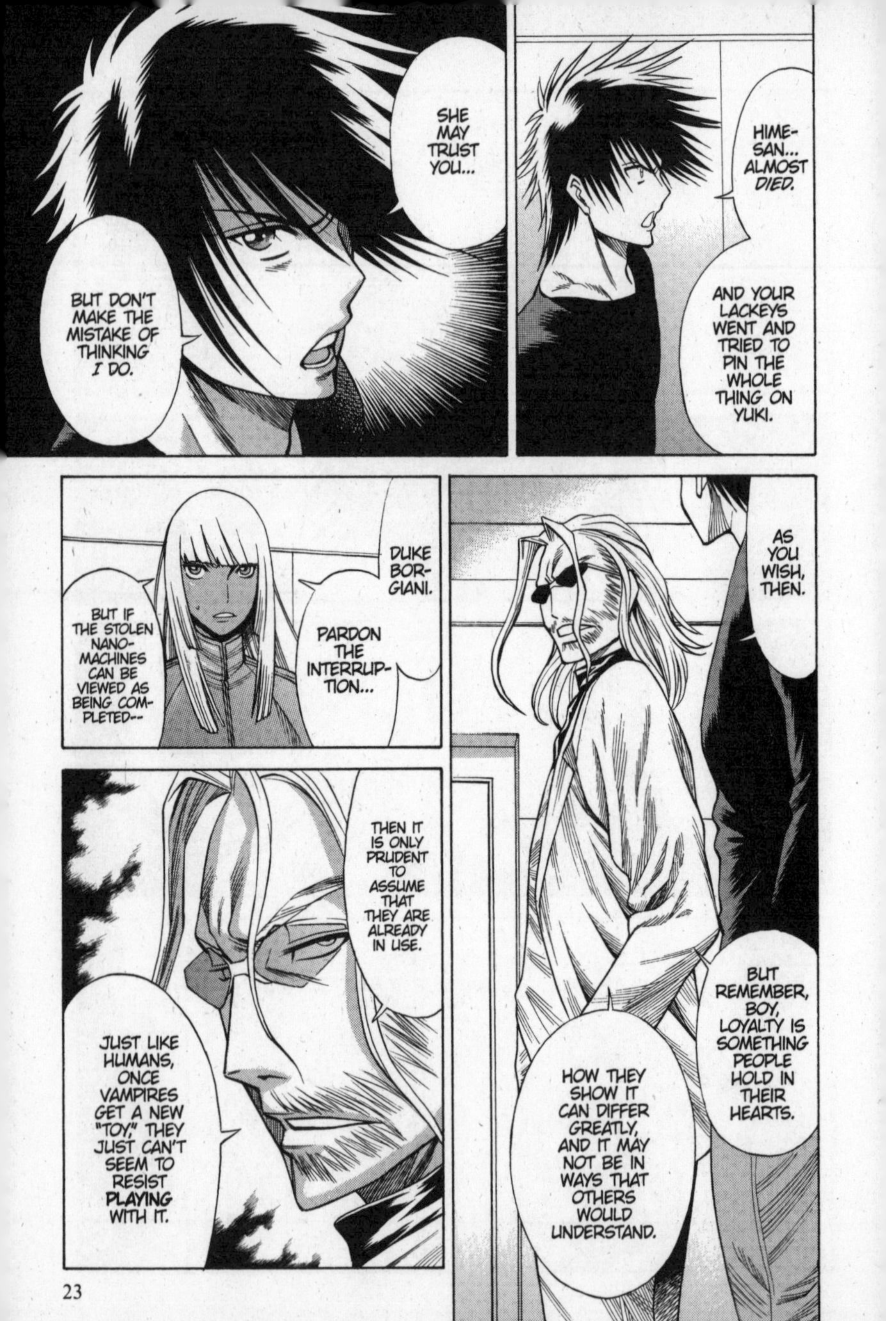
HIME-SAN... ALMOST *DIED.*
AND YOUR LACKEYS WENT AND TRIED TO PIN THE WHOLE THING ON YUKI.
SHE MAY TRUST YOU...
BUT DON'T MAKE THE MISTAKE OF THINKING *I* DO.
AS YOU WISH, THEN.
BUT REMEMBER, BOY, LOYALTY IS SOMETHING PEOPLE HOLD IN THEIR HEARTS.
HOW THEY SHOW IT CAN DIFFER GREATLY, AND IT MAY NOT BE IN WAYS THAT OTHERS WOULD UNDERSTAND.
DUKE BORGIANI.
PARDON THE INTERRUPTION...
BUT IF THE STOLEN NANO-MACHINES CAN BE VIEWED AS BEING COMPLETED--
THEN IT IS ONLY PRUDENT TO ASSUME THAT THEY ARE ALREADY IN USE.
JUST LIKE HUMANS, ONCE VAMPIRES GET A NEW "TOY," THEY JUST CAN'T SEEM TO RESIST **PLAYING** WITH IT.

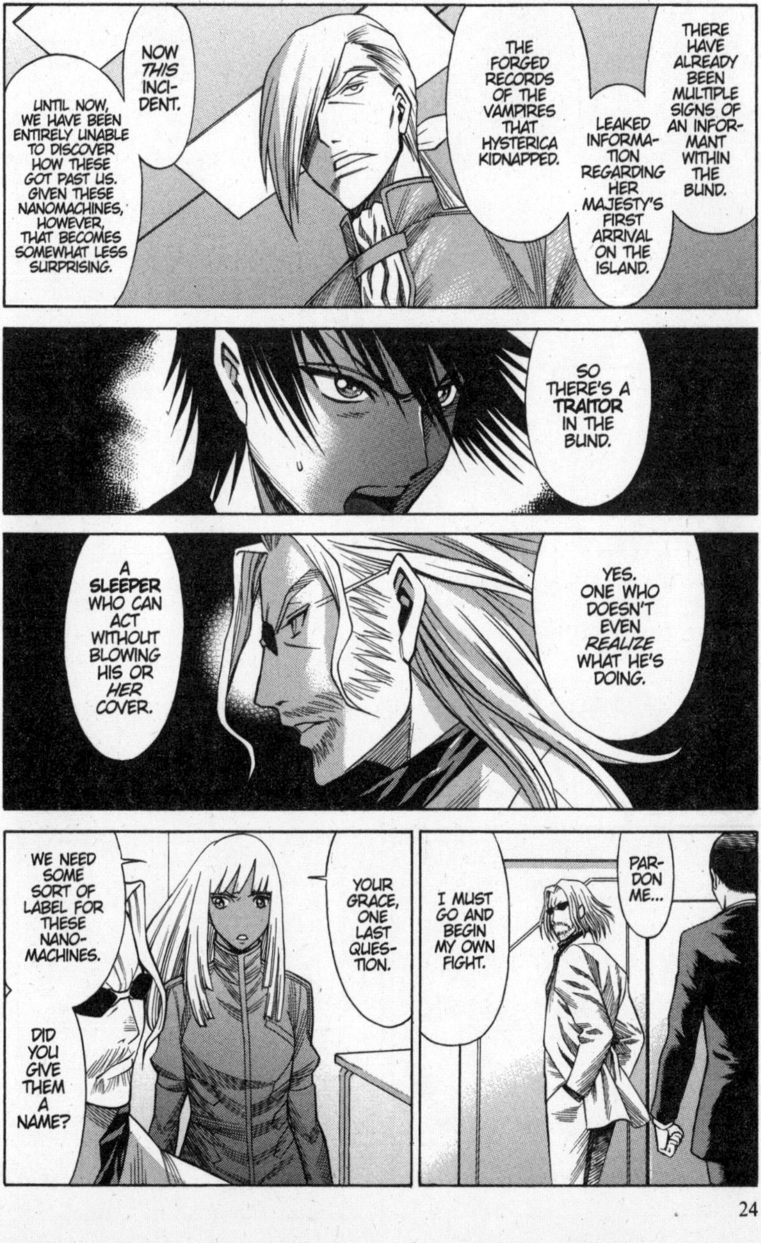
THERE HAVE ALREADY BEEN MULTIPLE SIGNS OF AN INFORMANT WITHIN THE BUND.
LEAKED INFORMATION REGARDING HER MAJESTY'S FIRST ARRIVAL ON THE ISLAND.
THE FORGED RECORDS OF THE VAMPIRES THAT HYSTERICA KIDNAPPED.
NOW *THIS* INCIDENT.
UNTIL NOW, WE HAVE BEEN ENTIRELY UNABLE TO DISCOVER HOW THESE GOT PAST US. GIVEN THESE NANOMACHINES, HOWEVER, THAT BECOMES SOMEWHAT LESS SURPRISING.
SO THERE'S A **TRAITOR** IN THE BUND.
YES. ONE WHO DOESN'T EVEN *REALIZE* WHAT HE'S DOING.
A **SLEEPER** WHO CAN ACT WITHOUT BLOWING HIS OR *HER* COVER.
PARDON ME...
I MUST GO AND BEGIN MY OWN FIGHT.
YOUR GRACE, ONE LAST QUESTION.
WE NEED SOME SORT OF LABEL FOR THESE NANOMACHINES.
DID YOU GIVE THEM A NAME?

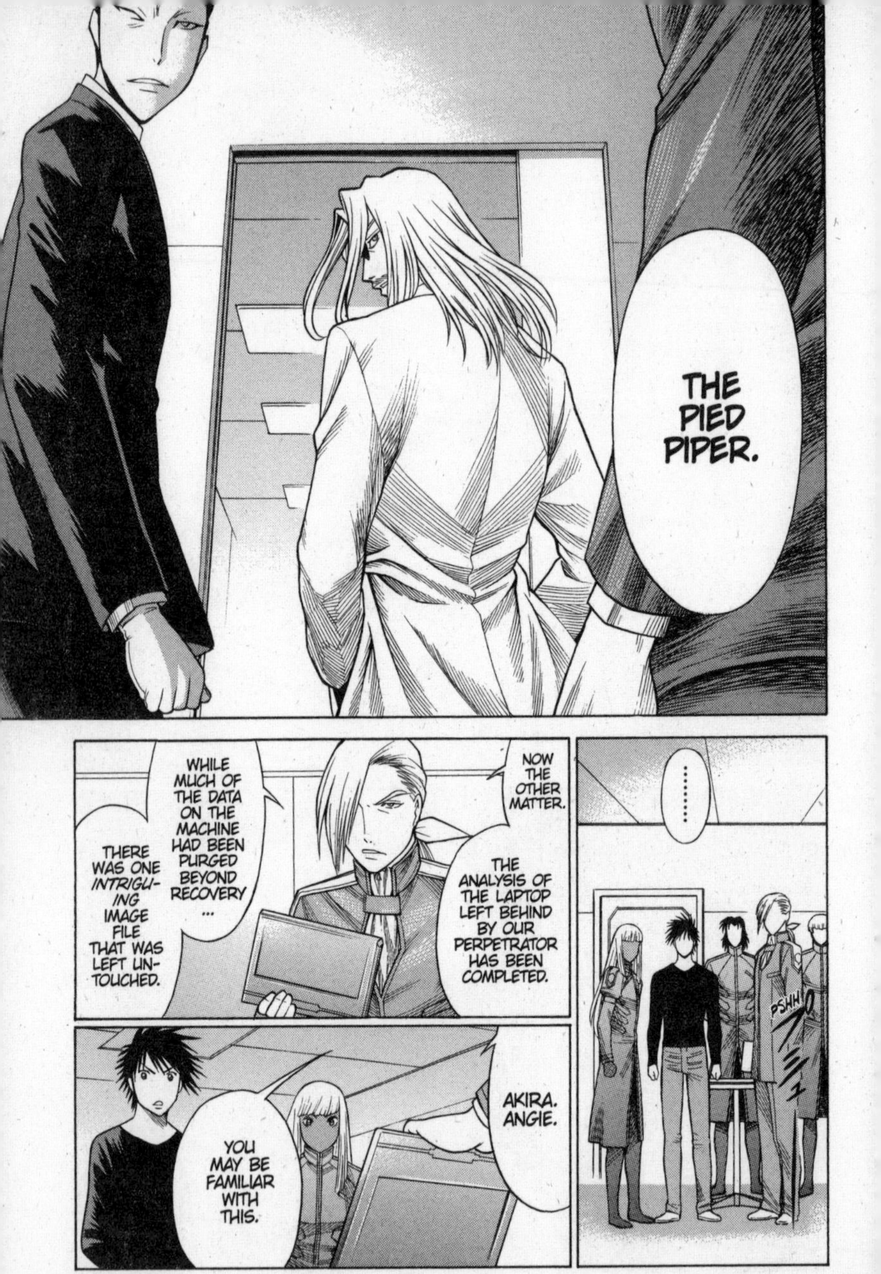
THE PIED PIPER.
......
PSHH
NOW THE OTHER MATTER.
THE ANALYSIS OF THE LAPTOP LEFT BEHIND BY OUR PERPETRATOR HAS BEEN COMPLETED.
WHILE MUCH OF THE DATA ON THE MACHINE HAD BEEN PURGED BEYOND RECOVERY ...
THERE WAS ONE *INTRIGUING* IMAGE FILE THAT WAS LEFT UNTOUCHED.
AKIRA. ANGIE.
YOU MAY BE FAMILIAR WITH THIS.

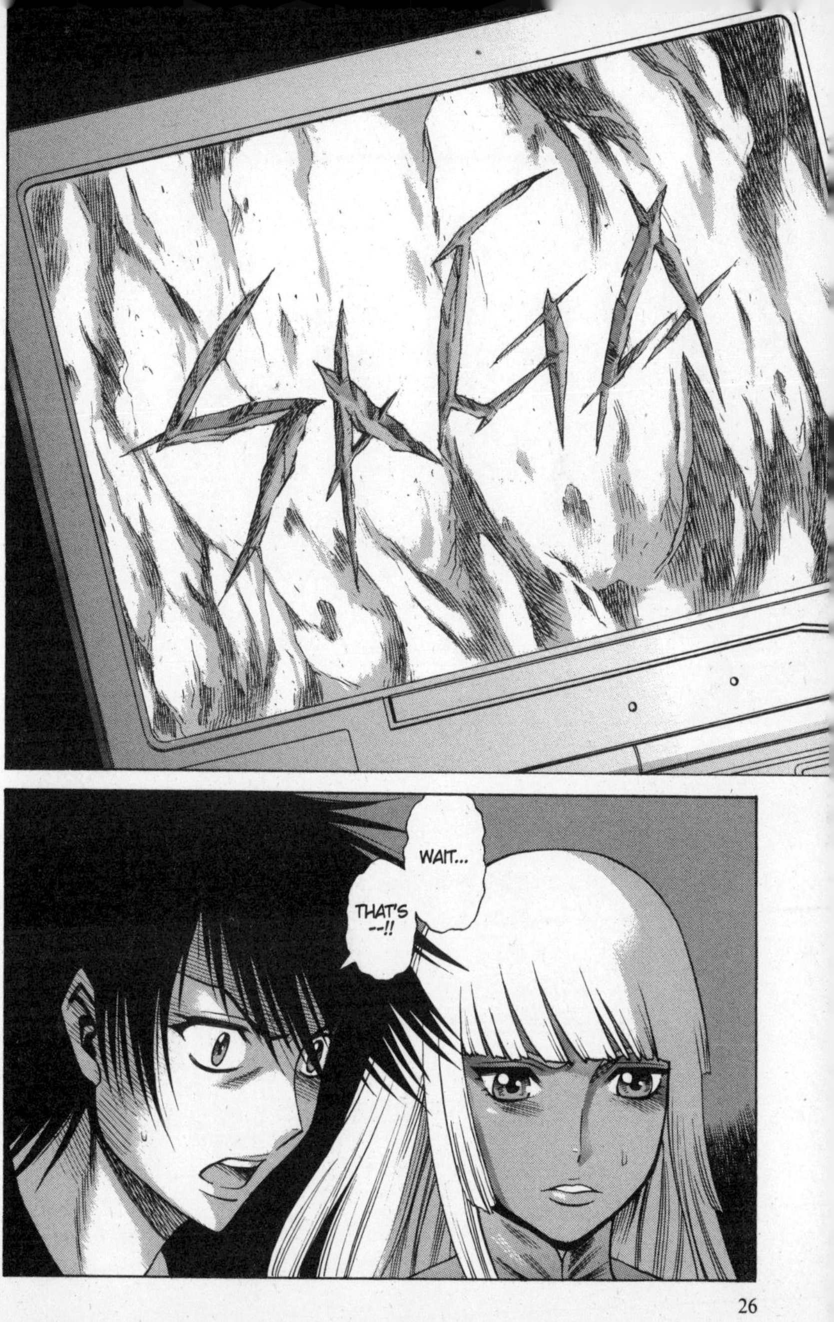
WAIT...
THAT'S --!!

Chapter 39: Crest of the Wolf

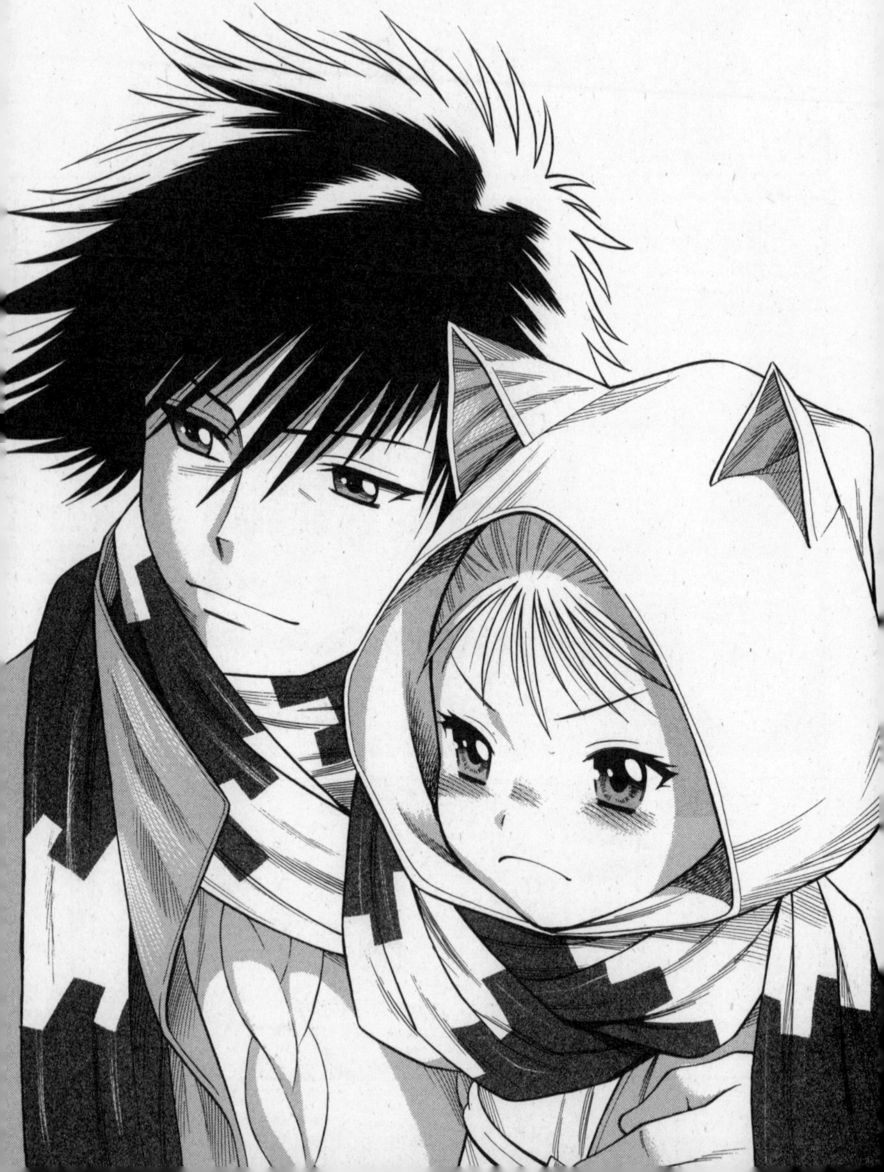

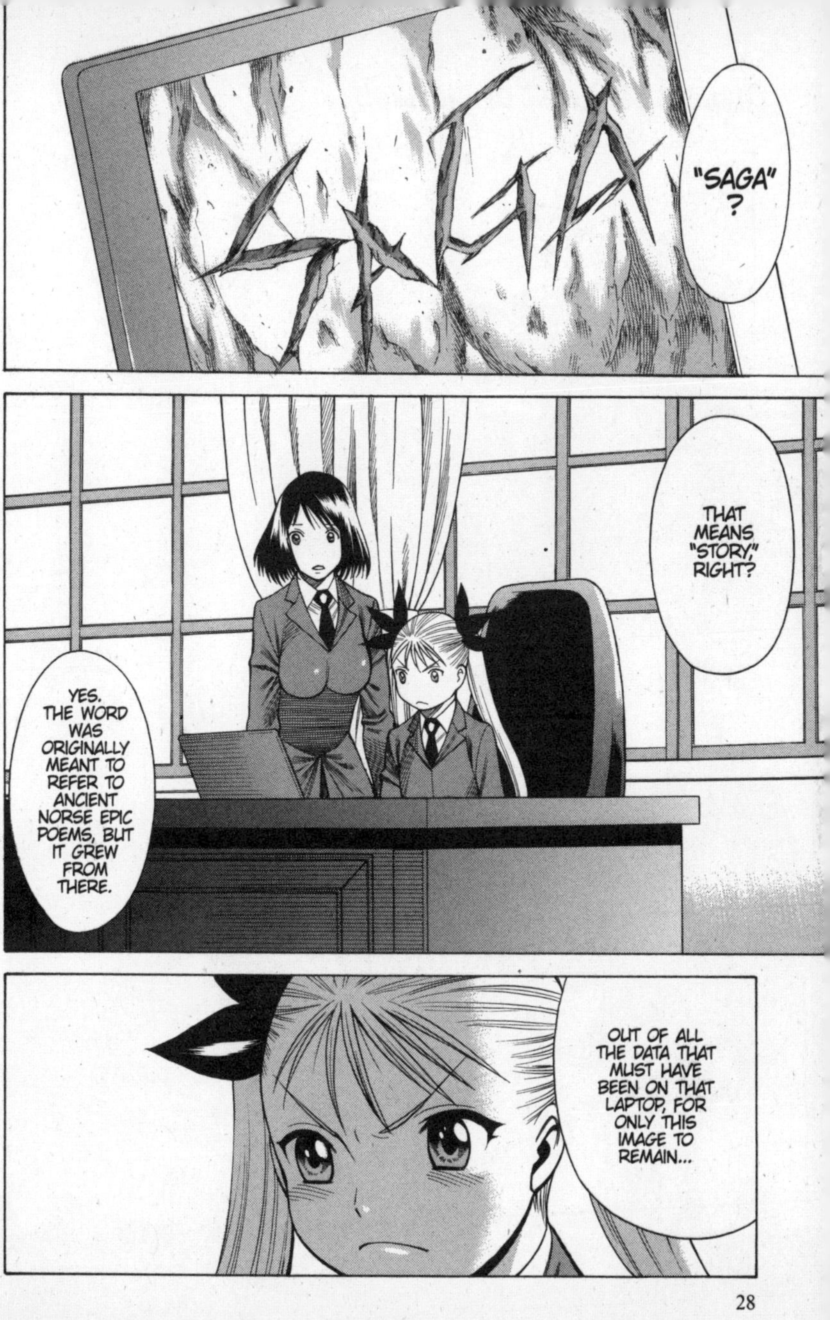
"SAGA"?
THAT MEANS "STORY," RIGHT?
YES. THE WORD WAS ORIGINALLY MEANT TO REFER TO ANCIENT NORSE EPIC POEMS, BUT IT GREW FROM THERE.
OUT OF ALL THE DATA THAT MUST HAVE BEEN ON THAT LAPTOP, FOR ONLY THIS IMAGE TO REMAIN...

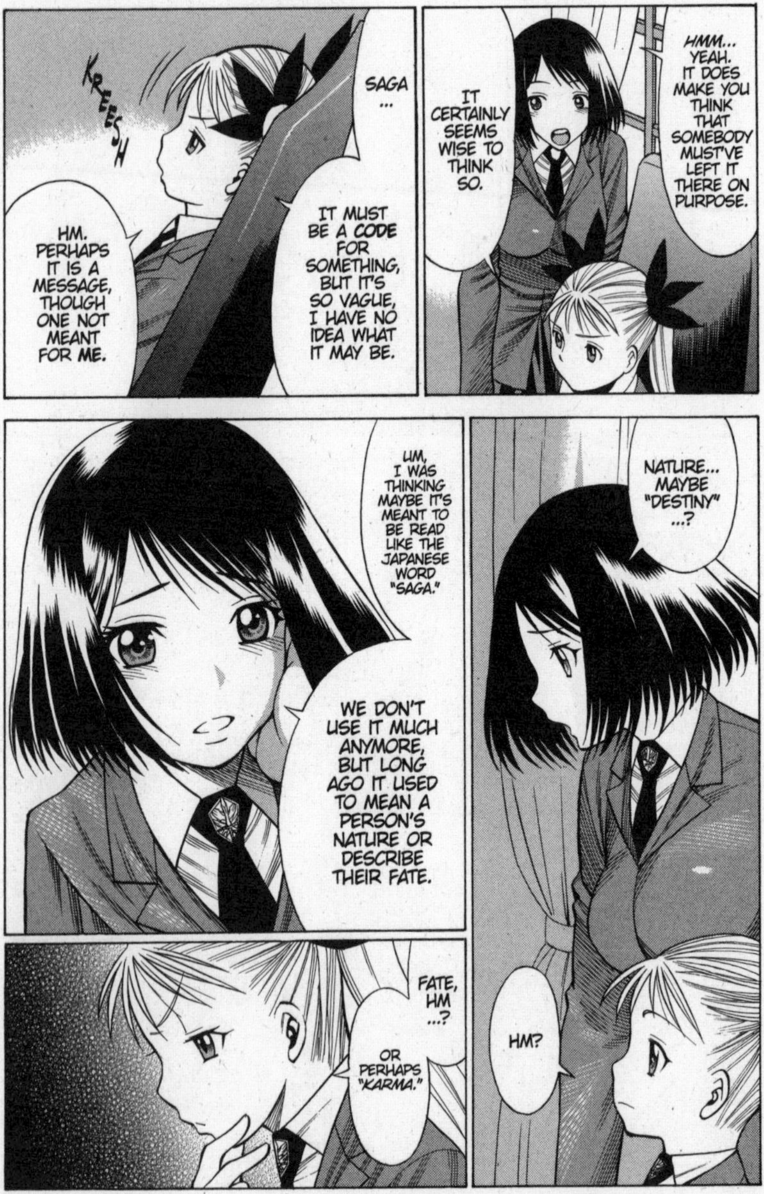
HMM... YEAH. IT DOES MAKE YOU THINK THAT SOMEBODY MUST'VE LEFT IT THERE ON PURPOSE.
IT CERTAINLY SEEMS WISE TO THINK SO.
SAGA ...
IT MUST BE A CODE FOR SOMETHING, BUT IT'S SO VAGUE, I HAVE NO IDEA WHAT IT MAY BE.
KREESH
HM. PERHAPS IT IS A MESSAGE, THOUGH ONE NOT MEANT FOR ME.
NATURE... MAYBE "DESTINY" ...?
HM?
UM, I WAS THINKING MAYBE IT'S MEANT TO BE READ LIKE THE JAPANESE WORD "SAGA."
WE DON'T USE IT MUCH ANYMORE, BUT LONG AGO IT USED TO MEAN A PERSON'S NATURE OR DESCRIBE THEIR FATE.
FATE, HM ...?
OR PERHAPS "KARMA."

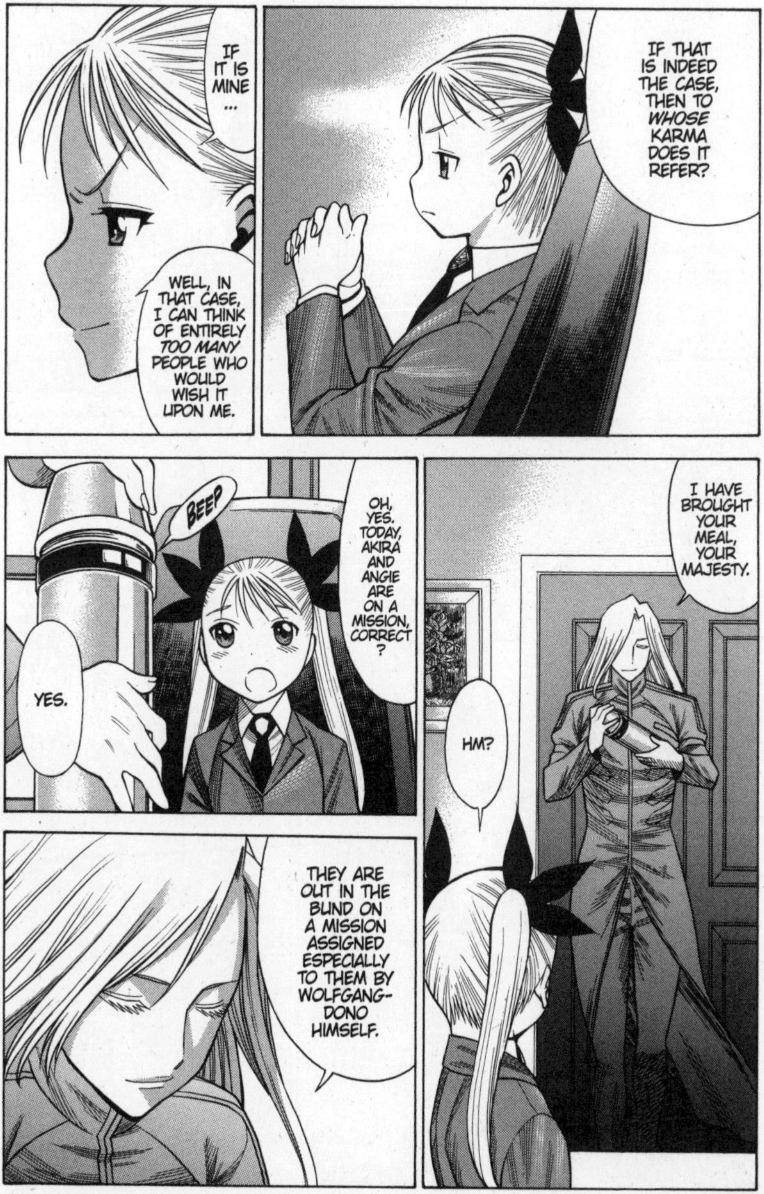
IF THAT IS INDEED THE CASE, THEN TO *WHOSE* KARMA DOES IT REFER?
IF IT IS MINE ...
WELL, IN THAT CASE, I CAN THINK OF ENTIRELY *TOO MANY* PEOPLE WHO WOULD WISH IT UPON ME.
I HAVE BROUGHT YOUR MEAL, YOUR MAJESTY.
HM?
BEEP
OH, YES. TODAY, AKIRA AND ANGIE ARE ON A MISSION, CORRECT?
YES.
THEY ARE OUT IN THE BUND ON A MISSION ASSIGNED ESPECIALLY TO THEM BY WOLFGANG-DONO HIMSELF.

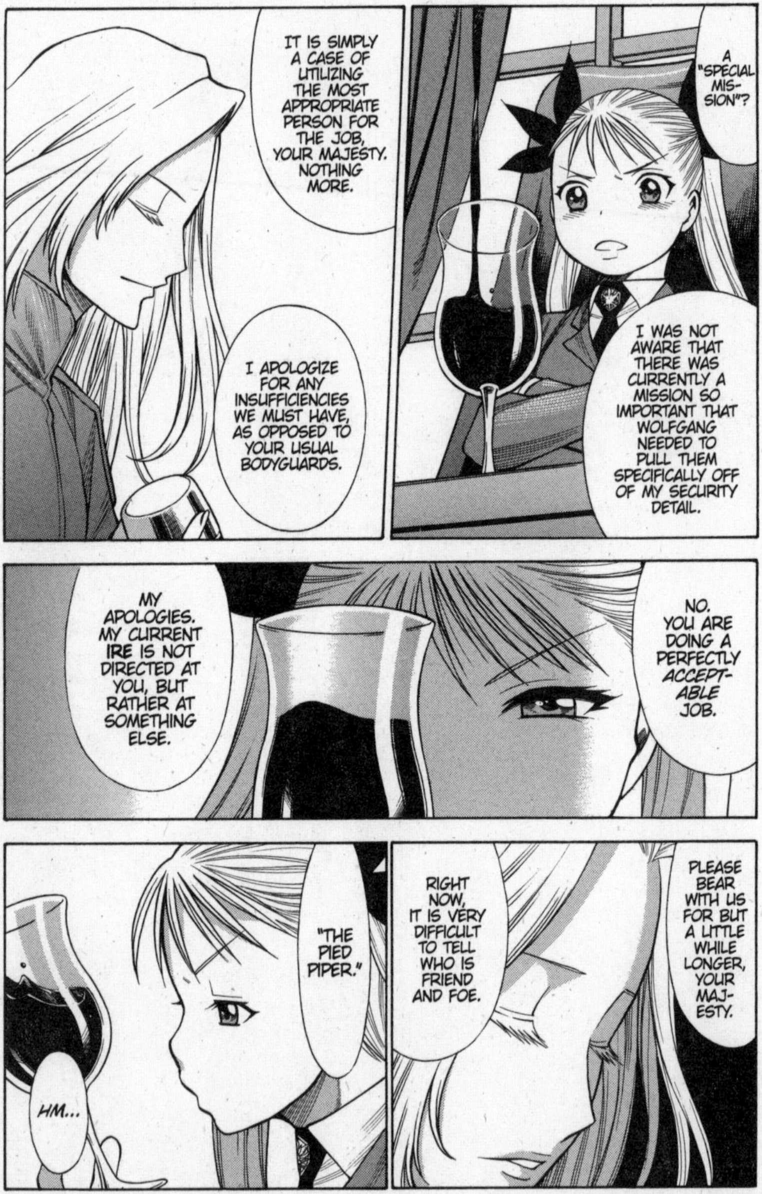
A "SPECIAL MISSION"?
I WAS NOT AWARE THAT THERE WAS CURRENTLY A MISSION SO IMPORTANT THAT WOLFGANG NEEDED TO PULL THEM SPECIFICALLY OFF OF MY SECURITY DETAIL.
IT IS SIMPLY A CASE OF UTILIZING THE MOST APPROPRIATE PERSON FOR THE JOB, YOUR MAJESTY. NOTHING MORE.
I APOLOGIZE FOR ANY INSUFFICIENCIES WE MUST HAVE, AS OPPOSED TO YOUR USUAL BODYGUARDS.
NO. YOU ARE DOING A PERFECTLY *ACCEPTABLE* JOB.
MY APOLOGIES. MY CURRENT **IRE** IS NOT DIRECTED AT YOU, BUT RATHER AT SOMETHING ELSE.
PLEASE BEAR WITH US FOR BUT A LITTLE WHILE LONGER, YOUR MAJESTY.
RIGHT NOW, IT IS VERY DIFFICULT TO TELL WHO IS FRIEND AND FOE.
"THE PIED PIPER."
HM...

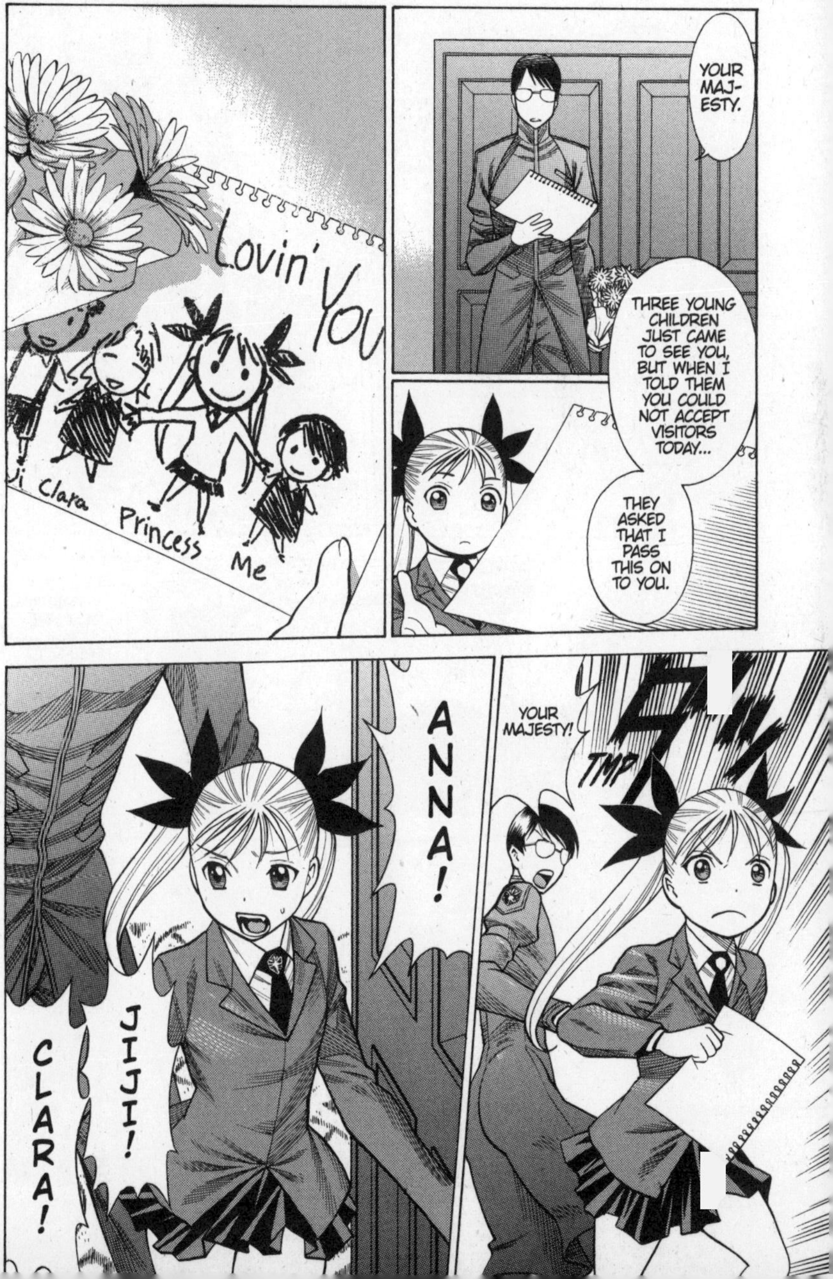

YOUR MAJ-ESTY.
THREE YOUNG CHILDREN JUST CAME TO SEE YOU, BUT WHEN I TOLD THEM YOU COULD NOT ACCEPT VISITORS TODAY...
THEY ASKED THAT I PASS THIS ON TO YOU.
Lovin' You
Ji
Clara
Princess
Me
TMP
YOUR MAJESTY!
ANNA!
JIJI!
CLARA!

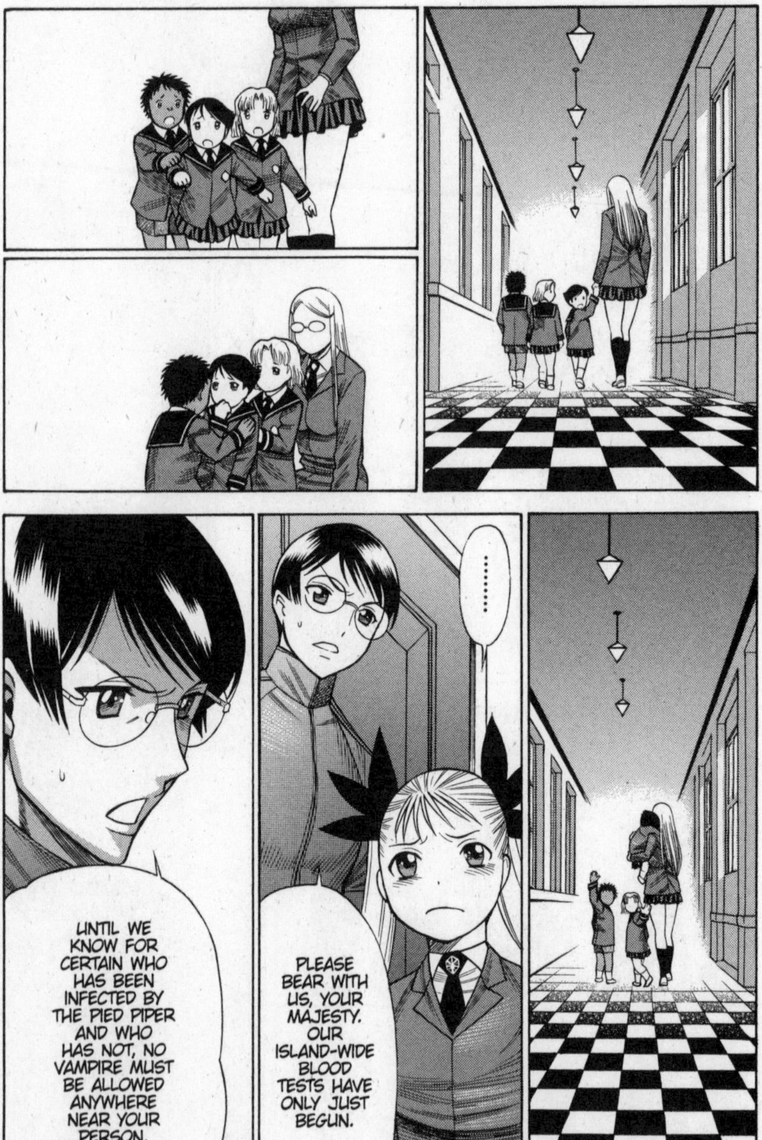
....
PLEASE BEAR WITH US, YOUR MAJESTY. OUR ISLAND-WIDE BLOOD TESTS HAVE ONLY JUST BEGUN.
UNTIL WE KNOW FOR CERTAIN WHO HAS BEEN INFECTED BY THE PIED PIPER AND WHO HAS NOT, NO VAMPIRE MUST BE ALLOWED ANYWHERE NEAR YOUR PERSON.

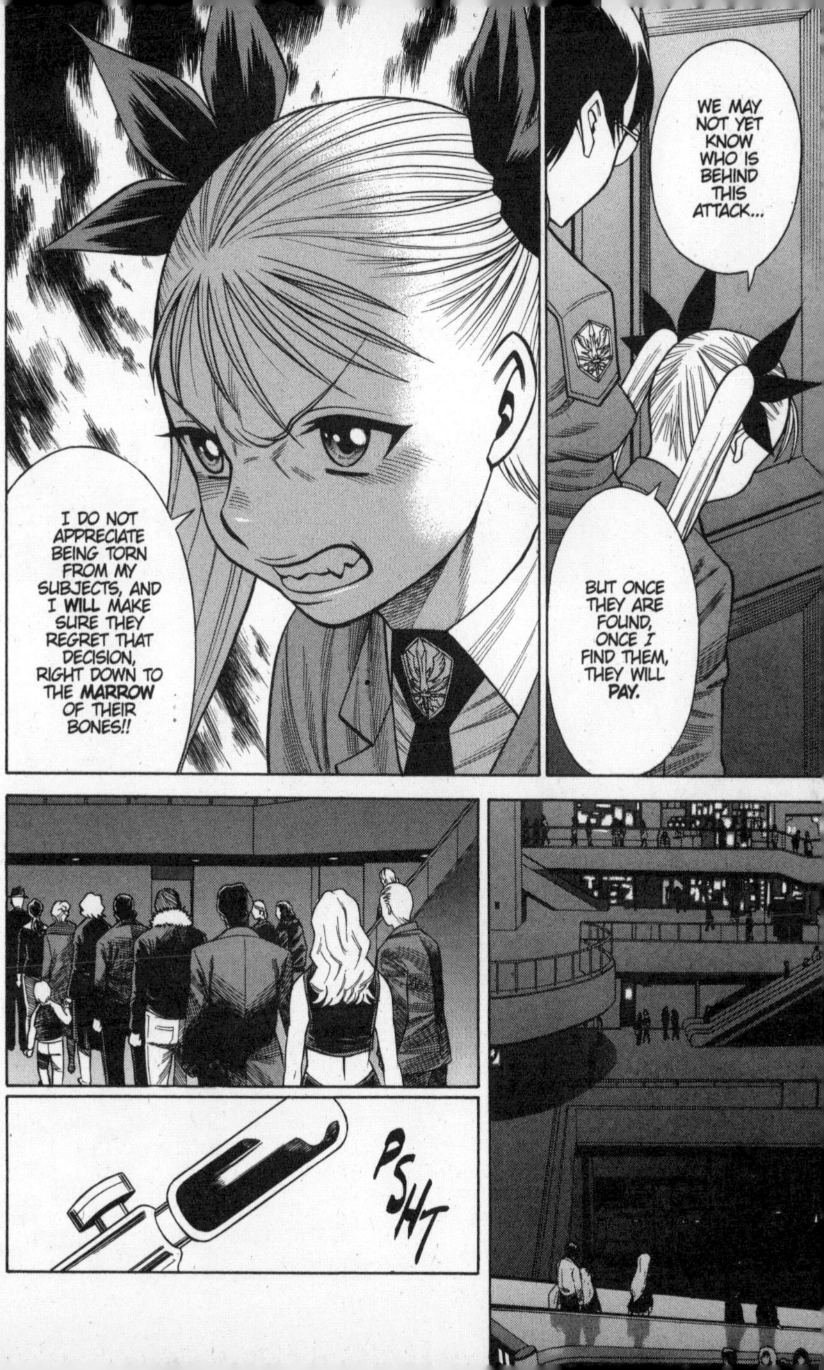
WE MAY NOT YET KNOW WHO IS BEHIND THIS ATTACK...
BUT ONCE THEY ARE FOUND, ONCE *I* FIND THEM, THEY WILL **PAY.**
I DO NOT APPRECIATE BEING TORN FROM MY SUBJECTS, AND I **WILL** MAKE SURE THEY REGRET THAT DECISION, RIGHT DOWN TO THE **MARROW** OF THEIR BONES!!
PSHT

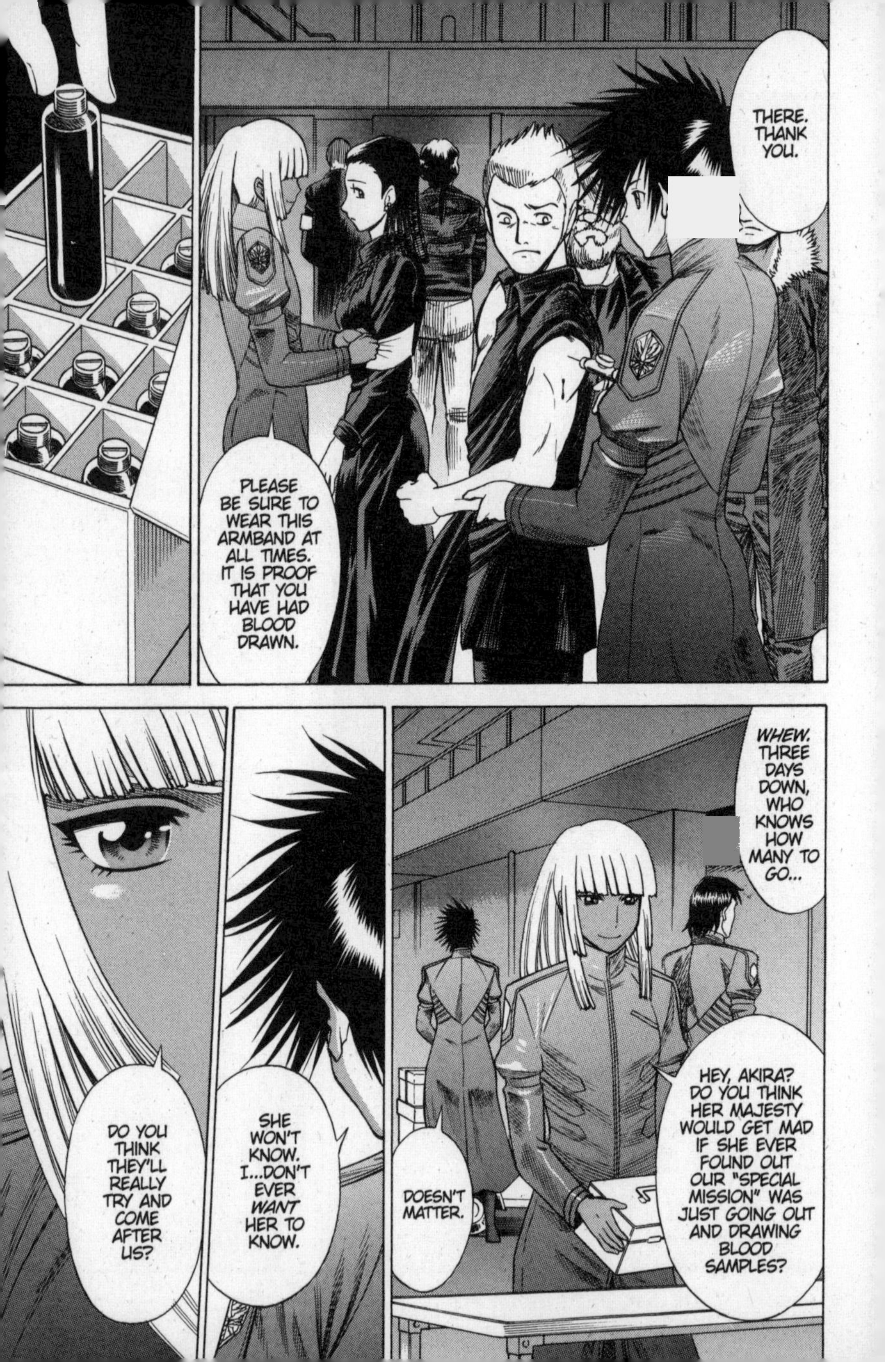
THERE. THANK YOU.
PLEASE BE SURE TO WEAR THIS ARMBAND AT ALL TIMES. IT IS PROOF THAT YOU HAVE HAD BLOOD DRAWN.
WHEW. THREE DAYS DOWN, WHO KNOWS HOW MANY TO GO...
HEY, AKIRA? DO YOU THINK HER MAJESTY WOULD GET MAD IF SHE EVER FOUND OUT OUR "SPECIAL MISSION" WAS JUST GOING OUT AND DRAWING BLOOD SAMPLES?
DOESN'T MATTER.
SHE WON'T KNOW. I...DON'T EVER WANT HER TO KNOW.
DO YOU THINK THEY'LL REALLY TRY AND COME AFTER US?

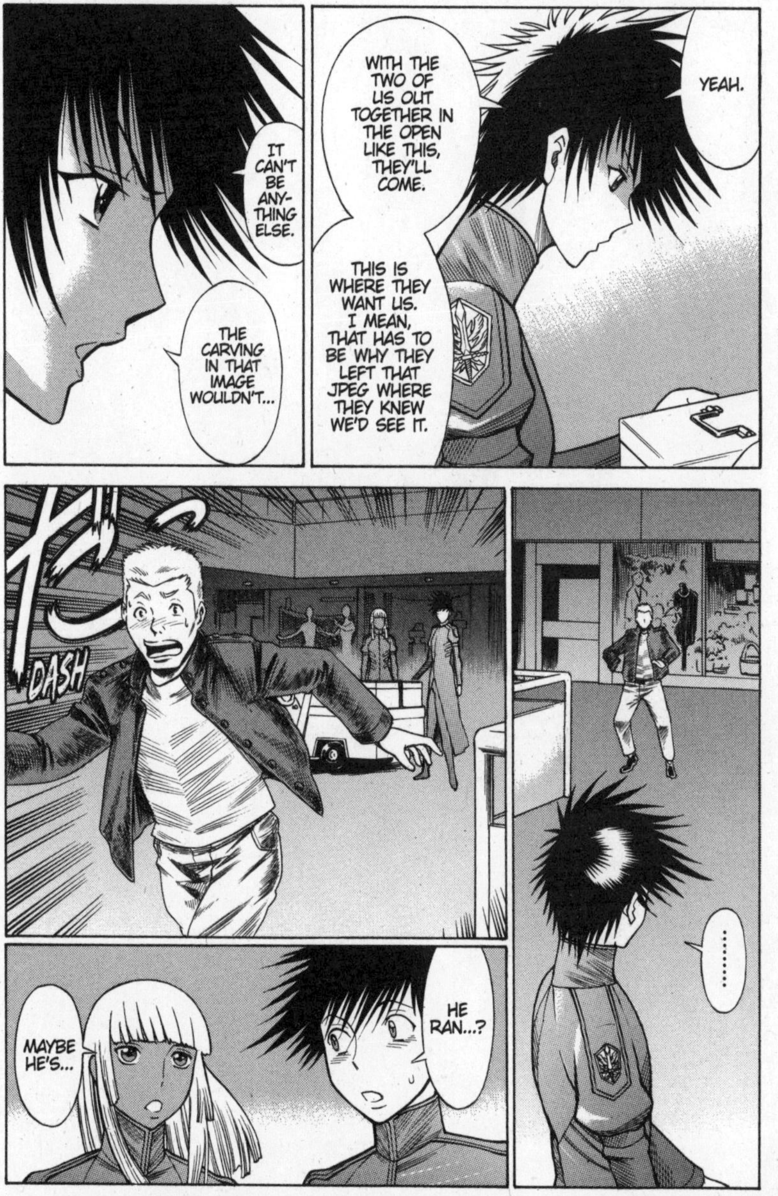
YEAH.
WITH THE TWO OF US OUT TOGETHER IN THE OPEN LIKE THIS, THEY'LL COME.
THIS IS WHERE THEY WANT US. I MEAN, THAT HAS TO BE WHY THEY LEFT THAT JPEG WHERE THEY KNEW WE'D SEE IT.
IT CAN'T BE ANY-THING ELSE.
THE CARVING IN THAT IMAGE WOULDN'T...
....
DASH
HE RAN...?
MAYBE HE'S...

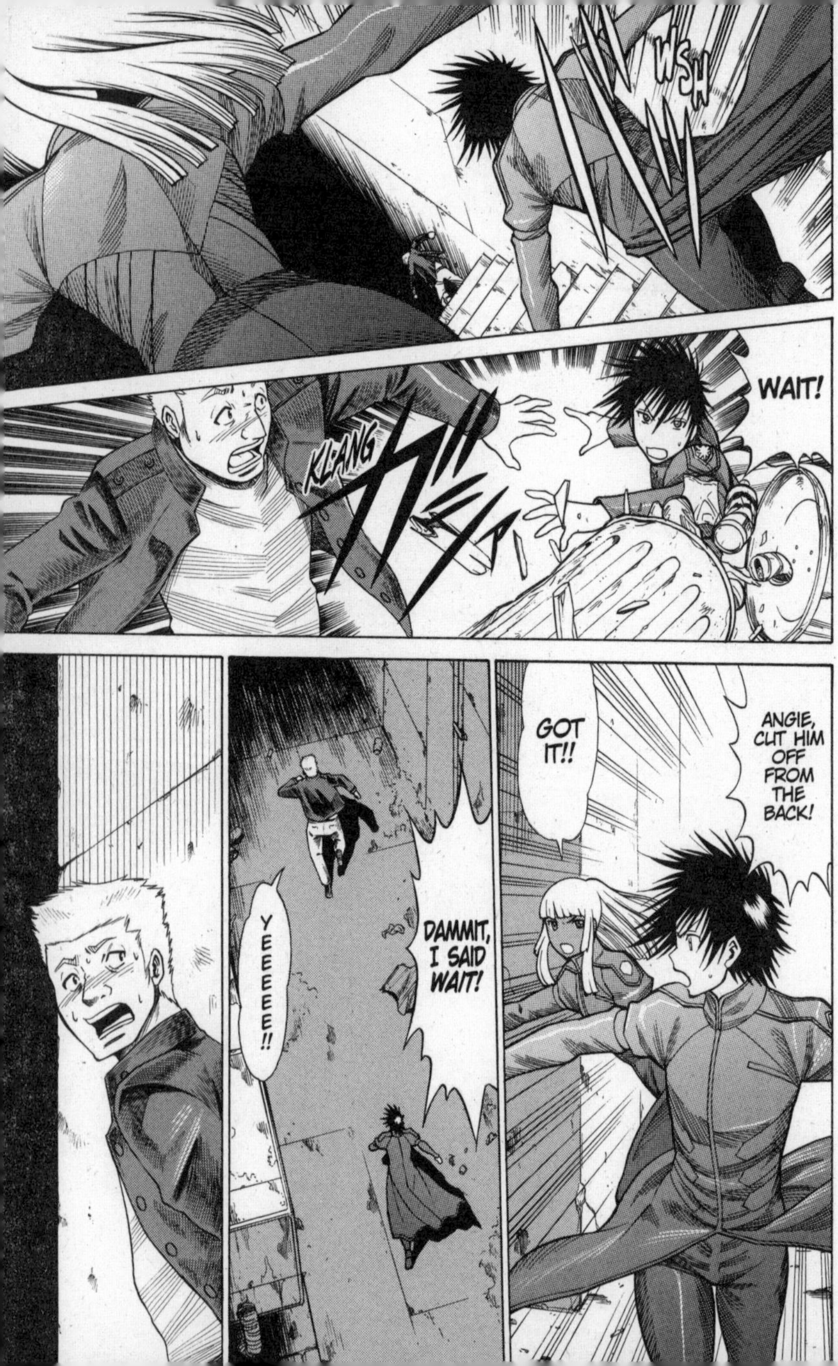
WSH
WAIT!
KLANG
ANGIE, CUT HIM OFF FROM THE BACK!
GOT IT!!
DAMMIT, I SAID WAIT!
YEEEEEE!!

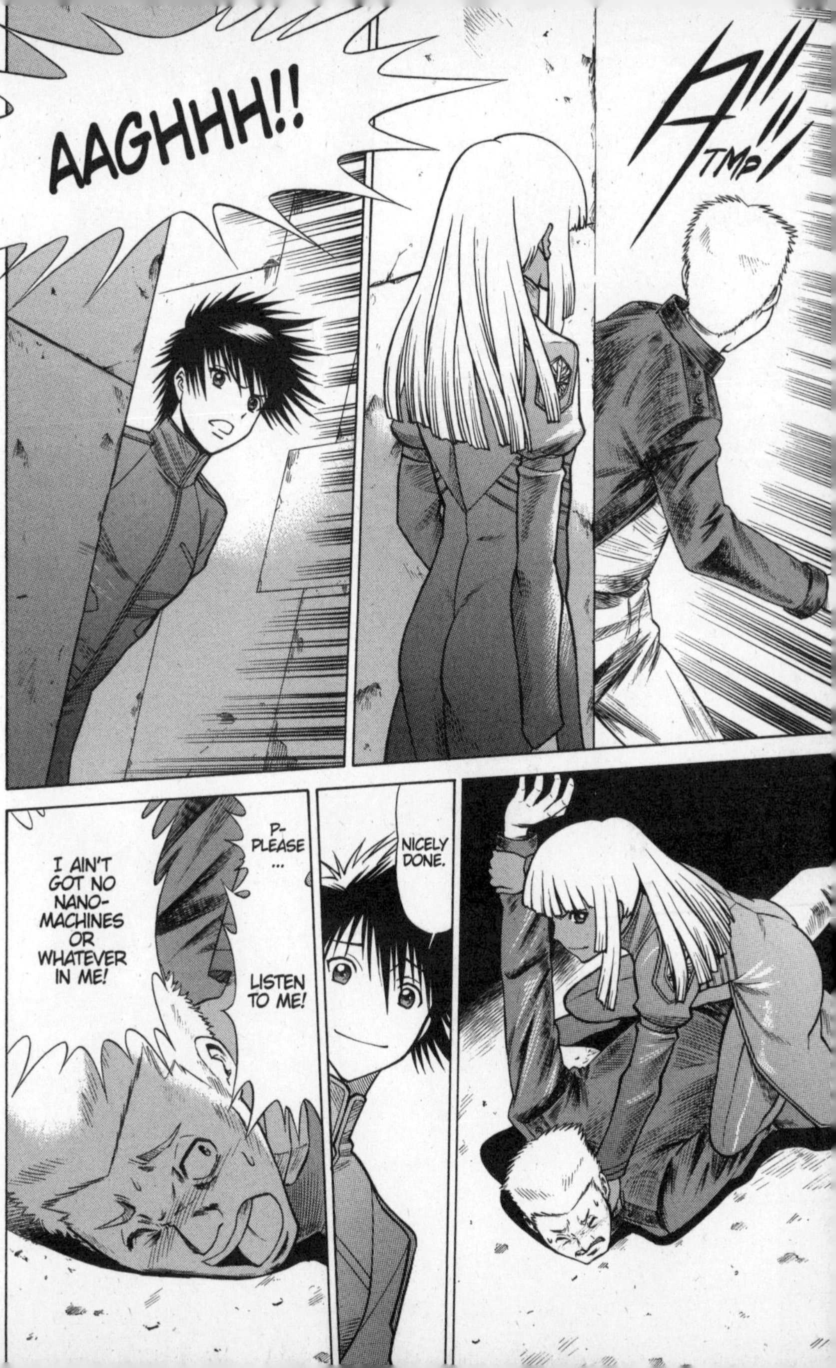
TMP!
AAGHHH!!
NICELY DONE.
P-PLEASE ...
LISTEN TO ME!
I AIN'T GOT NO NANO-MACHINES OR WHATEVER IN ME!

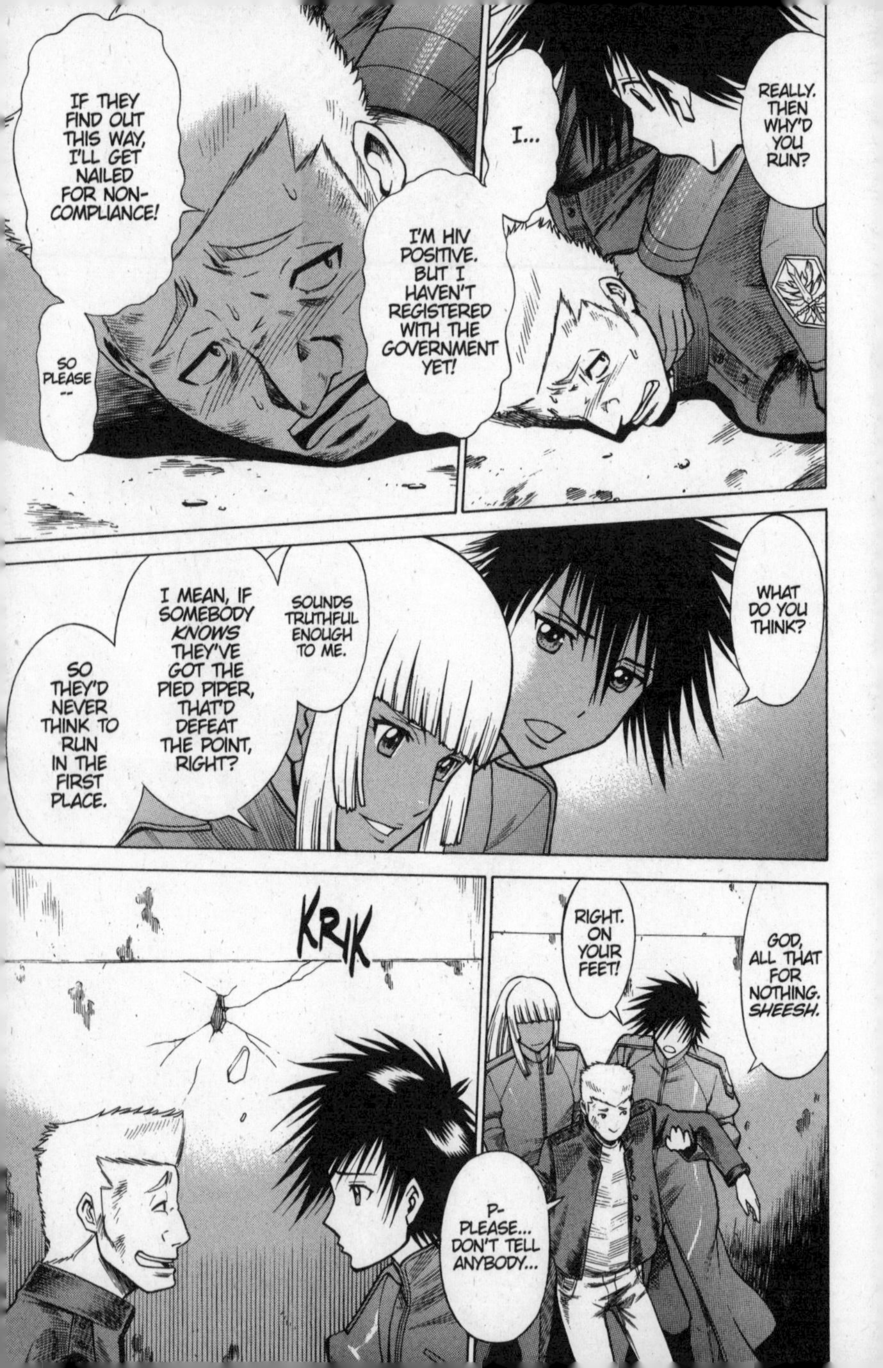
REALLY. THEN WHY'D YOU RUN?
I...
I'M HIV POSITIVE. BUT I HAVEN'T REGISTERED WITH THE GOVERNMENT YET!
IF THEY FIND OUT THIS WAY, I'LL GET NAILED FOR NON-COMPLIANCE!
SO PLEASE --
WHAT DO YOU THINK?
SOUNDS TRUTHFUL ENOUGH TO ME.
I MEAN, IF SOMEBODY *KNOWS* THEY'VE GOT THE PIED PIPER, THAT'D DEFEAT THE POINT, RIGHT?
SO THEY'D NEVER THINK TO RUN IN THE FIRST PLACE.
GOD, ALL THAT FOR NOTHING. *SHEESH.*
RIGHT. ON YOUR FEET!
P-PLEASE... DON'T TELL ANYBODY...
KRIK

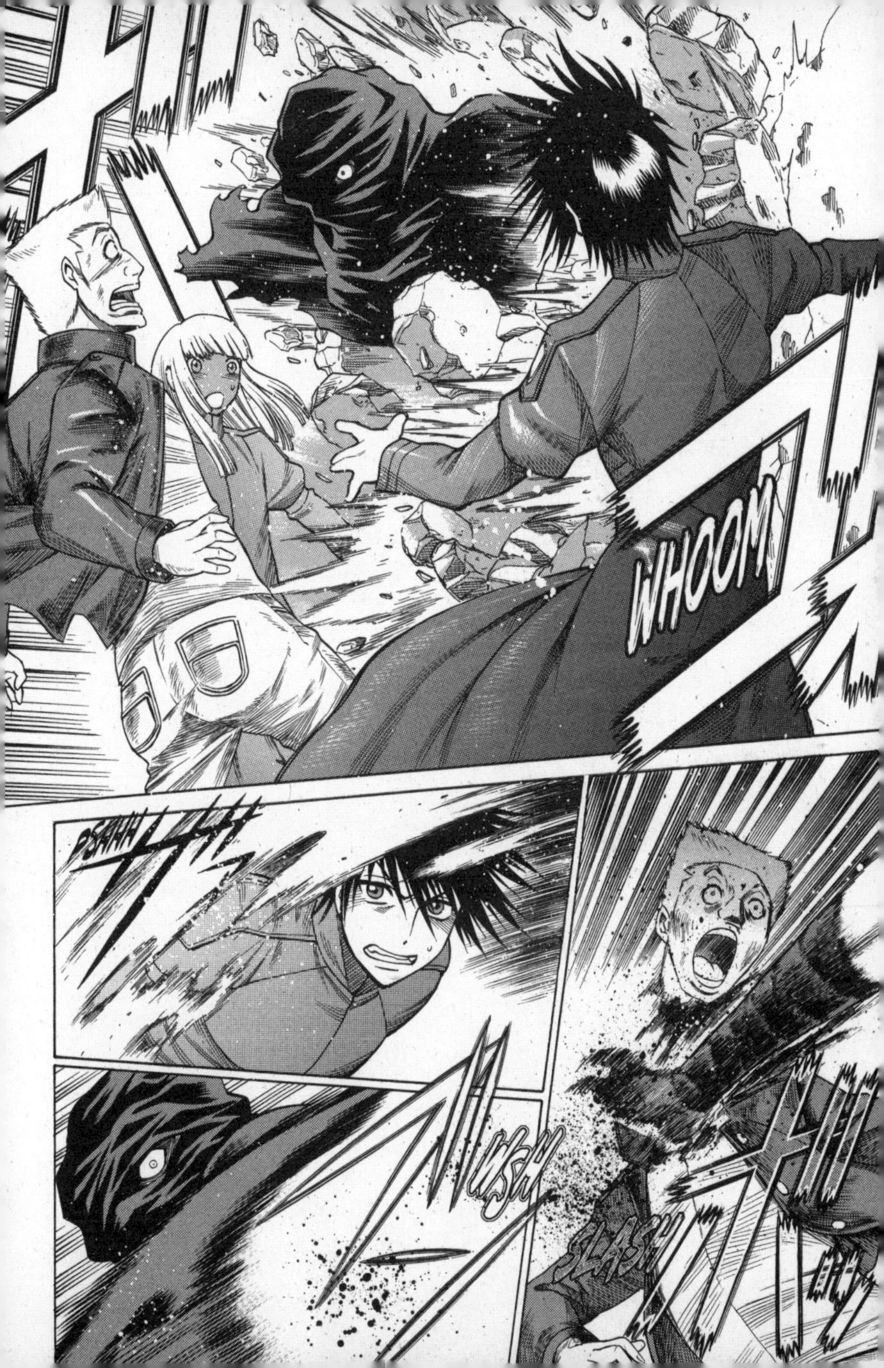
WHOOM
SLASH
PSHHH
WUSH

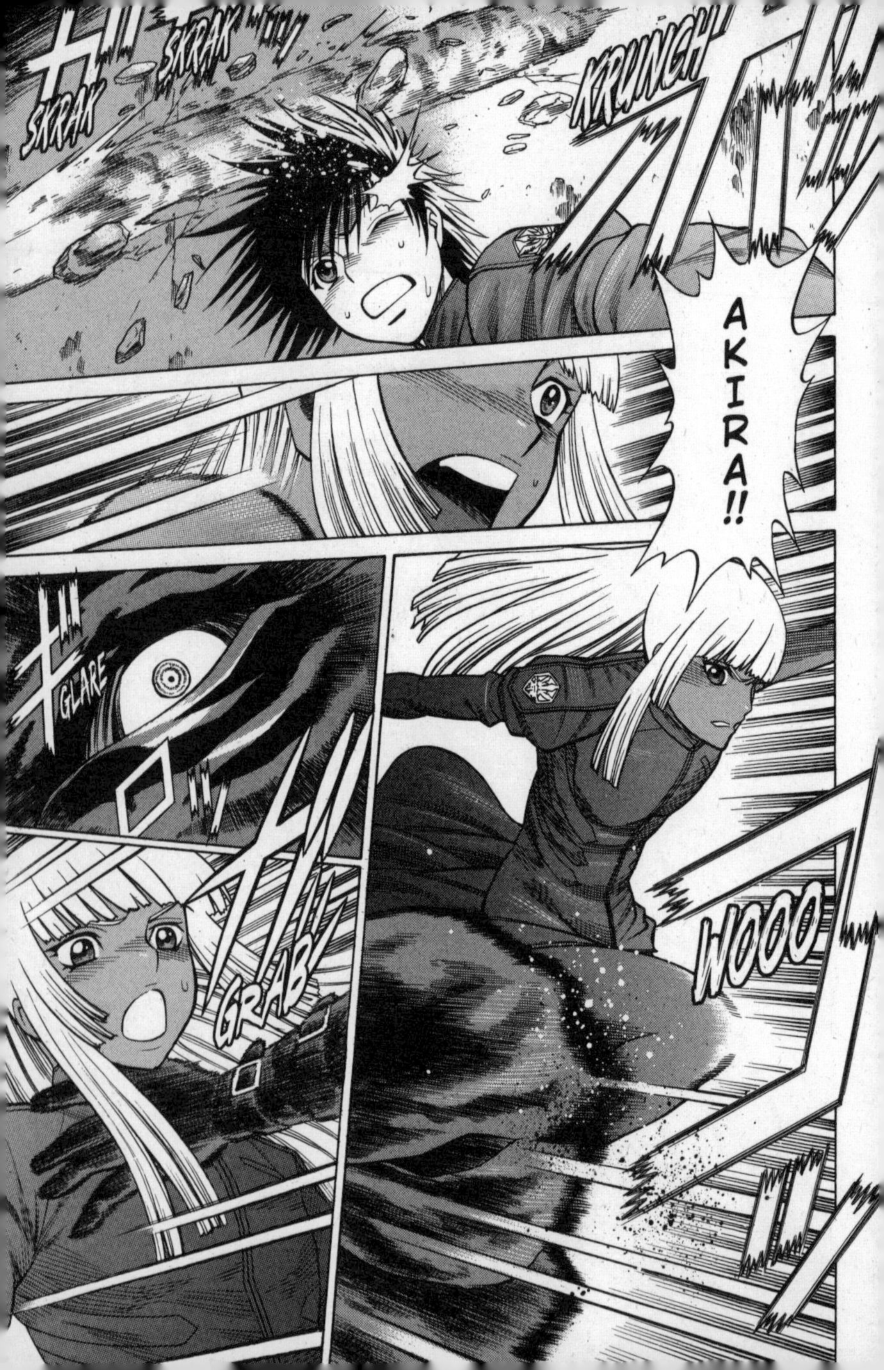
KRUNCH
SKRAK
SKRAK
AKIRA!!
WOOO
GLARE
GRAB

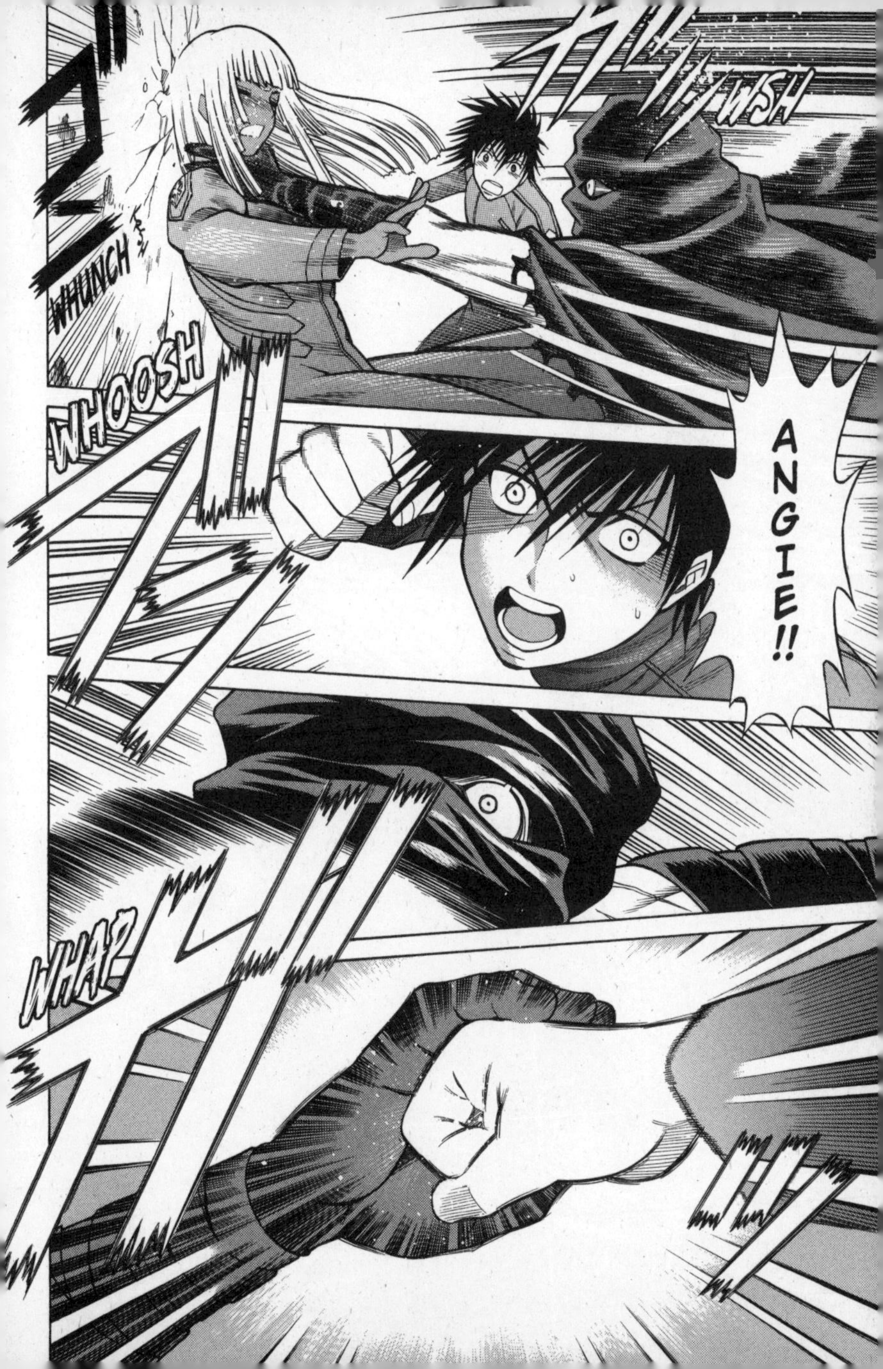
WSH
WHUNCH
WHOOSH
ANGIE!!
WHA?

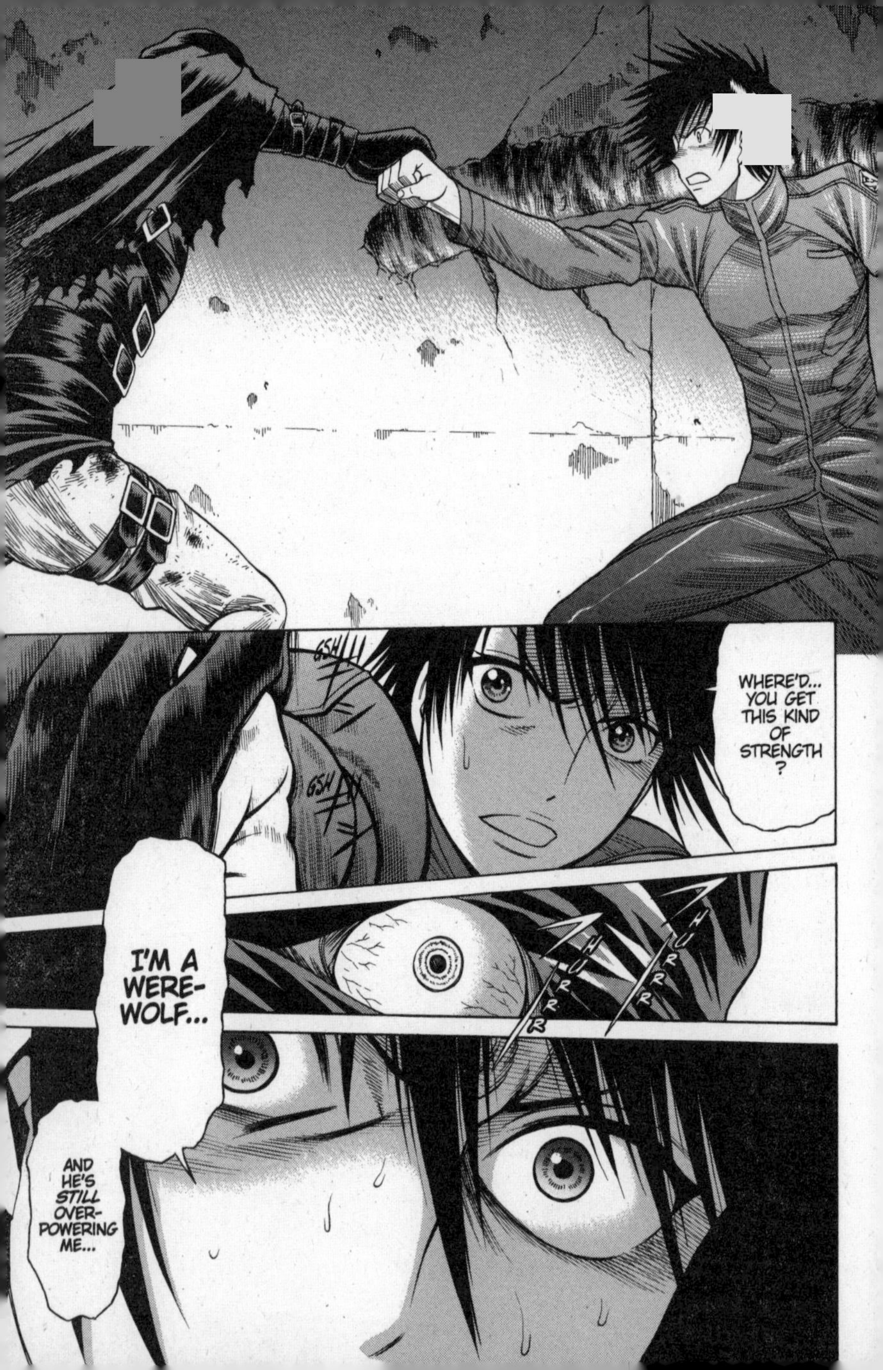
WHERE'D... YOU GET THIS KIND OF STRENGTH?
GSH
GSH
I'M A WERE-WOLF...
HURR
HURRR
AND HE'S STILL OVER-POWERING ME...

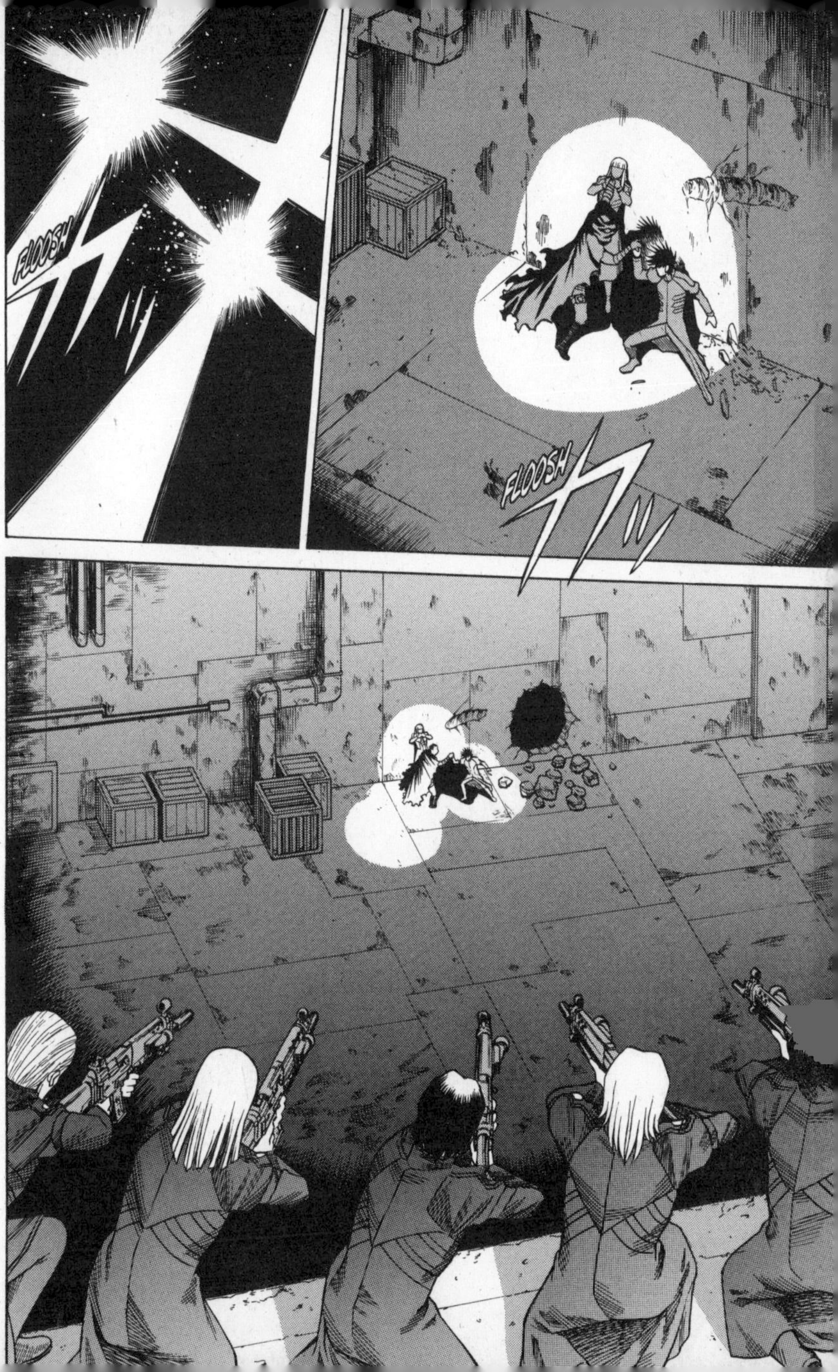
FLOOSH
FLOOSH

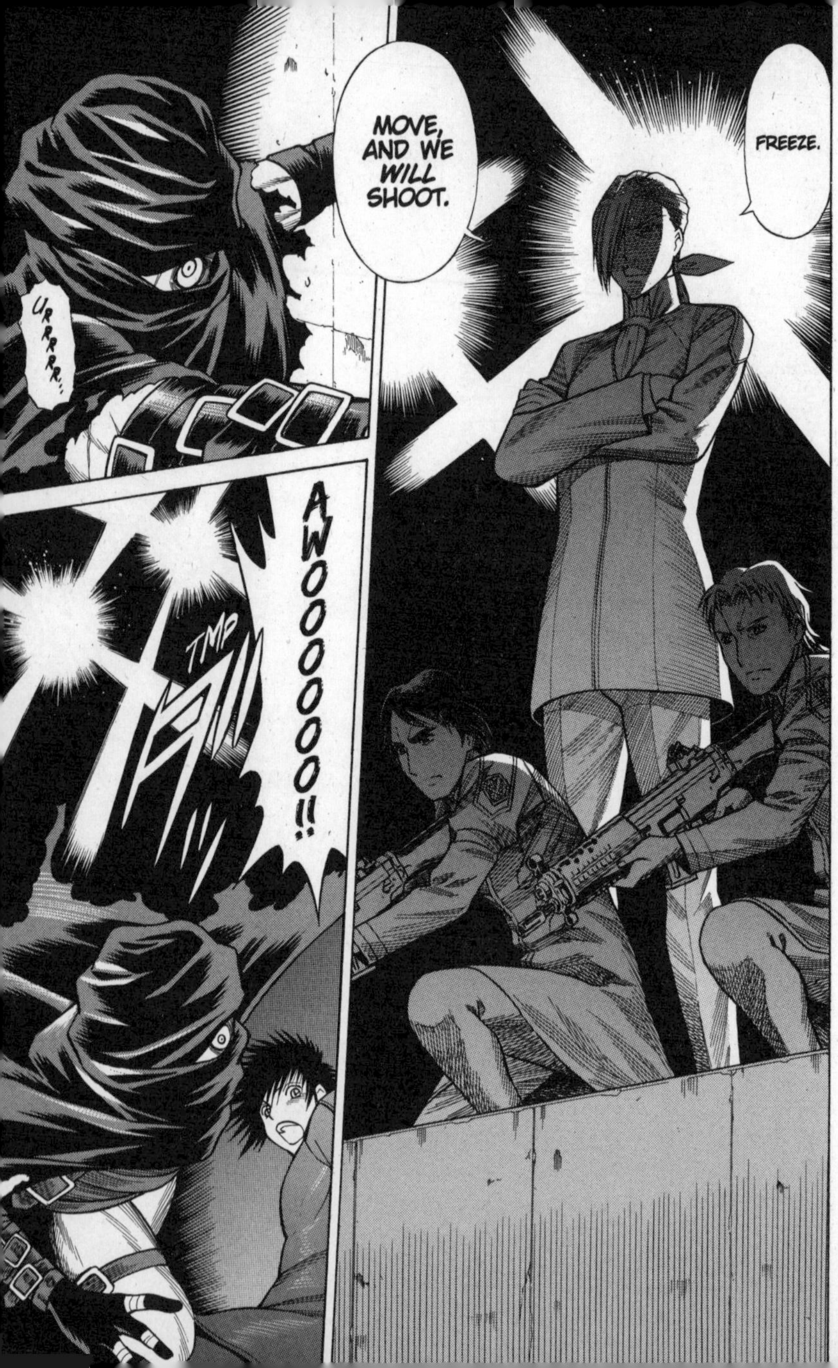
FREEZE.
MOVE, AND WE WILL SHOOT.
URRRRR...
AWOOOOOO!!
TMP

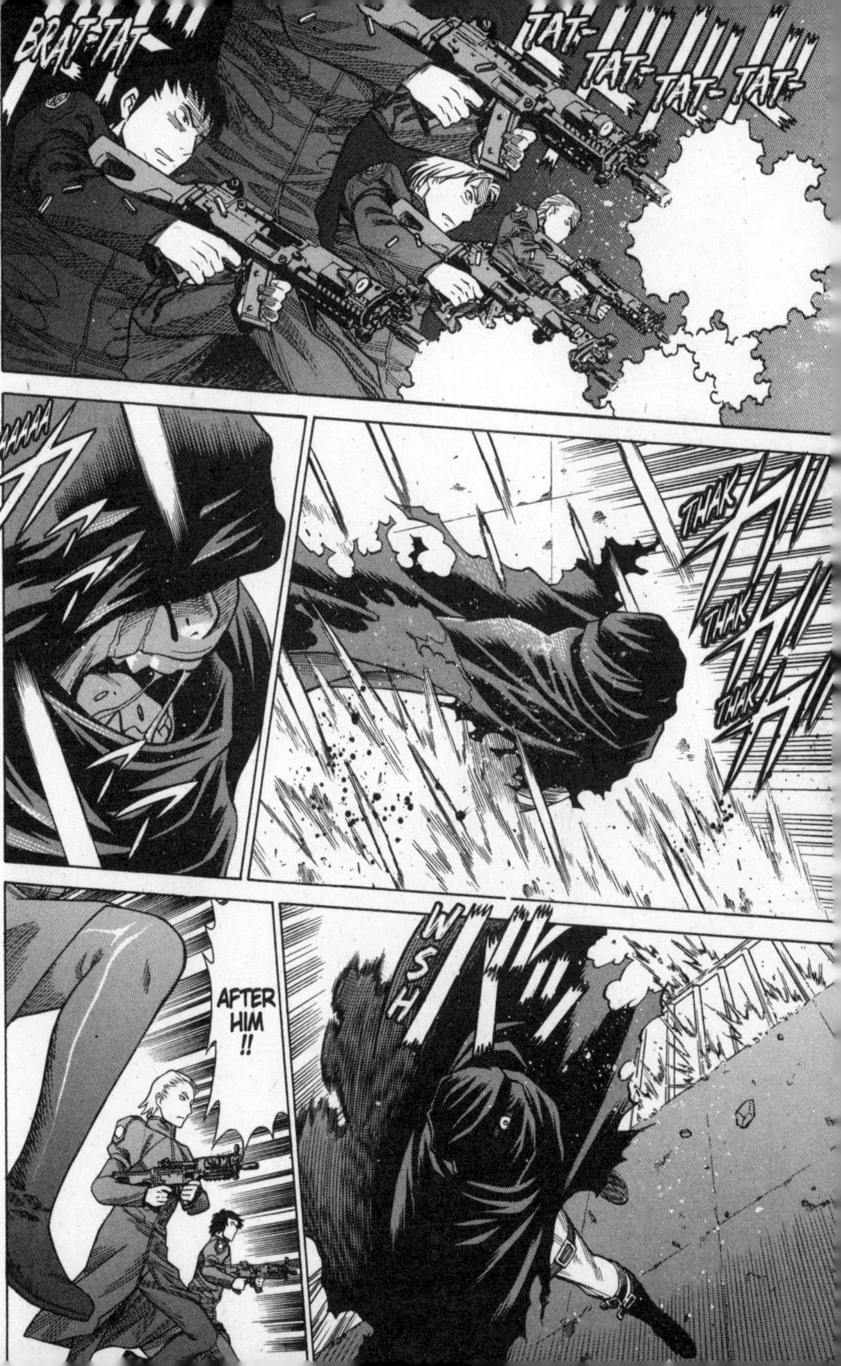
TAT-TAT-TAT-TAT-
BRAT-TAT
THAK THAK THAK
GRAAAAAH
WSH
AFTER HIM !!

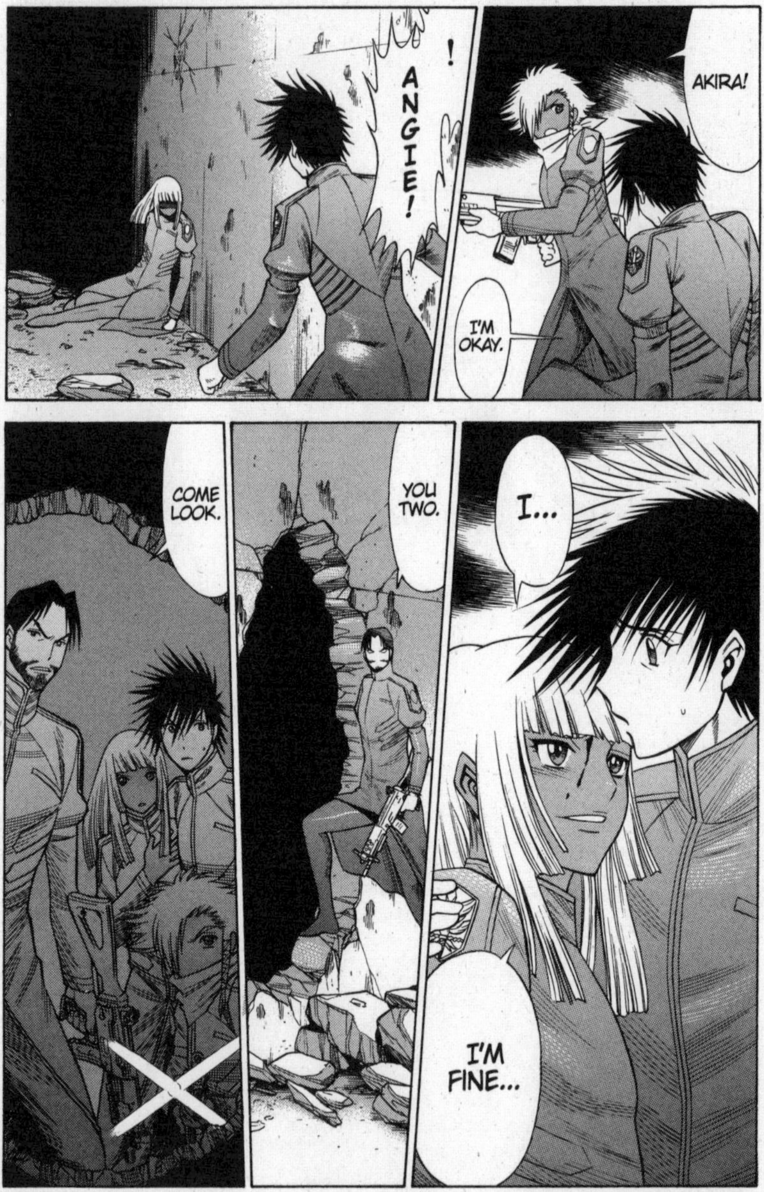
AKIRA!
I'M OKAY.
!
ANGIE!
I...
I'M FINE...
YOU TWO.
COME LOOK.

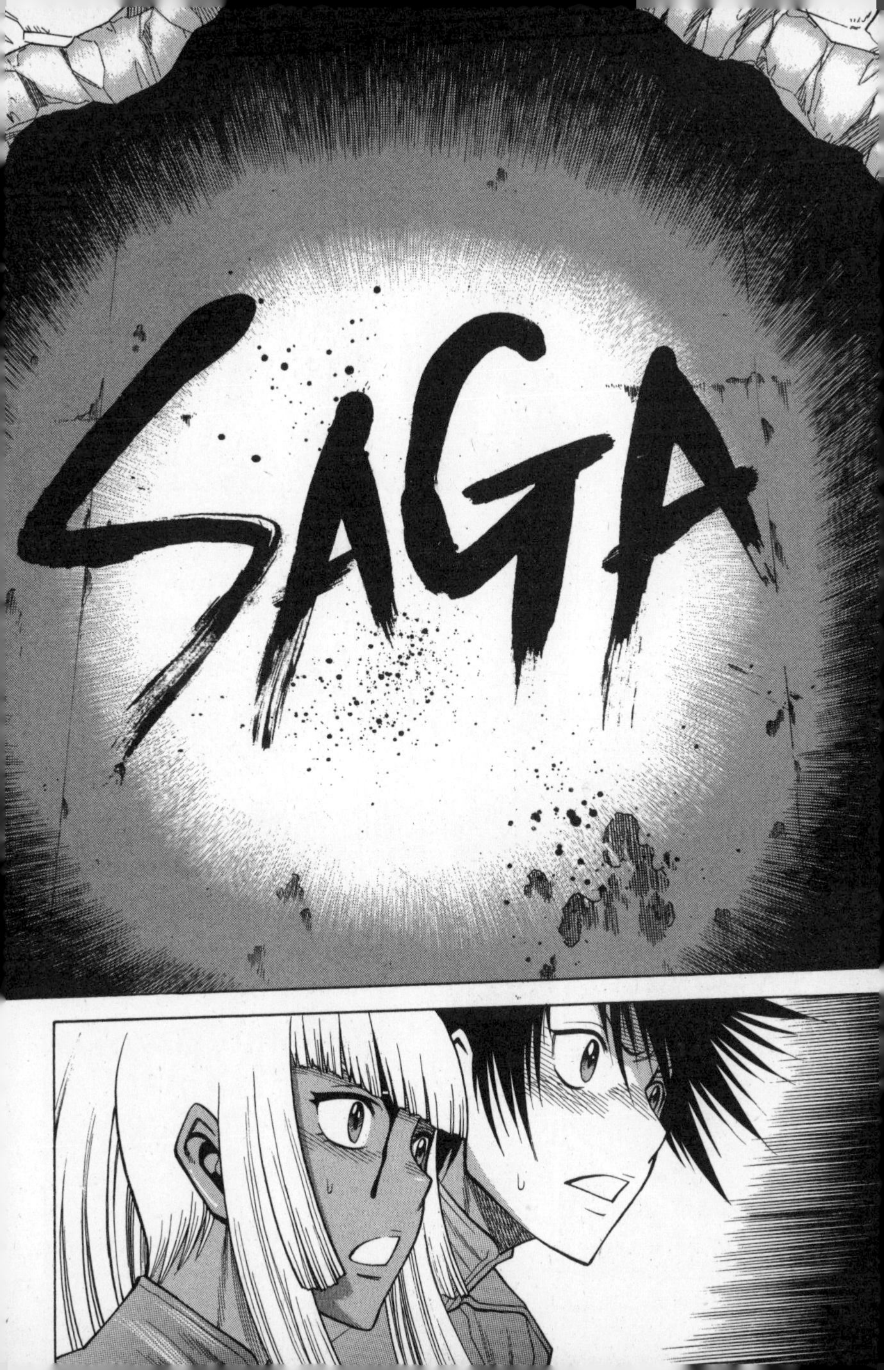
SAGA

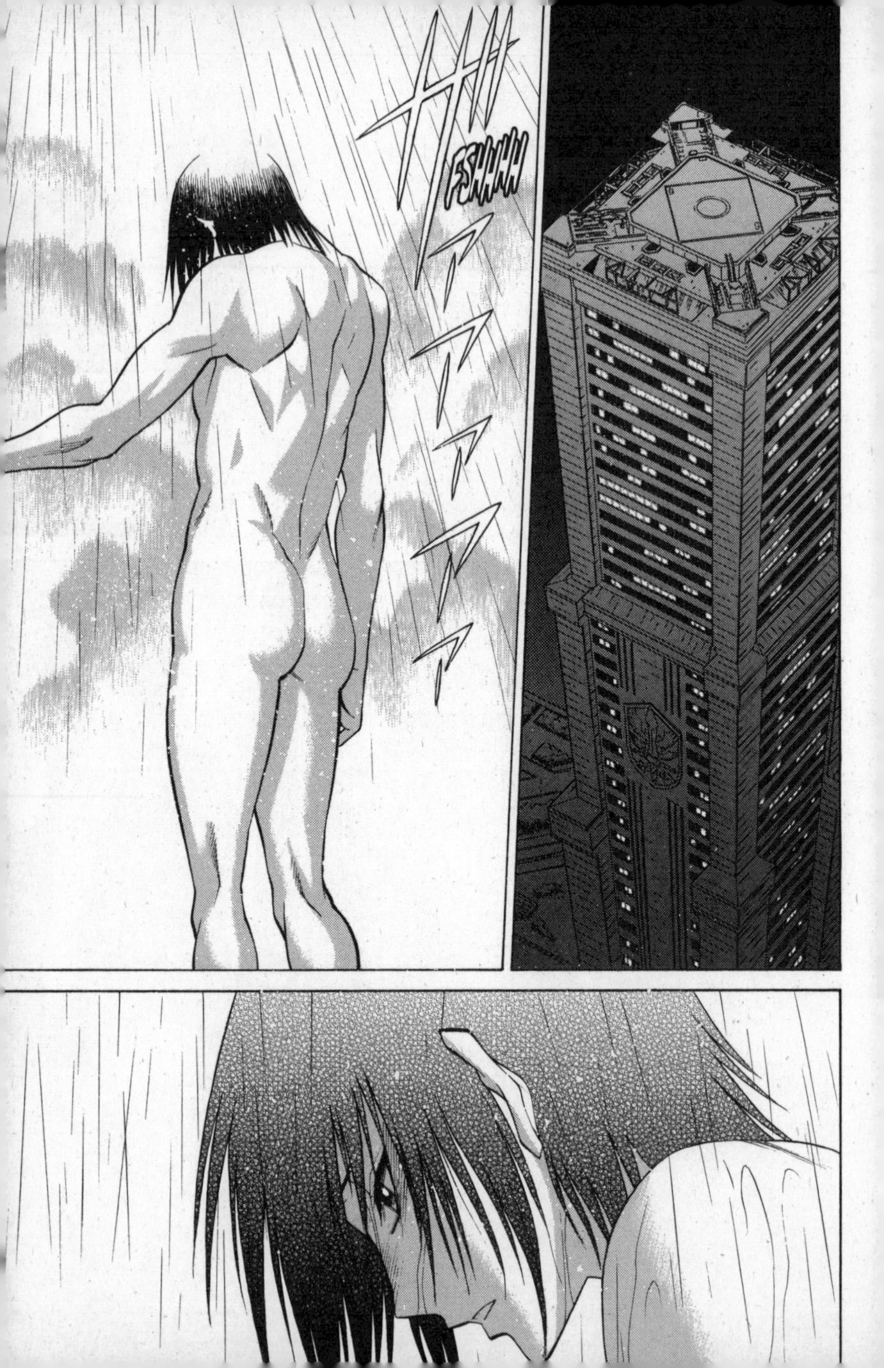
FSHHHH

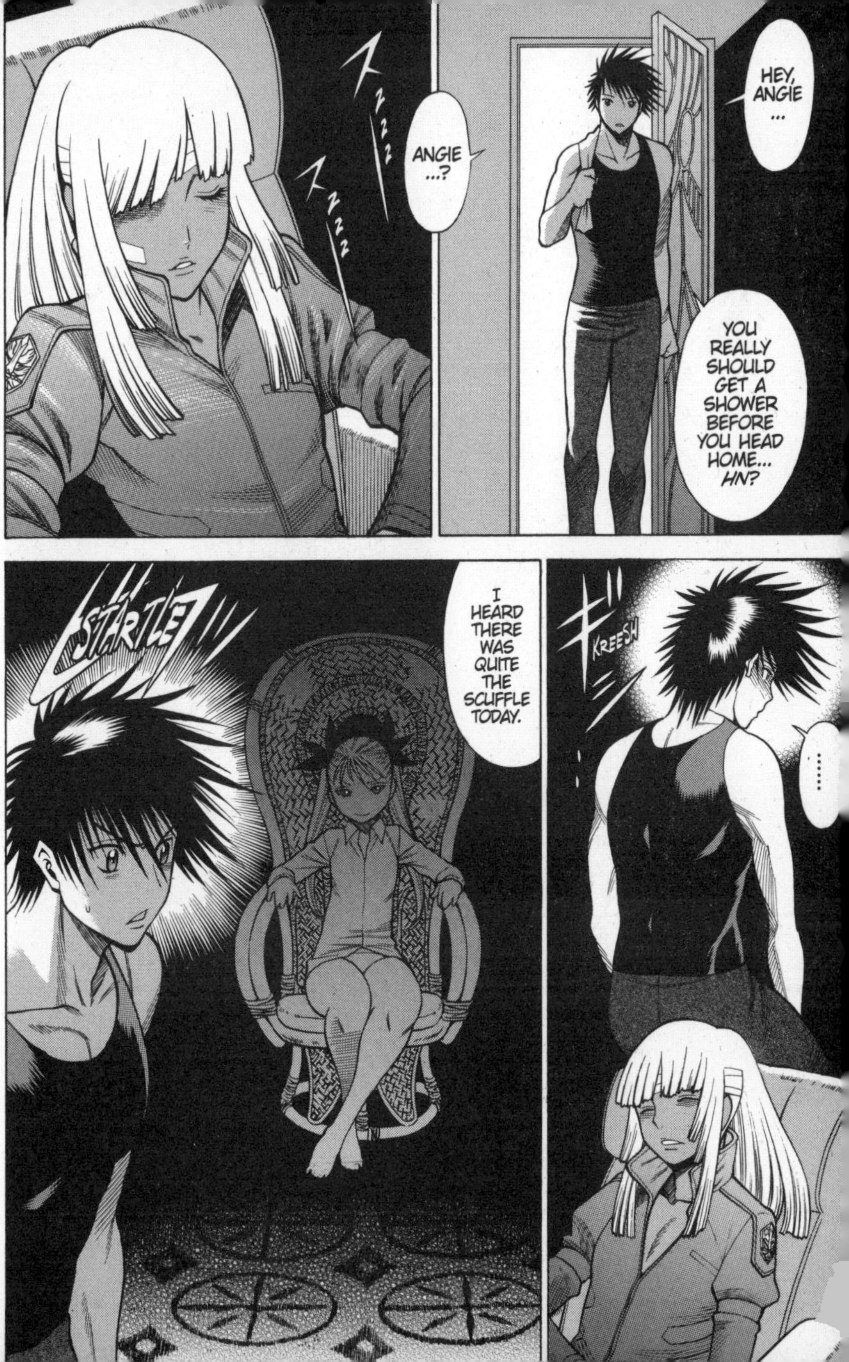
HEY, ANGIE ...
YOU REALLY SHOULD GET A SHOWER BEFORE YOU HEAD HOME... HN?
ANGIE ...?
KREESH
......
STARTLE
I HEARD THERE WAS QUITE THE SCUFFLE TODAY.

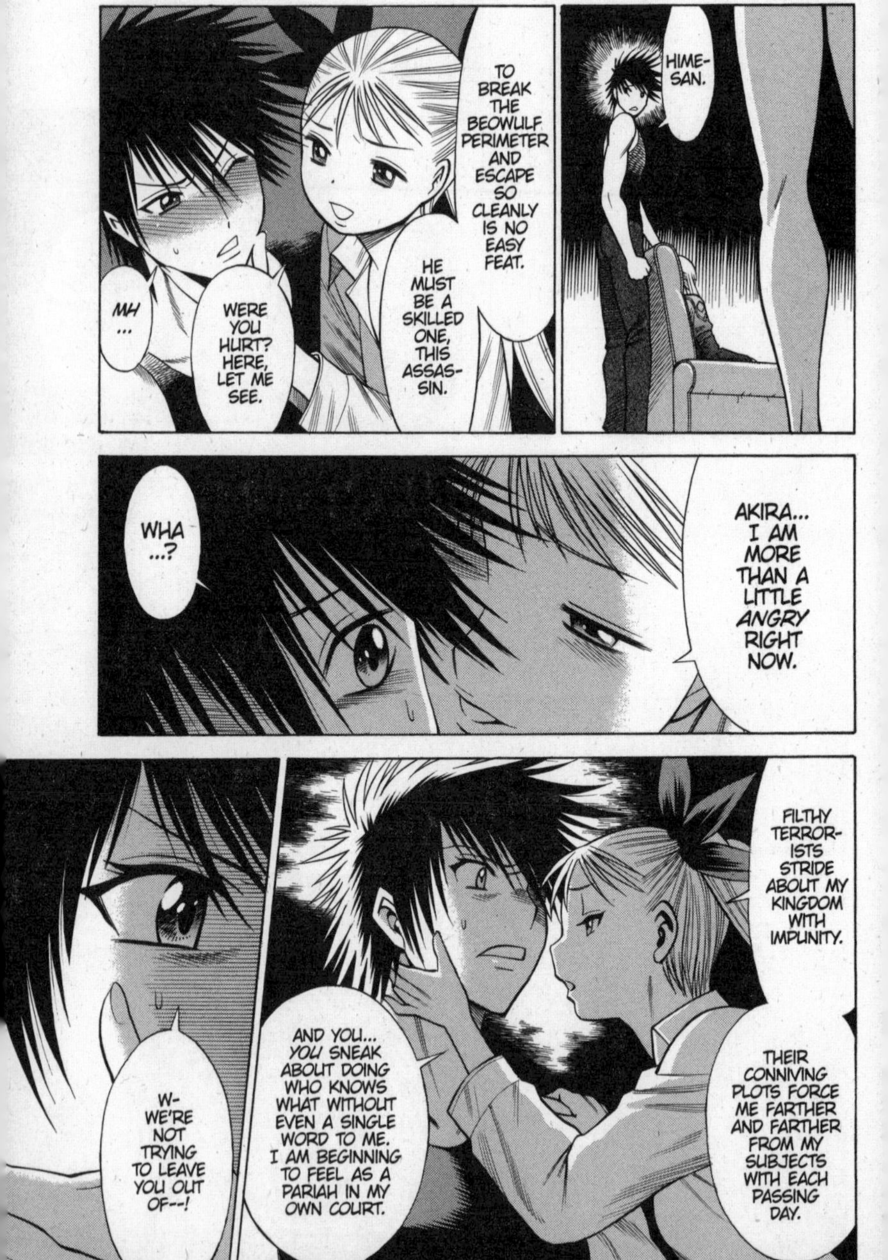
HIME-SAN.
TO BREAK THE BEOWULF PERIMETER AND ESCAPE SO CLEANLY IS NO EASY FEAT.
HE MUST BE A SKILLED ONE, THIS ASSAS-SIN.
WERE YOU HURT? HERE, LET ME SEE.
MH ...
AKIRA... I AM MORE THAN A LITTLE *ANGRY* RIGHT NOW.
WHA ...?
FILTHY TERROR-ISTS STRIDE ABOUT MY KINGDOM WITH IMPUNITY.
THEIR CONNIVING PLOTS FORCE ME FARTHER AND FARTHER FROM MY SUBJECTS WITH EACH PASSING DAY.
AND YOU... *YOU* SNEAK ABOUT DOING WHO KNOWS WHAT WITHOUT EVEN A SINGLE WORD TO ME. I AM BEGINNING TO FEEL AS A PARIAH IN MY OWN COURT.
W-WE'RE NOT TRYING TO LEAVE YOU OUT OF--!

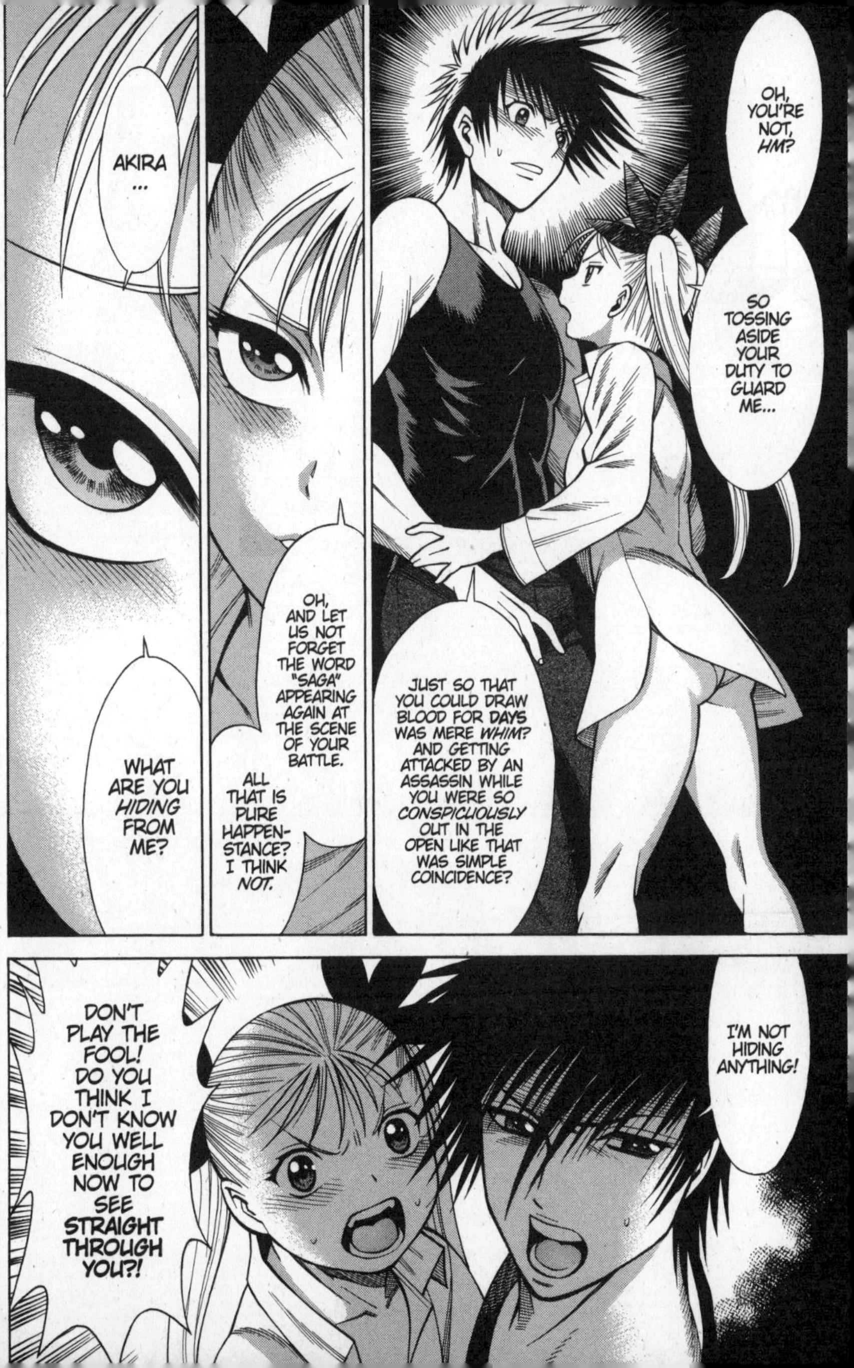
OH, YOU'RE NOT, HM?
SO TOSSING ASIDE YOUR DUTY TO GUARD ME...
JUST SO THAT YOU COULD DRAW BLOOD FOR DAYS WAS MERE WHIM? AND GETTING ATTACKED BY AN ASSASSIN WHILE YOU WERE SO CONSPICUOUSLY OUT IN THE OPEN LIKE THAT WAS SIMPLE COINCIDENCE?
OH, AND LET US NOT FORGET THE WORD "SAGA" APPEARING AGAIN AT THE SCENE OF YOUR BATTLE.
ALL THAT IS PURE HAPPEN-STANCE? I THINK NOT.
AKIRA ...
WHAT ARE YOU HIDING FROM ME?
I'M NOT HIDING ANYTHING!
DON'T PLAY THE FOOL! DO YOU THINK I DON'T KNOW YOU WELL ENOUGH NOW TO SEE STRAIGHT THROUGH YOU?!

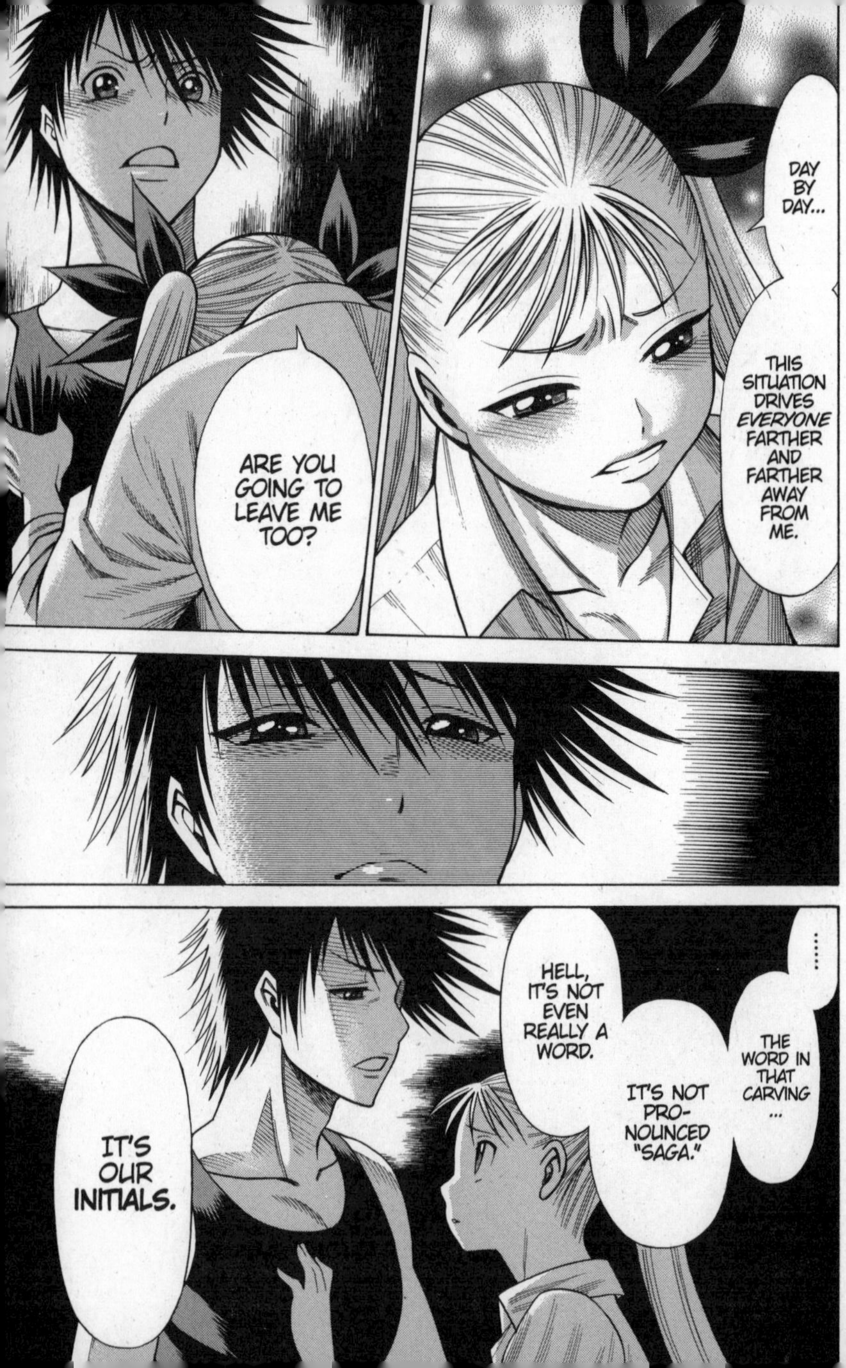
DAY BY DAY...
THIS SITUATION DRIVES *EVERYONE* FARTHER AND FARTHER AWAY FROM ME.
ARE YOU GOING TO LEAVE ME TOO?
......
THE WORD IN THAT CARVING...
IT'S NOT PRO-NOUNCED "SAGA."
HELL, IT'S NOT EVEN REALLY A WORD.
IT'S OUR INITIALS.

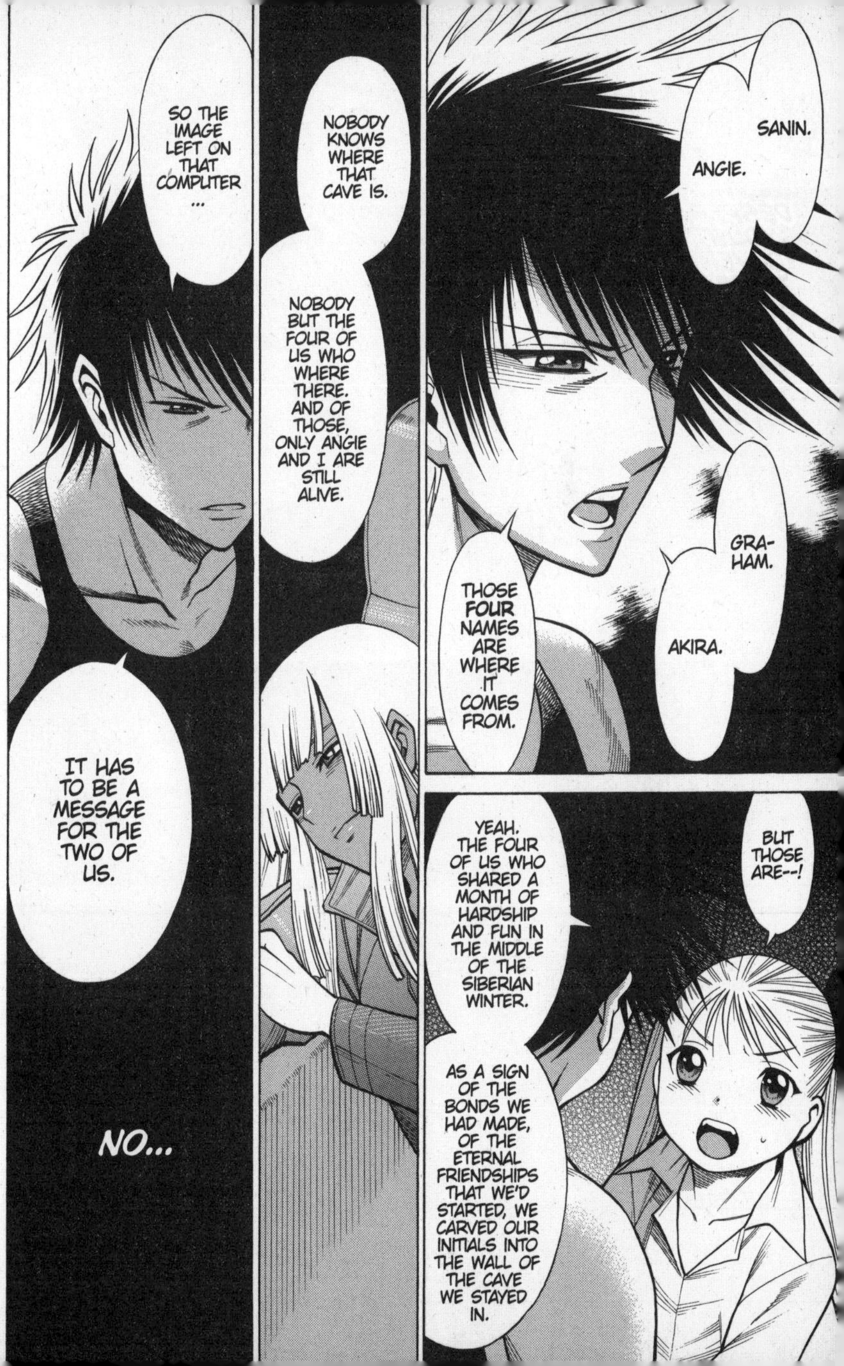
SANIN.
ANGIE.
GRA-HAM.
AKIRA.
THOSE FOUR NAMES ARE WHERE IT COMES FROM.
BUT THOSE ARE--!
YEAH. THE FOUR OF US WHO SHARED A MONTH OF HARDSHIP AND FUN IN THE MIDDLE OF THE SIBERIAN WINTER.
AS A SIGN OF THE BONDS WE HAD MADE, OF THE ETERNAL FRIENDSHIPS THAT WE'D STARTED, WE CARVED OUR INITIALS INTO THE WALL OF THE CAVE WE STAYED IN.
NOBODY KNOWS WHERE THAT CAVE IS.
NOBODY BUT THE FOUR OF US WHO WHERE THERE. AND OF THOSE, ONLY ANGIE AND I ARE STILL ALIVE.
SO THE IMAGE LEFT ON THAT COMPUTER ...
IT HAS TO BE A MESSAGE FOR THE TWO OF US.
NO...

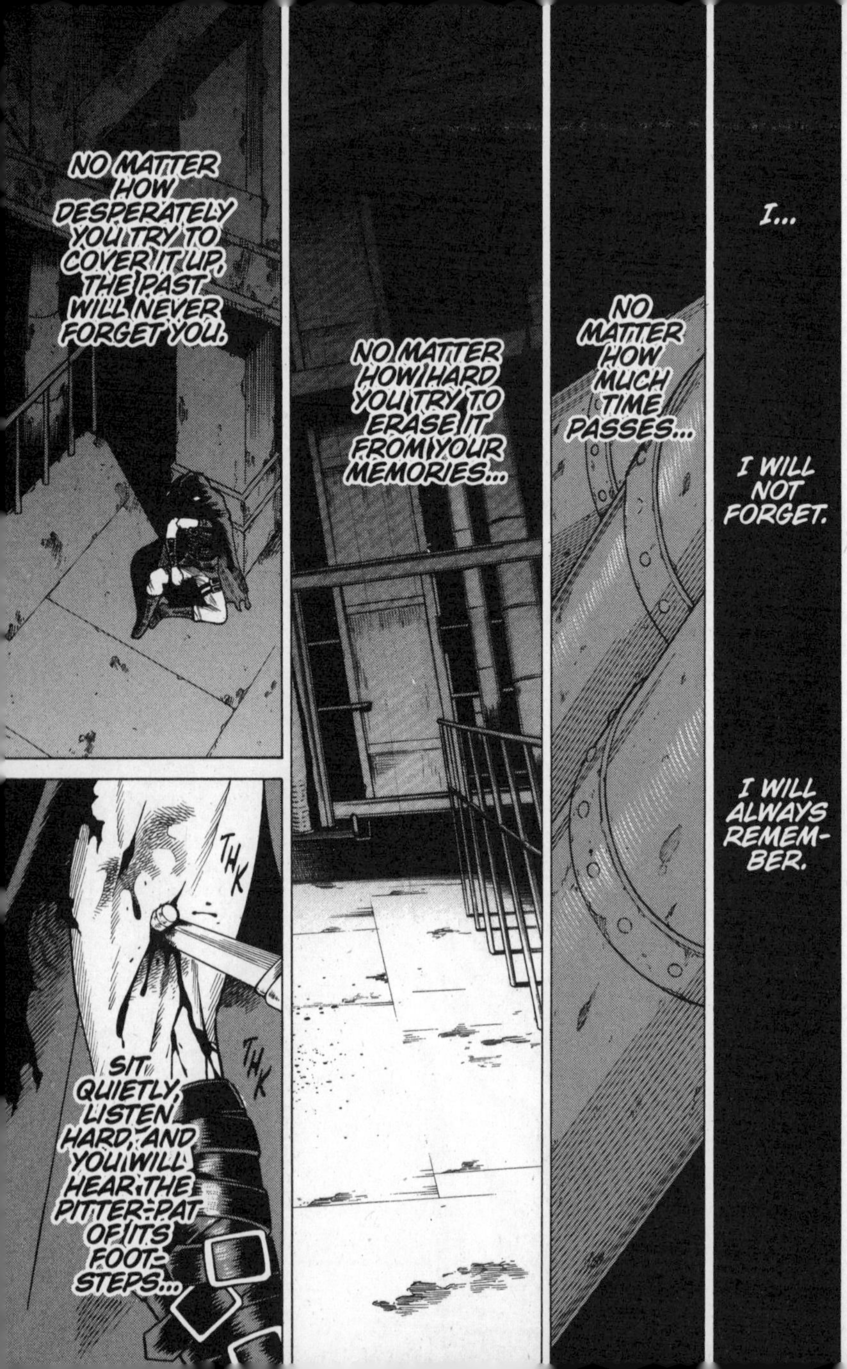
NO MATTER HOW DESPERATELY YOU TRY TO COVER IT UP, THE PAST WILL NEVER FORGET YOU.
THK
THK
SIT QUIETLY, LISTEN HARD, AND YOU WILL HEAR THE PITTER-PAT OF ITS FOOT-STEPS...
NO MATTER HOW HARD YOU TRY TO ERASE IT FROM YOUR MEMORIES...
NO MATTER HOW MUCH TIME PASSES...
I...
I WILL NOT FORGET.
I WILL ALWAYS REMEMBER.

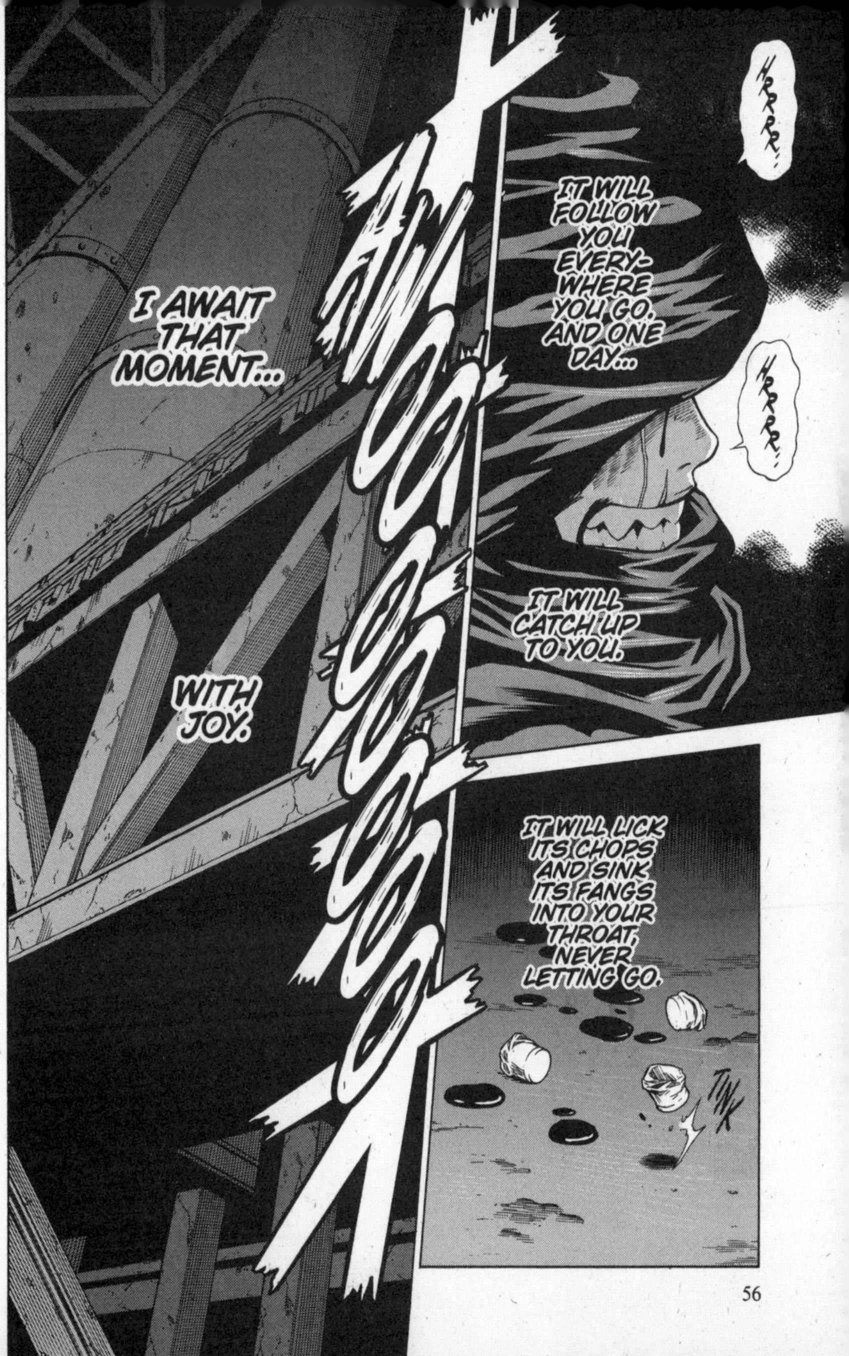
HRRRR!
IT WILL FOLLOW YOU EVERY-WHERE YOU GO. AND ONE DAY...
HRRRR!
IT WILL CATCH UP TO YOU.
IT WILL LICK ITS CHOPS AND SINK ITS FANGS INTO YOUR THROAT, NEVER LETTING GO.
TINK
I AWAIT THAT MOMENT...
WITH JOY.

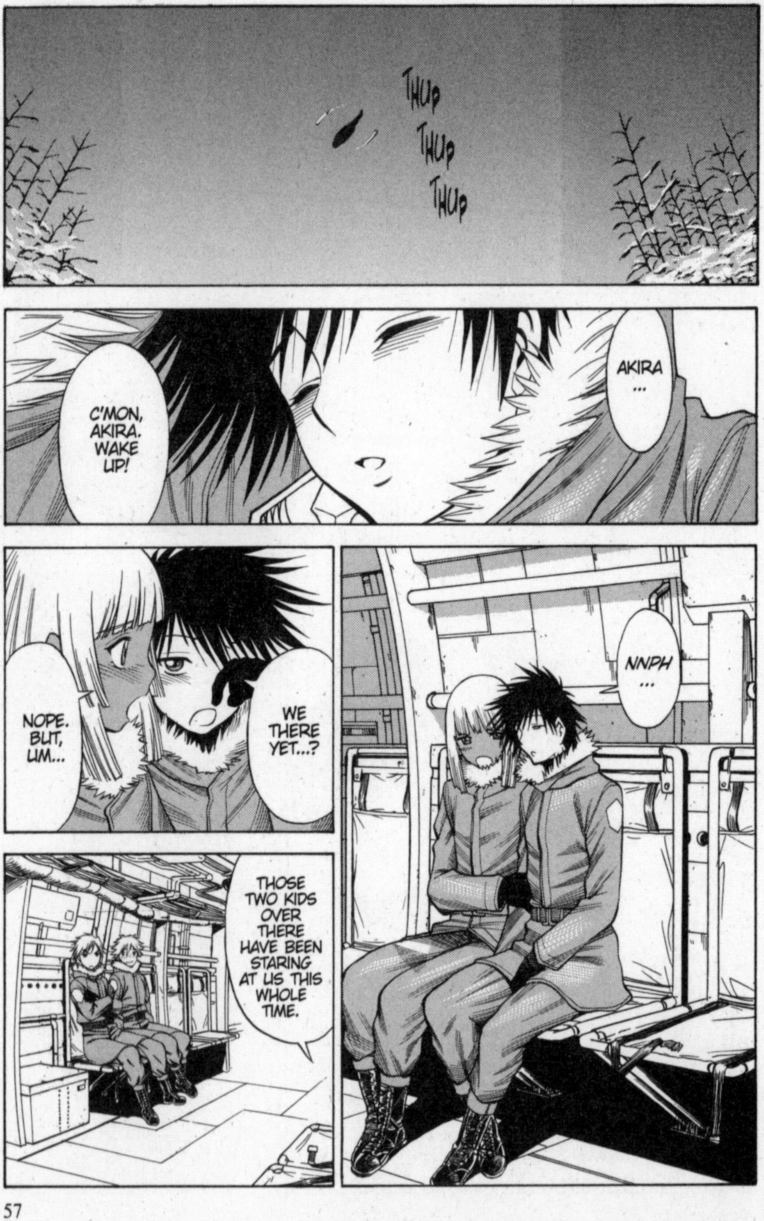
THUP
THUP
THUP
AKIRA ...
C'MON, AKIRA. WAKE UP!
NNPH ...
WE THERE YET...?
NOPE. BUT, UM...
THOSE TWO KIDS OVER THERE HAVE BEEN STARING AT US THIS WHOLE TIME.

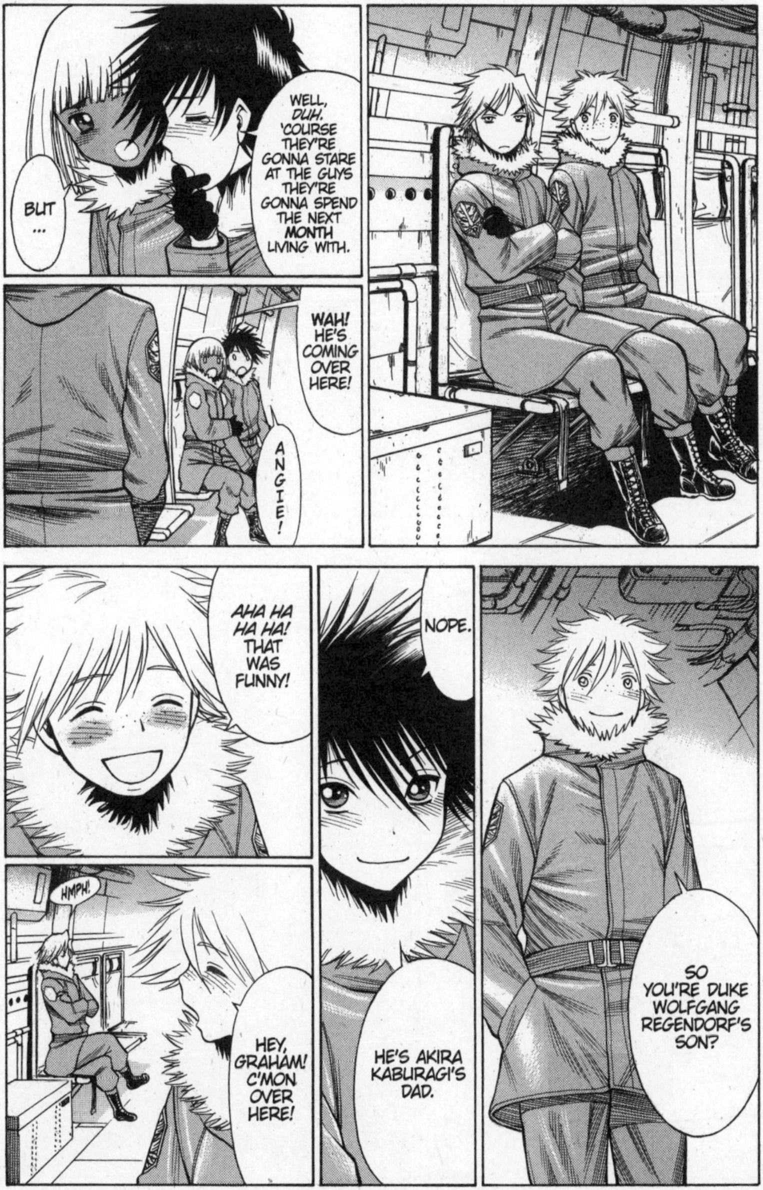
WELL, DUH. 'COURSE THEY'RE GONNA STARE AT THE GUYS THEY'RE GONNA SPEND THE NEXT MONTH LIVING WITH.
BUT ...
WAH! HE'S COMING OVER HERE!
ANGIE!
SO YOU'RE DUKE WOLFGANG REGENDORF'S SON?
NOPE.
HE'S AKIRA KABURAGI'S DAD.
AHA HA HA HA! THAT WAS FUNNY!
HEY, GRAHAM! C'MON OVER HERE!
HMPH!

Chapter 40: Hour of the Wolf

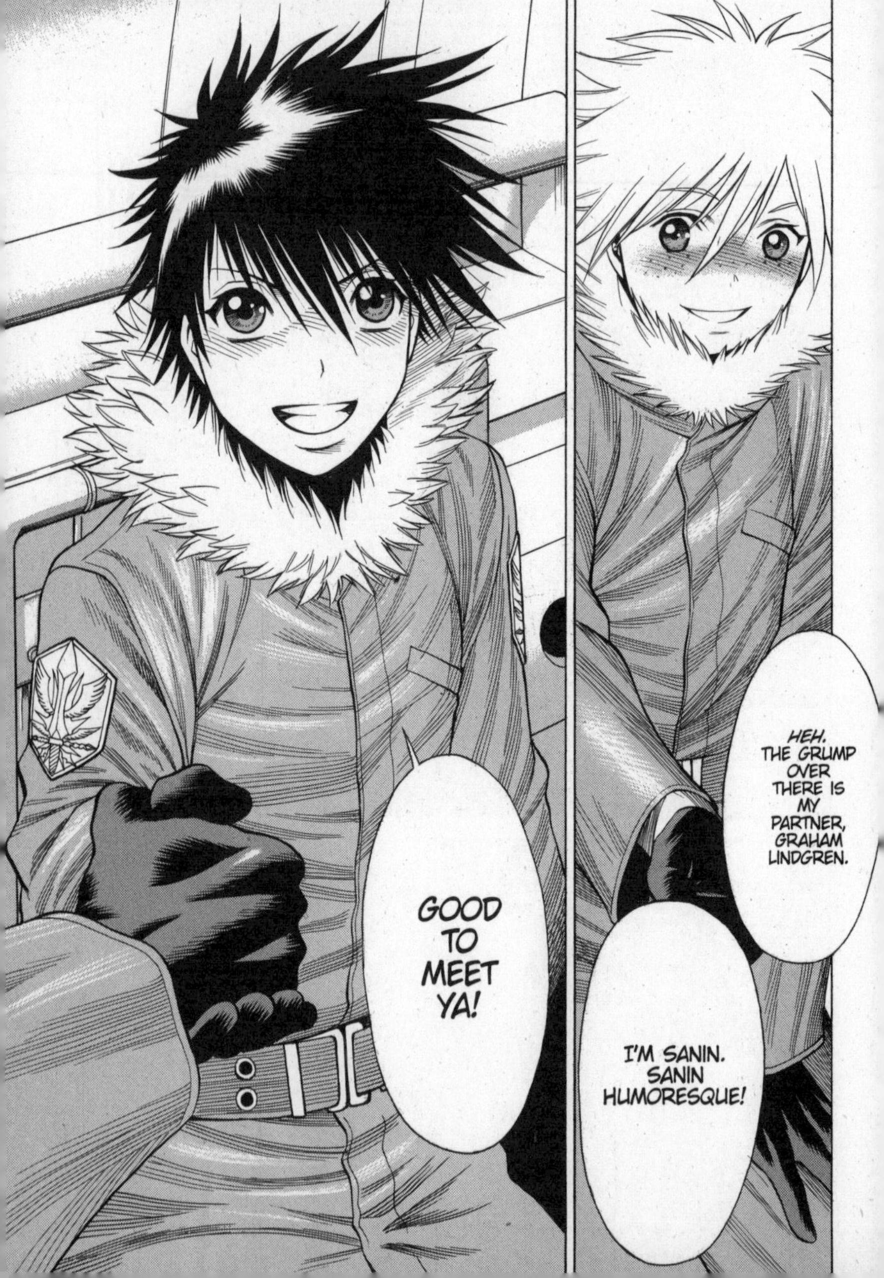
HEH. THE GRUMP OVER THERE IS MY PARTNER, GRAHAM LINDGREN.
I'M SANIN. SANIN HUMORESQUE!
GOOD TO MEET YA!

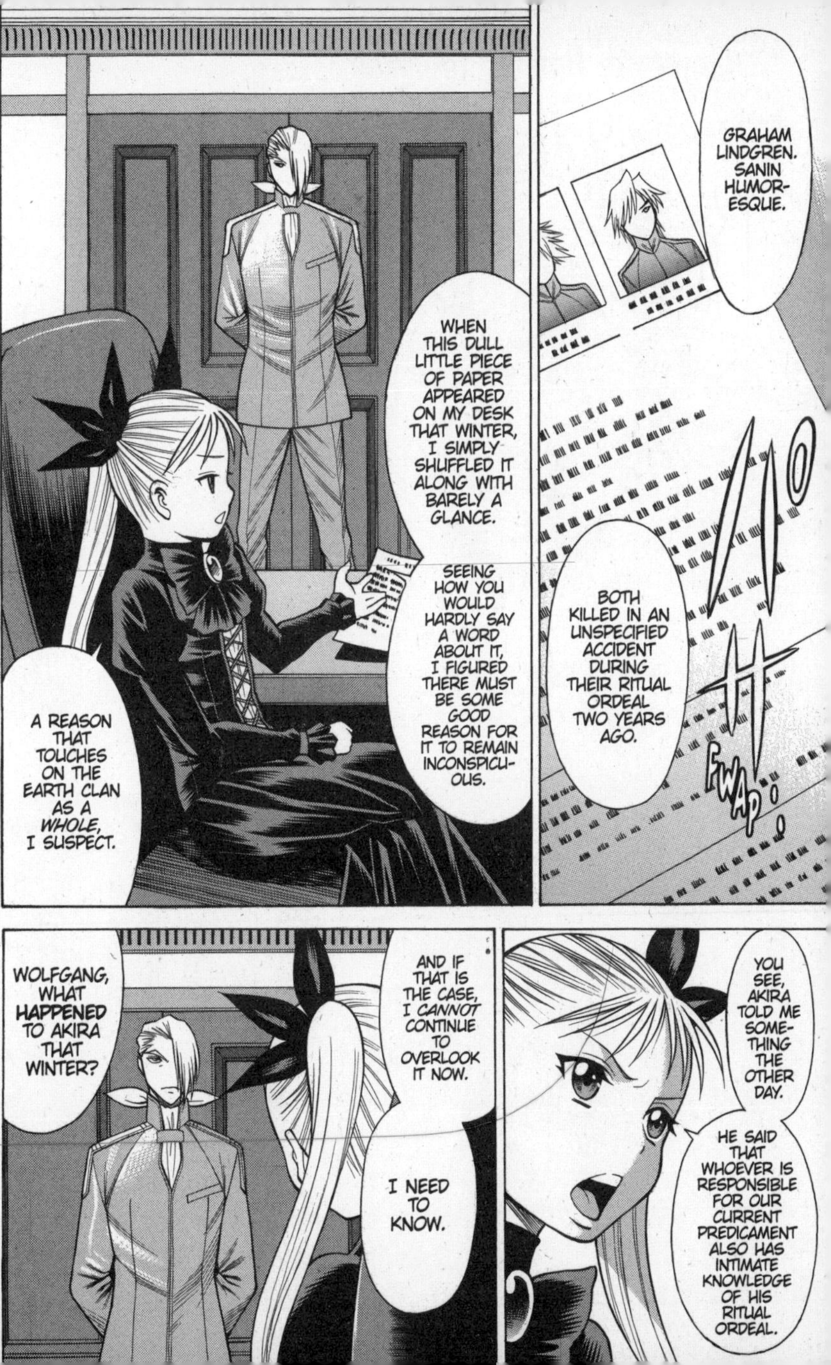
GRAHAM LINDGREN. SANIN HUMOR-ESQUE.
BOTH KILLED IN AN UNSPECIFIED ACCIDENT DURING THEIR RITUAL ORDEAL TWO YEARS AGO.
FWAP!
WHEN THIS DULL LITTLE PIECE OF PAPER APPEARED ON MY DESK THAT WINTER, I SIMPLY SHUFFLED IT ALONG WITH BARELY A GLANCE.
SEEING HOW YOU WOULD HARDLY SAY A WORD ABOUT IT, I FIGURED THERE MUST BE SOME GOOD REASON FOR IT TO REMAIN INCONSPICU-OUS.
A REASON THAT TOUCHES ON THE EARTH CLAN AS A *WHOLE*, I SUSPECT.
YOU SEE, AKIRA TOLD ME SOME-THING THE OTHER DAY.
HE SAID THAT WHOEVER IS RESPONSIBLE FOR OUR CURRENT PREDICAMENT ALSO HAS INTIMATE KNOWLEDGE OF HIS RITUAL ORDEAL.
AND IF THAT IS THE CASE, I *CANNOT* CONTINUE TO OVERLOOK IT NOW.
I NEED TO KNOW.
WOLFGANG, WHAT **HAPPENED** TO AKIRA THAT WINTER?

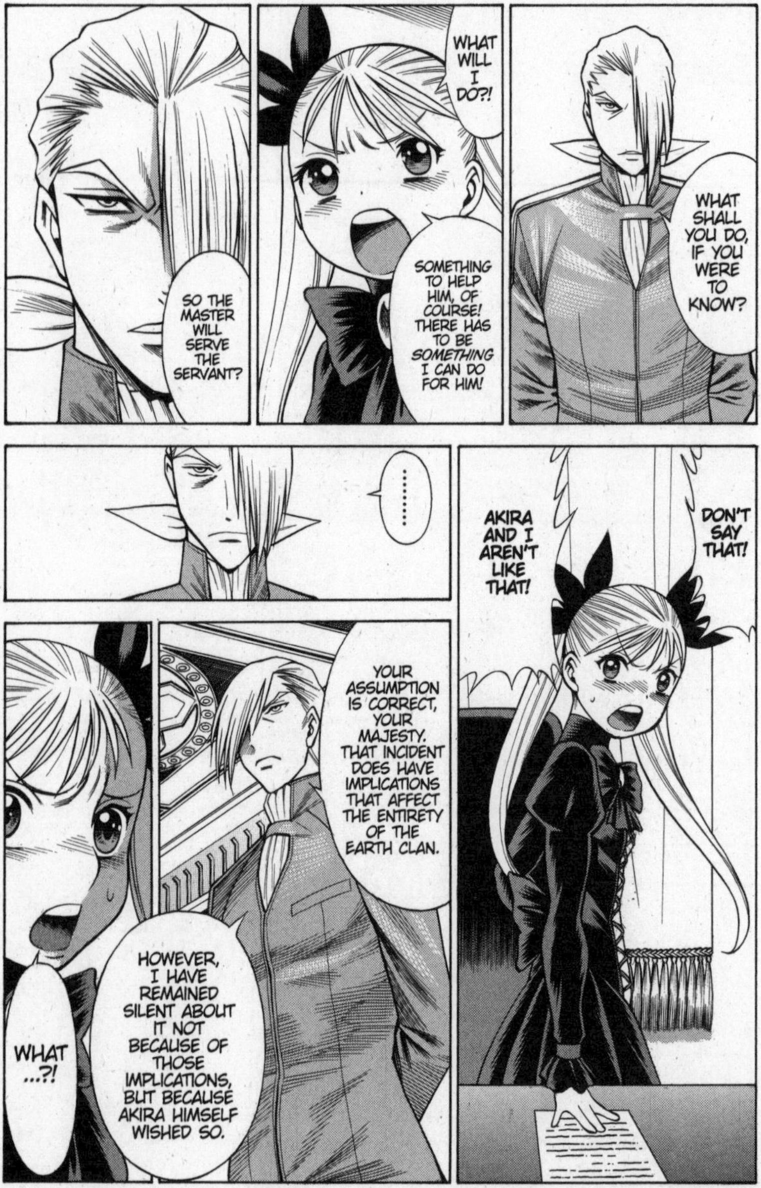
WHAT SHALL YOU DO, IF YOU WERE TO KNOW?
WHAT WILL I DO?!
SOMETHING TO HELP HIM, OF COURSE! THERE HAS TO BE *SOMETHING* I CAN DO FOR HIM!
SO THE MASTER WILL SERVE THE SERVANT?
DON'T SAY THAT!
AKIRA AND I AREN'T LIKE THAT!
....
YOUR ASSUMPTION IS CORRECT, YOUR MAJESTY. THAT INCIDENT DOES HAVE IMPLICATIONS THAT AFFECT THE ENTIRETY OF THE EARTH CLAN.
HOWEVER, I HAVE REMAINED SILENT ABOUT IT NOT BECAUSE OF THOSE IMPLICATIONS, BUT BECAUSE AKIRA HIMSELF WISHED SO.
WHAT ...?!

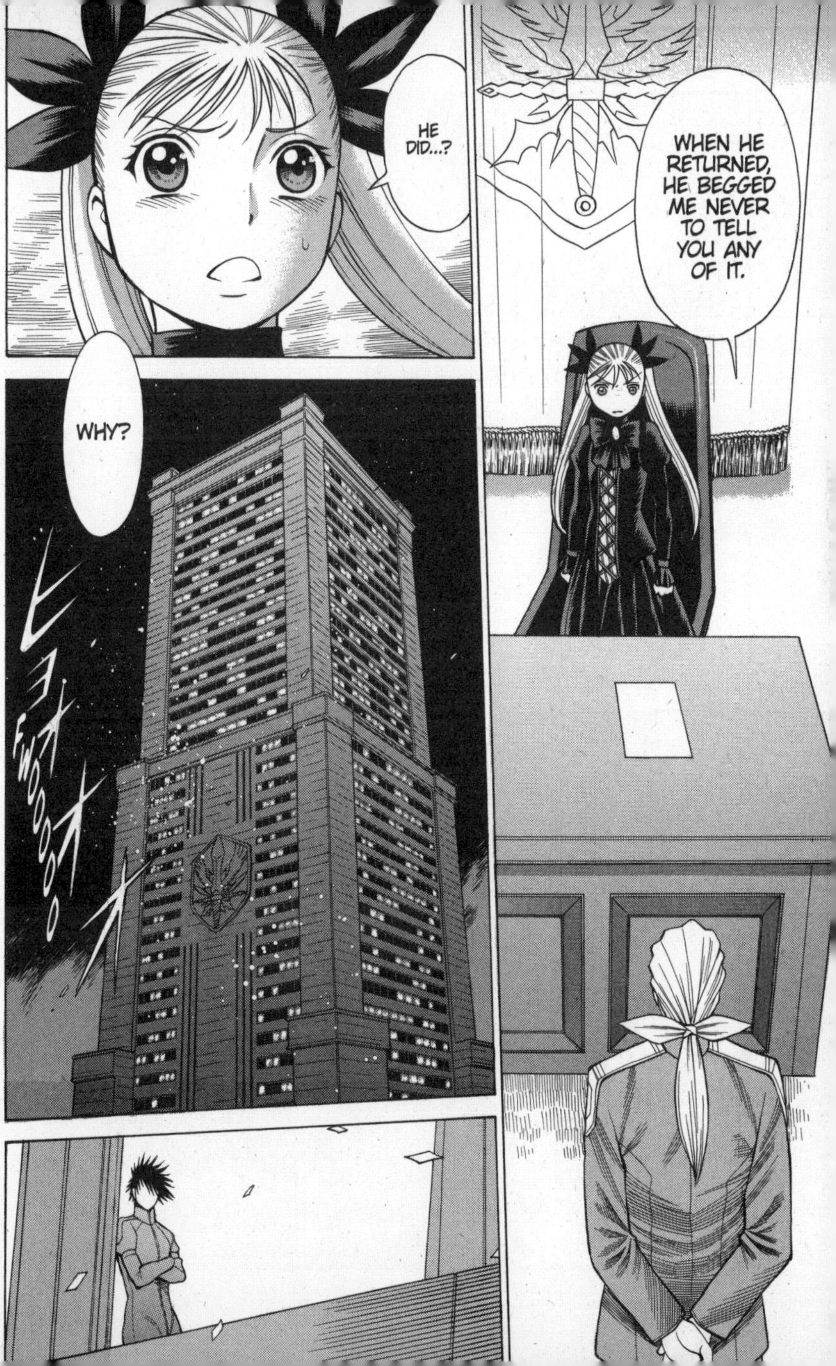
WHEN HE RETURNED, HE BEGGED ME NEVER TO TELL YOU ANY OF IT.
HE DID...?
WHY?
FWOOOOO

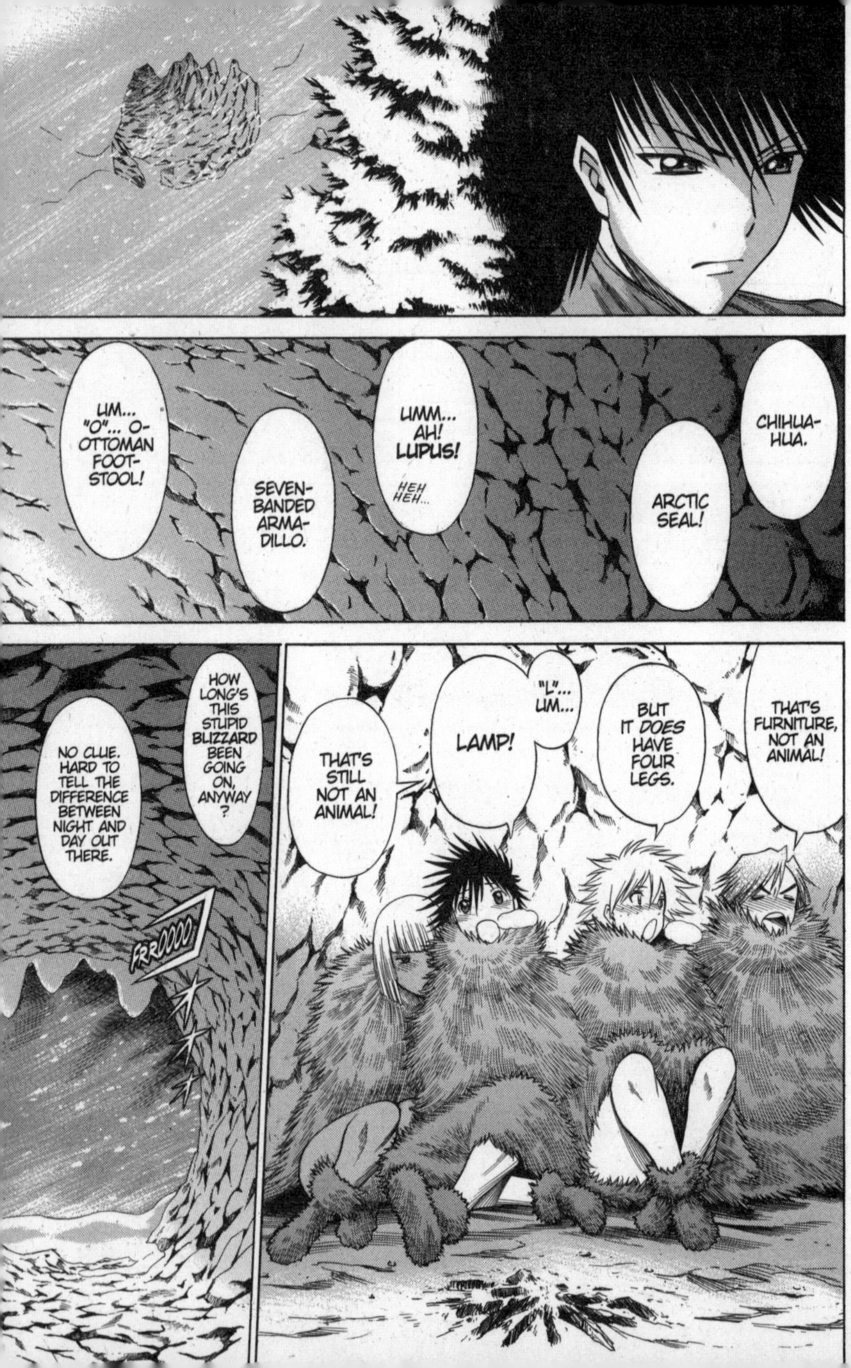
CHIHUA-HUA.
ARCTIC SEAL!
UMM... AH! LUPUS!
HEH HEH...
SEVEN-BANDED ARMA-DILLO.
UM... "O"... O-OTTOMAN FOOT-STOOL!
THAT'S FURNITURE, NOT AN ANIMAL!
BUT IT DOES HAVE FOUR LEGS.
"L"... UM...
LAMP!
THAT'S STILL NOT AN ANIMAL!
HOW LONG'S THIS STUPID BLIZZARD BEEN GOING ON, ANYWAY?
NO CLUE. HARD TO TELL THE DIFFERENCE BETWEEN NIGHT AND DAY OUT THERE.
FRROOOO

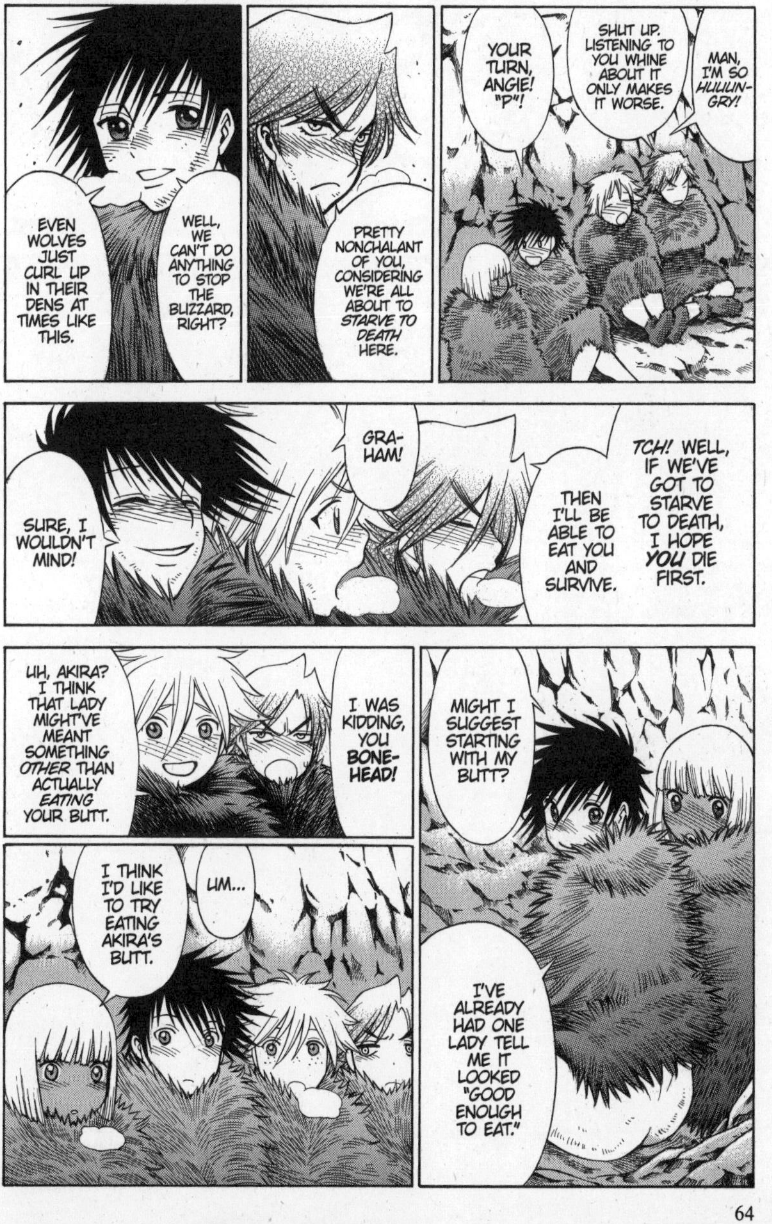
MAN, I'M SO *HUUUNGRY!*
SHUT UP. LISTENING TO YOU WHINE ABOUT IT ONLY MAKES IT WORSE.
YOUR TURN, ANGIE! "P"!
PRETTY NONCHALANT OF YOU, CONSIDERING WE'RE ALL ABOUT TO *STARVE TO DEATH* HERE.
WELL, WE CAN'T DO ANYTHING TO STOP THE BLIZZARD, RIGHT?
EVEN WOLVES JUST CURL UP IN THEIR DENS AT TIMES LIKE THIS.
TCH! WELL, IF WE'VE GOT TO STARVE TO DEATH, I HOPE ***YOU*** DIE FIRST.
THEN I'LL BE ABLE TO EAT YOU AND SURVIVE.
GRA-HAM!
SURE, I WOULDN'T MIND!
MIGHT I SUGGEST STARTING WITH MY BUTT?
I'VE ALREADY HAD ONE LADY TELL ME IT LOOKED "GOOD ENOUGH TO EAT."
I WAS KIDDING, YOU **BONE-HEAD!**
UH, AKIRA? I THINK THAT LADY MIGHT'VE MEANT SOMETHING *OTHER* THAN ACTUALLY *EATING* YOUR BUTT.
UM...
I THINK I'D LIKE TO TRY EATING AKIRA'S BUTT.

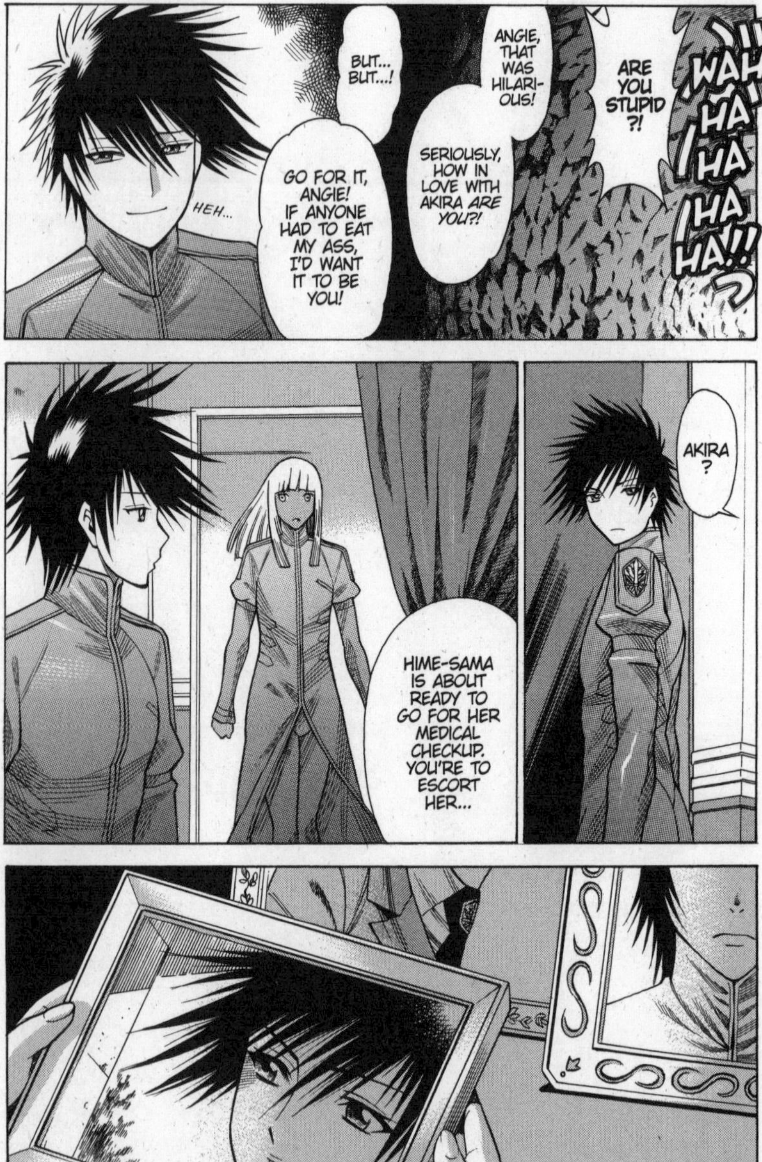
WAH HA HA HA HA!!
ARE YOU STUPID?!
ANGIE, THAT WAS HILARIOUS!
SERIOUSLY, HOW IN LOVE WITH AKIRA ARE YOU?!
BUT... BUT...!
GO FOR IT, ANGIE! IF ANYONE HAD TO EAT MY ASS, I'D WANT IT TO BE YOU!
HEH...
AKIRA?
HIME-SAMA IS ABOUT READY TO GO FOR HER MEDICAL CHECKUP. YOU'RE TO ESCORT HER...

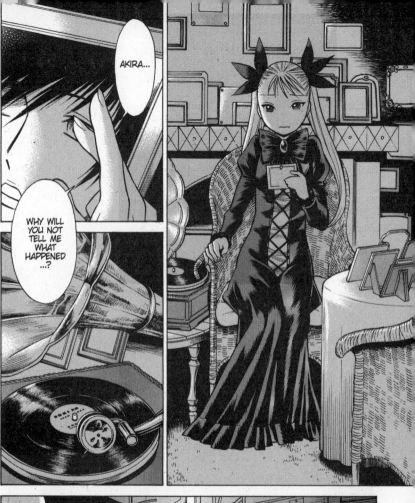

AKIRA...

WHY WILL YOU NOT TELL ME WHAT HAPPENED ...?

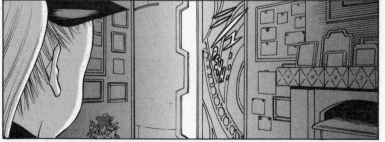

66

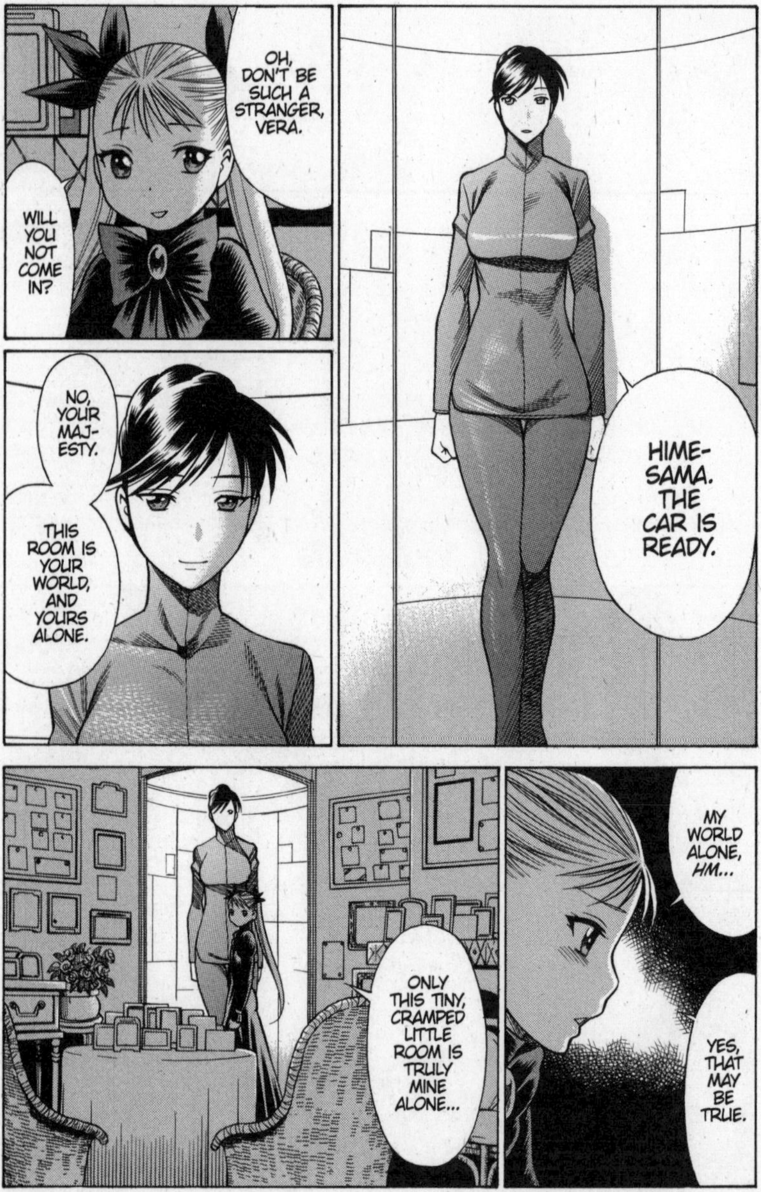
HIME-SAMA. THE CAR IS READY.
OH, DON'T BE SUCH A STRANGER, VERA.
WILL YOU NOT COME IN?
NO, YOUR MAJ-ESTY.
THIS ROOM IS YOUR WORLD, AND YOURS ALONE.
MY WORLD ALONE, HM...
YES, THAT MAY BE TRUE.
ONLY THIS TINY, CRAMPED LITTLE ROOM IS TRULY MINE ALONE...

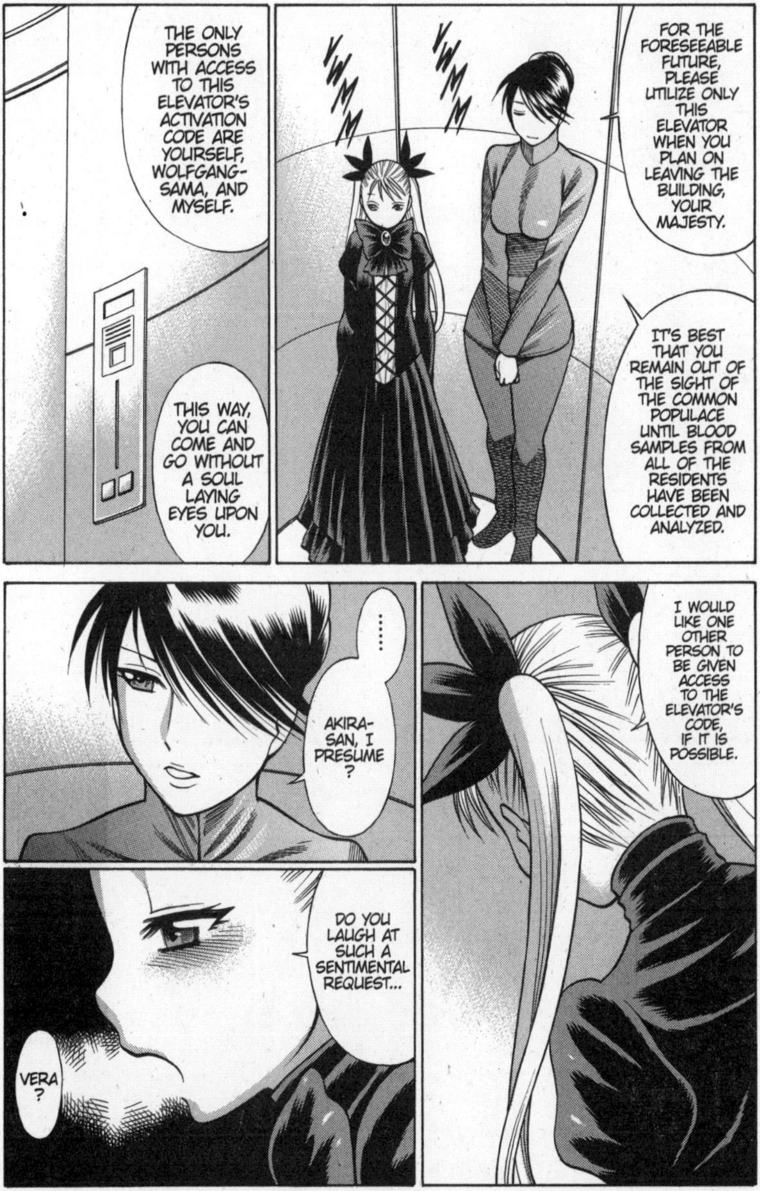
FOR THE FORESEEABLE FUTURE, PLEASE UTILIZE ONLY THIS ELEVATOR WHEN YOU PLAN ON LEAVING THE BUILDING, YOUR MAJESTY.
VWMM
VWMM
IT'S BEST THAT YOU REMAIN OUT OF THE SIGHT OF THE COMMON POPULACE UNTIL BLOOD SAMPLES FROM ALL OF THE RESIDENTS HAVE BEEN COLLECTED AND ANALYZED.
THE ONLY PERSONS WITH ACCESS TO THIS ELEVATOR'S ACTIVATION CODE ARE YOURSELF, WOLFGANG-SAMA, AND MYSELF.
THIS WAY, YOU CAN COME AND GO WITHOUT A SOUL LAYING EYES UPON YOU.
I WOULD LIKE ONE OTHER PERSON TO BE GIVEN ACCESS TO THE ELEVATOR'S CODE, IF IT IS POSSIBLE.
......
AKIRA-SAN, I PRESUME?
DO YOU LAUGH AT SUCH A SENTIMENTAL REQUEST...
VERA?

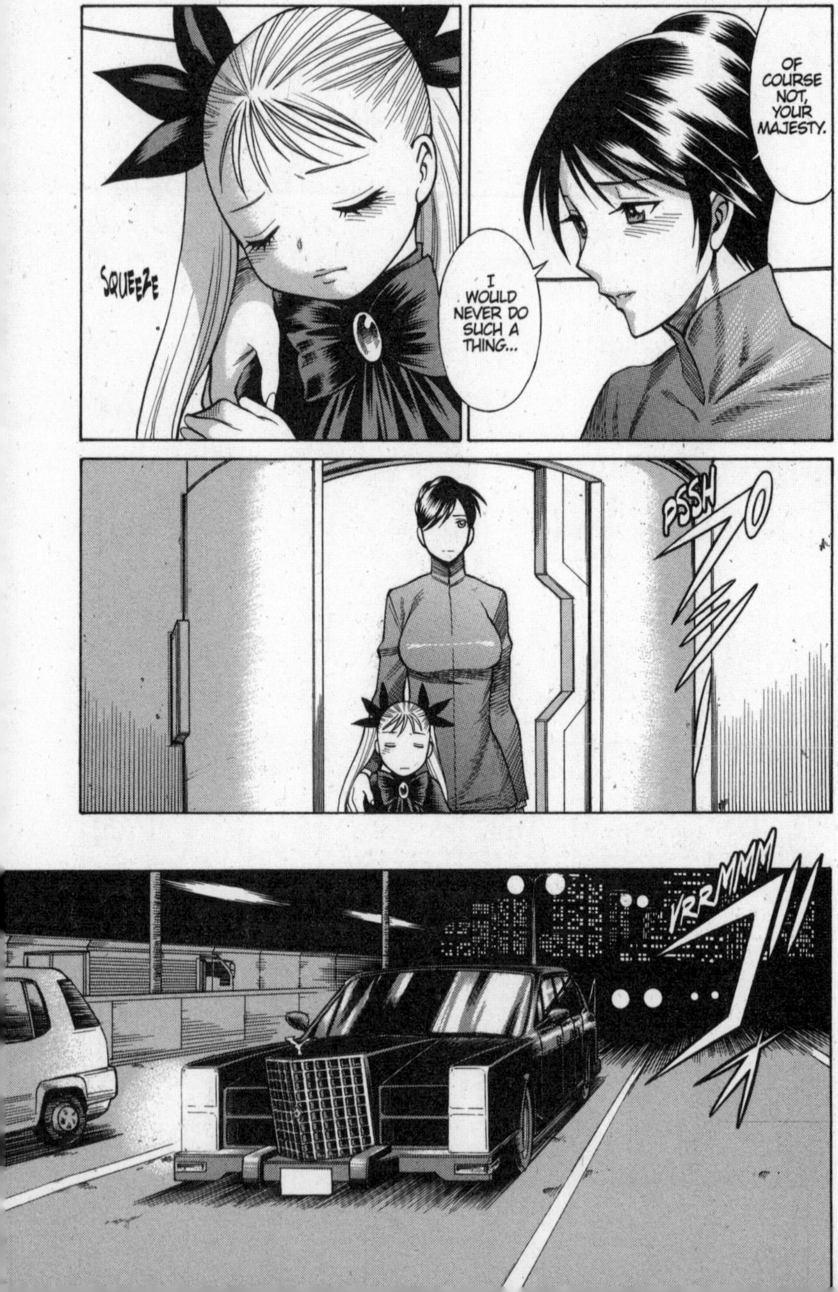
OF COURSE NOT, YOUR MAJESTY.
I WOULD NEVER DO SUCH A THING...
SQUEEZE
PSSH
VRRMMM

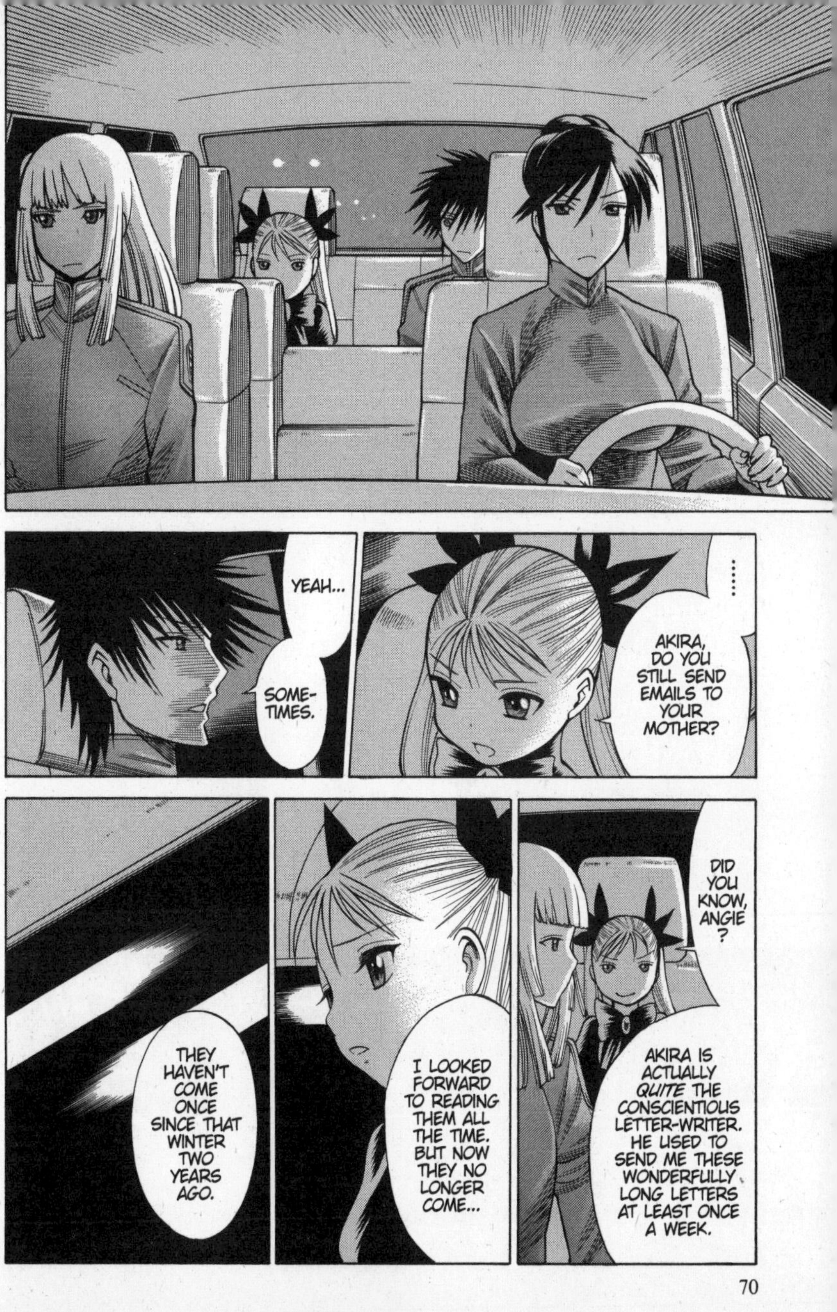
……
AKIRA, DO YOU STILL SEND EMAILS TO YOUR MOTHER?
YEAH...
SOME-TIMES.
DID YOU KNOW, ANGIE?
AKIRA IS ACTUALLY *QUITE* THE CONSCIENTIOUS LETTER-WRITER. HE USED TO SEND ME THESE WONDERFULLY LONG LETTERS AT LEAST ONCE A WEEK.
I LOOKED FORWARD TO READING THEM ALL THE TIME. BUT NOW THEY NO LONGER COME...
THEY HAVEN'T COME ONCE SINCE THAT WINTER TWO YEARS AGO.

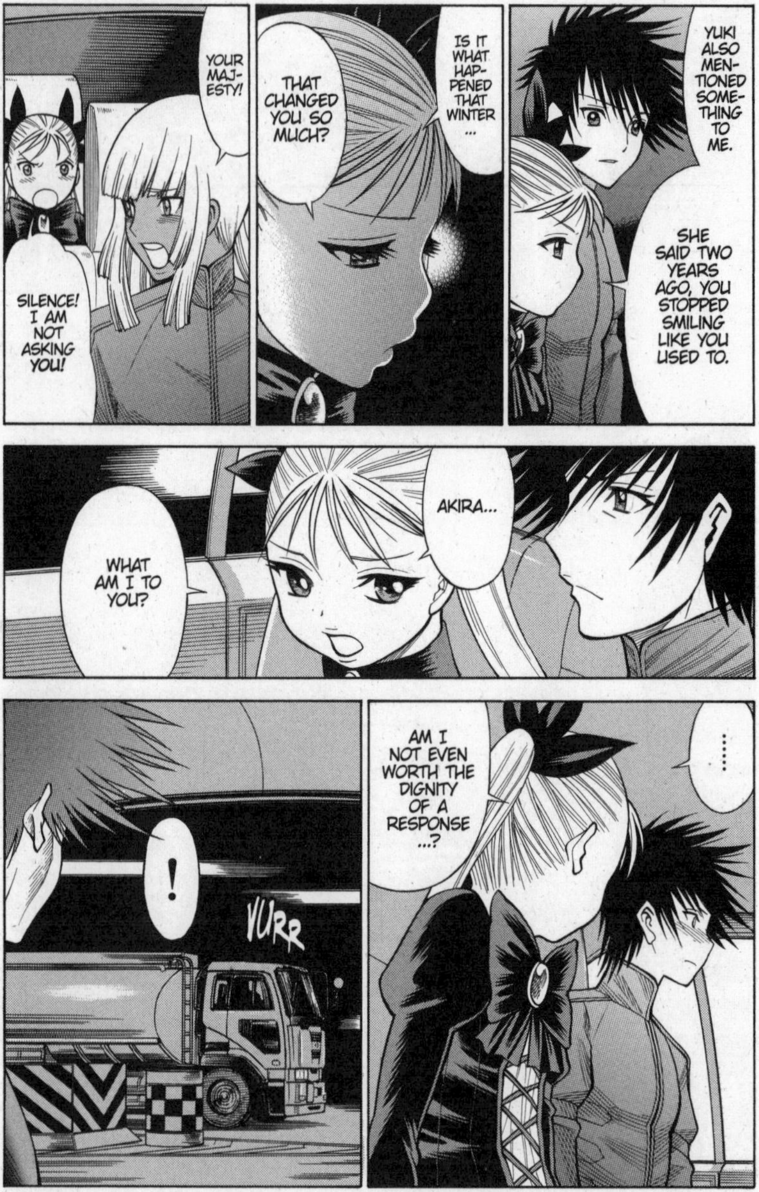
YUKI ALSO MEN-TIONED SOME-THING TO ME.
SHE SAID TWO YEARS AGO, YOU STOPPED SMILING LIKE YOU USED TO.
IS IT WHAT HAP-PENED THAT WINTER ...
THAT CHANGED YOU SO MUCH?
YOUR MAJ-ESTY!
SILENCE! I AM NOT ASKING YOU!
AKIRA...
WHAT AM I TO YOU?
......
AM I NOT EVEN WORTH THE DIGNITY OF A RESPONSE ...?
!
VURR

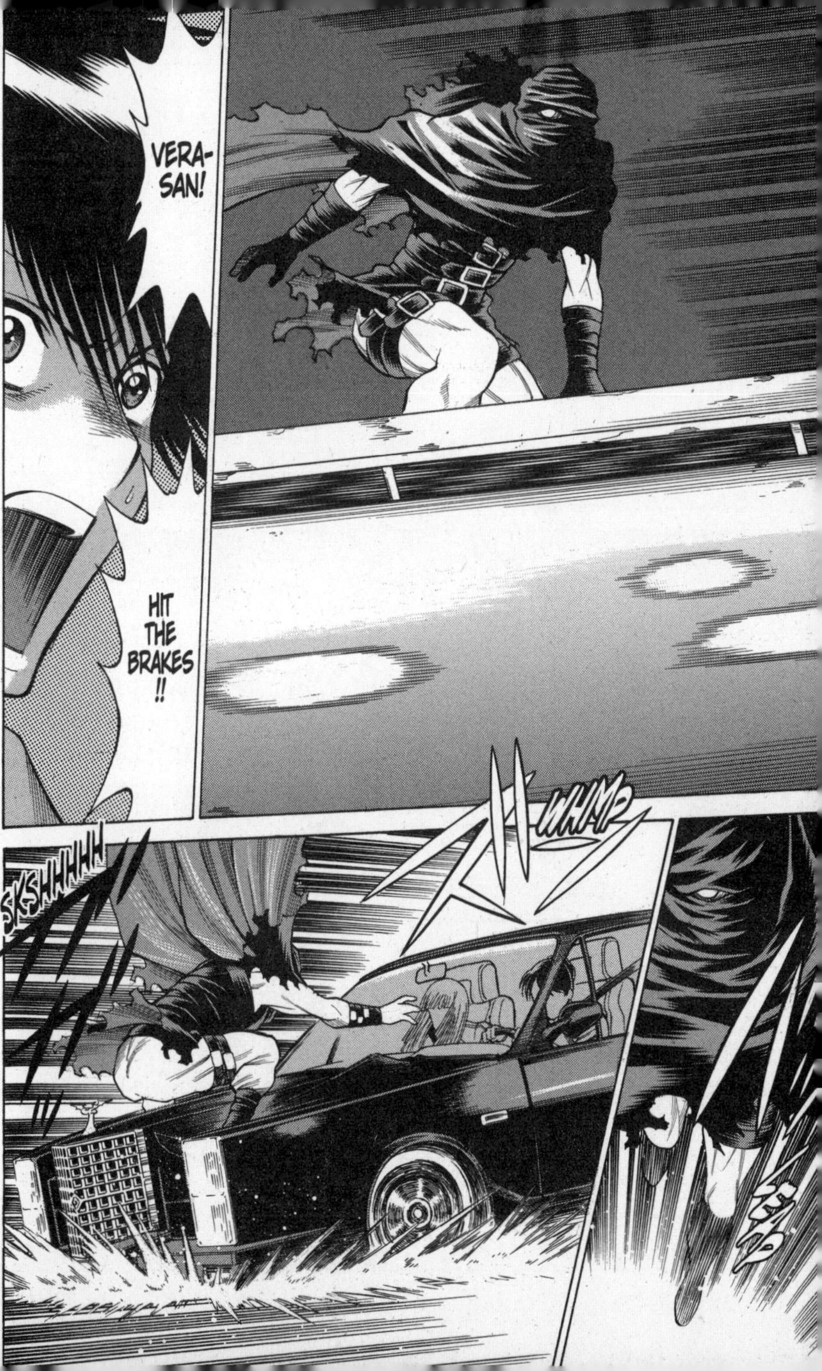
VERA-SAN!
HIT THE BRAKES!!
WHMP
SKSHHHHH

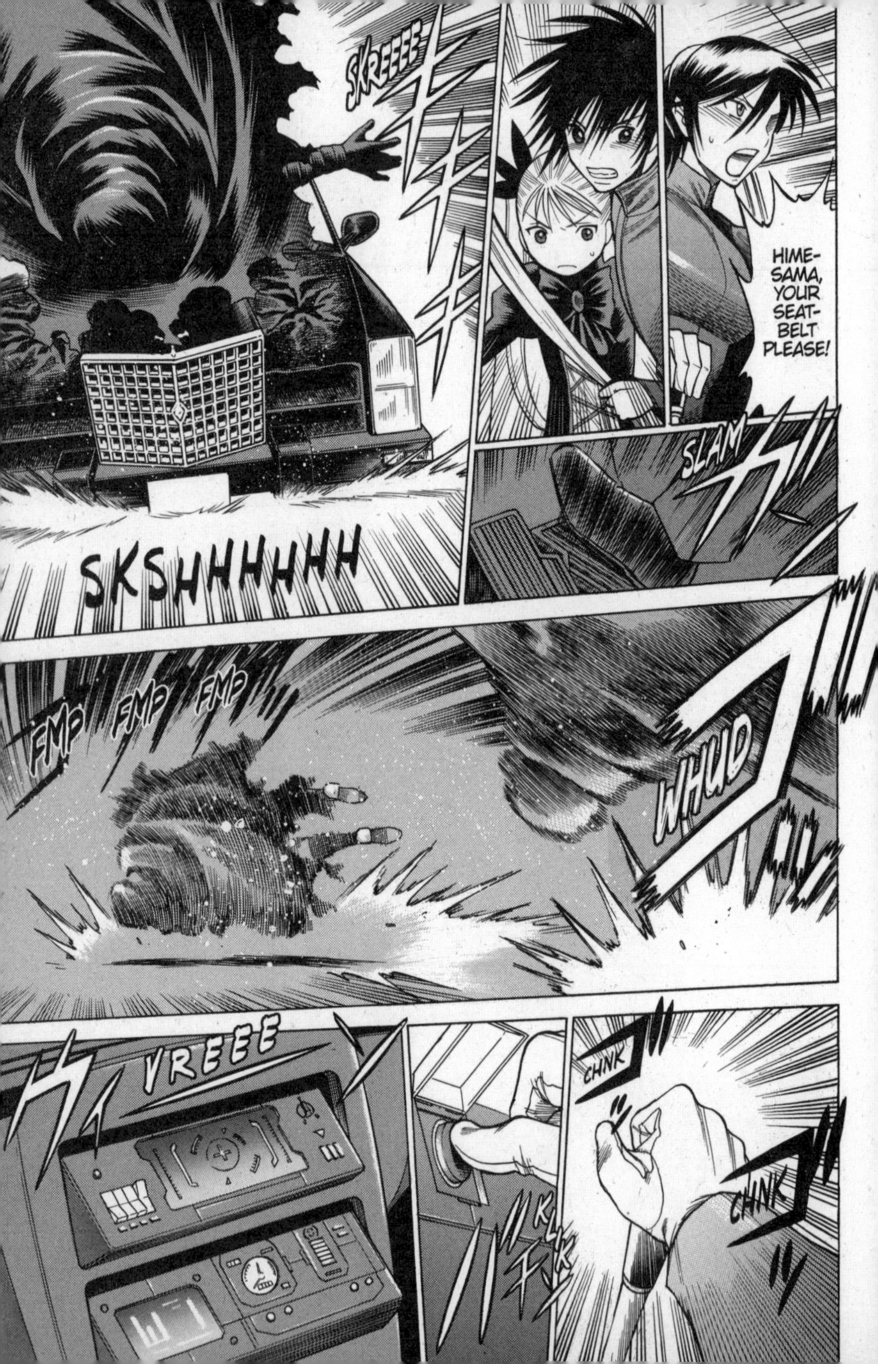
HIME-SAMA, YOUR SEAT-BELT PLEASE!
SLAM
SKREEEE
SKSHHHHHH
WHUD
FMP FMP FMP
CHNK
CHNK
KLK
VREEE

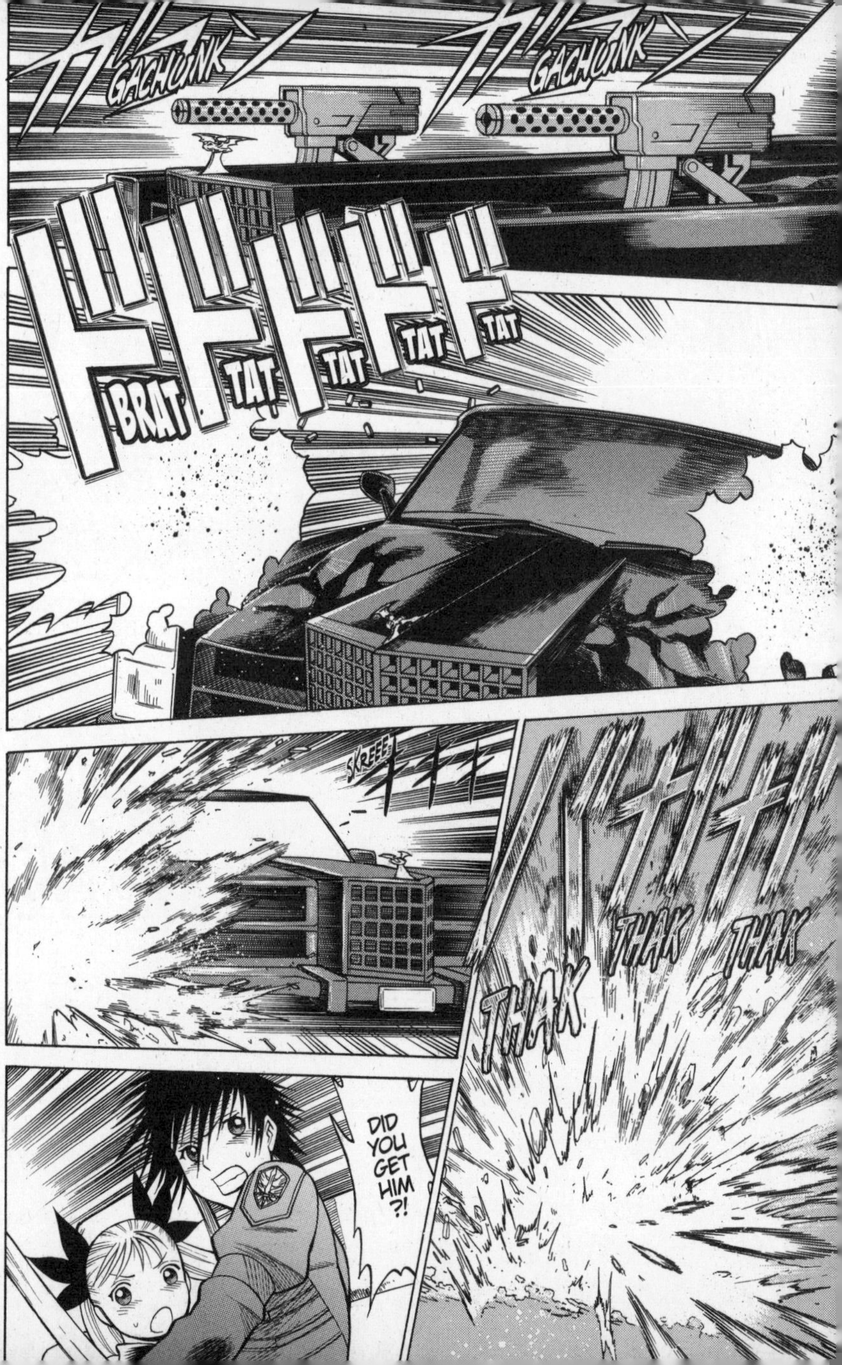
GACHUNK
GACHUNK
BRAT TAT TAT TAT TAT
THAK THAK THAK
SKREEE
DID YOU GET HIM?!

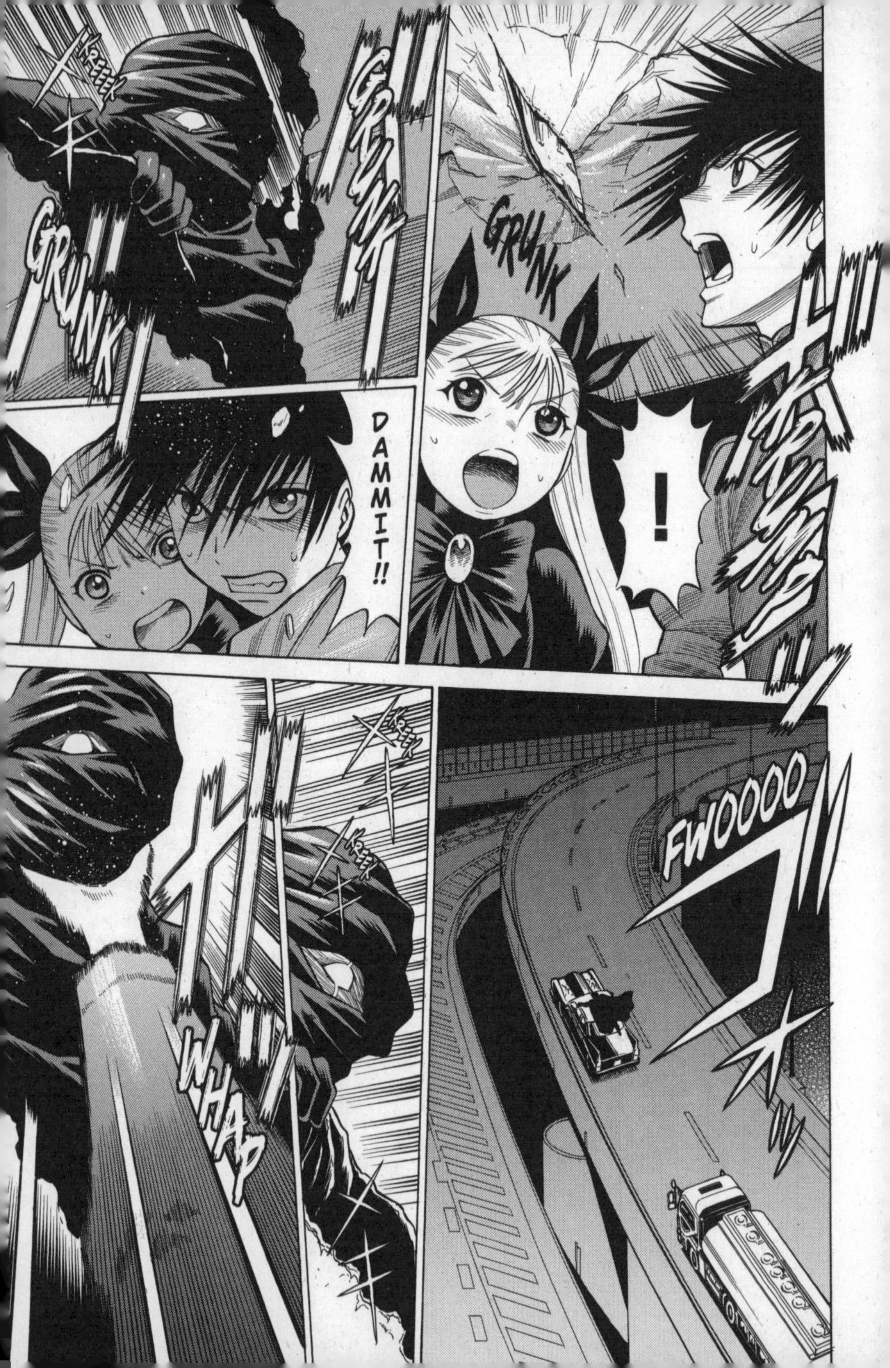

GRUNK
KREEEK
GRUNK
GRUNK
!
DAMMIT!!
FWOOOO
WHAP

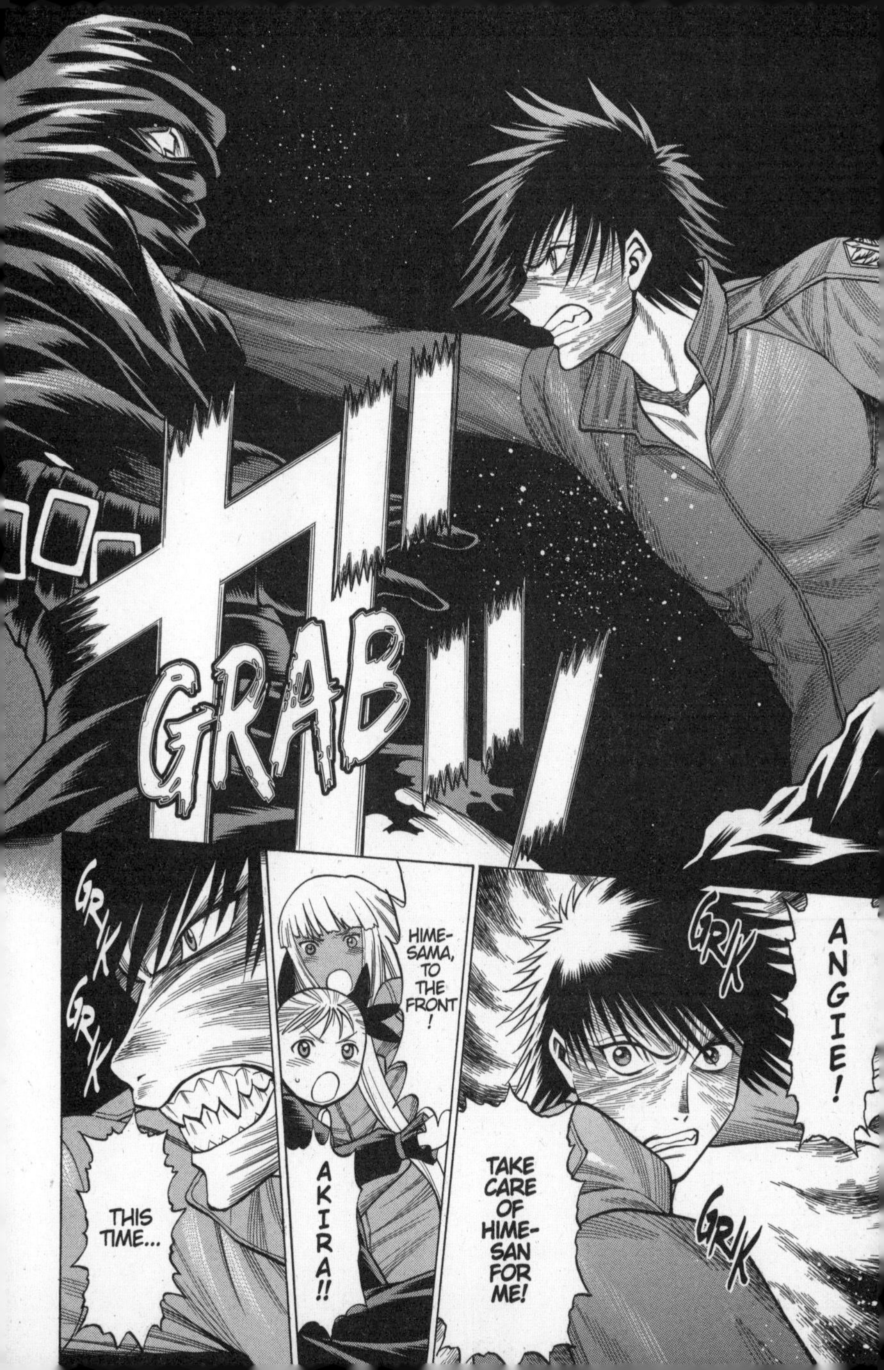
GRAB
ANGIE!
GRIK
TAKE CARE OF HIME-SAN FOR ME!
GRIK
HIME-SAMA, TO THE FRONT!
AKIRA!!
GRIK GRIK
THIS TIME...

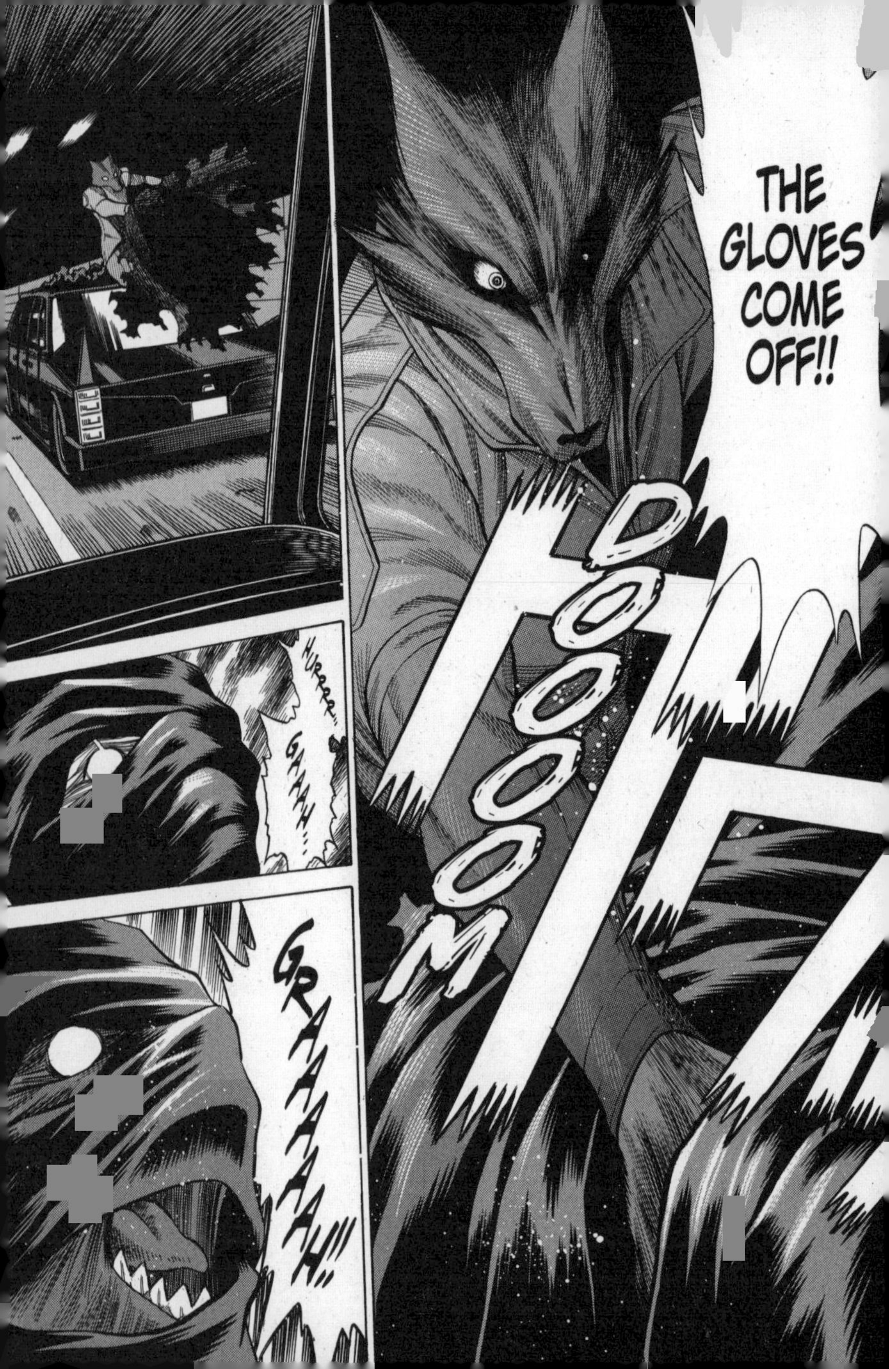
THE GLOVES COME OFF!!
DOOOOOM
HURRRR..
GAAAH!!
GRAAAAAAAH!!

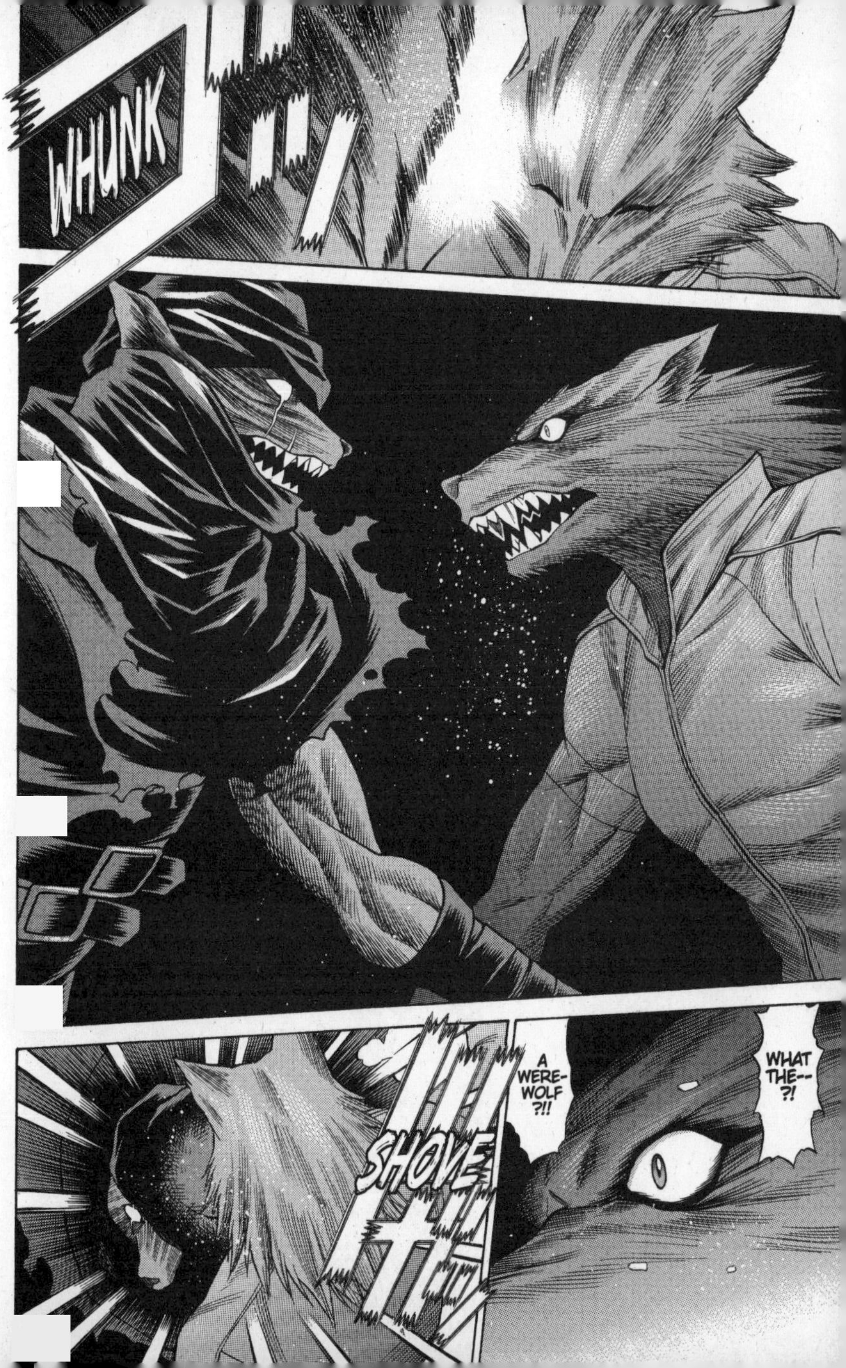
WHUNK
WHAT THE--?!
A WERE-WOLF?!!
SHOVE

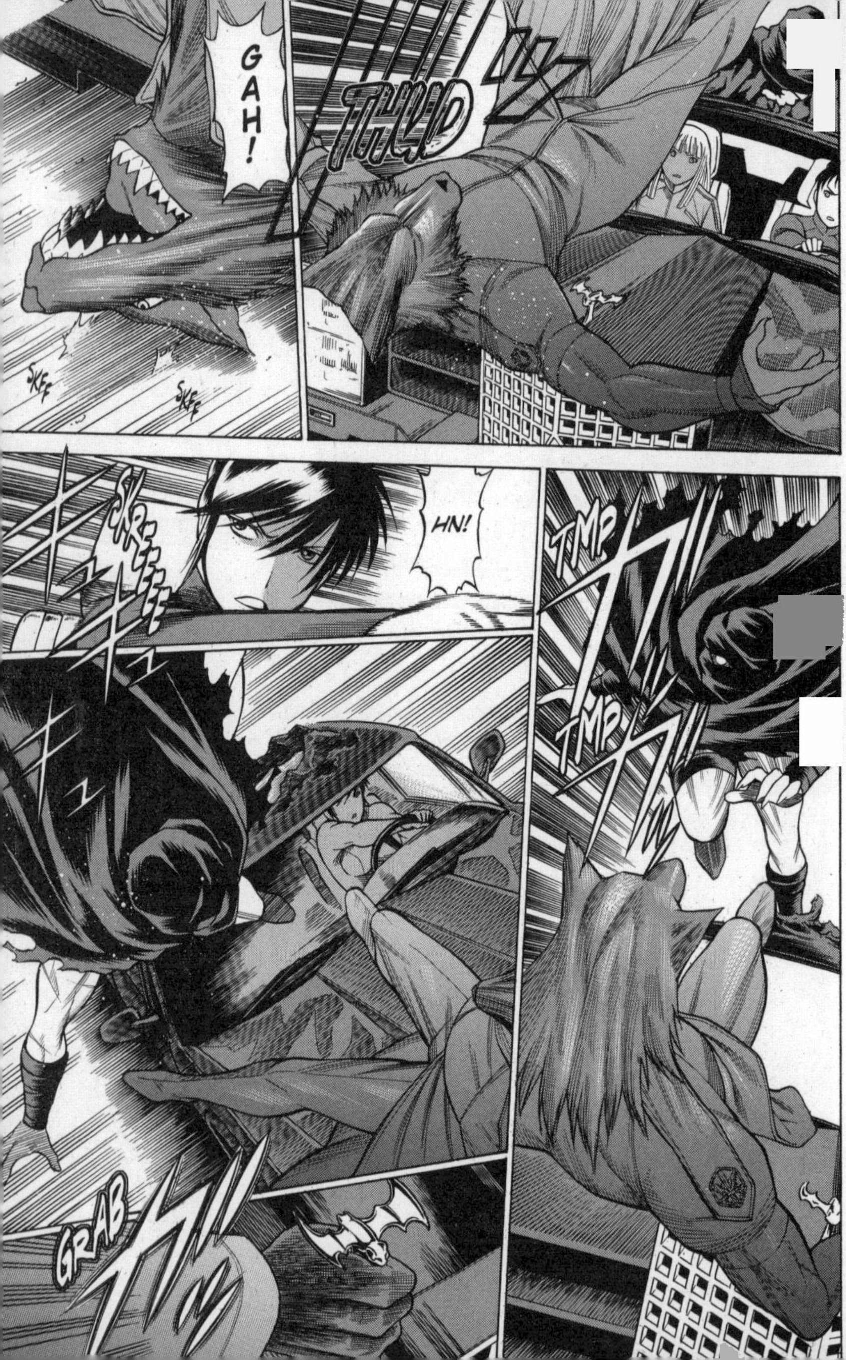
THUD
GAH!
SKFF
SKFF
TMP
TMP
HN!
SKREEEE
GRAB

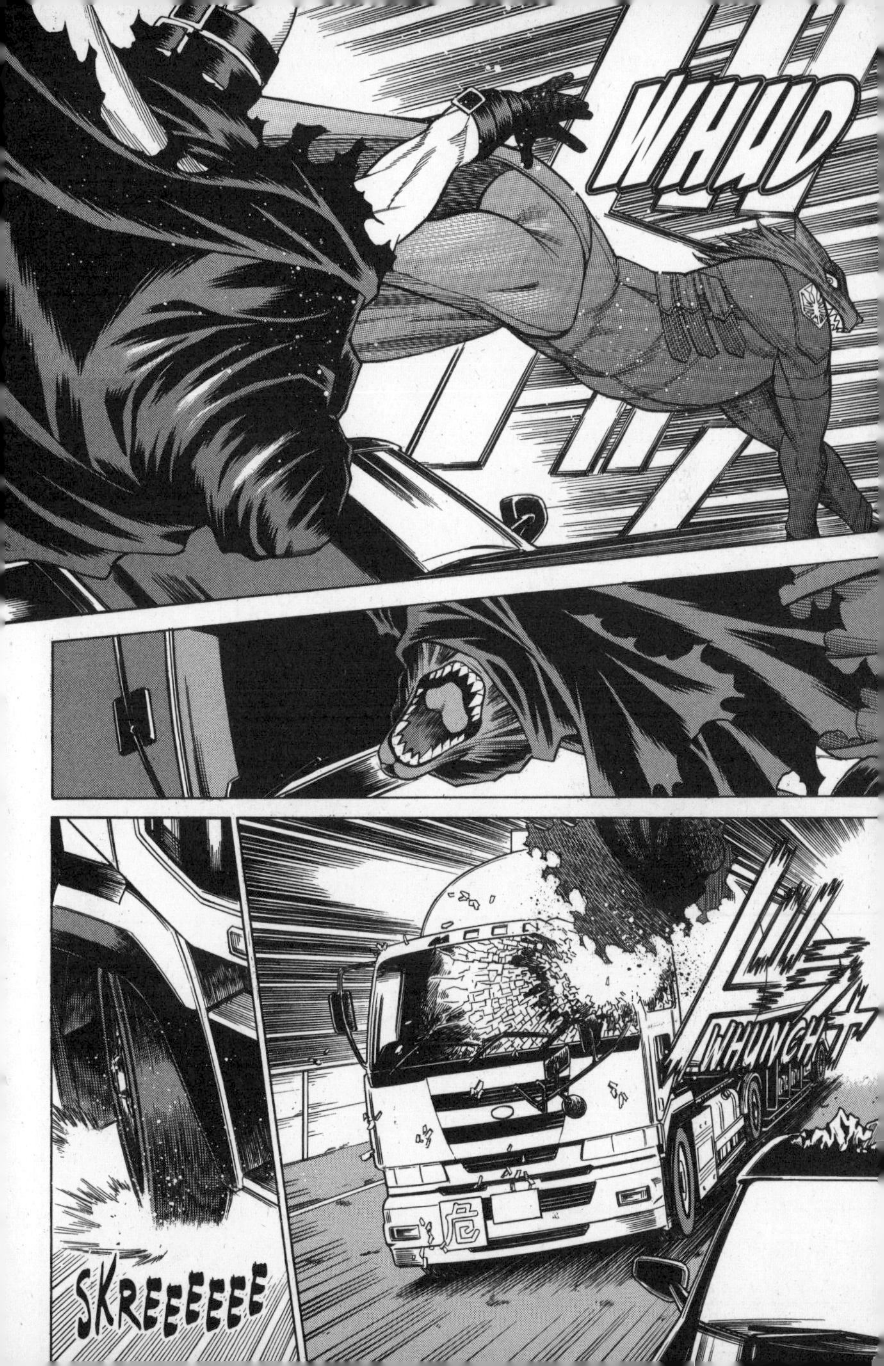
WHUD
WHUNCH
危
SKREEEEEEE

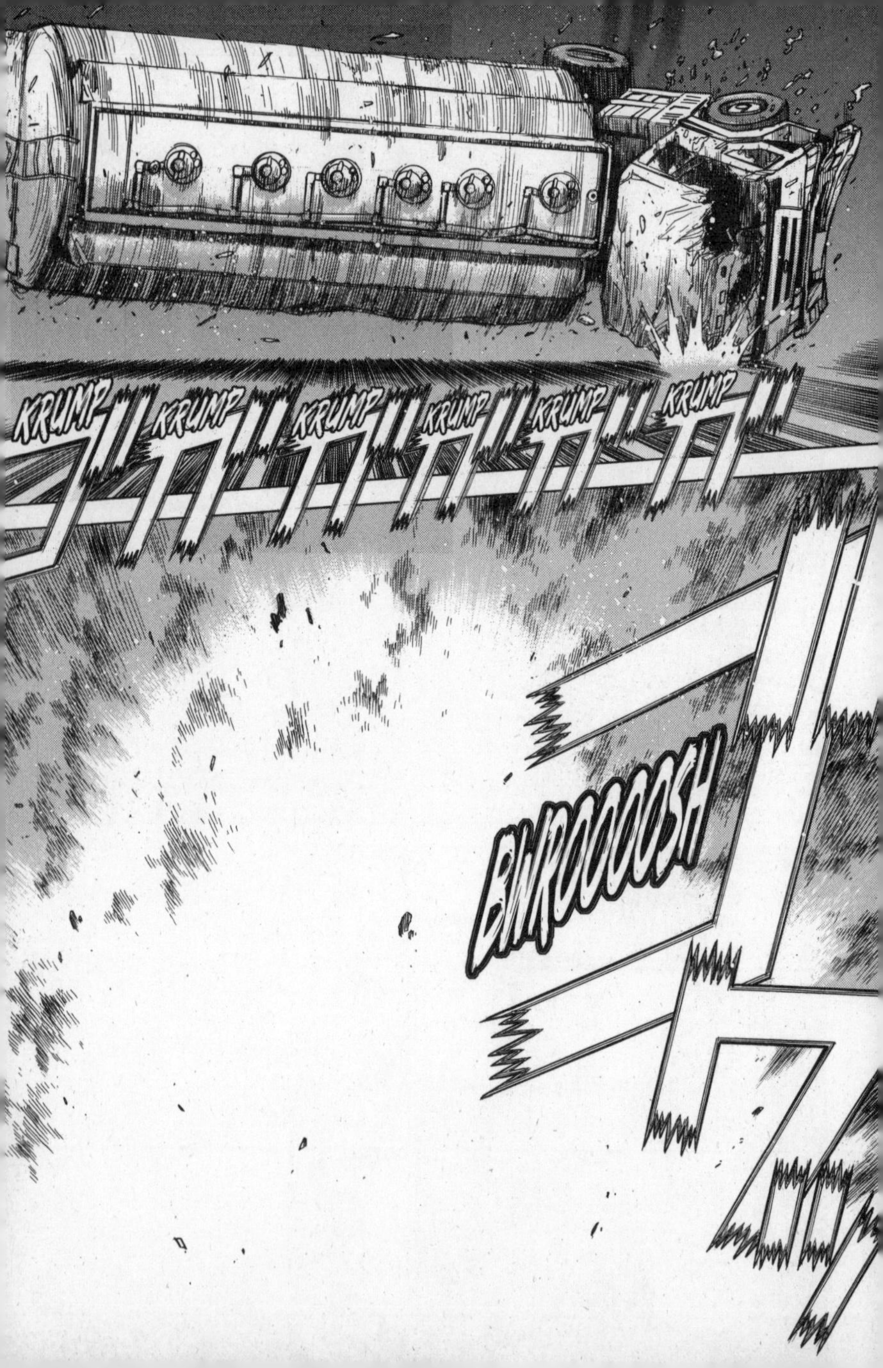
KRUMP
KRUMP
KRUMP
KRUMP
KRUMP
KRUMP
BWROOOOSH

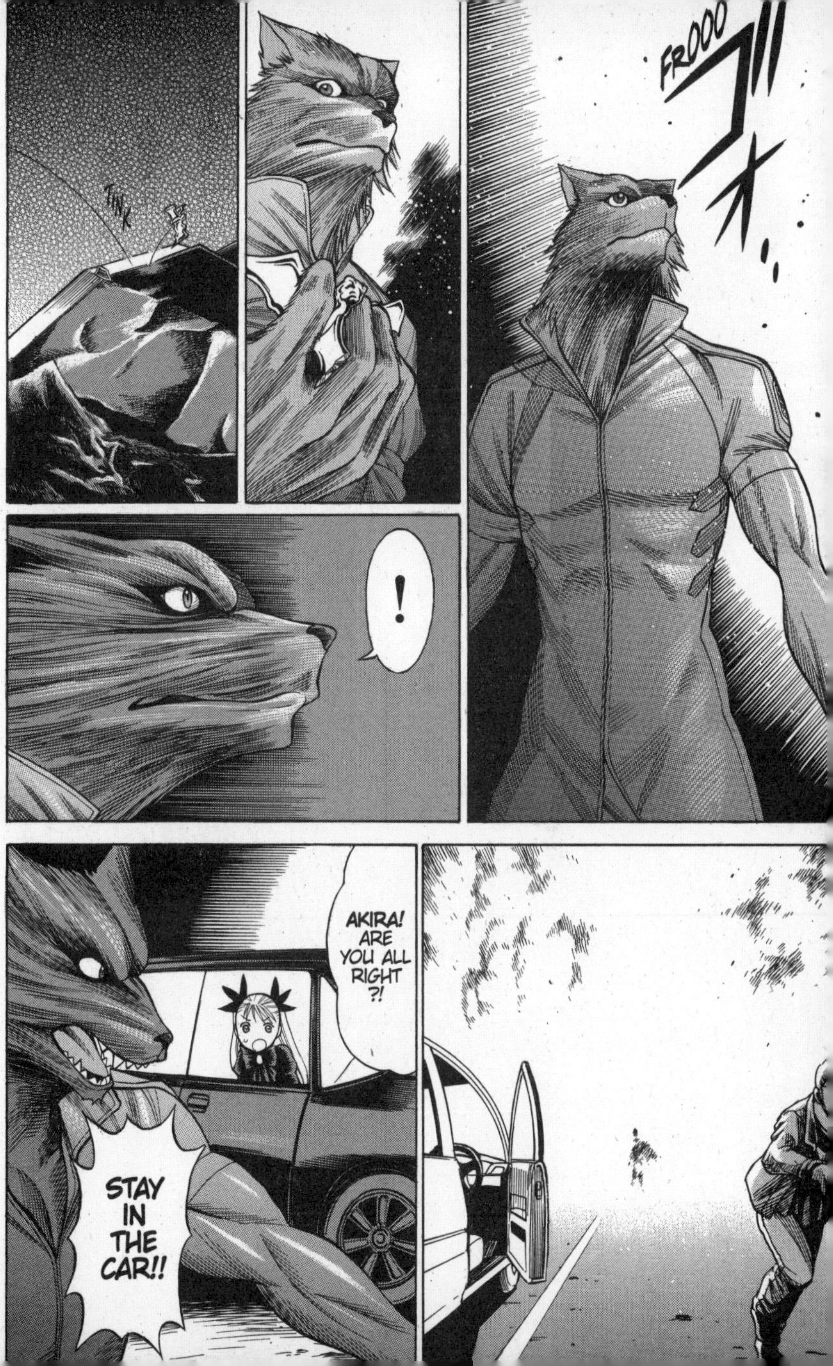
FROOO
TINK
!
AKIRA! ARE YOU ALL RIGHT ?!
STAY IN THE CAR!!

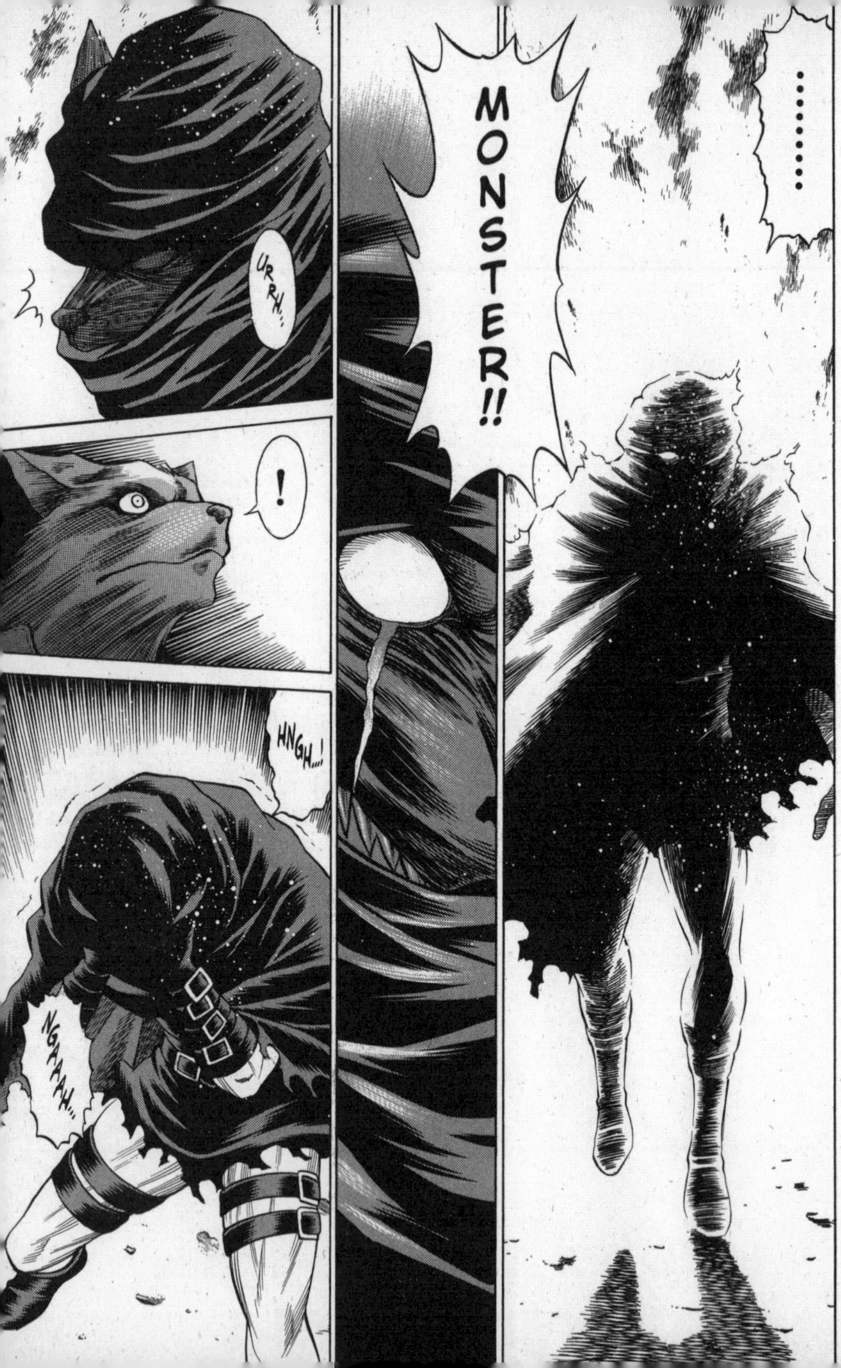
......
MONSTER!!
URRH...
!
HNGH...!
NGAAAAH...

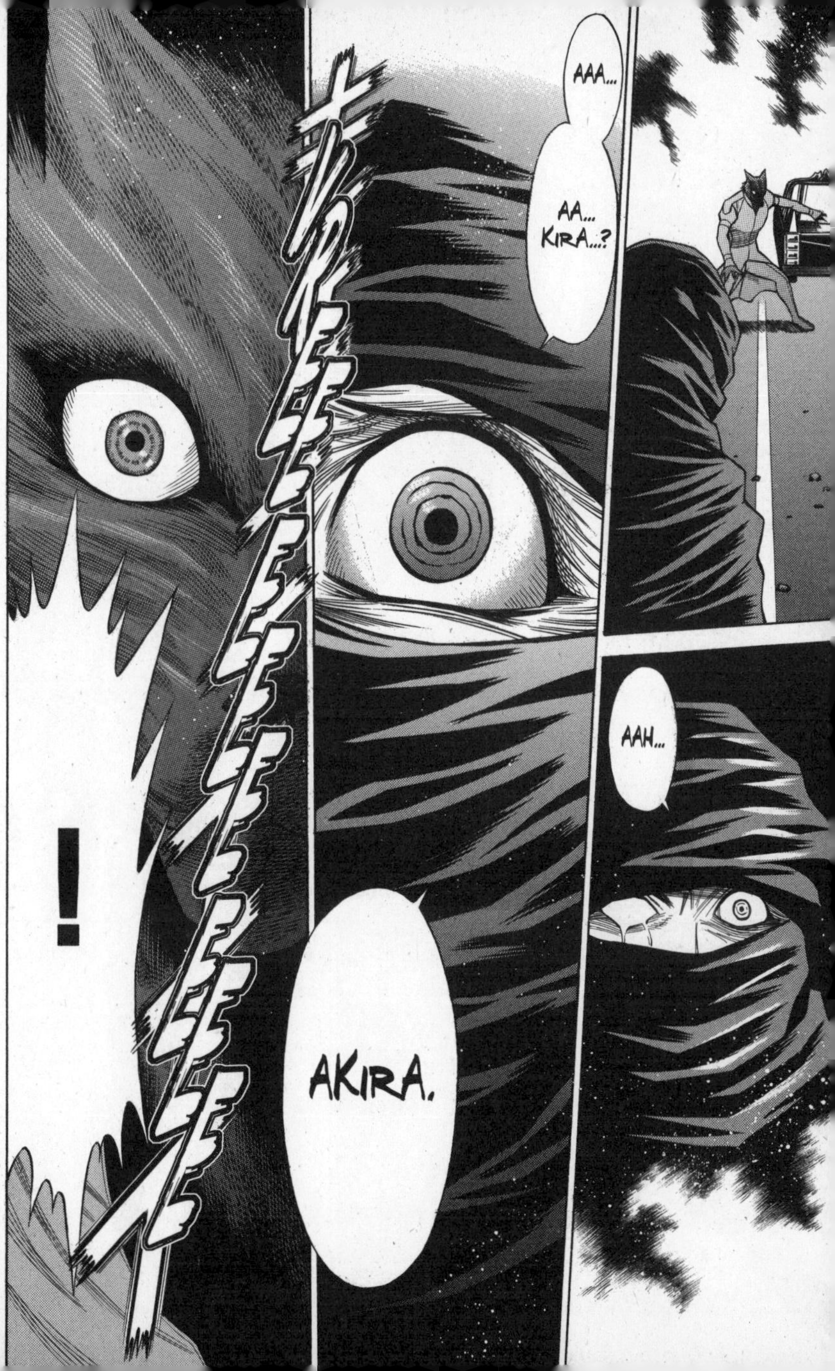
AAH...
AAA...
AA... KIRA...?
AKIRA.
!

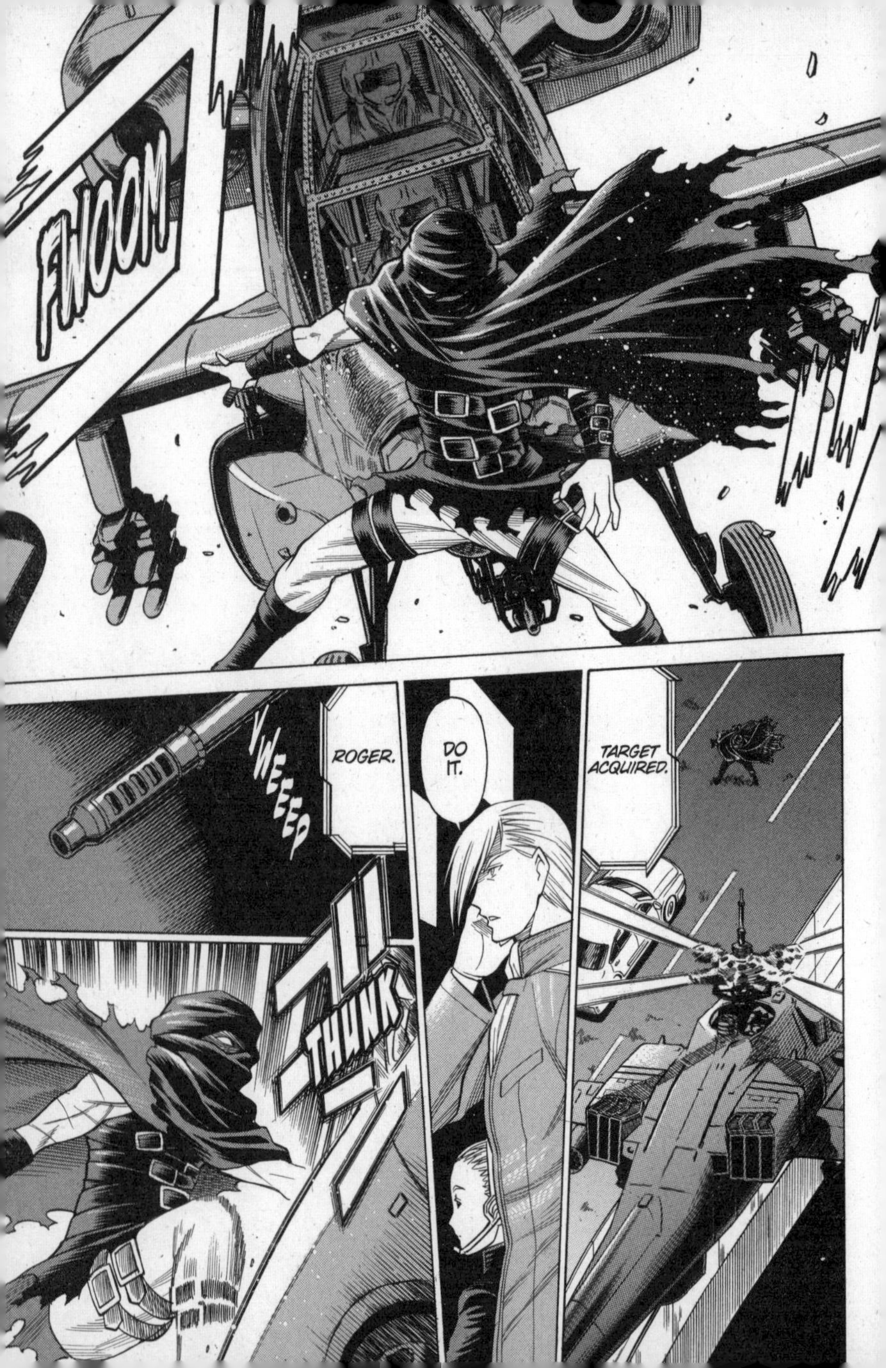
FWOOM
TARGET ACQUIRED.
DO IT.
ROGER.
VWEEEP
THUNK

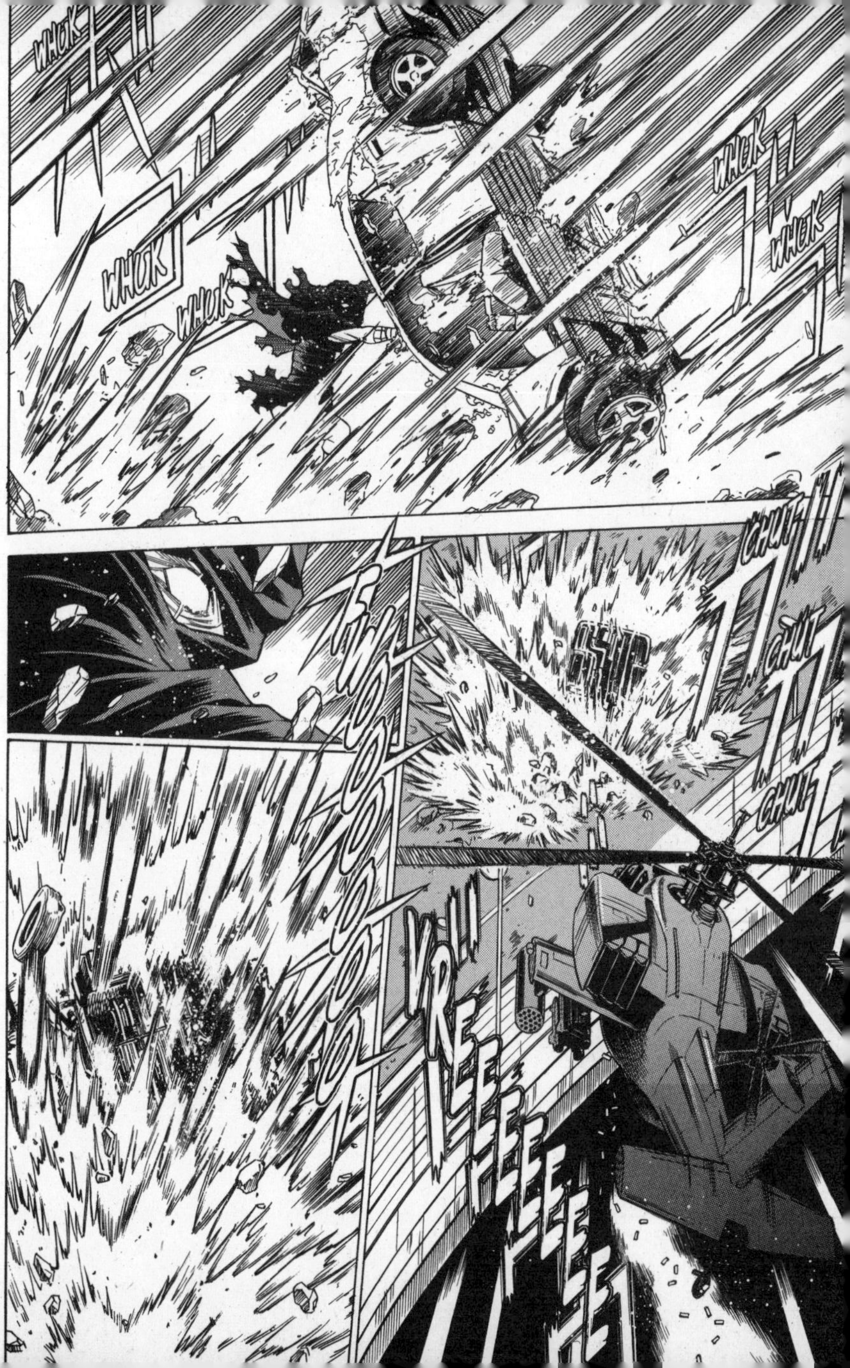
WHUK
WHUK
WHUK
WHUK
WHUK
CHUT
CHUT
CHUT

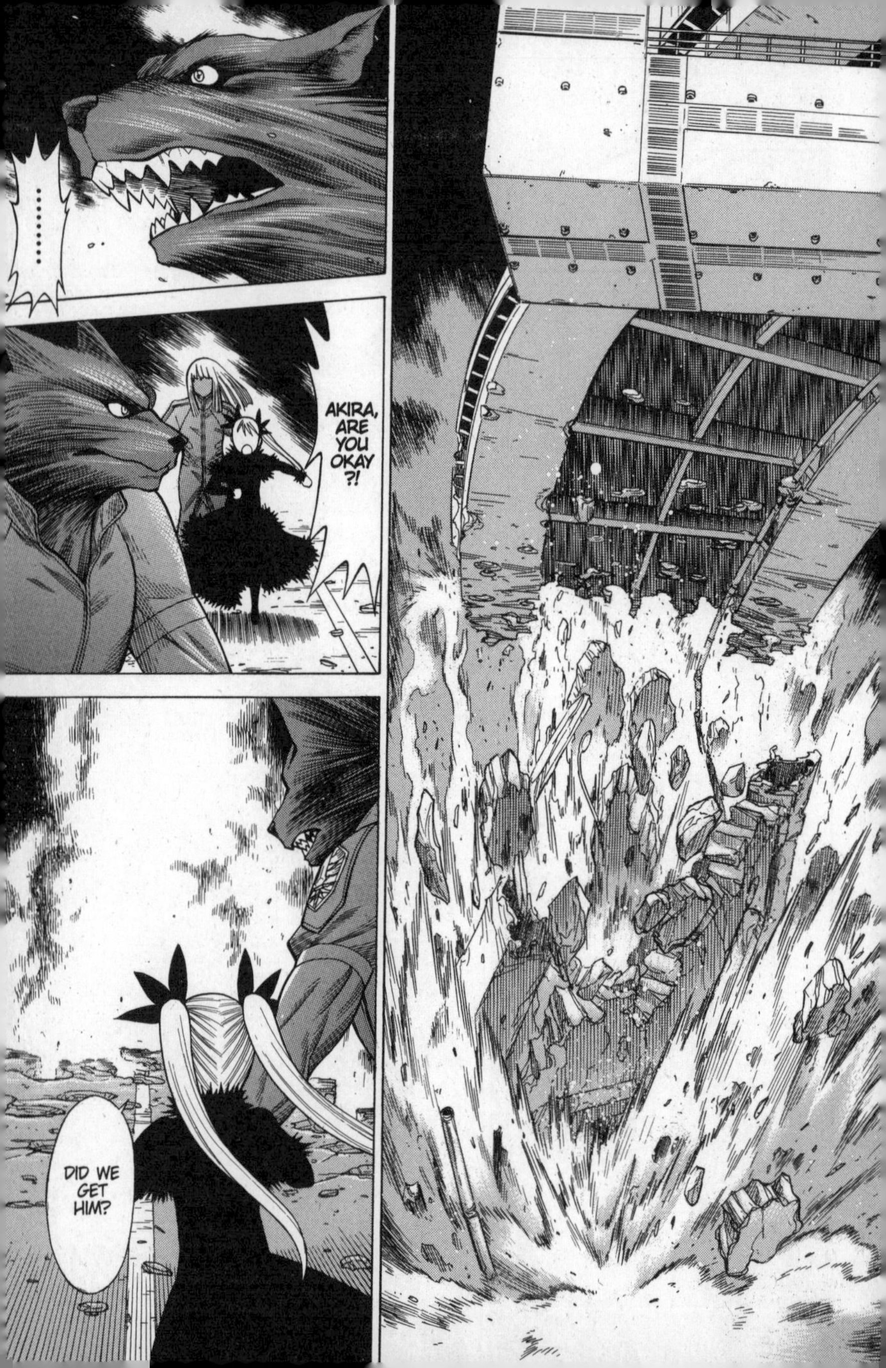
......
AKIRA, ARE YOU OKAY?!
DID WE GET HIM?

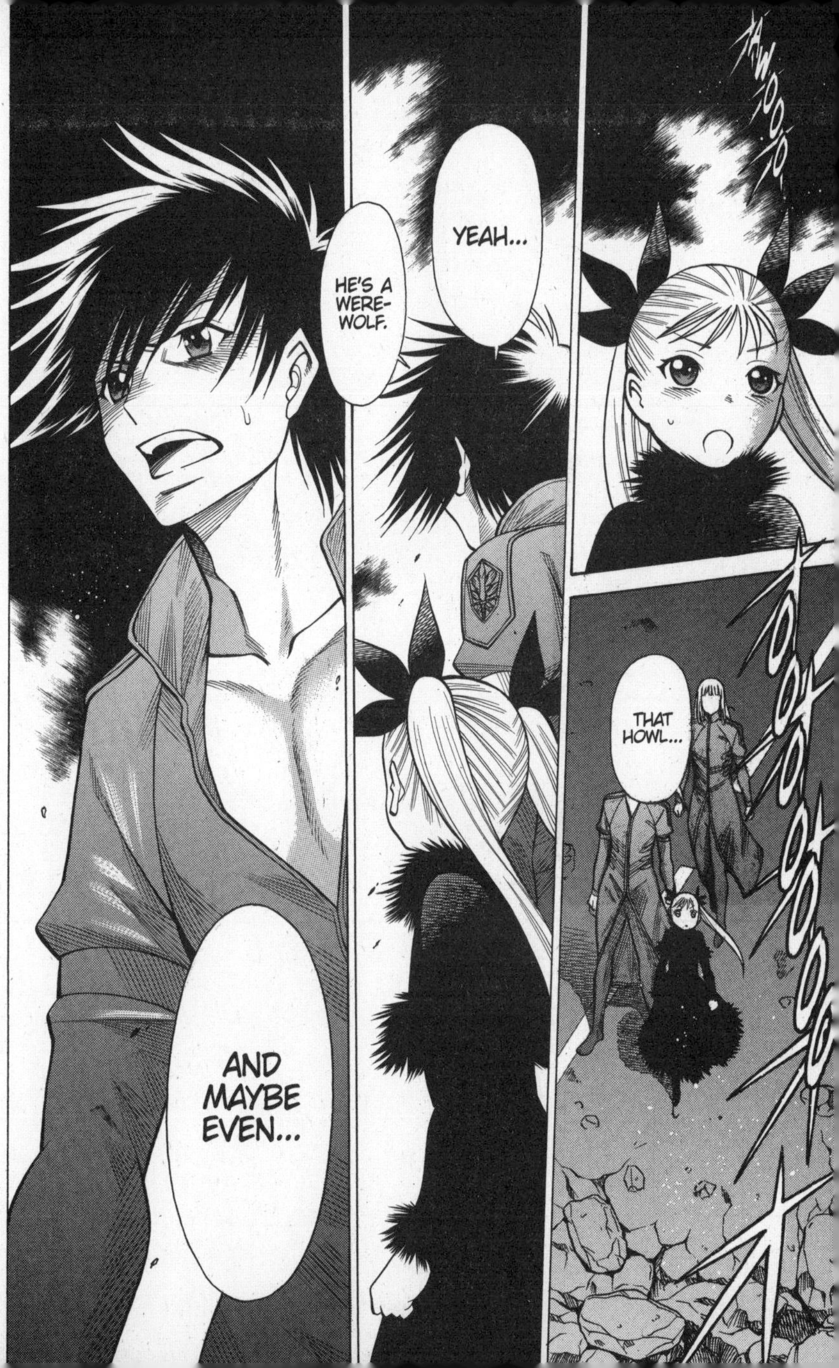
AWOOO...
THAT HOWL...
YEAH...
HE'S A WERE-WOLF.
AND MAYBE EVEN...

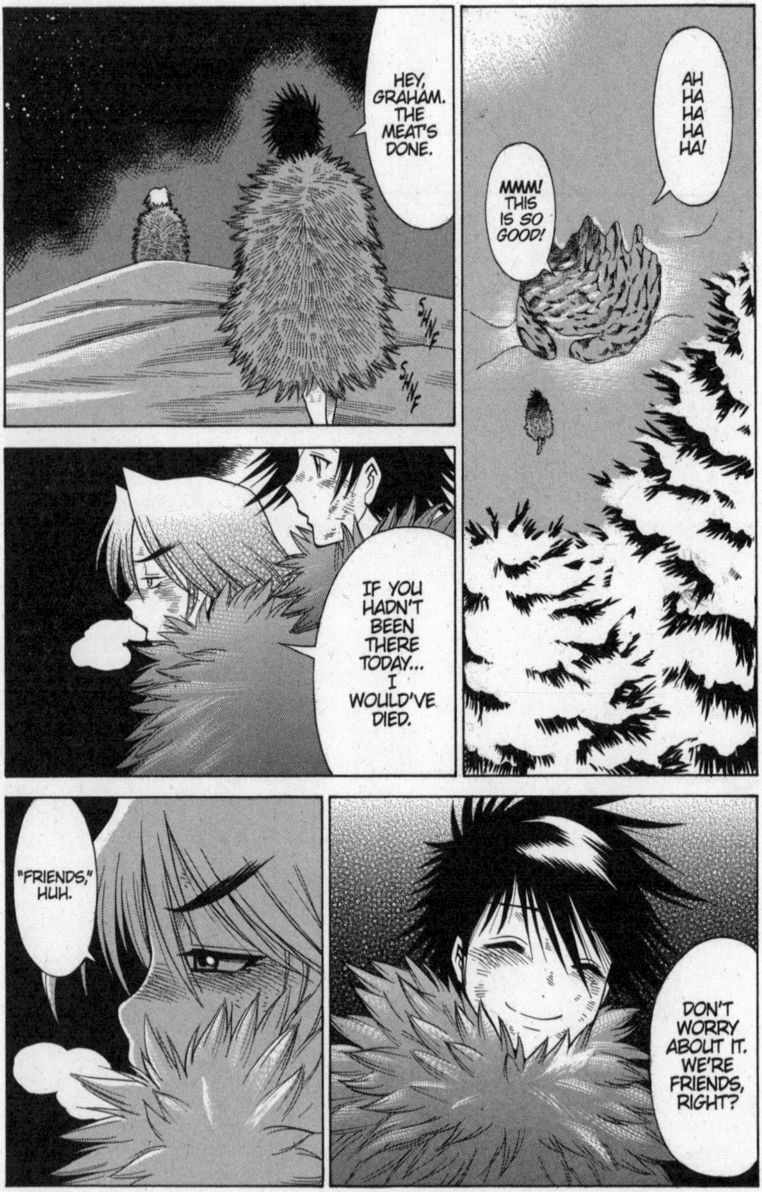
AH HA HA HA HA!
MMM! THIS IS SO GOOD!
HEY, GRAHAM. THE MEAT'S DONE.
SHNF
SHNF
IF YOU HADN'T BEEN THERE TODAY... I WOULD'VE DIED.
DON'T WORRY ABOUT IT. WE'RE FRIENDS, RIGHT?
"FRIENDS," HUH.

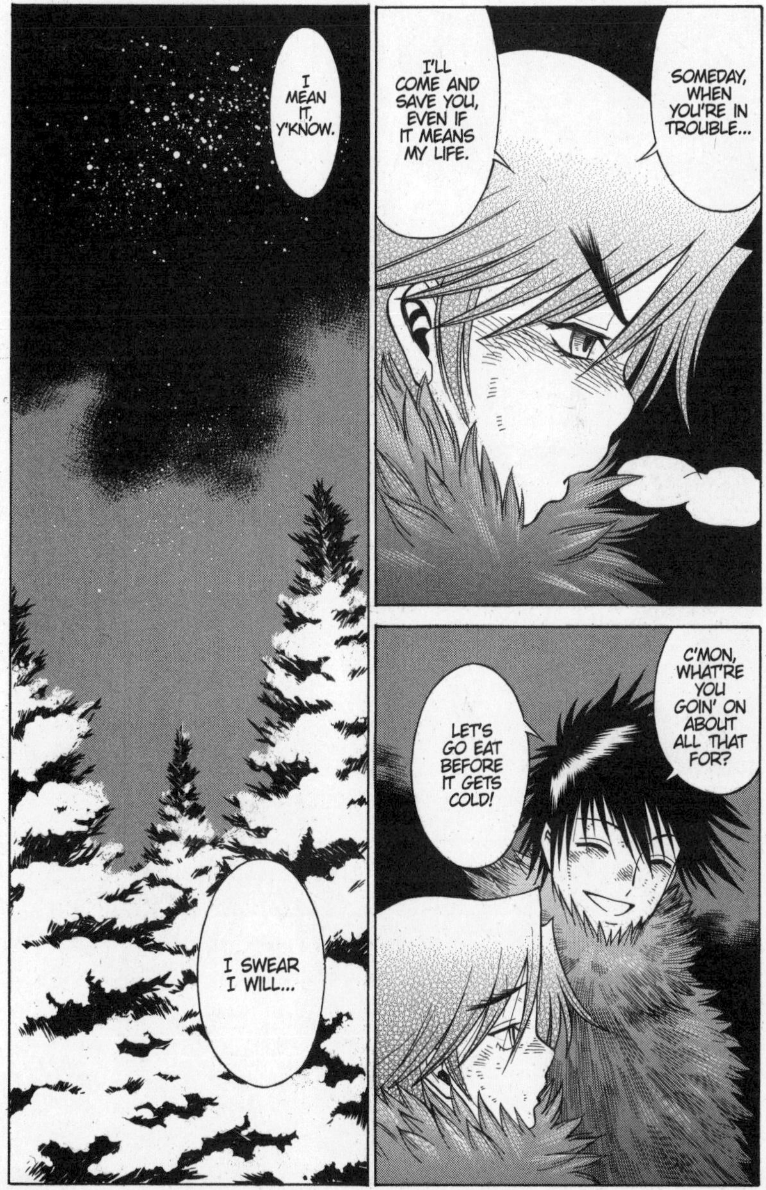
SOMEDAY, WHEN YOU'RE IN TROUBLE...
I'LL COME AND SAVE YOU, EVEN IF IT MEANS MY LIFE.
C'MON, WHAT'RE YOU GOIN' ON ABOUT ALL THAT FOR?
LET'S GO EAT BEFORE IT GETS COLD!
I MEAN IT, Y'KNOW.
I SWEAR I WILL...

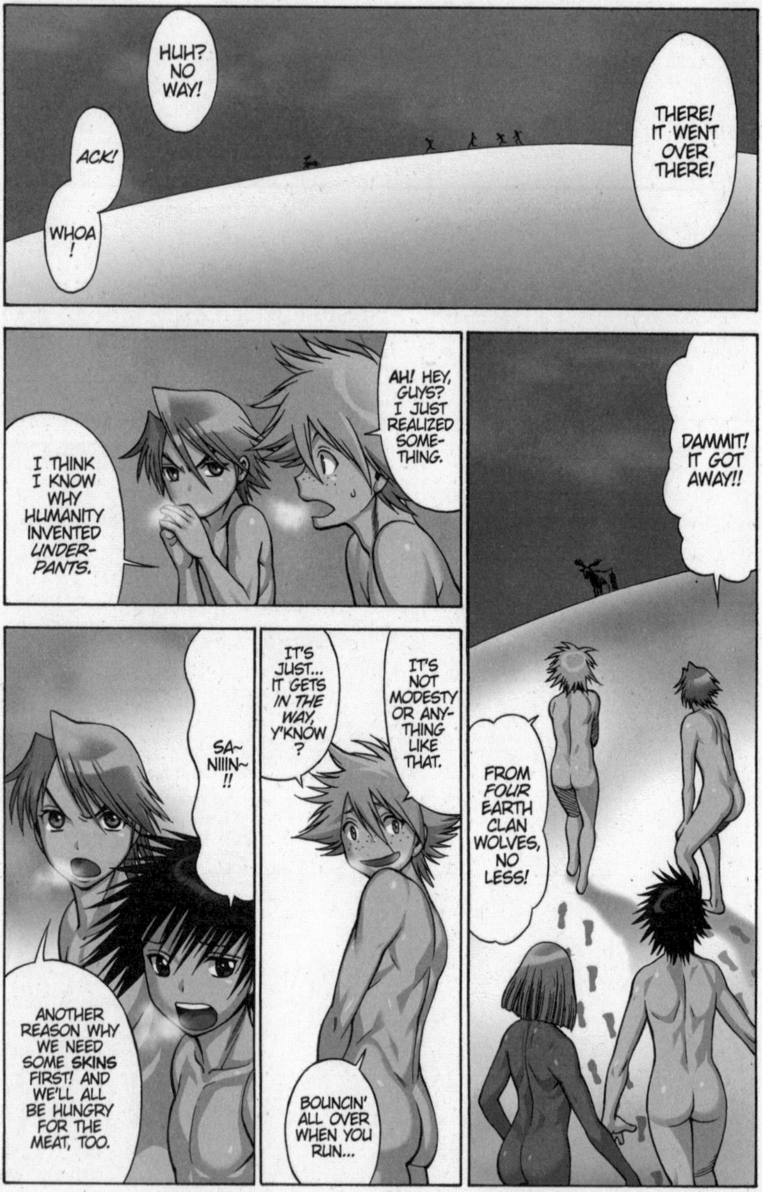
THERE! IT WENT OVER THERE!
HUH? NO WAY!
ACK!
WHOA!
DAMMIT! IT GOT AWAY!!
FROM FOUR EARTH CLAN WOLVES, NO LESS!
AH! HEY, GUYS? I JUST REALIZED SOME-THING.
I THINK I KNOW WHY HUMANITY INVENTED UNDER-PANTS.
IT'S NOT MODESTY OR ANY-THING LIKE THAT.
IT'S JUST... IT GETS IN THE WAY, Y'KNOW?
BOUNCIN' ALL OVER WHEN YOU RUN...
SA~NIIIN~!!
ANOTHER REASON WHY WE NEED SOME SKINS FIRST! AND WE'LL ALL BE HUNGRY FOR THE MEAT, TOO.

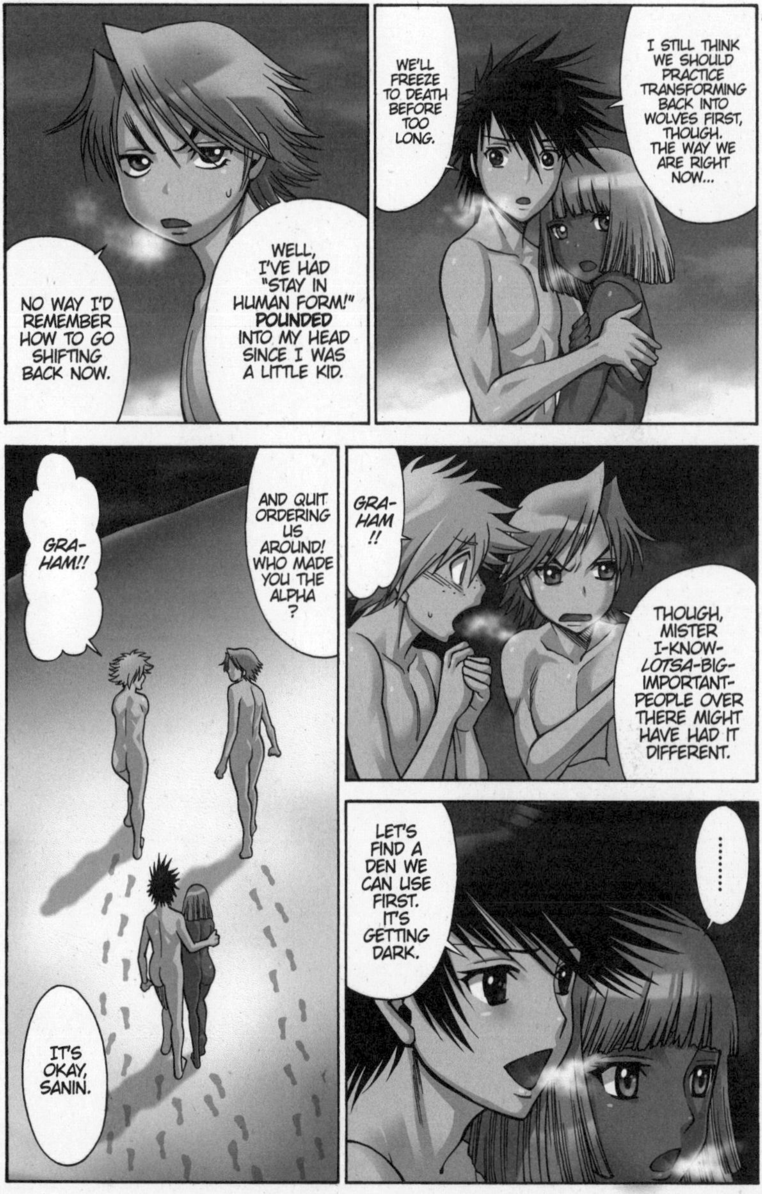
I STILL THINK WE SHOULD PRACTICE TRANSFORMING BACK INTO WOLVES FIRST, THOUGH. THE WAY WE ARE RIGHT NOW...
WE'LL FREEZE TO DEATH BEFORE TOO LONG.
WELL, I'VE HAD "STAY IN HUMAN FORM!" POUNDED INTO MY HEAD SINCE I WAS A LITTLE KID.
NO WAY I'D REMEMBER HOW TO GO SHIFTING BACK NOW.
THOUGH, MISTER I-KNOW-LOTSA-BIG-IMPORTANT-PEOPLE OVER THERE MIGHT HAVE HAD IT DIFFERENT.
GRA-HAM!!
......
LET'S FIND A DEN WE CAN USE FIRST. IT'S GETTING DARK.
AND QUIT ORDERING US AROUND! WHO MADE YOU THE ALPHA?
GRA-HAM!!
IT'S OKAY, SANIN.

Chapter 41: An Afternoon with Wolves

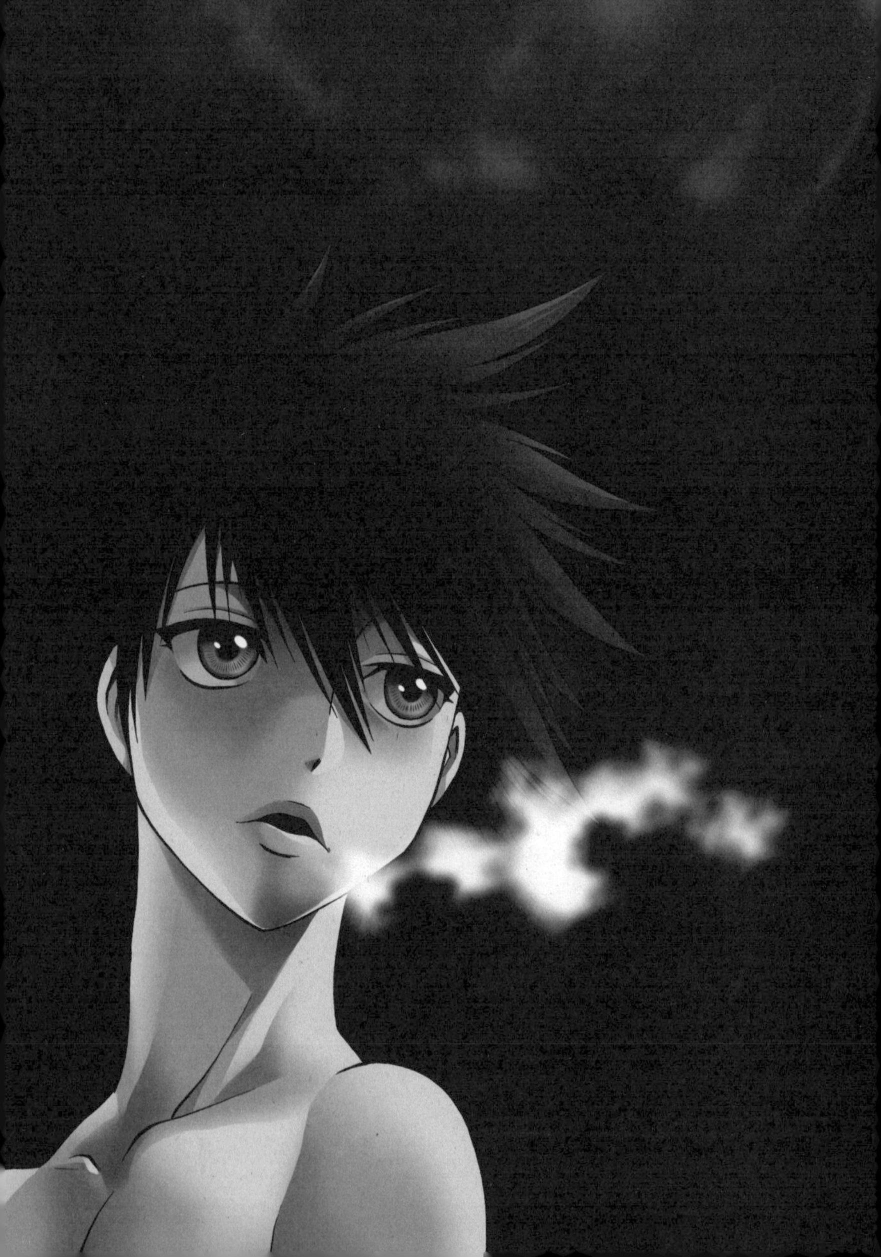

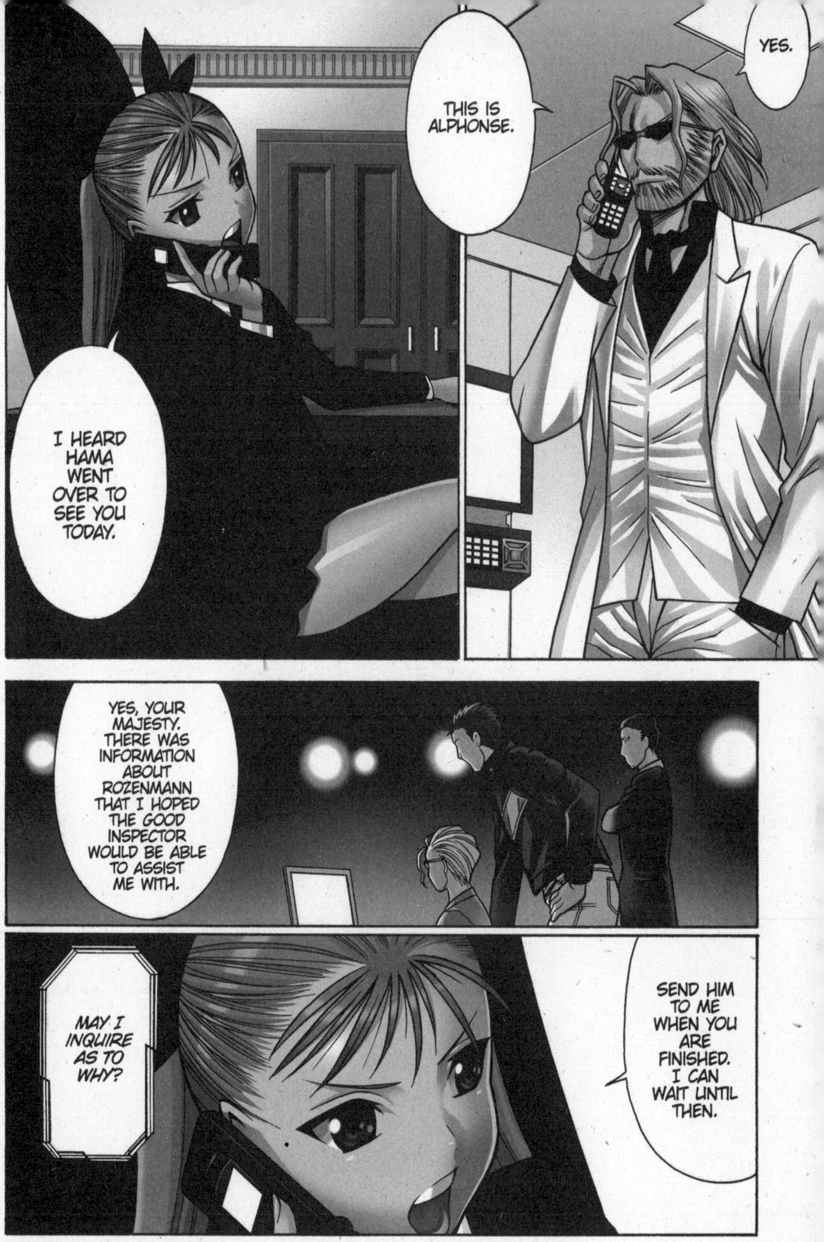
YES.
THIS IS ALPHONSE.
I HEARD HAMA WENT OVER TO SEE YOU TODAY.
YES, YOUR MAJESTY. THERE WAS INFORMATION ABOUT ROZENMANN THAT I HOPED THE GOOD INSPECTOR WOULD BE ABLE TO ASSIST ME WITH.
SEND HIM TO ME WHEN YOU ARE FINISHED. I CAN WAIT UNTIL THEN.
MAY I INQUIRE AS TO WHY?

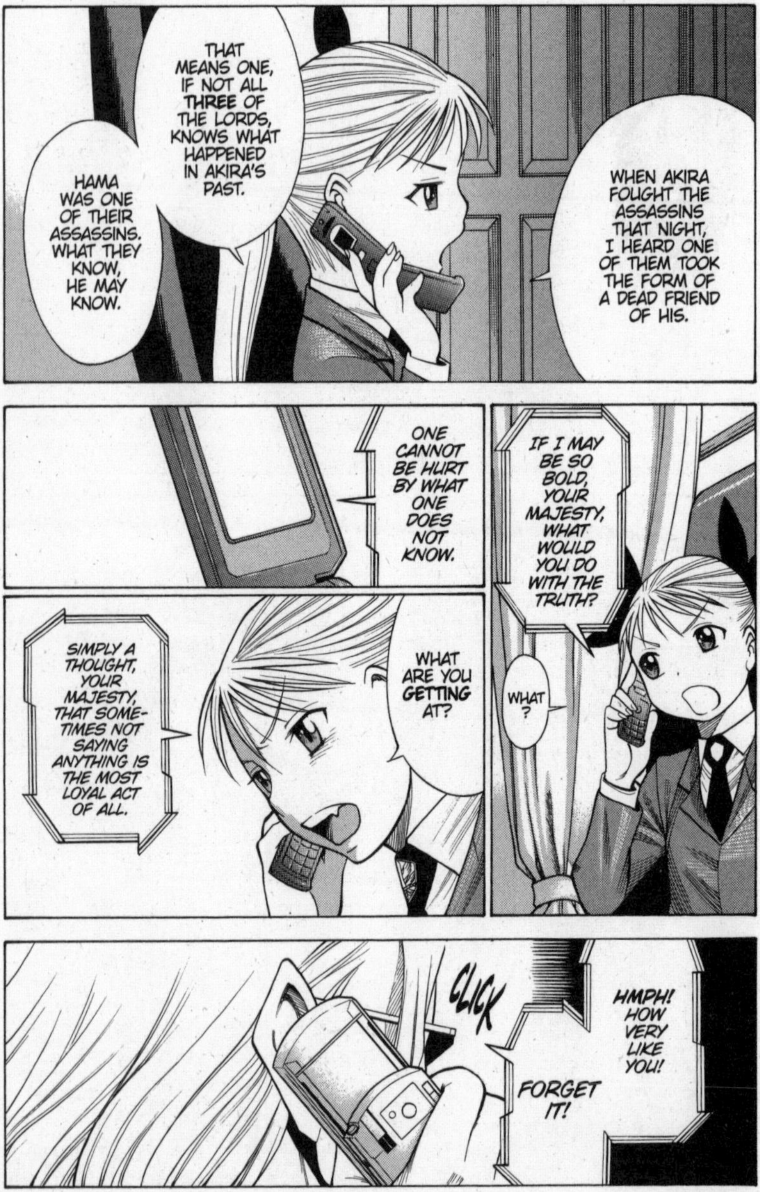
WHEN AKIRA FOUGHT THE ASSASSINS THAT NIGHT, I HEARD ONE OF THEM TOOK THE FORM OF A DEAD FRIEND OF HIS.
THAT MEANS ONE, IF NOT ALL THREE OF THE LORDS, KNOWS WHAT HAPPENED IN AKIRA'S PAST.
HAMA WAS ONE OF THEIR ASSASSINS. WHAT THEY KNOW, HE MAY KNOW.
IF I MAY BE SO BOLD, YOUR MAJESTY, WHAT WOULD YOU DO WITH THE TRUTH?
WHAT?
ONE CANNOT BE HURT BY WHAT ONE DOES NOT KNOW.
WHAT ARE YOU GETTING AT?
SIMPLY A THOUGHT, YOUR MAJESTY, THAT SOMETIMES NOT SAYING ANYTHING IS THE MOST LOYAL ACT OF ALL.
HMPH! HOW VERY LIKE YOU!
CLICK
FORGET IT!

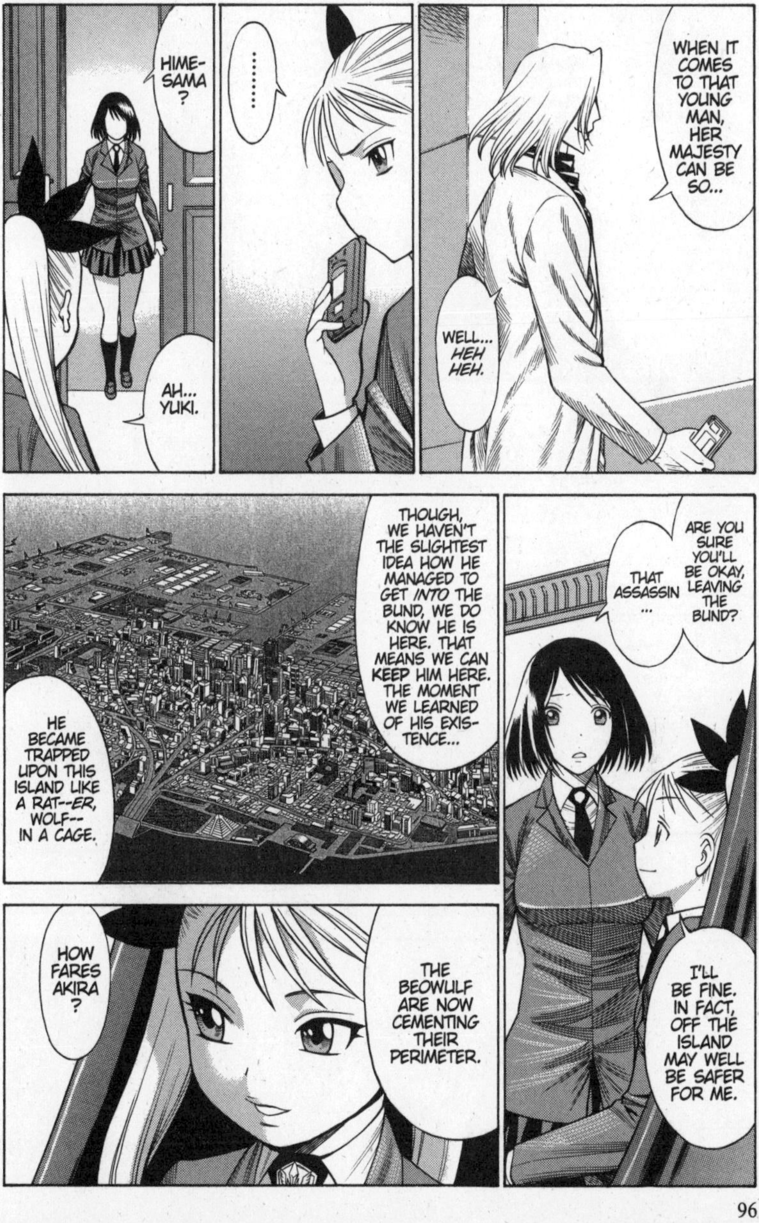
WHEN IT COMES TO THAT YOUNG MAN, HER MAJESTY CAN BE SO...
WELL... HEH HEH.
......
HIME-SAMA?
AH... YUKI.
ARE YOU SURE YOU'LL BE OKAY, LEAVING THE BUND?
THAT ASSASSIN...
I'LL BE FINE. IN FACT, OFF THE ISLAND MAY WELL BE SAFER FOR ME.
THOUGH, WE HAVEN'T THE SLIGHTEST IDEA HOW HE MANAGED TO GET *INTO* THE BUND, WE DO KNOW HE IS HERE. THAT MEANS WE CAN KEEP HIM HERE. THE MOMENT WE LEARNED OF HIS EXISTENCE...
HE BECAME TRAPPED UPON THIS ISLAND LIKE A RAT--*ER*, WOLF-- IN A CAGE.
THE BEOWULF ARE NOW CEMENTING THEIR PERIMETER.
HOW FARES AKIRA?

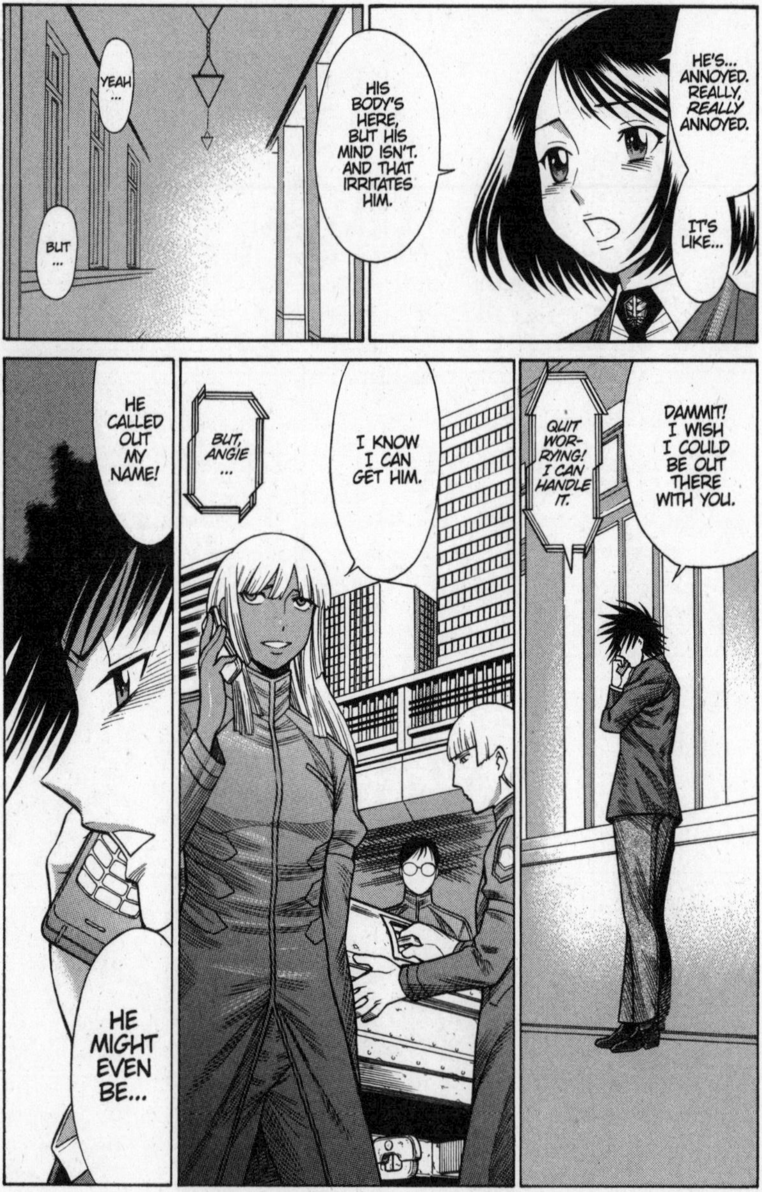
HE'S... ANNOYED. REALLY, *REALLY* ANNOYED.
IT'S LIKE...
HIS BODY'S HERE, BUT HIS MIND ISN'T. AND THAT IRRITATES HIM.
YEAH ...
BUT ...
DAMMIT! I WISH I COULD BE OUT THERE WITH YOU.
QUIT WOR-RYING! I CAN HANDLE IT.
I KNOW I CAN GET HIM.
BUT, ANGIE ...
HE CALLED OUT MY NAME!
HE MIGHT EVEN BE...

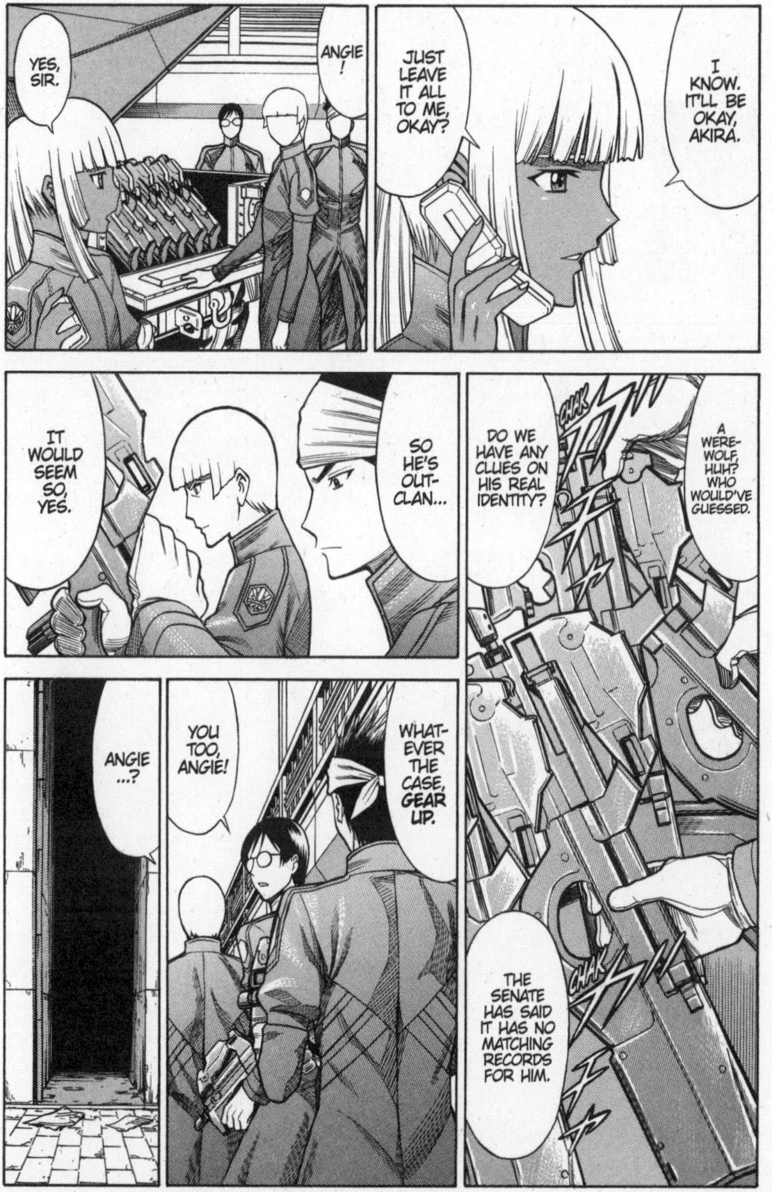
I KNOW. IT'LL BE OKAY, AKIRA.
JUST LEAVE IT ALL TO ME, OKAY?
ANGIE!
YES, SIR.
A WERE-WOLF, HUH? WHO WOULD'VE GUESSED.
CHAK
DO WE HAVE ANY CLUES ON HIS REAL IDENTITY?
CHAK
THE SENATE HAS SAID IT HAS NO MATCHING RECORDS FOR HIM.
SO HE'S OUT-CLAN...
IT WOULD SEEM SO, YES.
WHAT-EVER THE CASE, GEAR UP.
YOU TOO, ANGIE!
ANGIE ...?

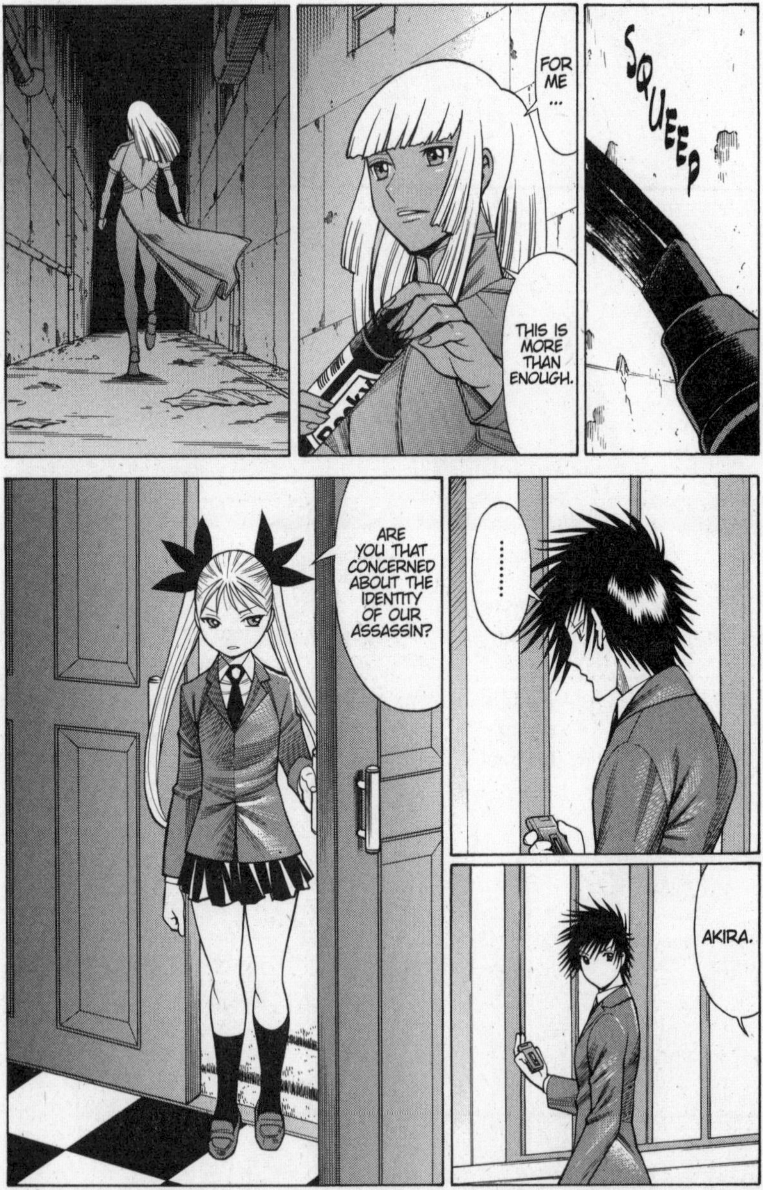
SQUEEP
FOR ME ...
THIS IS MORE THAN ENOUGH.
......
AKIRA.
ARE YOU THAT CONCERNED ABOUT THE IDENTITY OF OUR ASSASSIN?

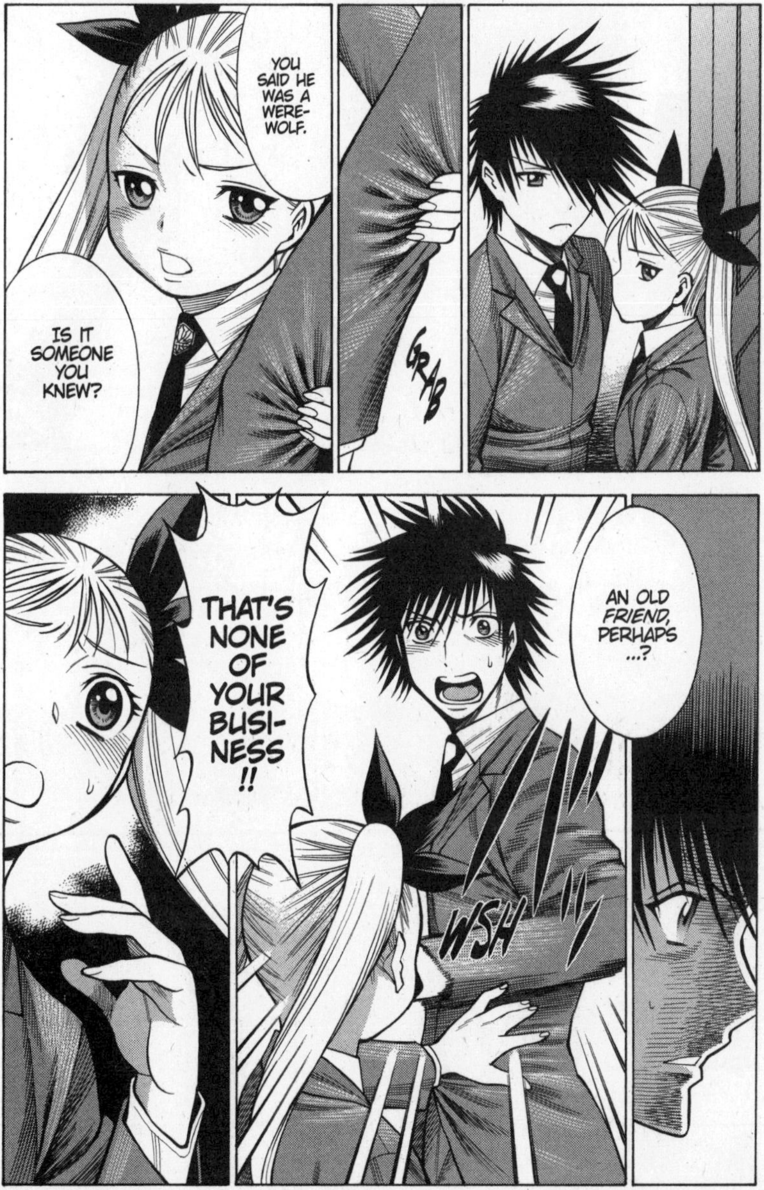
GRAB
YOU SAID HE WAS A WERE-WOLF.
IS IT SOMEONE YOU KNEW?
AN OLD FRIEND, PERHAPS ...?
THAT'S NONE OF YOUR BUSI-NESS !!
WSH

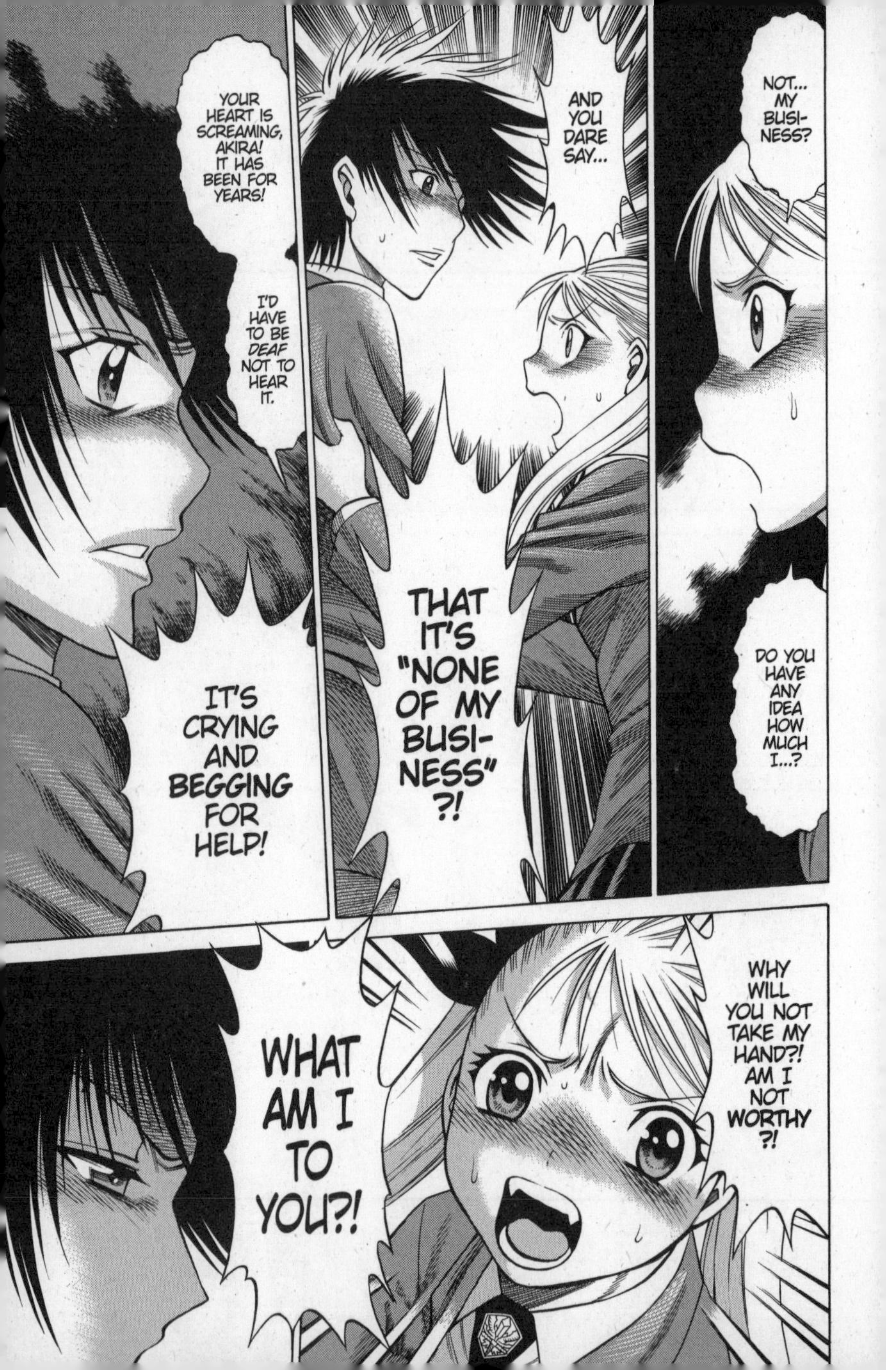
NOT... MY BUSI-NESS?
DO YOU HAVE ANY IDEA HOW MUCH I...?
AND YOU DARE SAY...
THAT IT'S "NONE OF MY BUSI-NESS"?!
YOUR HEART IS SCREAMING, AKIRA! IT HAS BEEN FOR YEARS!
I'D HAVE TO BE *DEAF* NOT TO HEAR IT.
IT'S CRYING AND BEGGING FOR HELP!
WHY WILL YOU NOT TAKE MY HAND?! AM I NOT WORTHY?!
WHAT AM I TO YOU?!

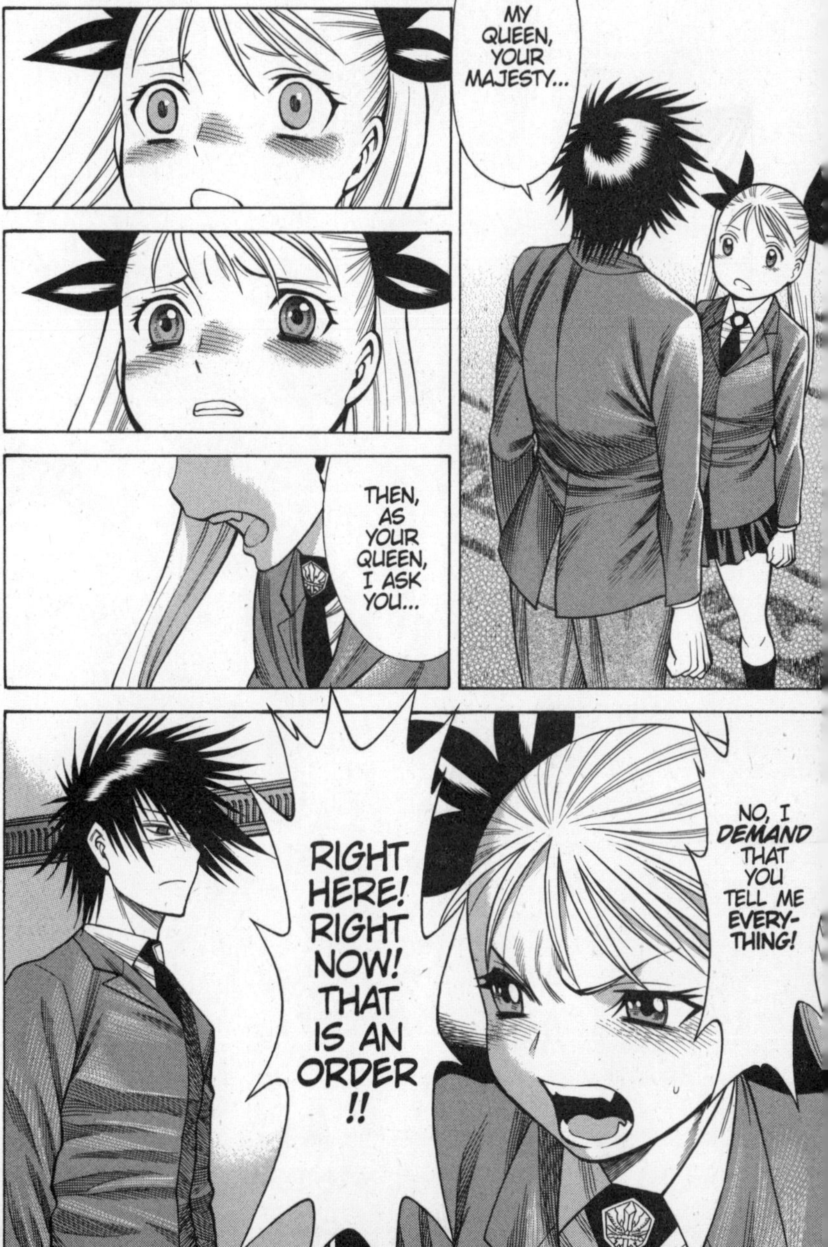
MY QUEEN, YOUR MAJESTY...
THEN, AS YOUR QUEEN, I ASK YOU...
NO, I ***DEMAND*** THAT YOU TELL ME EVERY-THING!
RIGHT HERE! RIGHT NOW! THAT IS AN ORDER!!

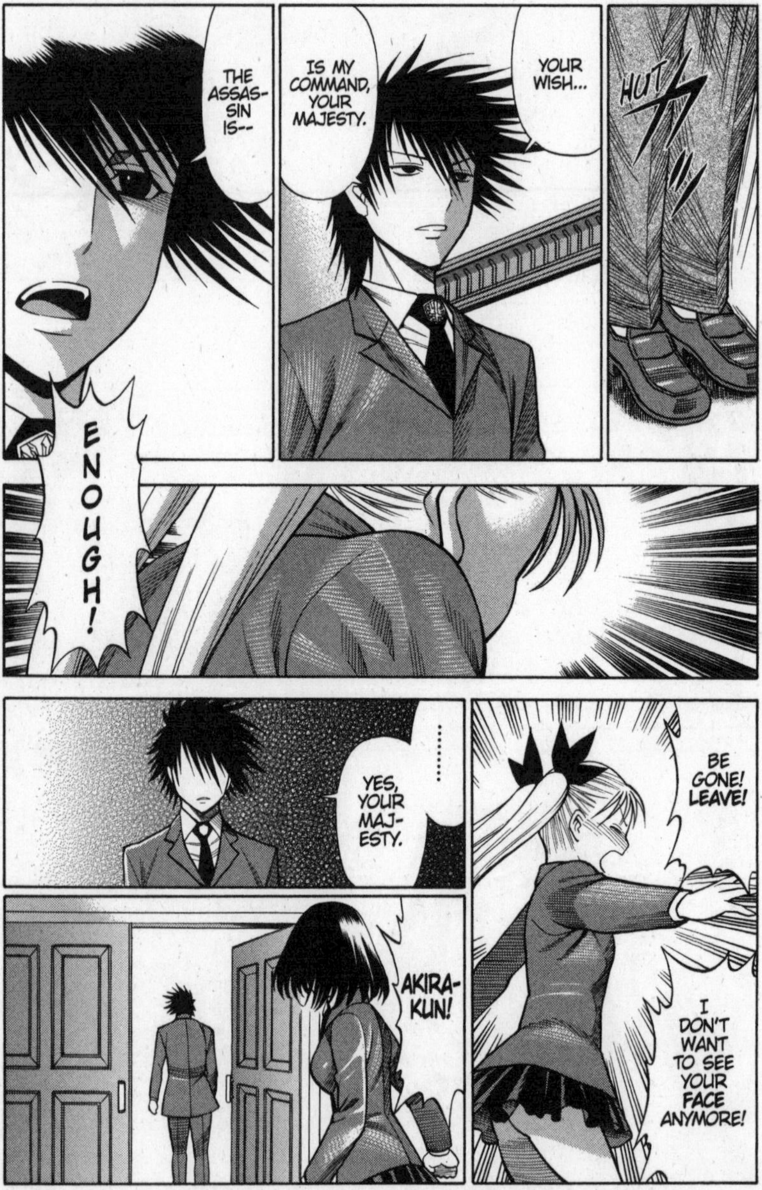
HUT
YOUR WISH...
IS MY COMMAND, YOUR MAJESTY.
THE ASSAS-SIN IS--
ENOUGH!
BE GONE! LEAVE!
I DON'T WANT TO SEE YOUR FACE ANYMORE!
......
YES, YOUR MAJ-ESTY.
AKIRA-KUN!

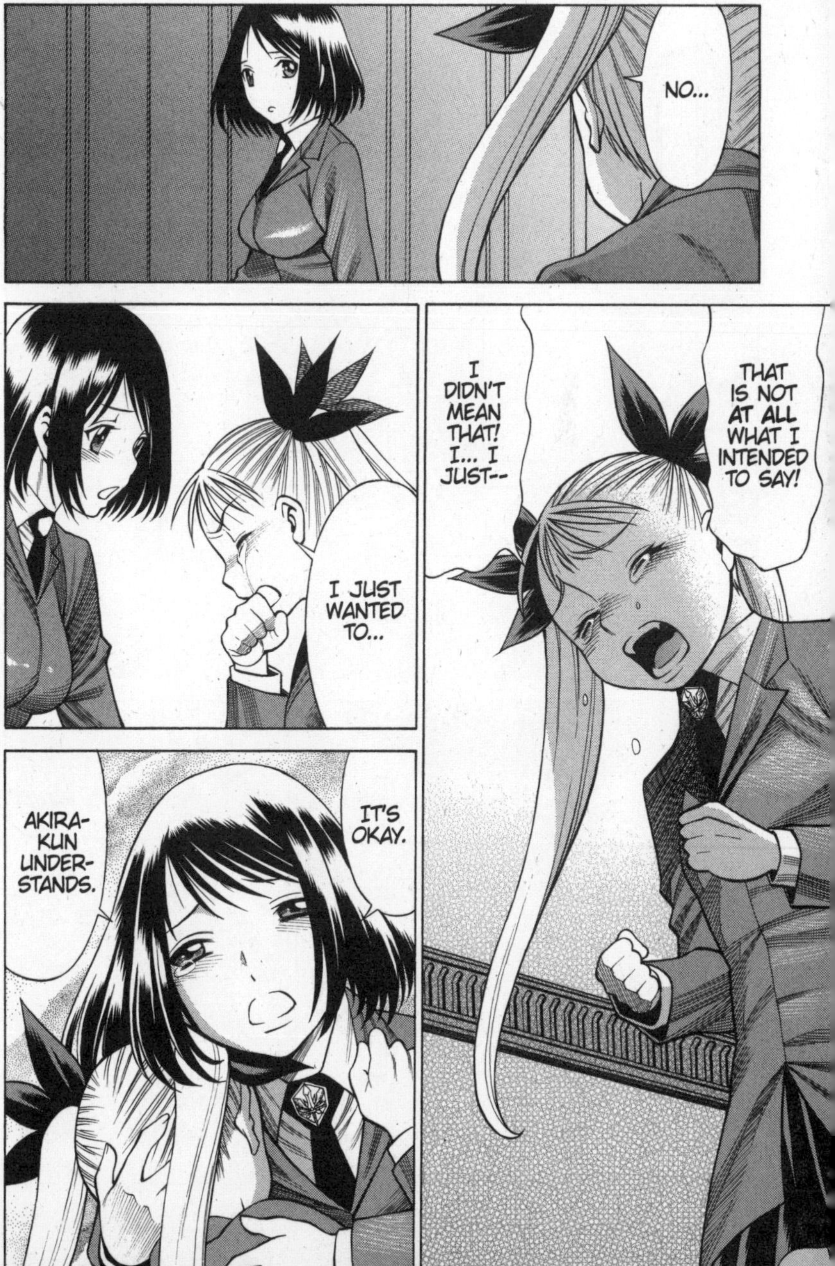
NO...
THAT IS NOT AT ALL WHAT I INTENDED TO SAY!
I DIDN'T MEAN THAT! I... I JUST--
I JUST WANTED TO...
IT'S OKAY.
AKIRA-KUN UNDERSTANDS.

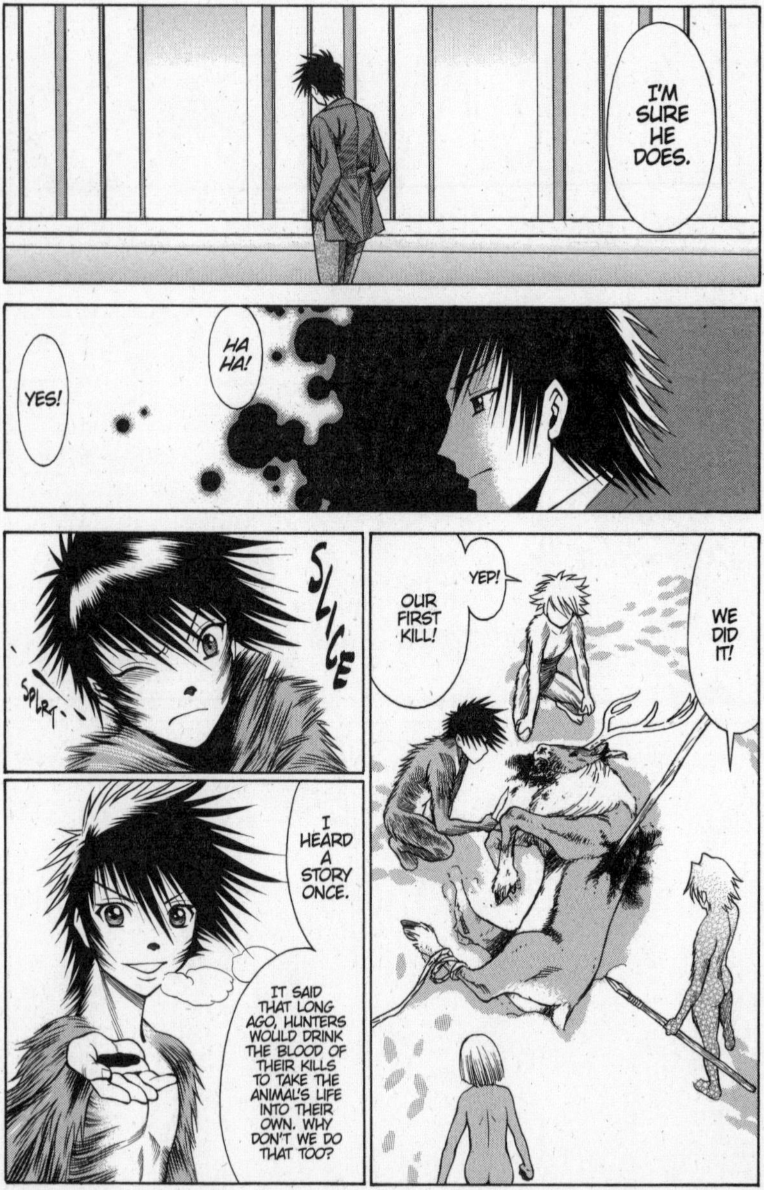
I'M SURE HE DOES.
HA HA!
YES!
WE DID IT!
YEP!
OUR FIRST KILL!
SLICE
SPLRT
I HEARD A STORY ONCE.
IT SAID THAT LONG AGO, HUNTERS WOULD DRINK THE BLOOD OF THEIR KILLS TO TAKE THE ANIMAL'S LIFE INTO THEIR OWN. WHY DON'T WE DO THAT TOO?

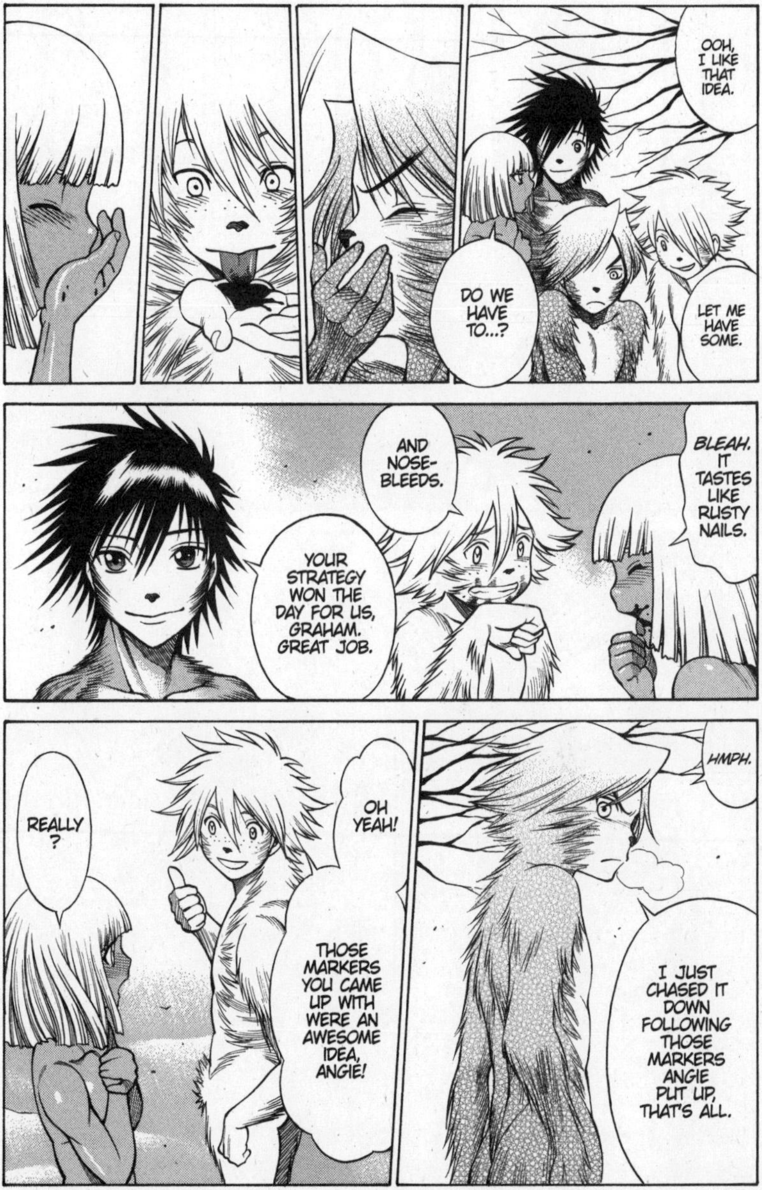
OOH, I LIKE THAT IDEA.
LET ME HAVE SOME.
DO WE HAVE TO...?
BLEAH. IT TASTES LIKE RUSTY NAILS.
AND NOSE-BLEEDS.
YOUR STRATEGY WON THE DAY FOR US, GRAHAM. GREAT JOB.
HMPH.
I JUST CHASED IT DOWN FOLLOWING THOSE MARKERS ANGIE PUT UP, THAT'S ALL.
OH YEAH!
REALLY?
THOSE MARKERS YOU CAME UP WITH WERE AN AWESOME IDEA, ANGIE!

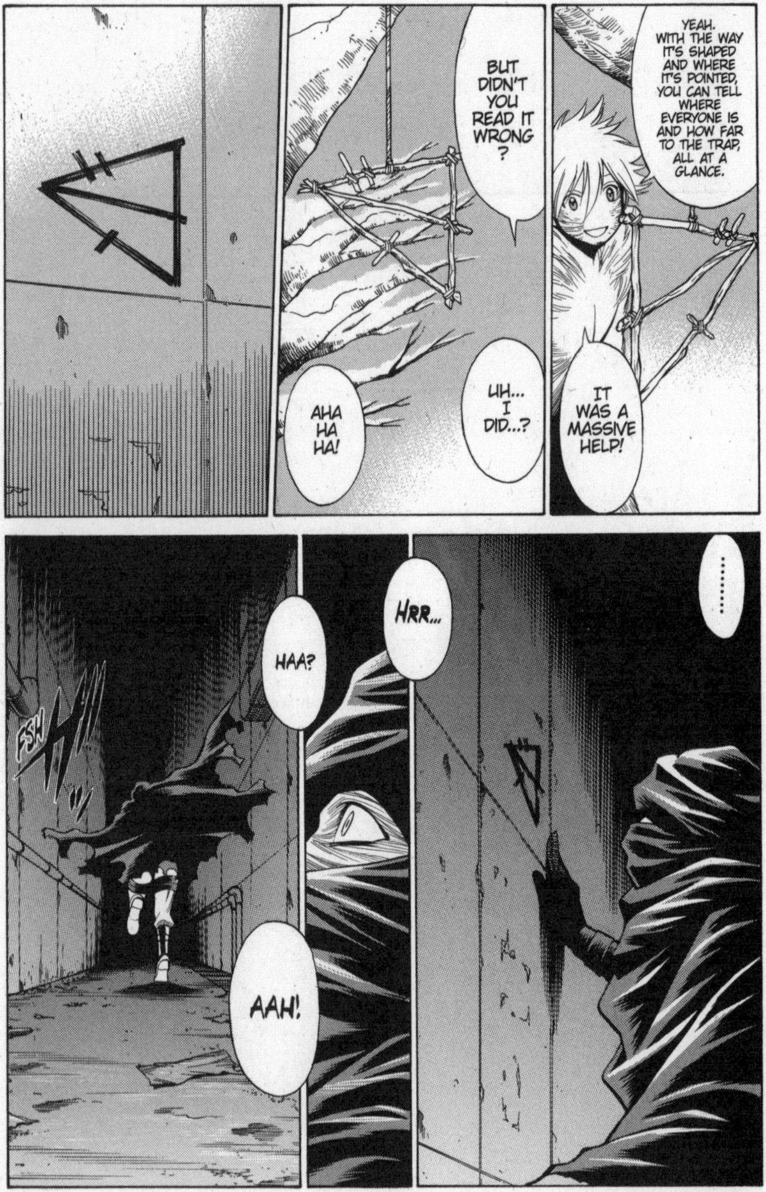
YEAH. WITH THE WAY IT'S SHAPED AND WHERE IT'S POINTED, YOU CAN TELL WHERE EVERYONE IS AND HOW FAR TO THE TRAP, ALL AT A GLANCE.
IT WAS A MASSIVE HELP!
BUT DIDN'T YOU READ IT WRONG?
UH... I DID...?
AHA HA HA!
......
HRR...
HAA?
FSH
AAH!

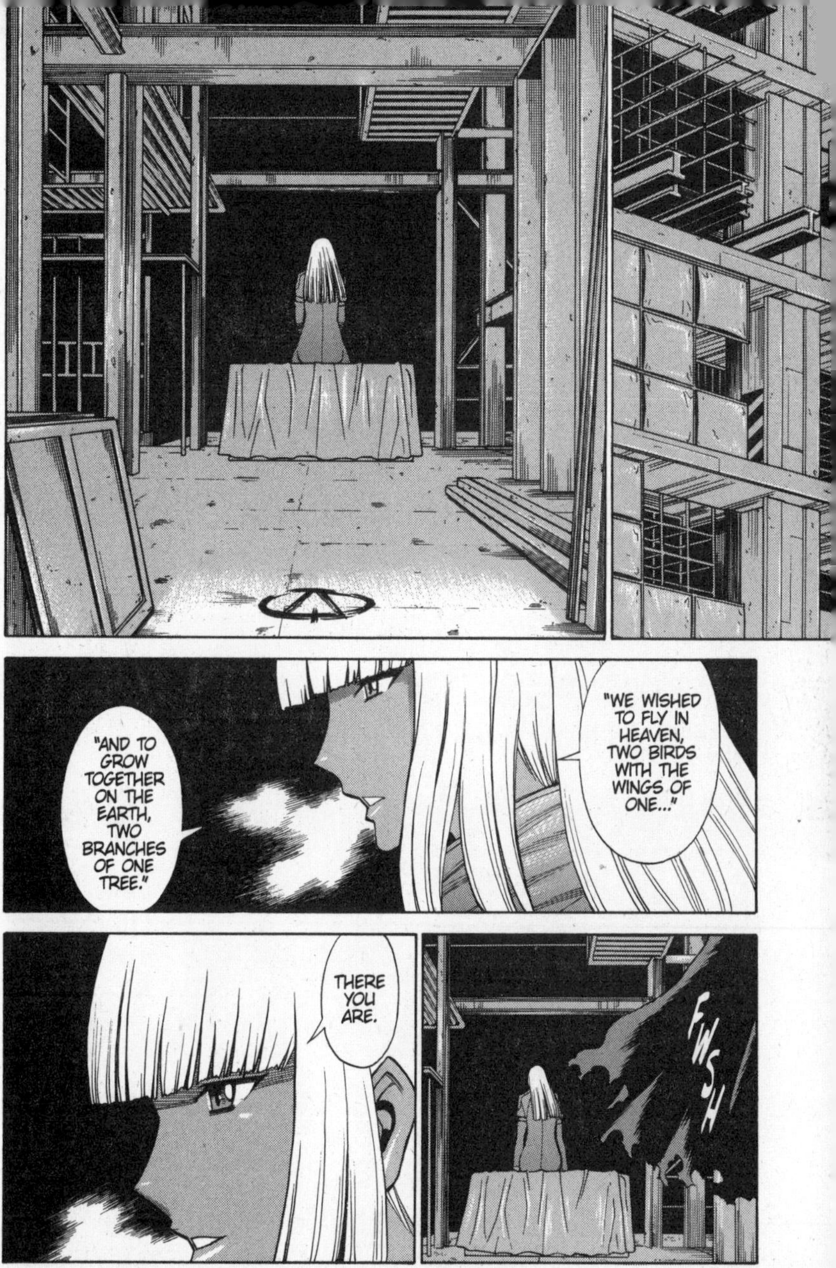
"WE WISHED TO FLY IN HEAVEN, TWO BIRDS WITH THE WINGS OF ONE..."
"AND TO GROW TOGETHER ON THE EARTH, TWO BRANCHES OF ONE TREE."
FWSH
THERE YOU ARE.

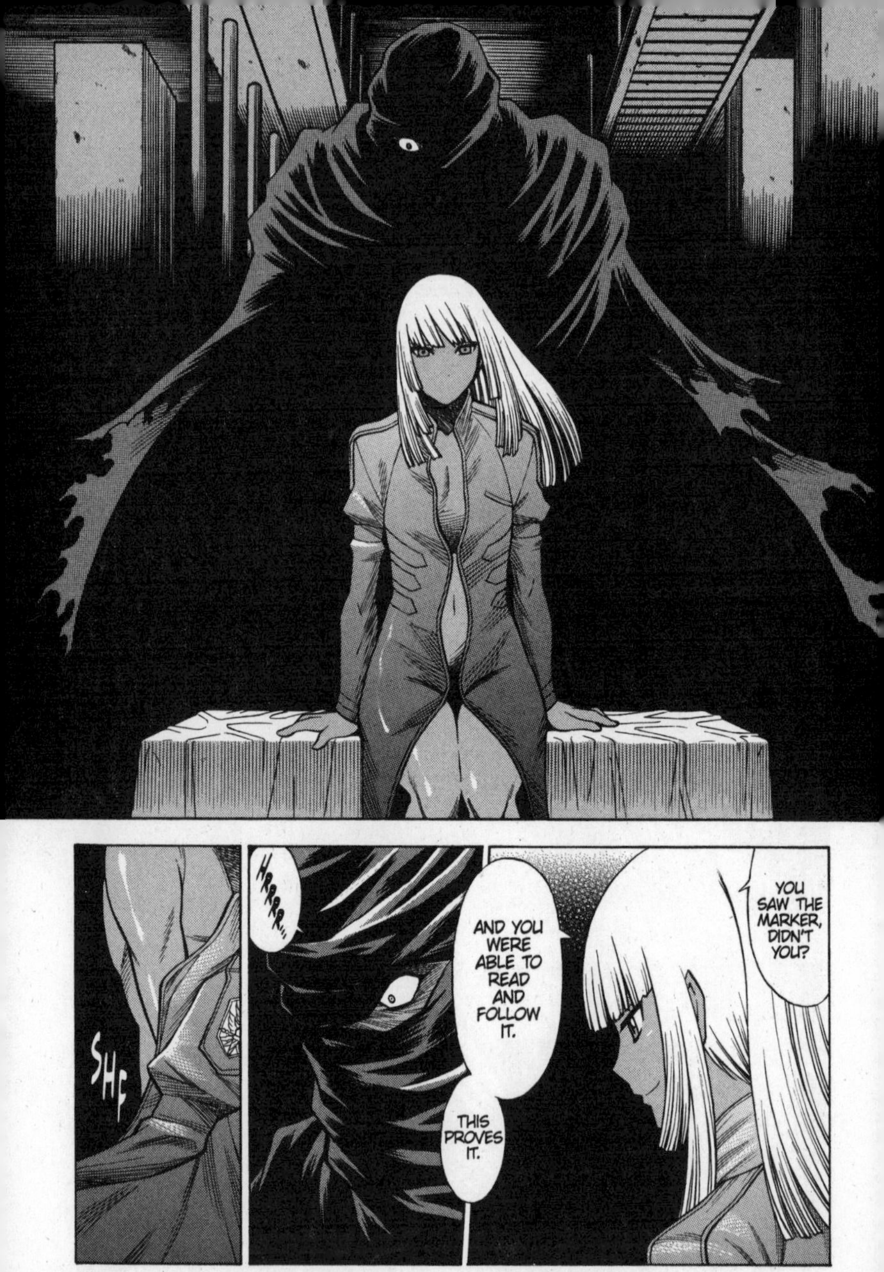
YOU SAW THE MARKER, DIDN'T YOU?
AND YOU WERE ABLE TO READ AND FOLLOW IT.
THIS PROVES IT.
HRRRR...
SHF

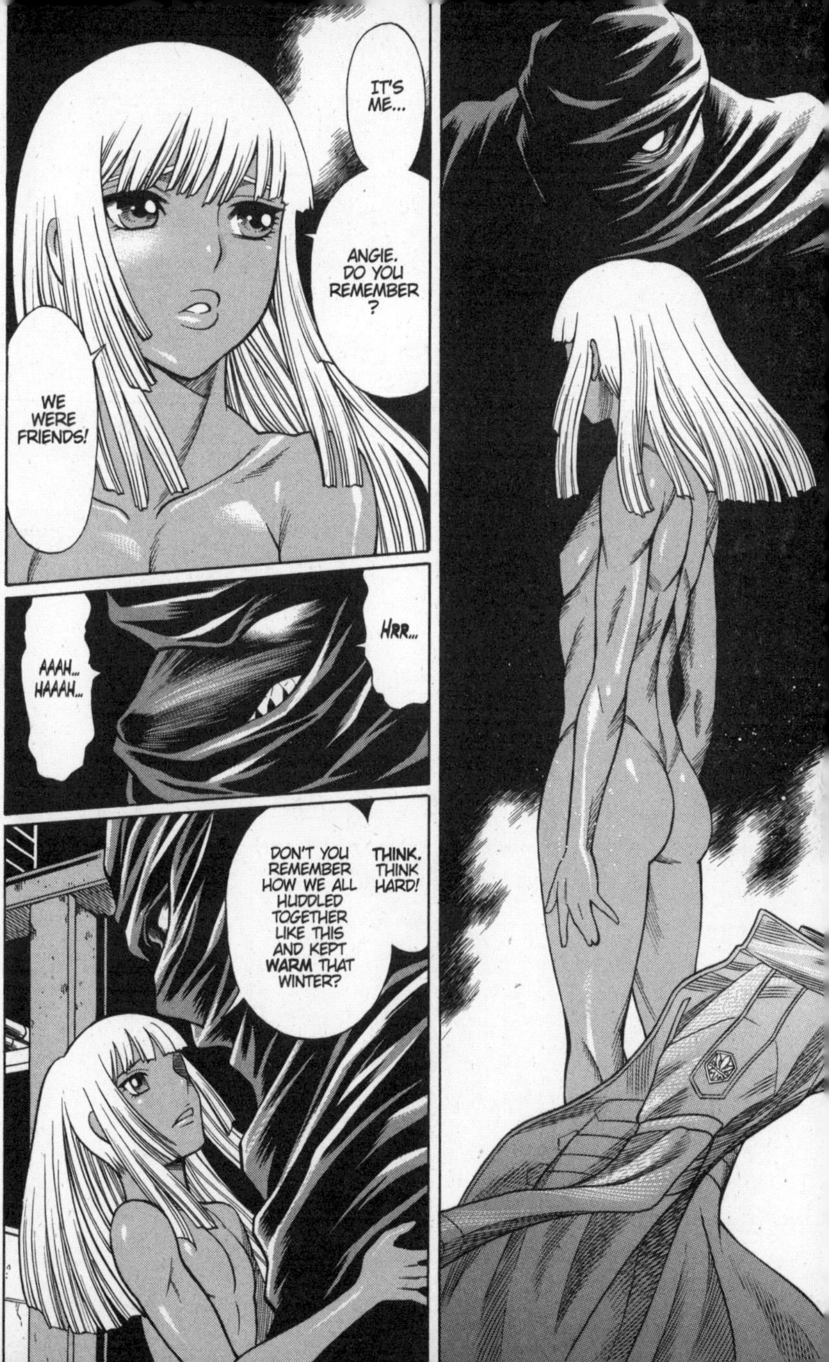
IT'S ME...
ANGIE. DO YOU REMEMBER?
WE WERE FRIENDS!
HRR...
AAAH... HAAAH...
THINK. THINK HARD!
DON'T YOU REMEMBER HOW WE ALL HUDDLED TOGETHER LIKE THIS AND KEPT WARM THAT WINTER?

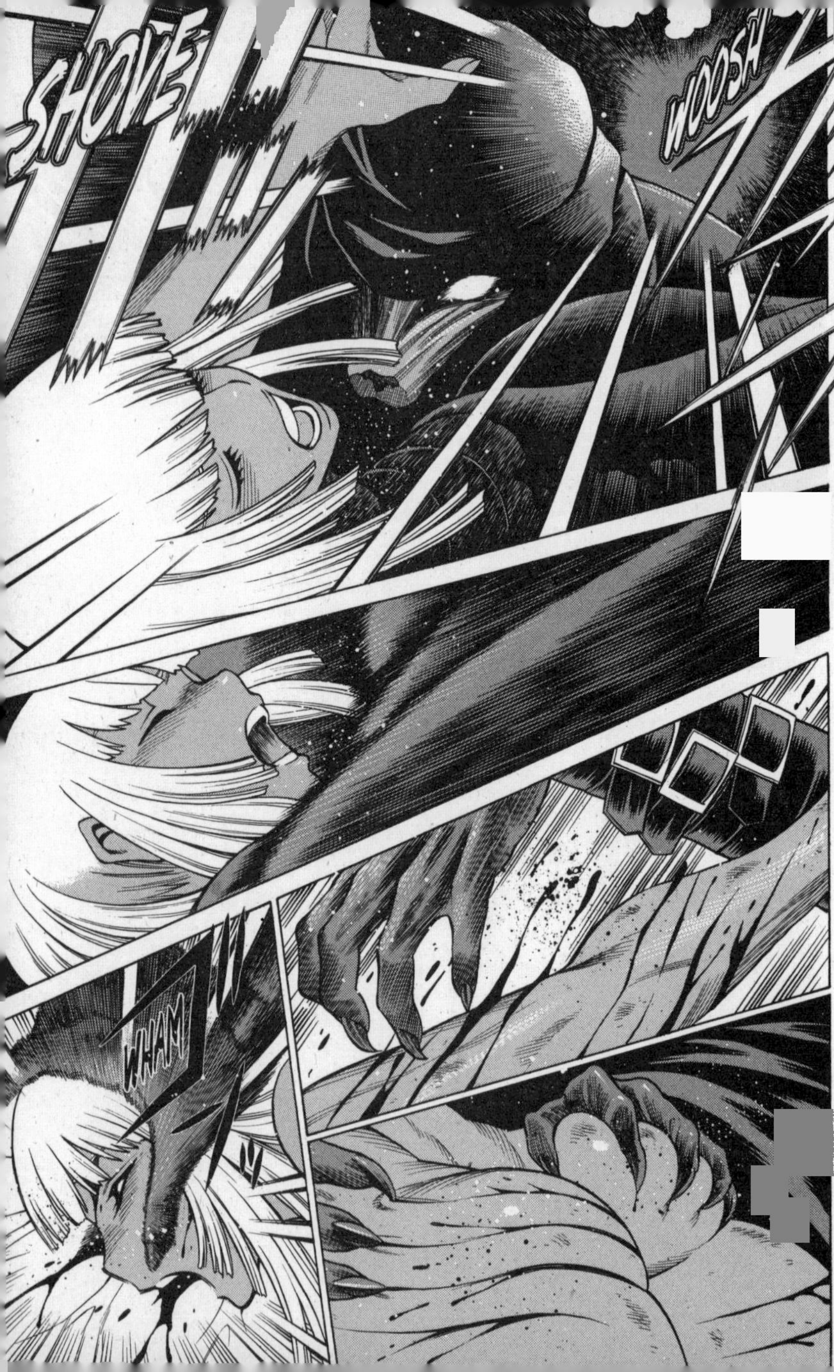
WOOSH
SHOVE
WHAM

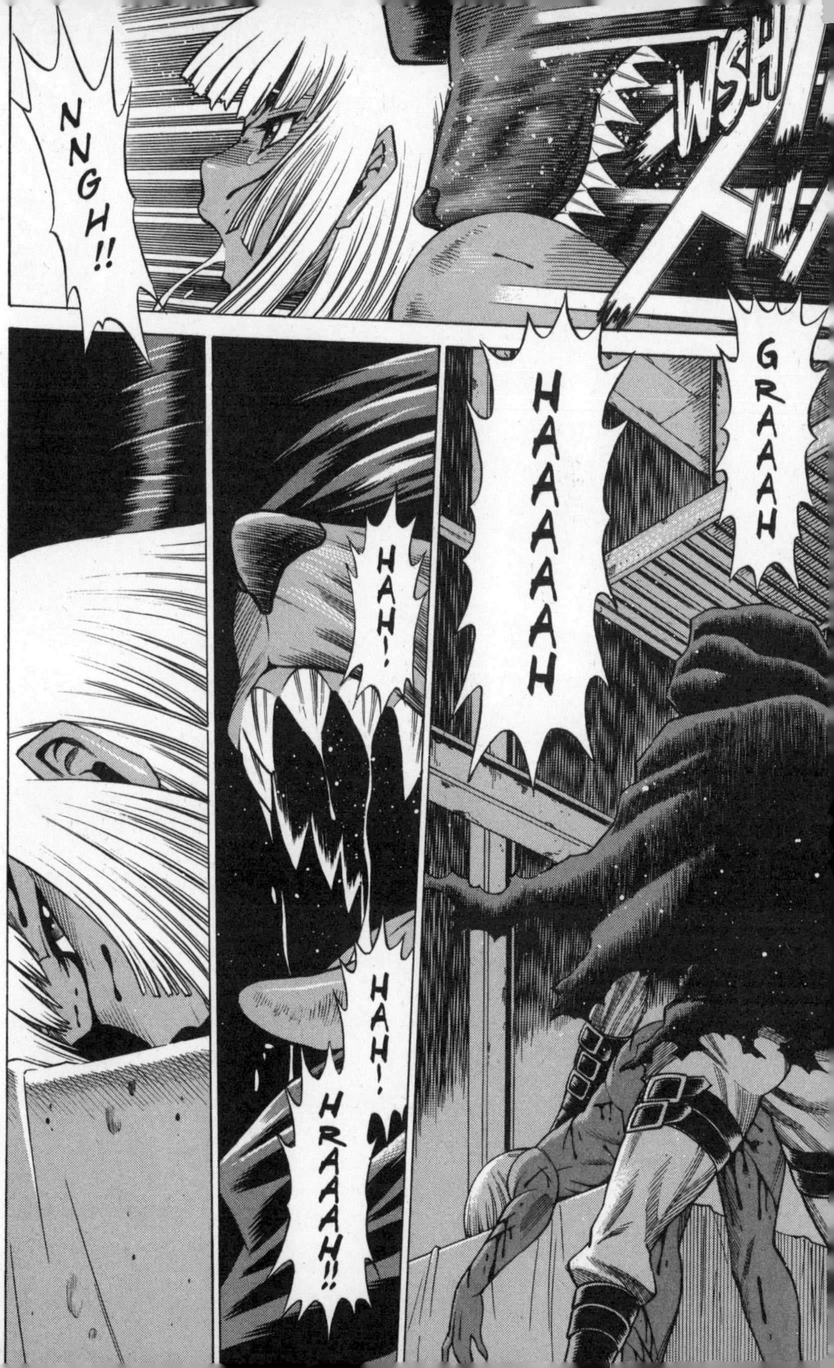
WSH
NNGH!!
GRAAAAH
HAAAAAAAH
HAH!
HAH!
HRAAAAH!!

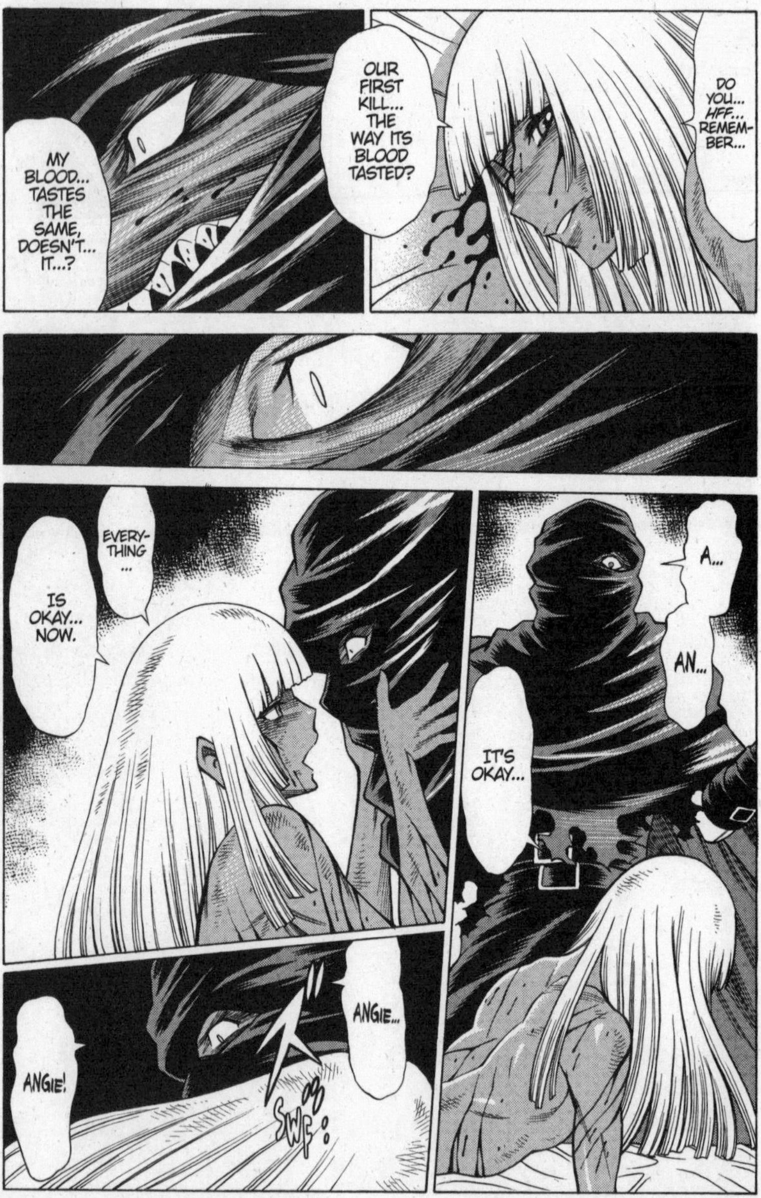
DO YOU... HFF... REMEMBER...
OUR FIRST KILL... THE WAY ITS BLOOD TASTED?
MY BLOOD... TASTES THE SAME, DOESN'T... IT...?
A...
AN...
IT'S OKAY...
EVERYTHING...
IS OKAY... NOW.
ANGIE...
ANGIE!
SWF

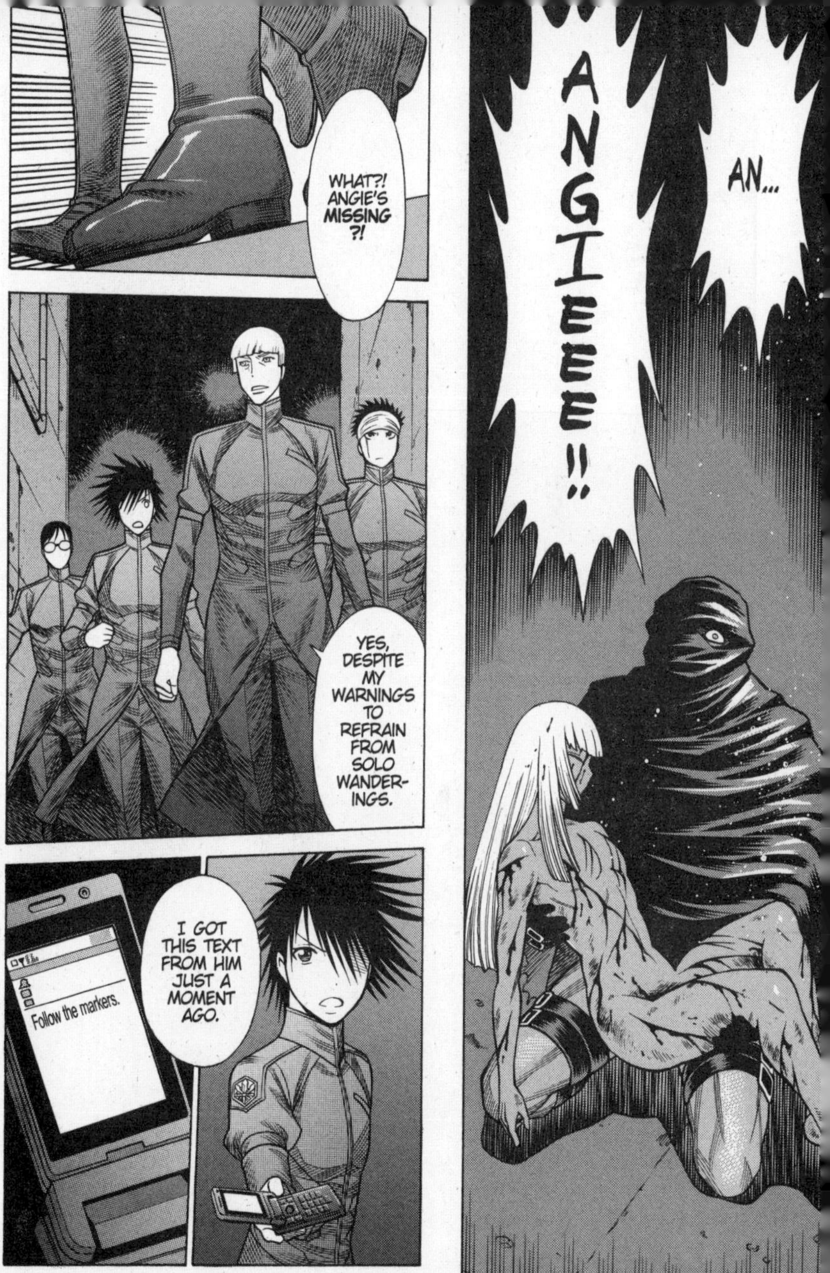
AN...
ANGIEEE!!
WHAT?! ANGIE'S MISSING?!
YES, DESPITE MY WARNINGS TO REFRAIN FROM SOLO WANDER-INGS.
I GOT THIS TEXT FROM HIM JUST A MOMENT AGO.
Follow the markers.

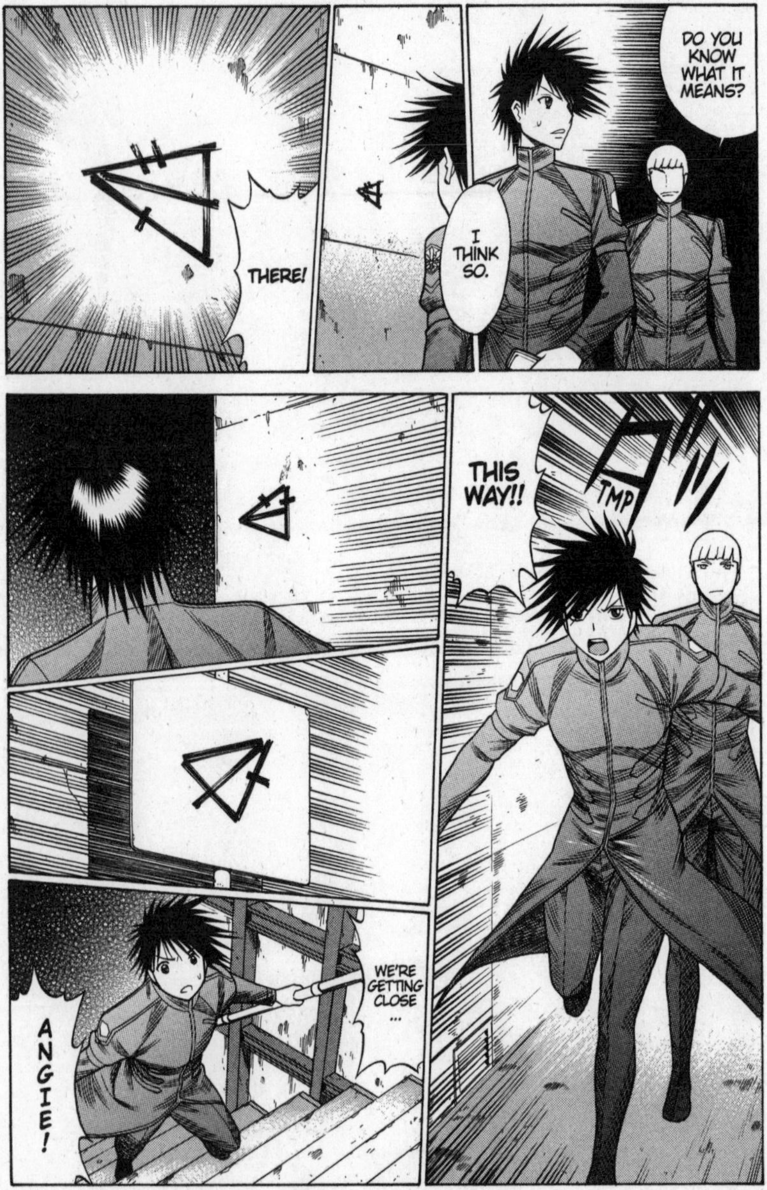
DO YOU KNOW WHAT IT MEANS?
I THINK SO.
THERE!
THIS WAY!!
TMP
WE'RE GETTING CLOSE ...
ANGIE!

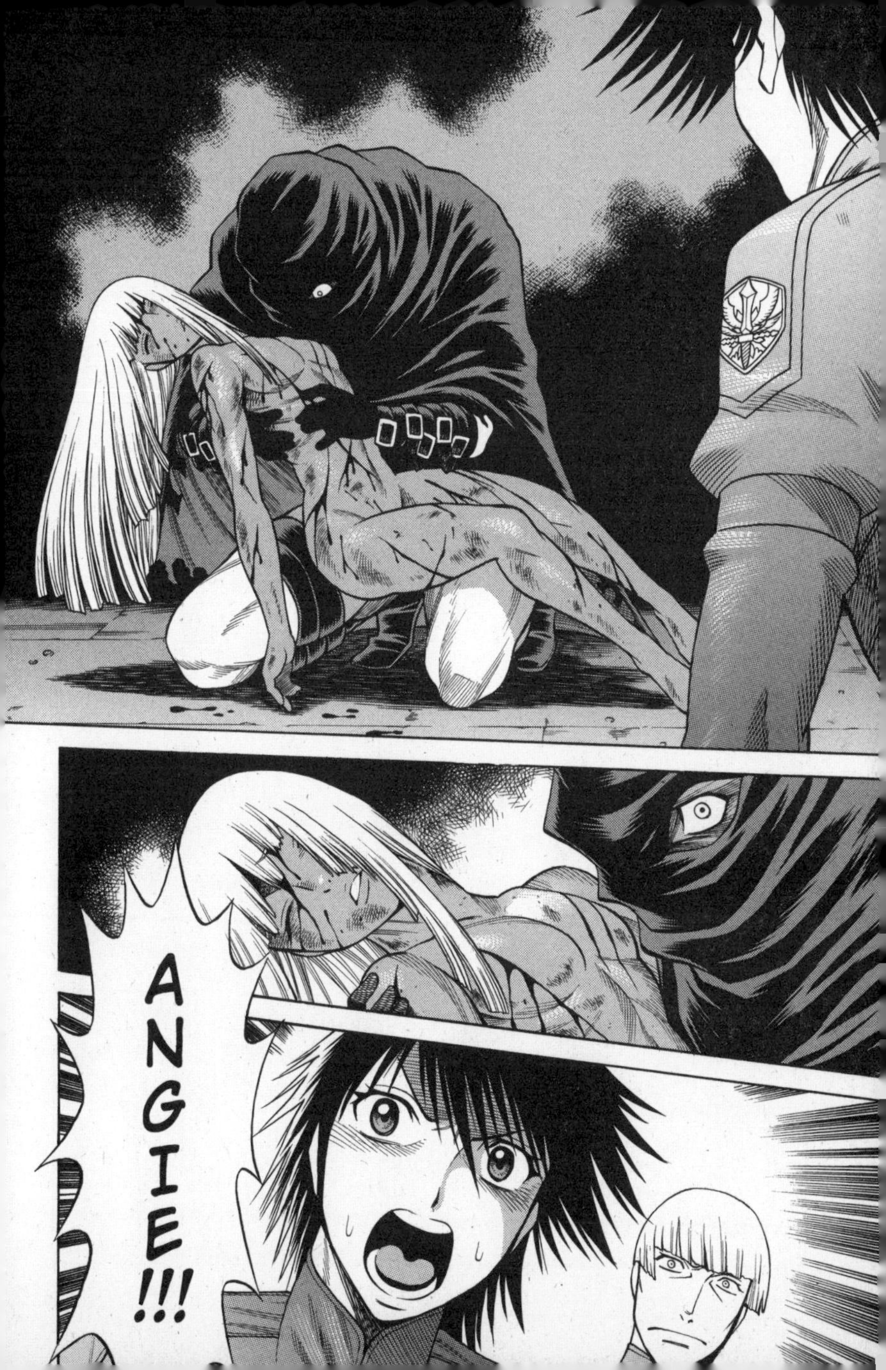
ANGIE!!!

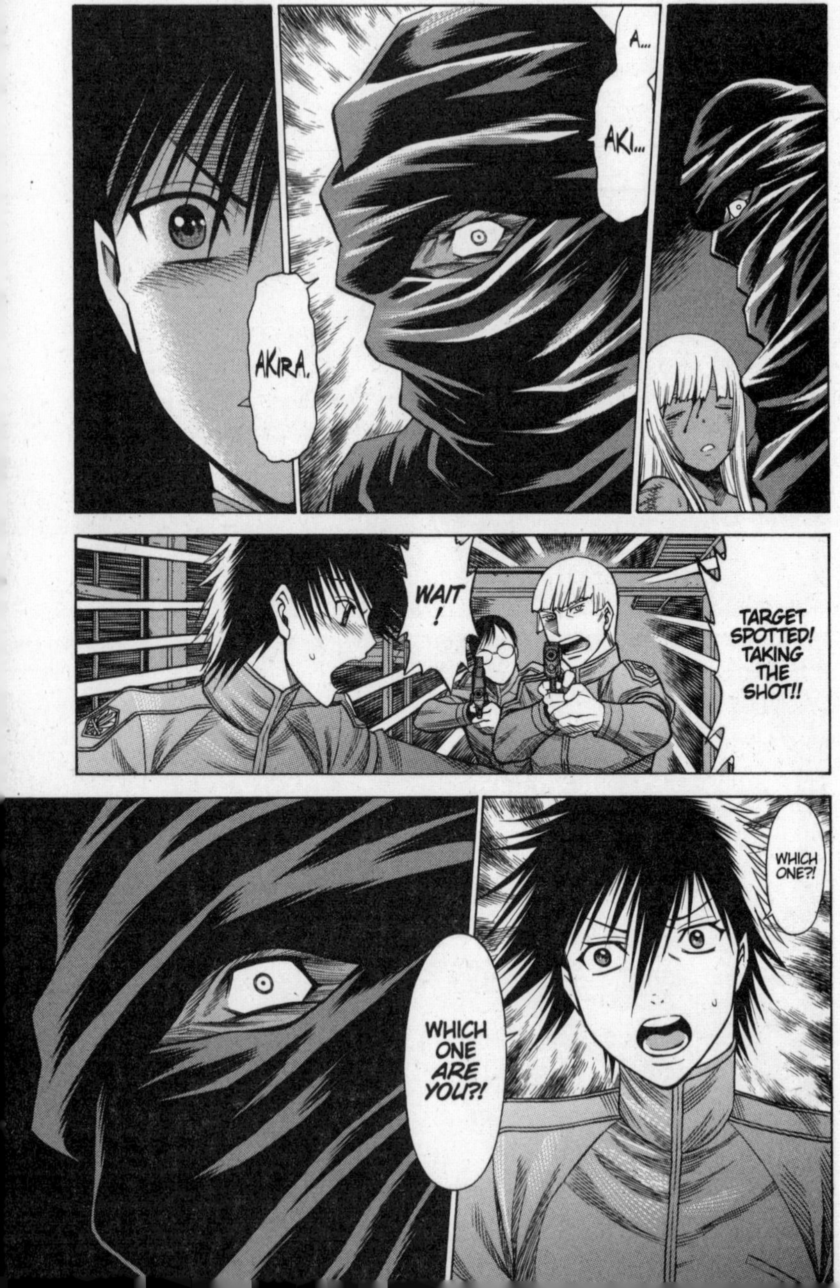
A...
AKI...
AKIRA.
TARGET SPOTTED! TAKING THE SHOT!!
WAIT!
WHICH ONE?!
WHICH ONE ARE YOU?!

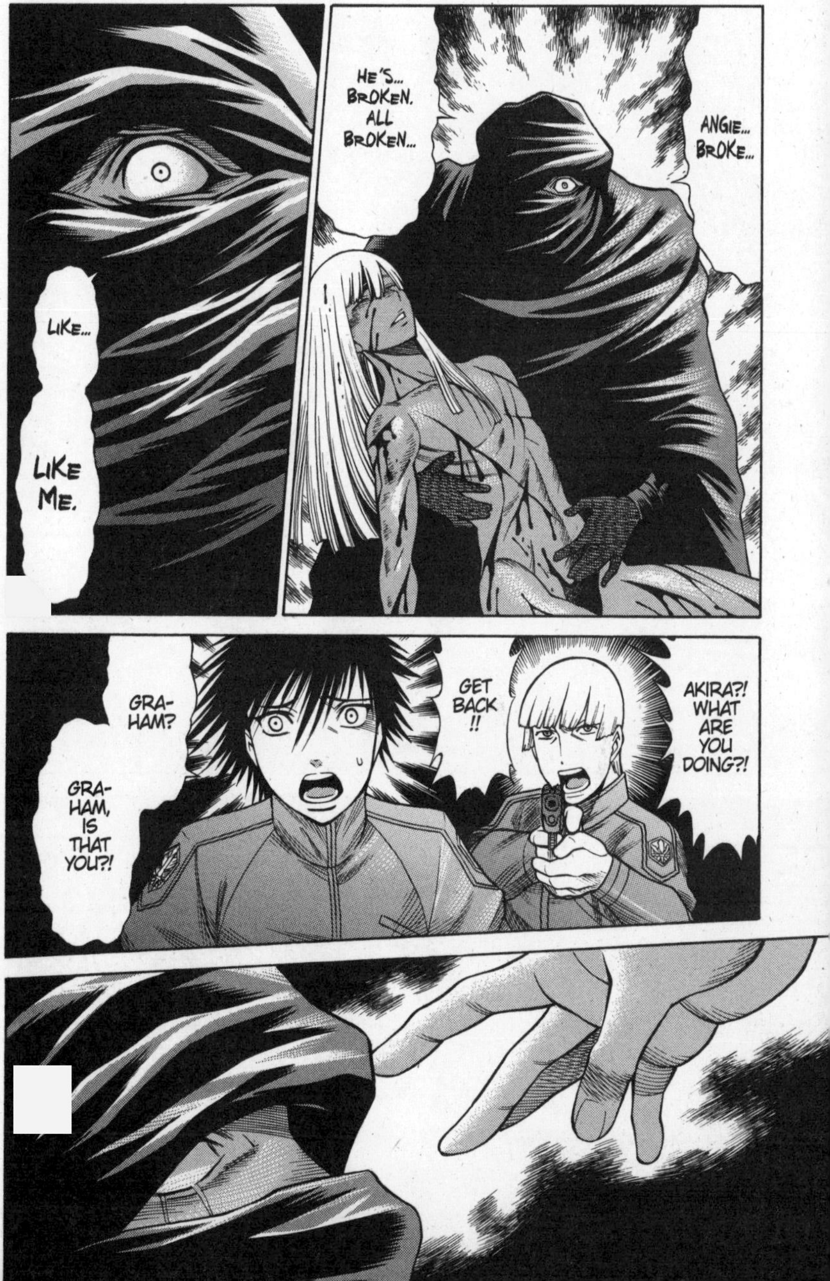
ANGIE... BROKE...
HE'S... BROKEN. ALL BROKEN...
LIKE...
LIKE ME.
AKIRA?! WHAT ARE YOU DOING?!
GET BACK!!
GRA-HAM?
GRA-HAM, IS THAT YOU?!

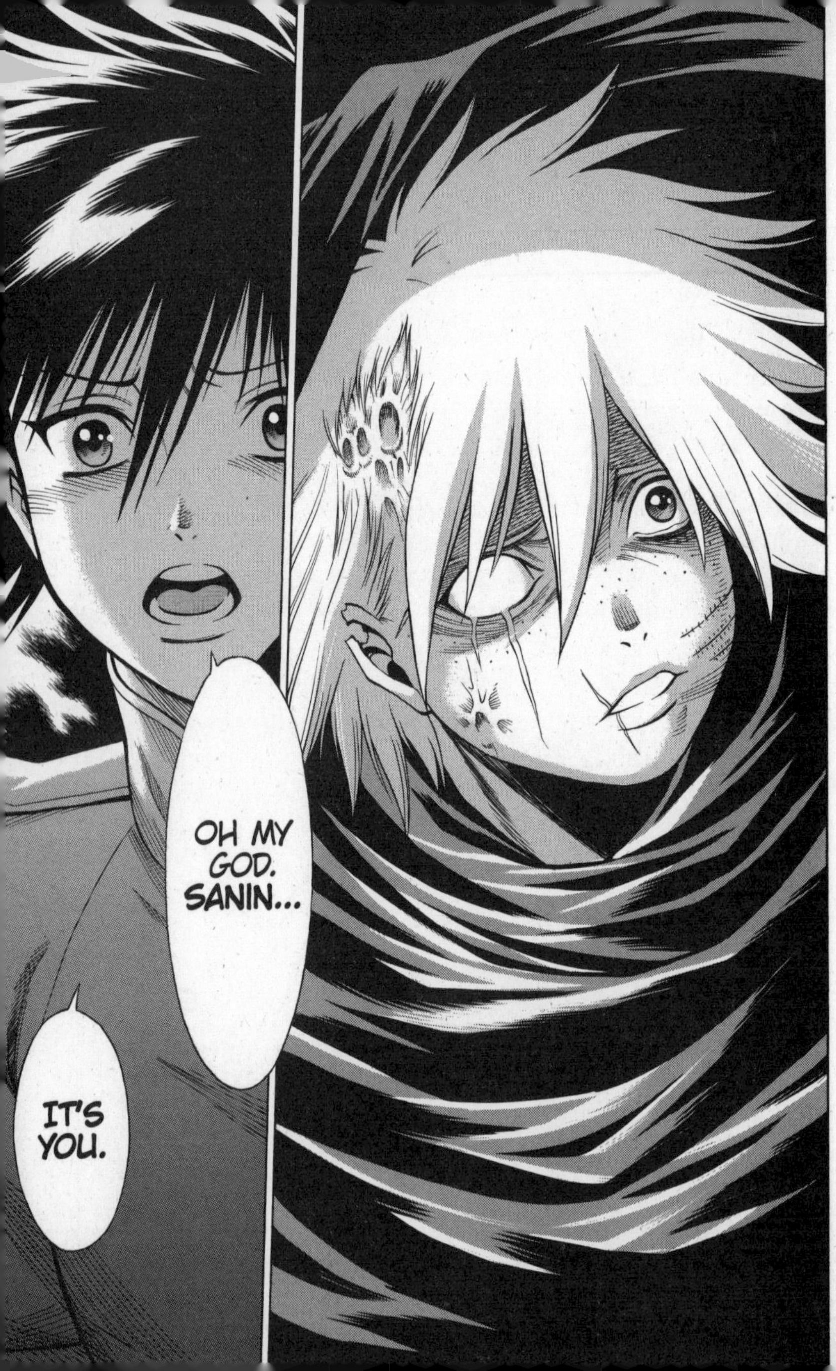
OH MY GOD. SANIN...
IT'S YOU.

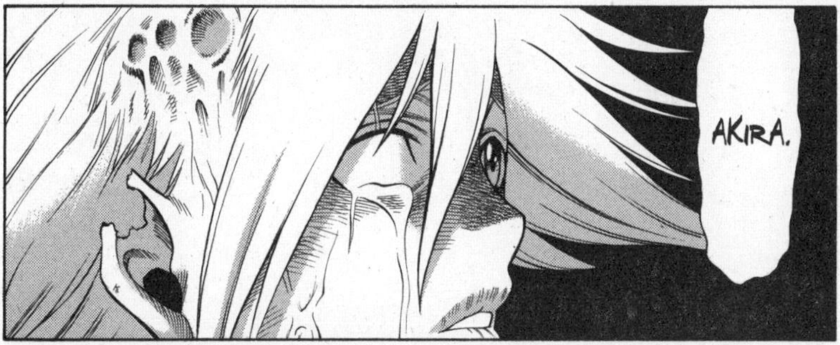
AKIRA.

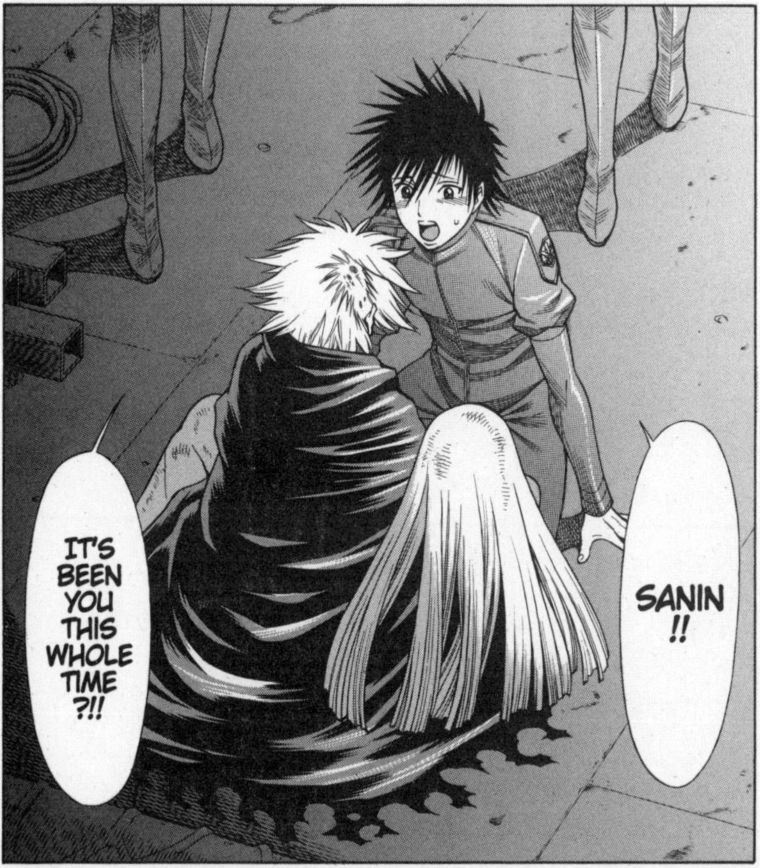
SANIN !!
IT'S BEEN YOU THIS WHOLE TIME ?!!

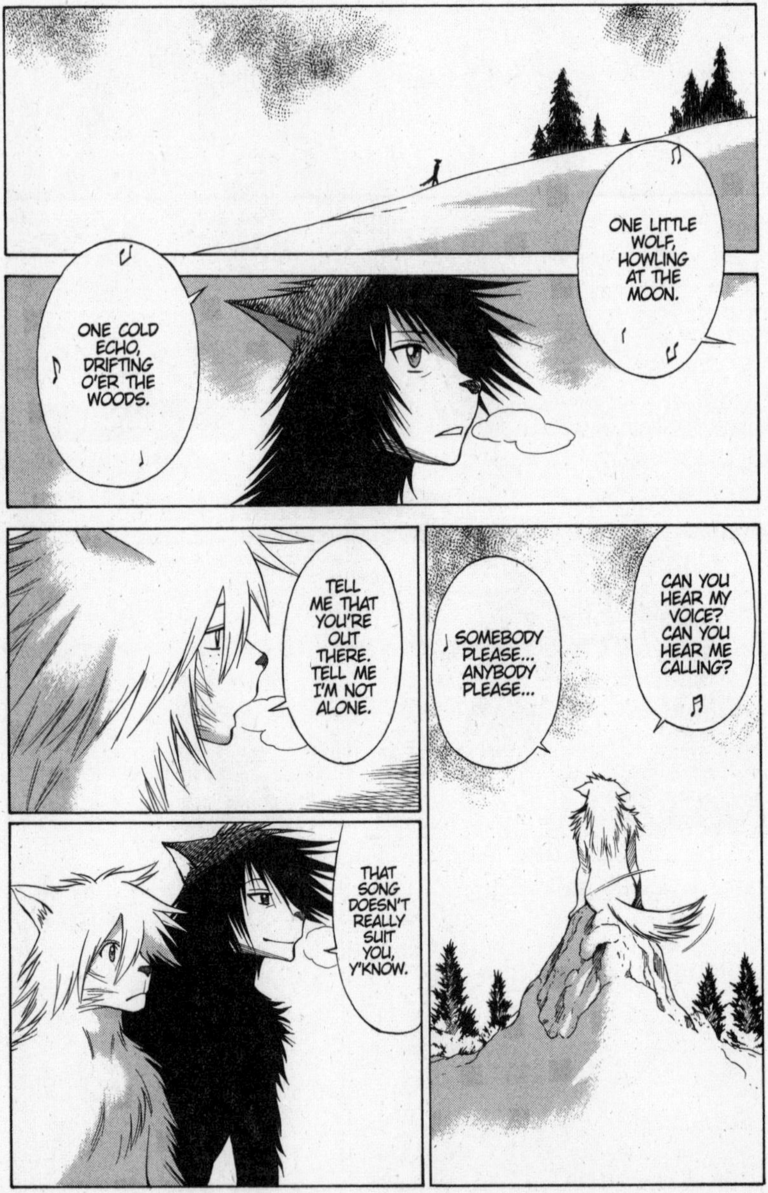
ONE LITTLE WOLF, HOWLING AT THE MOON.
ONE COLD ECHO, DRIFTING O'ER THE WOODS.
CAN YOU HEAR MY VOICE? CAN YOU HEAR ME CALLING?
SOMEBODY PLEASE... ANYBODY PLEASE...
TELL ME THAT YOU'RE OUT THERE. TELL ME I'M NOT ALONE.
THAT SONG DOESN'T REALLY SUIT YOU, Y'KNOW.

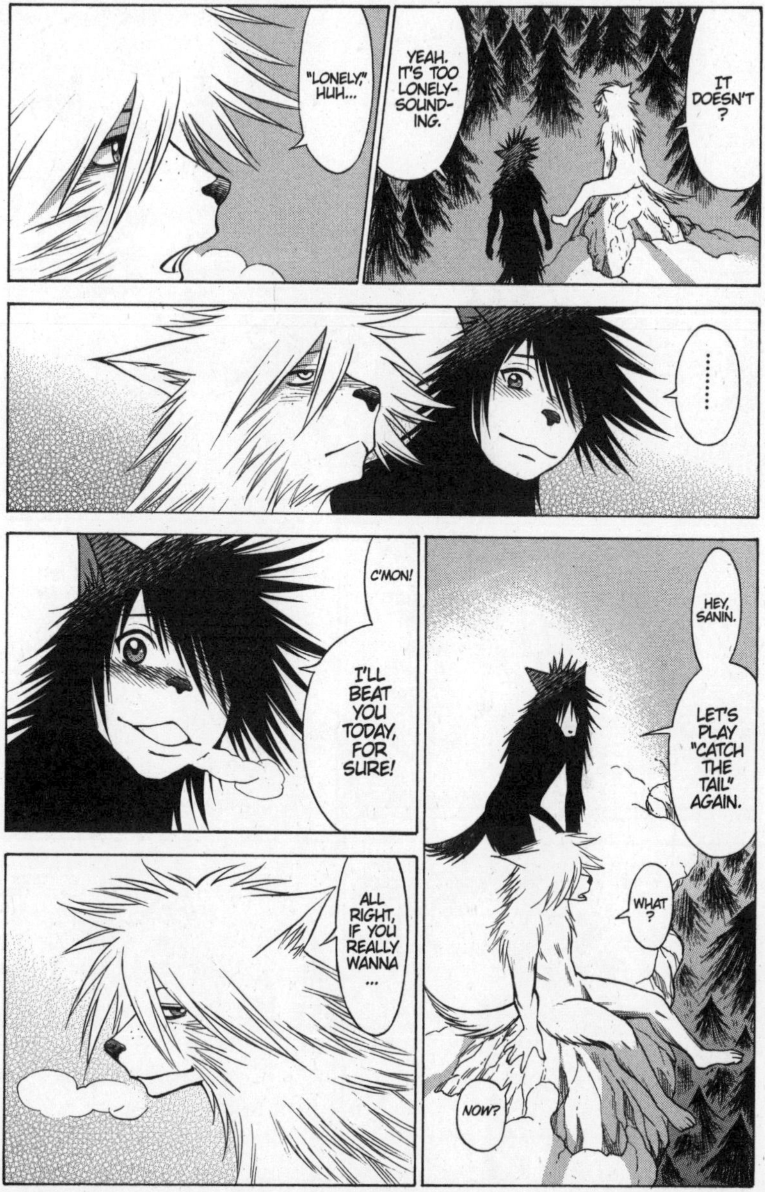
IT DOESN'T ?
YEAH. IT'S TOO LONELY-SOUNDING.
"LONELY," HUH...
....
HEY, SANIN.
LET'S PLAY "CATCH THE TAIL" AGAIN.
WHAT ?
NOW?
C'MON!
I'LL BEAT YOU TODAY, FOR SURE!
ALL RIGHT, IF YOU REALLY WANNA ...

Chapter 42: Elegy for a Wolf

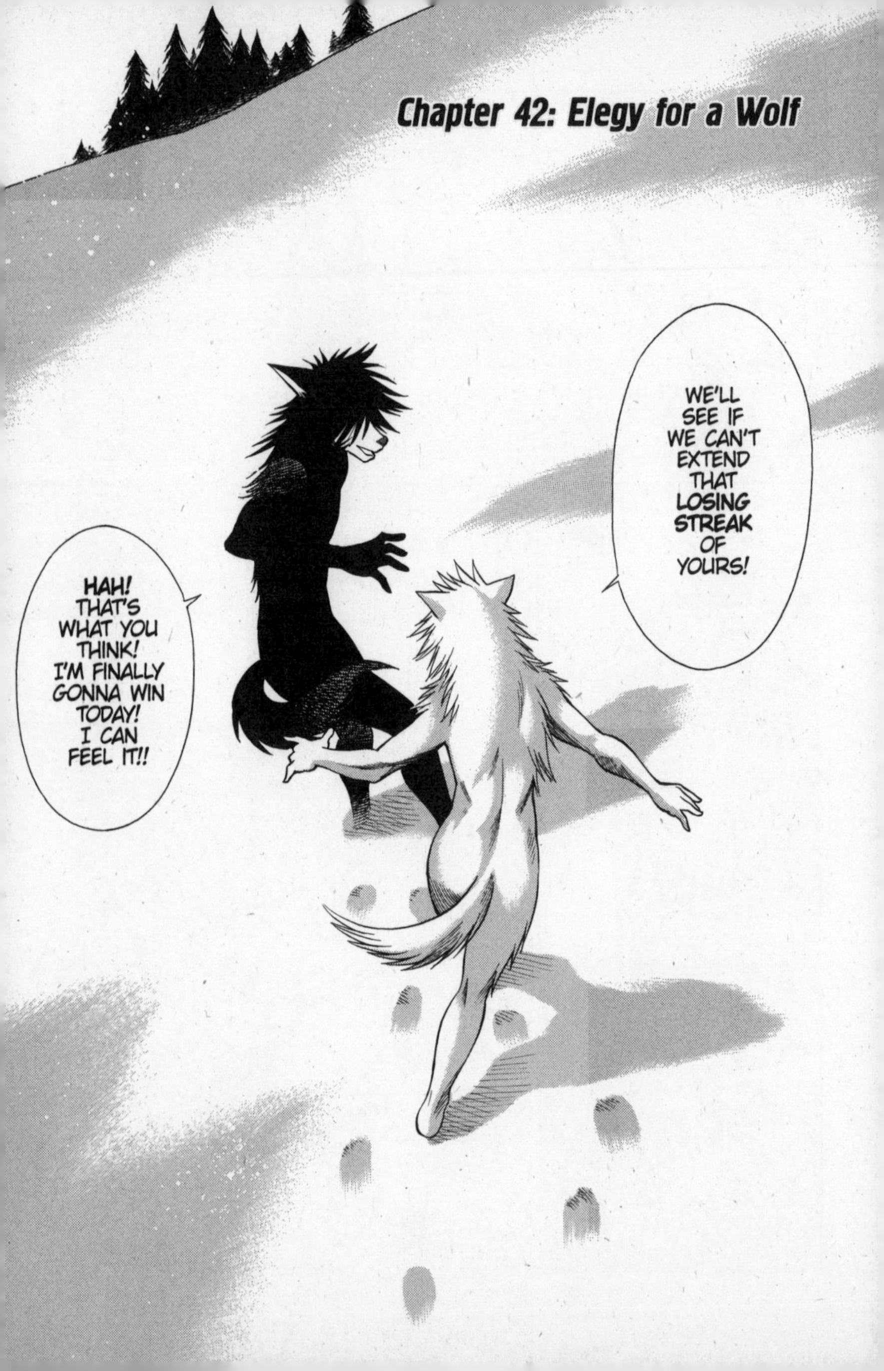
HAH! THAT'S WHAT YOU THINK! I'M FINALLY GONNA WIN TODAY! I CAN FEEL IT!!
WE'LL SEE IF WE CAN'T EXTEND THAT LOSING STREAK OF YOURS!

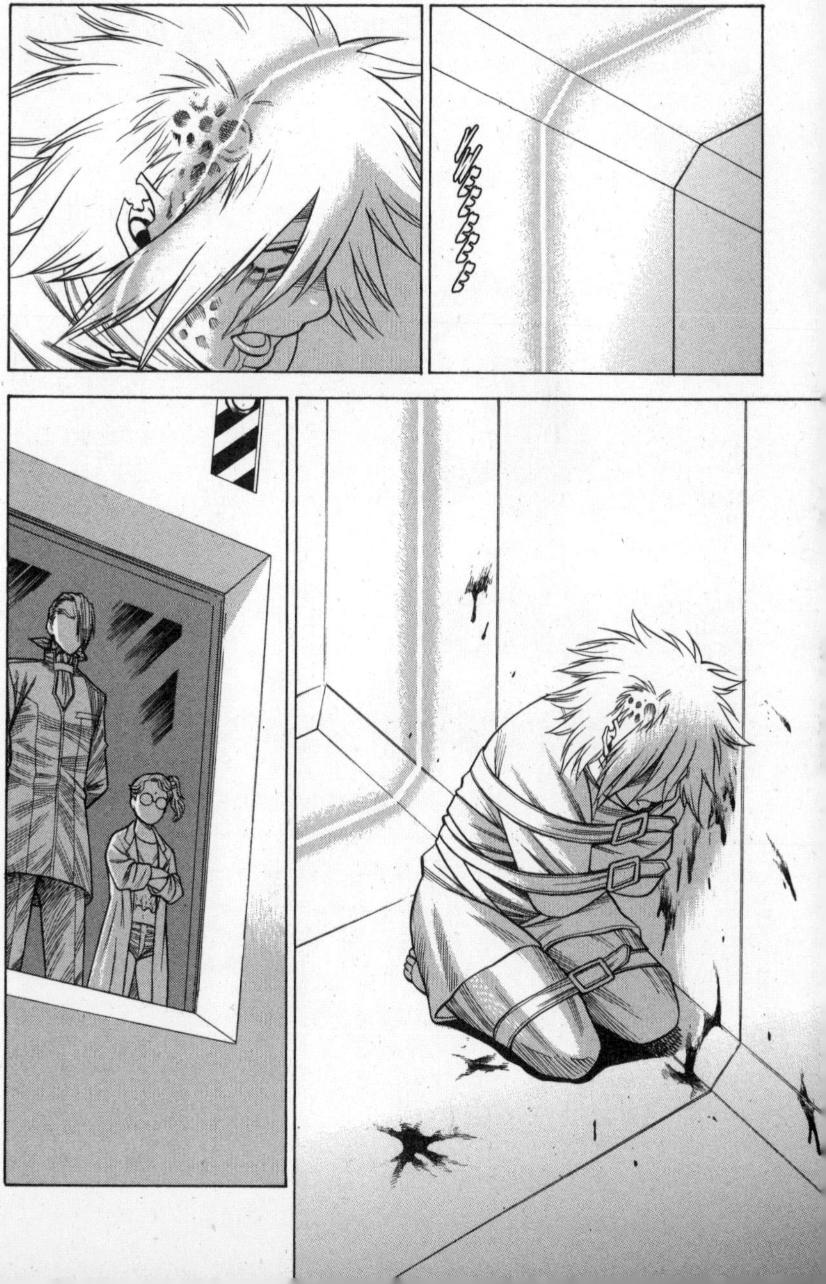

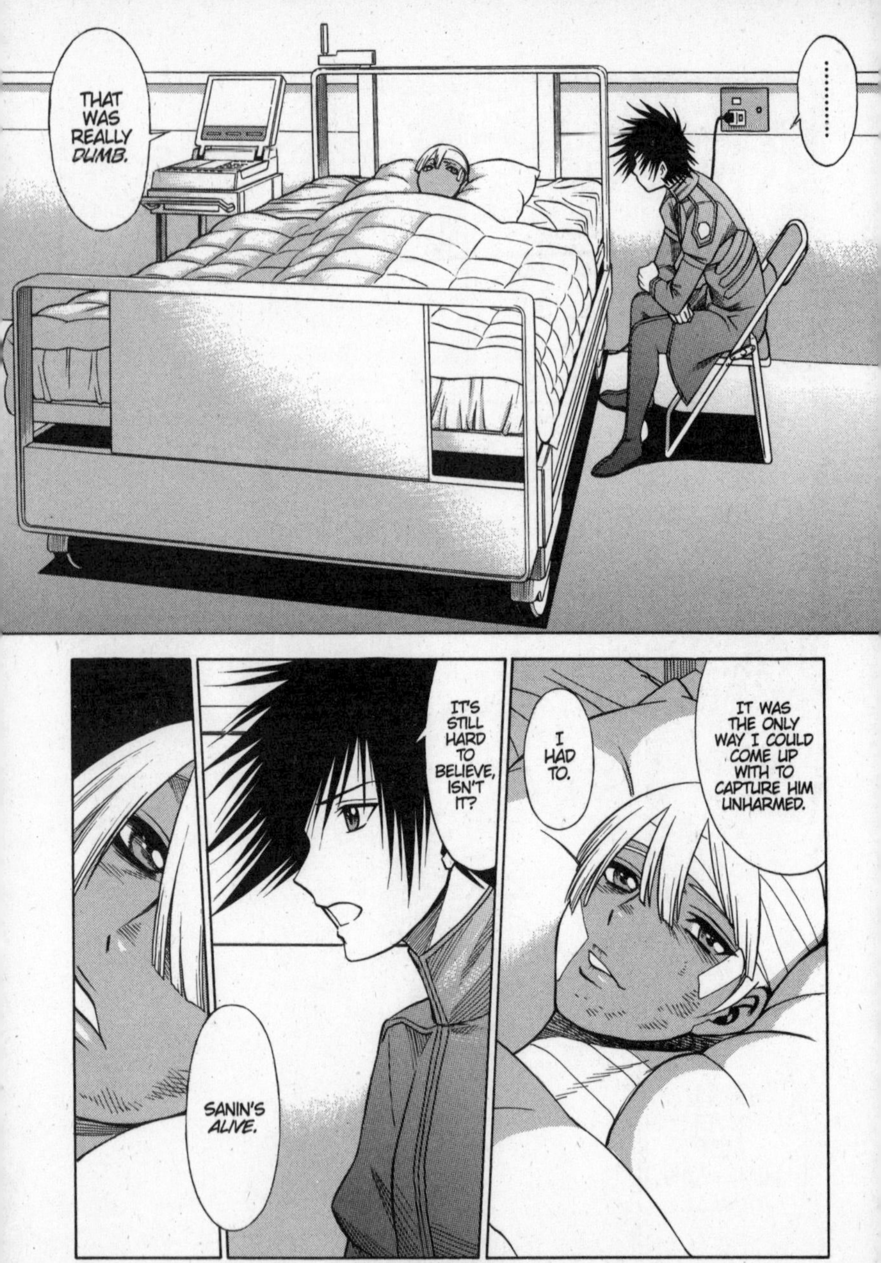
......
THAT WAS REALLY *DUMB.*
IT WAS THE ONLY WAY I COULD COME UP WITH TO CAPTURE HIM UNHARMED.
I HAD TO.
IT'S STILL HARD TO BELIEVE, ISN'T IT?
SANIN'S *ALIVE.*

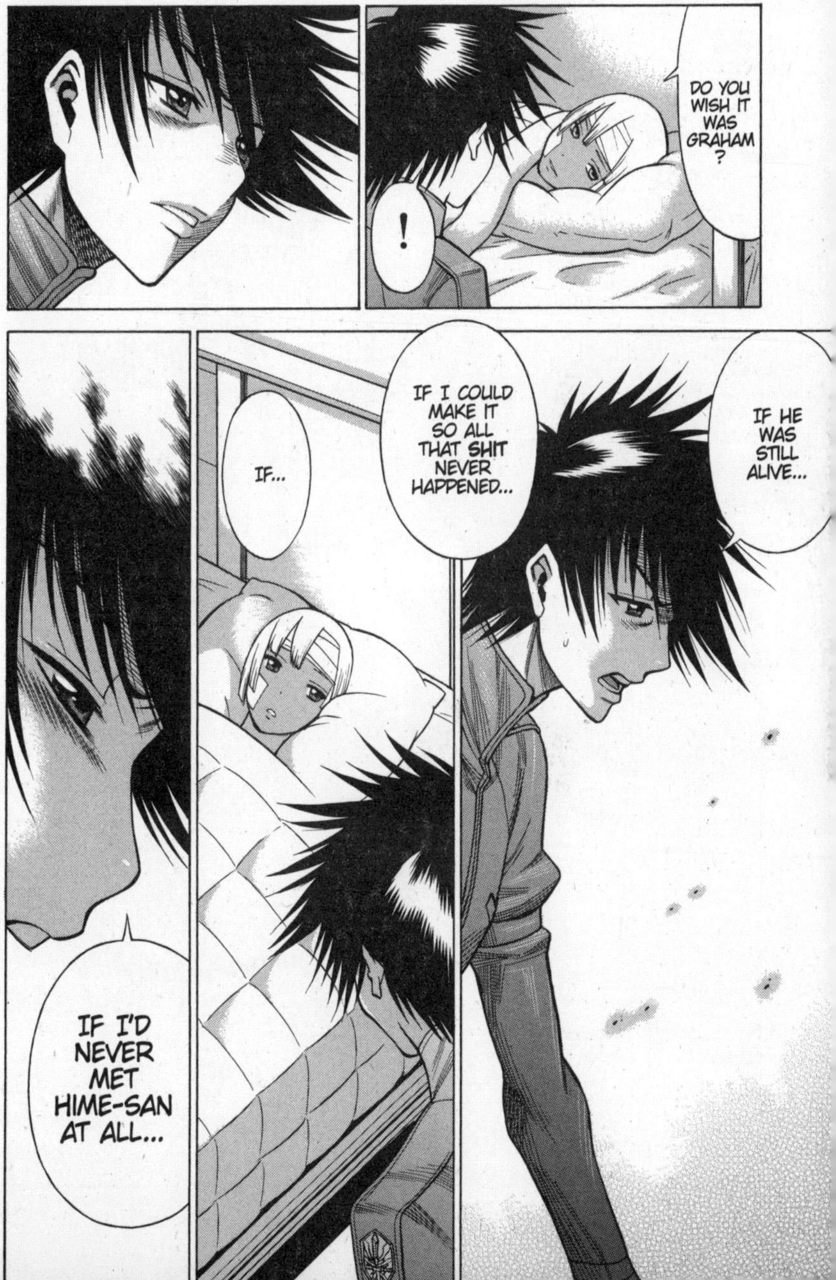
DO YOU WISH IT WAS GRAHAM ?
!
IF HE WAS STILL ALIVE...
IF I COULD MAKE IT SO ALL THAT SHIT NEVER HAPPENED...
IF...
IF I'D NEVER MET HIME-SAN AT ALL...

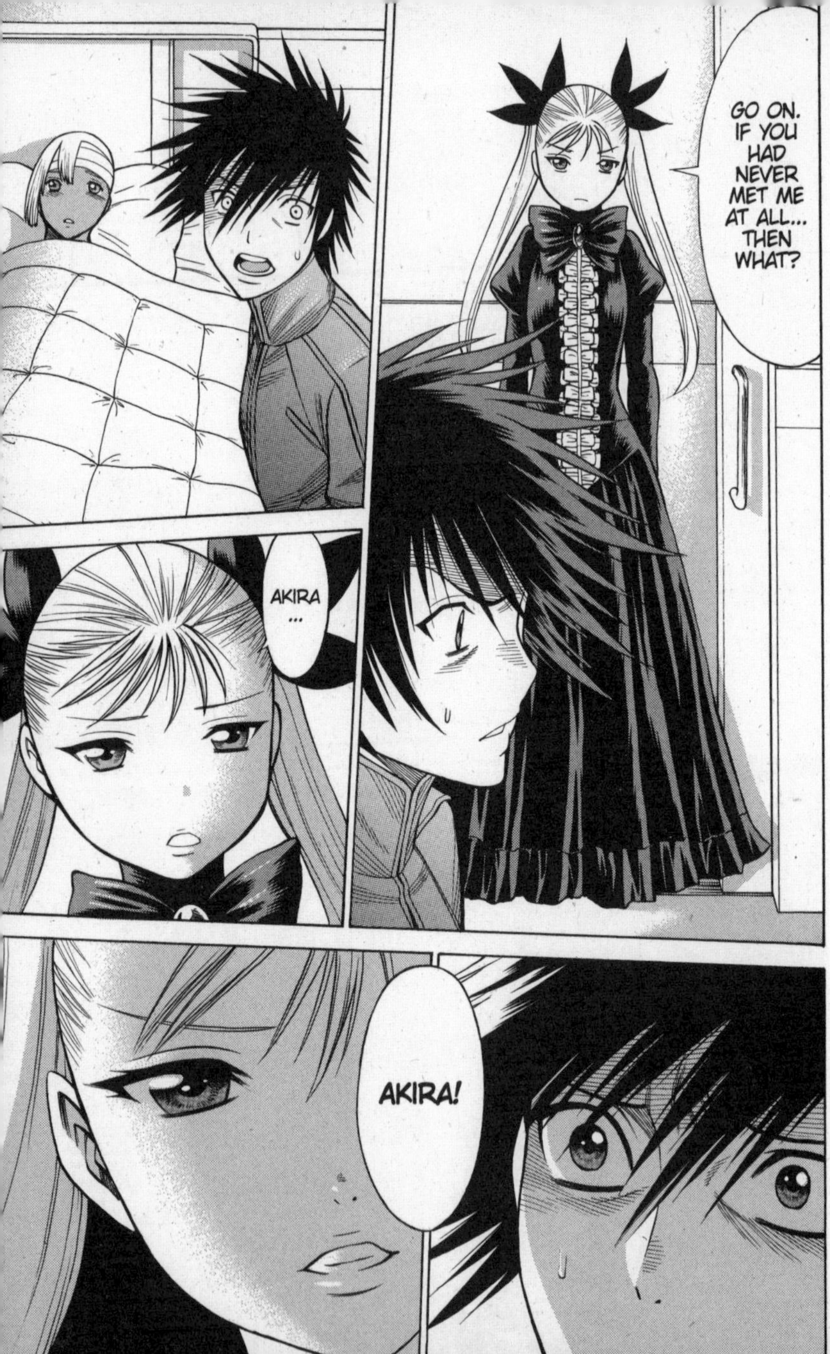
GO ON. IF YOU HAD NEVER MET ME AT ALL... THEN WHAT?
AKIRA ...
AKIRA!

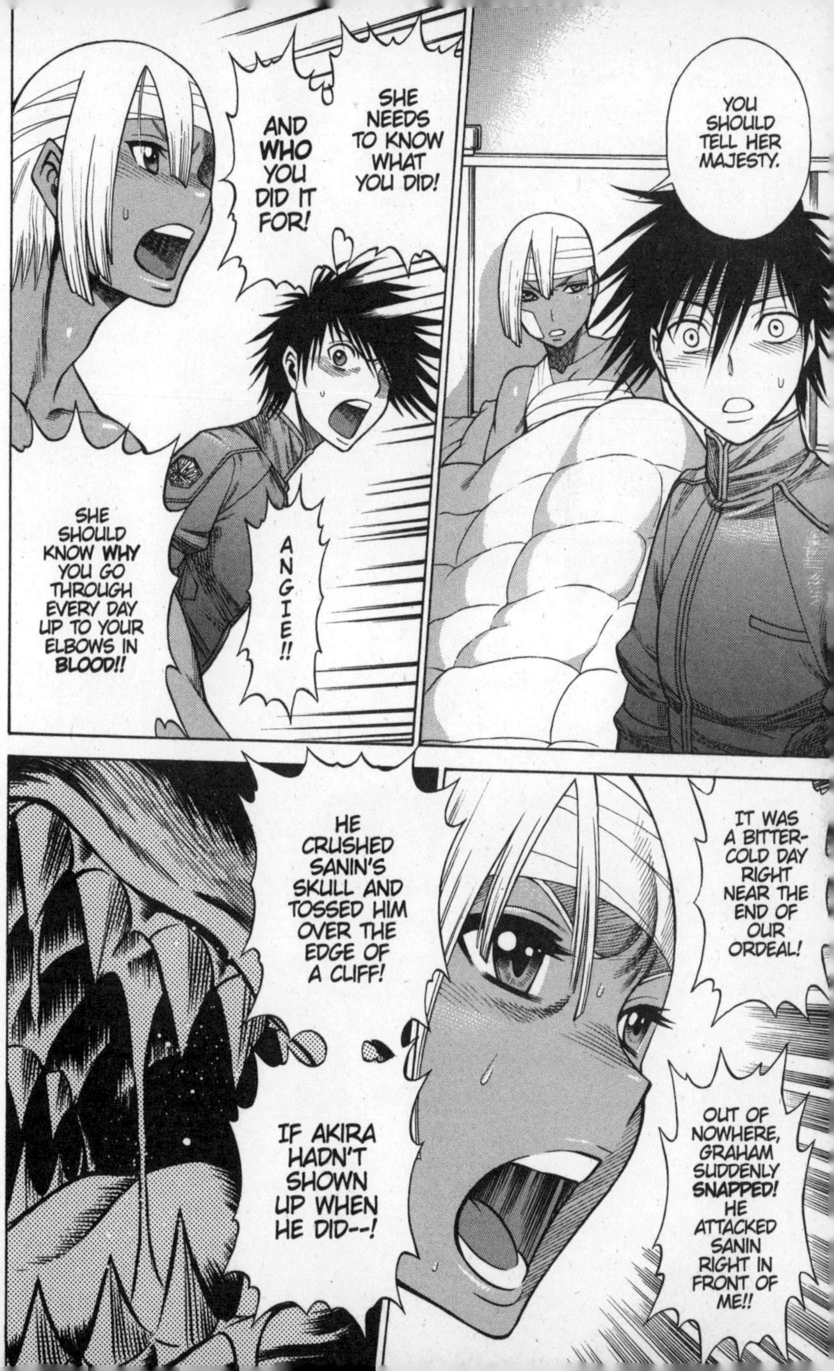
YOU SHOULD TELL HER MAJESTY.
SHE NEEDS TO KNOW WHAT YOU DID!
AND WHO YOU DID IT FOR!
ANGIE!!
SHE SHOULD KNOW WHY YOU GO THROUGH EVERY DAY UP TO YOUR ELBOWS IN BLOOD!!
IT WAS A BITTER-COLD DAY RIGHT NEAR THE END OF OUR ORDEAL!
OUT OF NOWHERE, GRAHAM SUDDENLY SNAPPED! HE ATTACKED SANIN RIGHT IN FRONT OF ME!!
HE CRUSHED SANIN'S SKULL AND TOSSED HIM OVER THE EDGE OF A CLIFF!
IF AKIRA HADN'T SHOWN UP WHEN HE DID--!

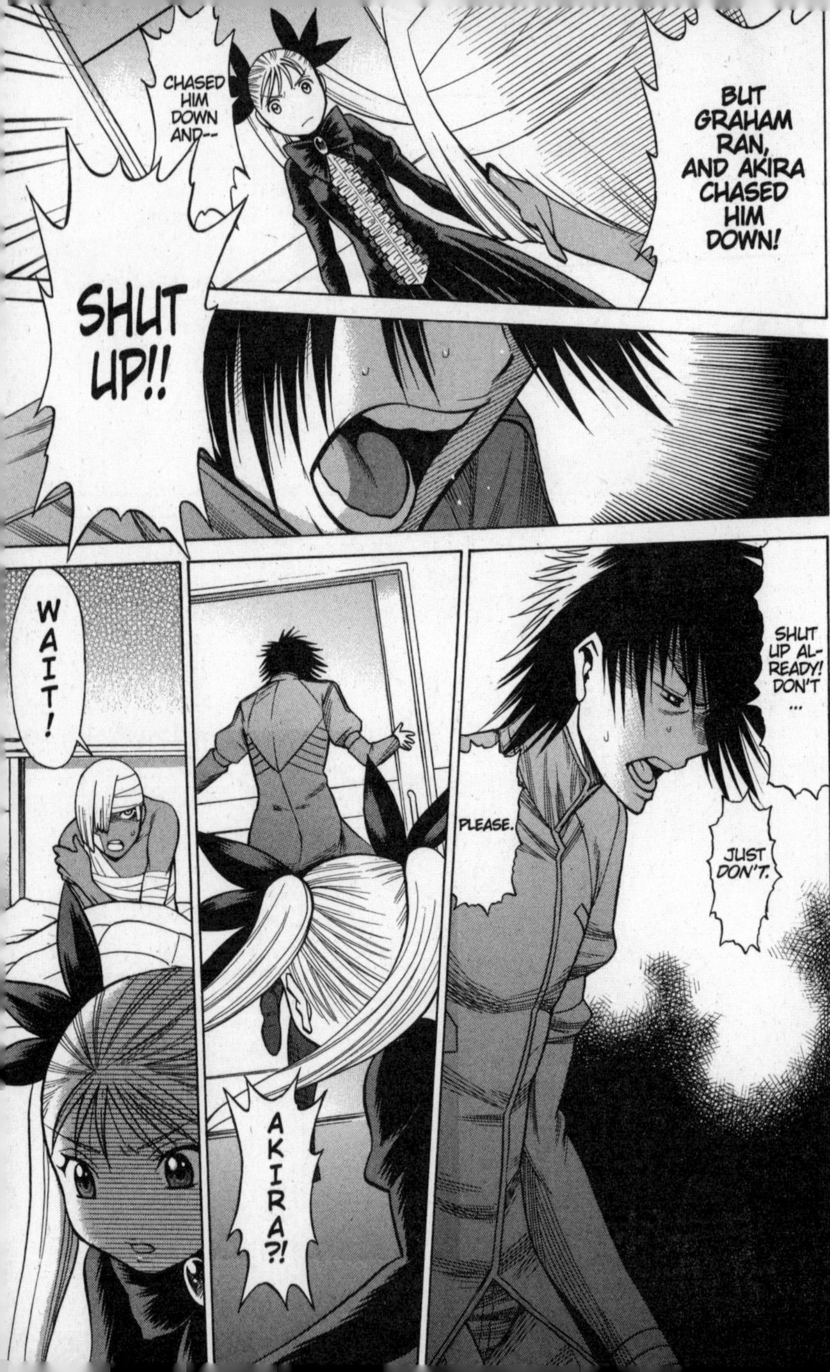
BUT GRAHAM RAN, AND AKIRA CHASED HIM DOWN!
CHASED HIM DOWN AND--
SHUT UP!!
SHUT UP AL- READY! DON'T ...
JUST DON'T.
PLEASE.
AKIRA?!
WAIT!

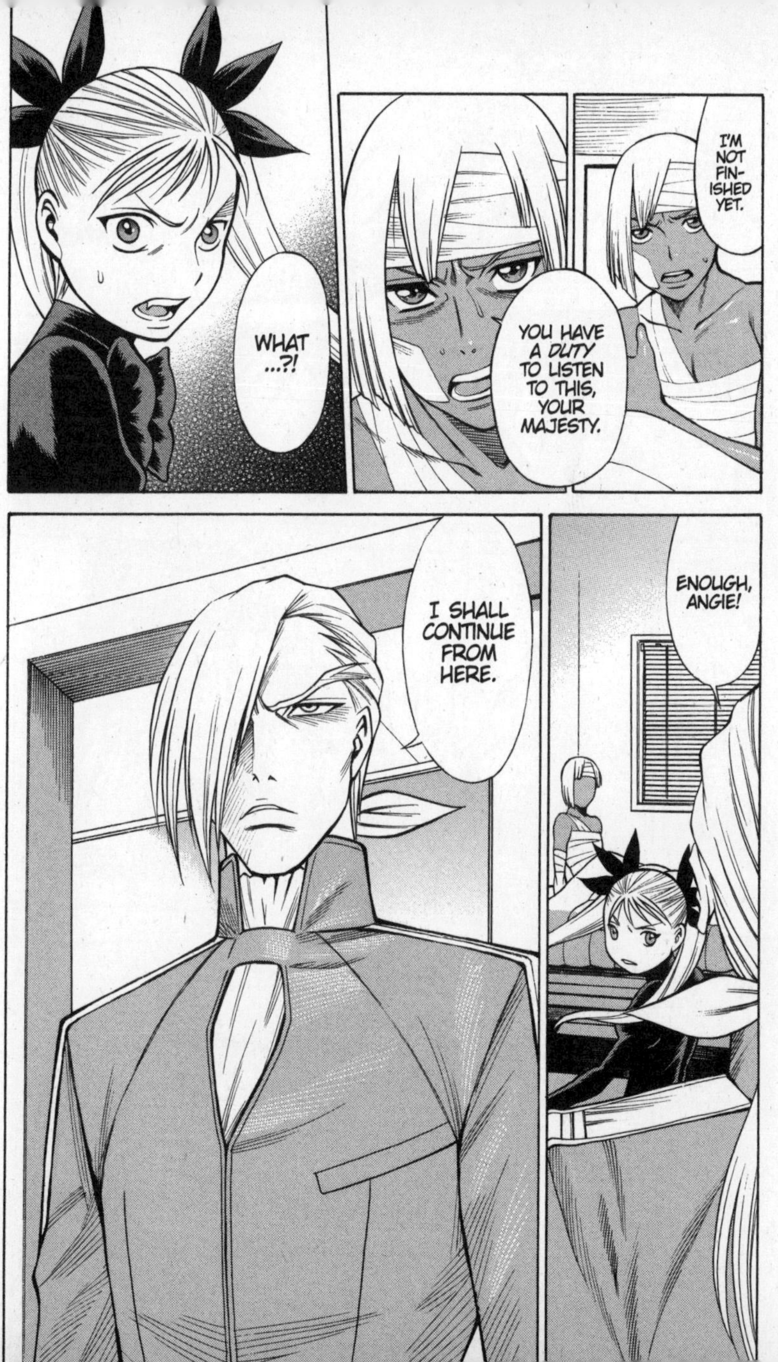
I'M NOT FIN- ISHED YET.
YOU HAVE A *DUTY* TO LISTEN TO THIS, YOUR MAJESTY.
WHAT ...?!
ENOUGH, ANGIE!
I SHALL CONTINUE FROM HERE.

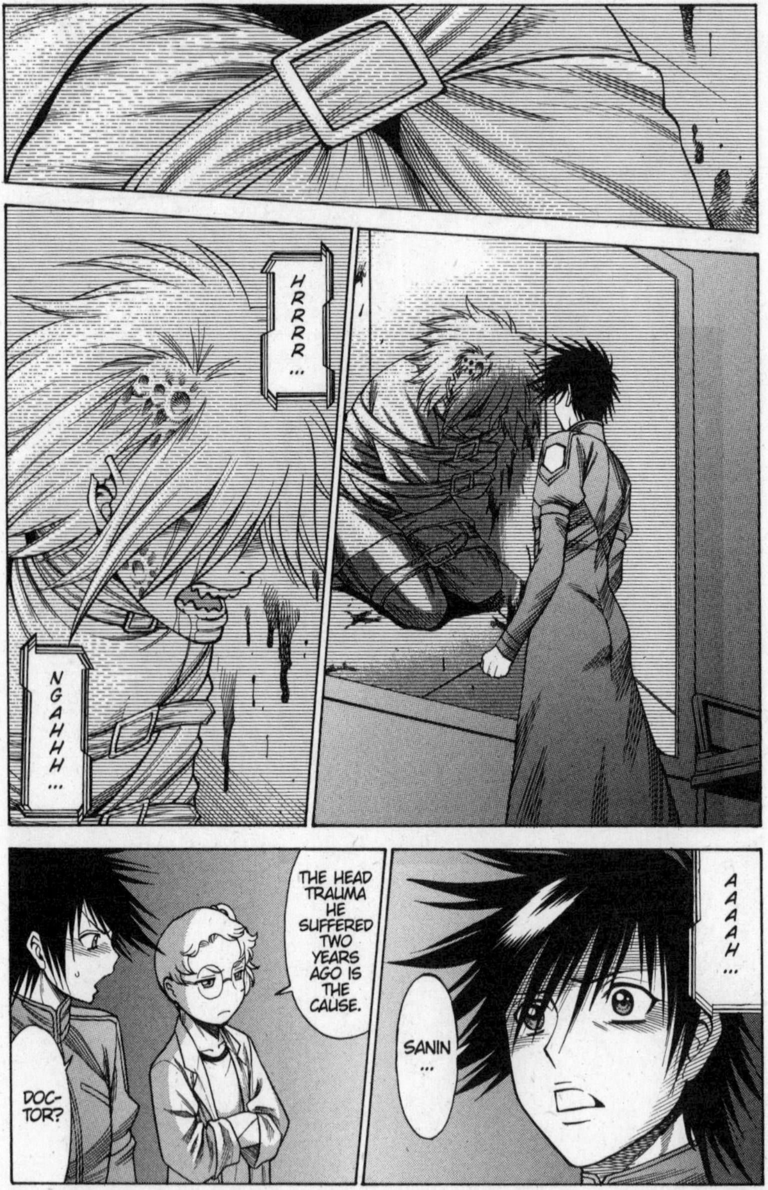
HRRRR...
NGAHHH...
AAAAH...
SANIN...
THE HEAD TRAUMA HE SUFFERED TWO YEARS AGO IS THE CAUSE.
DOC-TOR?

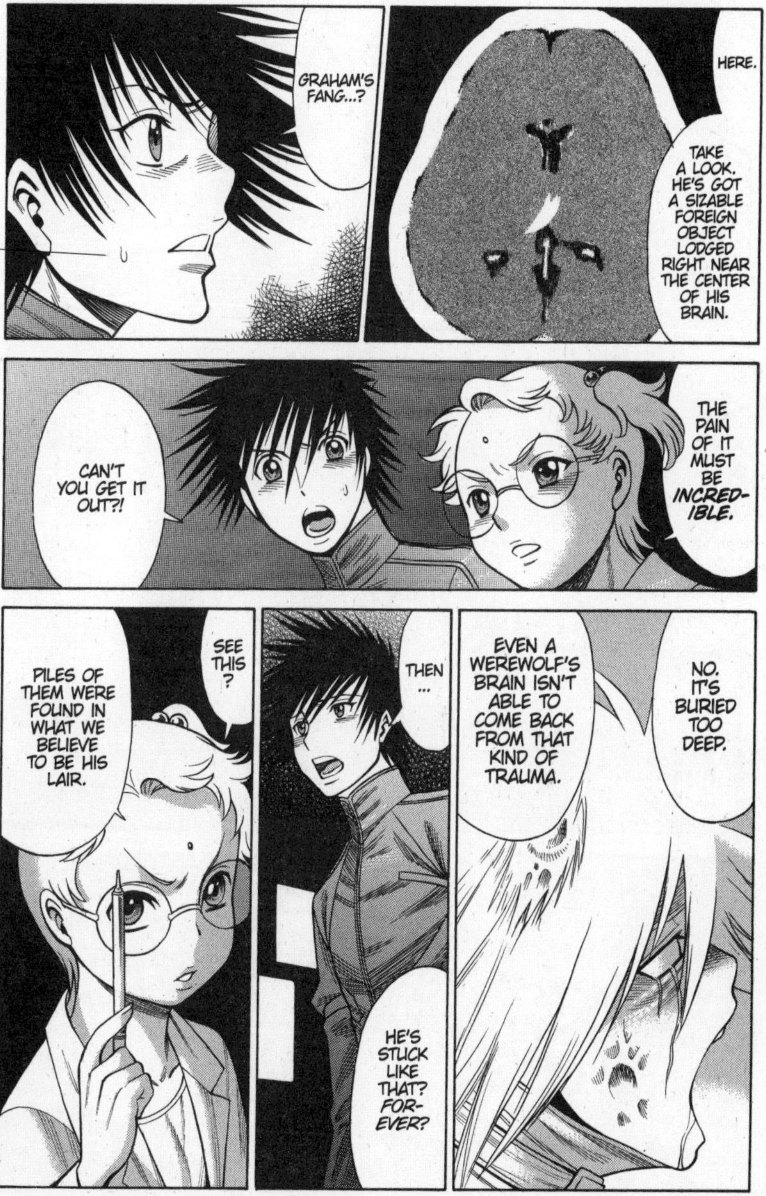
HERE.
TAKE A LOOK. HE'S GOT A SIZABLE FOREIGN OBJECT LODGED RIGHT NEAR THE CENTER OF HIS BRAIN.
GRAHAM'S FANG...?
THE PAIN OF IT MUST BE *INCREDIBLE.*
CAN'T YOU GET IT OUT?!
NO. IT'S BURIED TOO DEEP.
EVEN A WEREWOLF'S BRAIN ISN'T ABLE TO COME BACK FROM THAT KIND OF TRAUMA.
THEN ...
HE'S STUCK LIKE THAT? *FOREVER?*
SEE THIS?
PILES OF THEM WERE FOUND IN WHAT WE BELIEVE TO BE HIS LAIR.

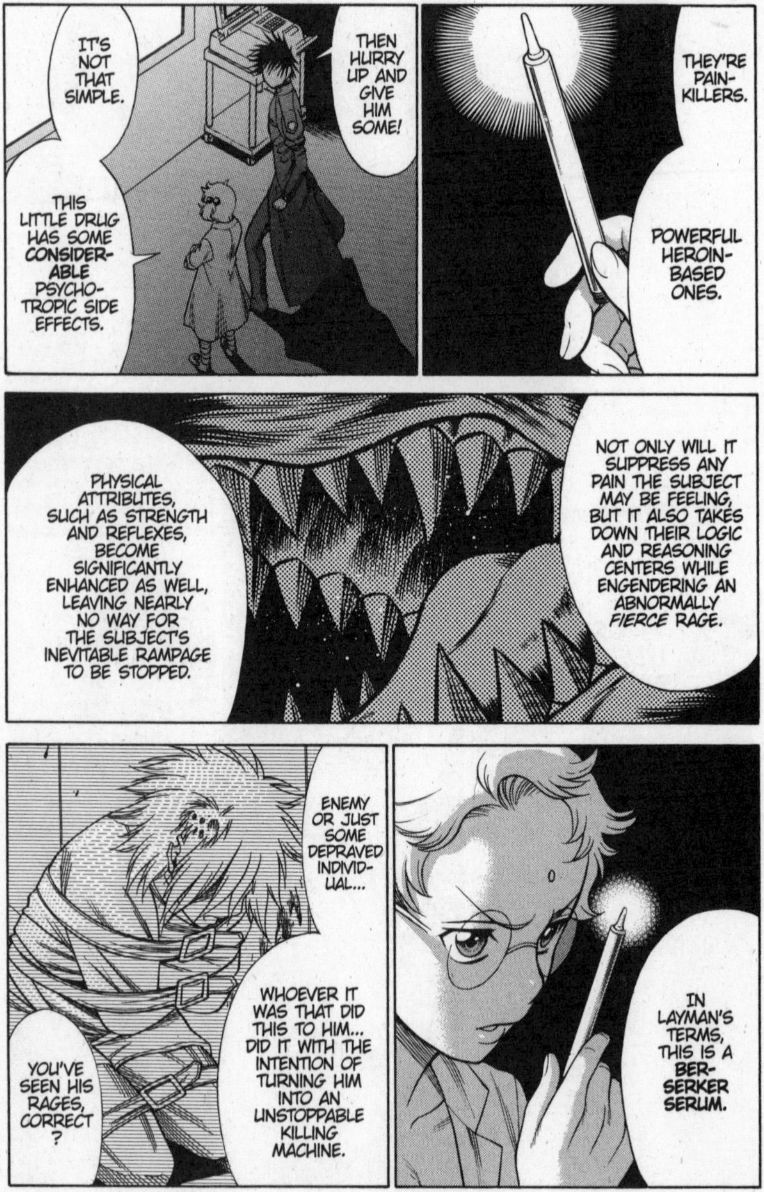
THEY'RE PAIN-KILLERS.
POWERFUL HEROIN-BASED ONES.
THEN HURRY UP AND GIVE HIM SOME!
IT'S NOT THAT SIMPLE.
THIS LITTLE DRUG HAS SOME CONSIDER-ABLE PSYCHO-TROPIC SIDE EFFECTS.
NOT ONLY WILL IT SUPPRESS ANY PAIN THE SUBJECT MAY BE FEELING, BUT IT ALSO TAKES DOWN THEIR LOGIC AND REASONING CENTERS WHILE ENGENDERING AN ABNORMALLY *FIERCE* RAGE.
PHYSICAL ATTRIBUTES, SUCH AS STRENGTH AND REFLEXES, BECOME SIGNIFICANTLY ENHANCED AS WELL, LEAVING NEARLY NO WAY FOR THE SUBJECT'S INEVITABLE RAMPAGE TO BE STOPPED.
IN LAYMAN'S TERMS, THIS IS A **BER-SERKER SERUM.**
ENEMY OR JUST SOME DEPRAVED INDIVID-UAL...
WHOEVER IT WAS THAT DID THIS TO HIM... DID IT WITH THE INTENTION OF TURNING HIM INTO AN UNSTOPPABLE KILLING MACHINE.
YOU'VE SEEN HIS RAGES, CORRECT ?

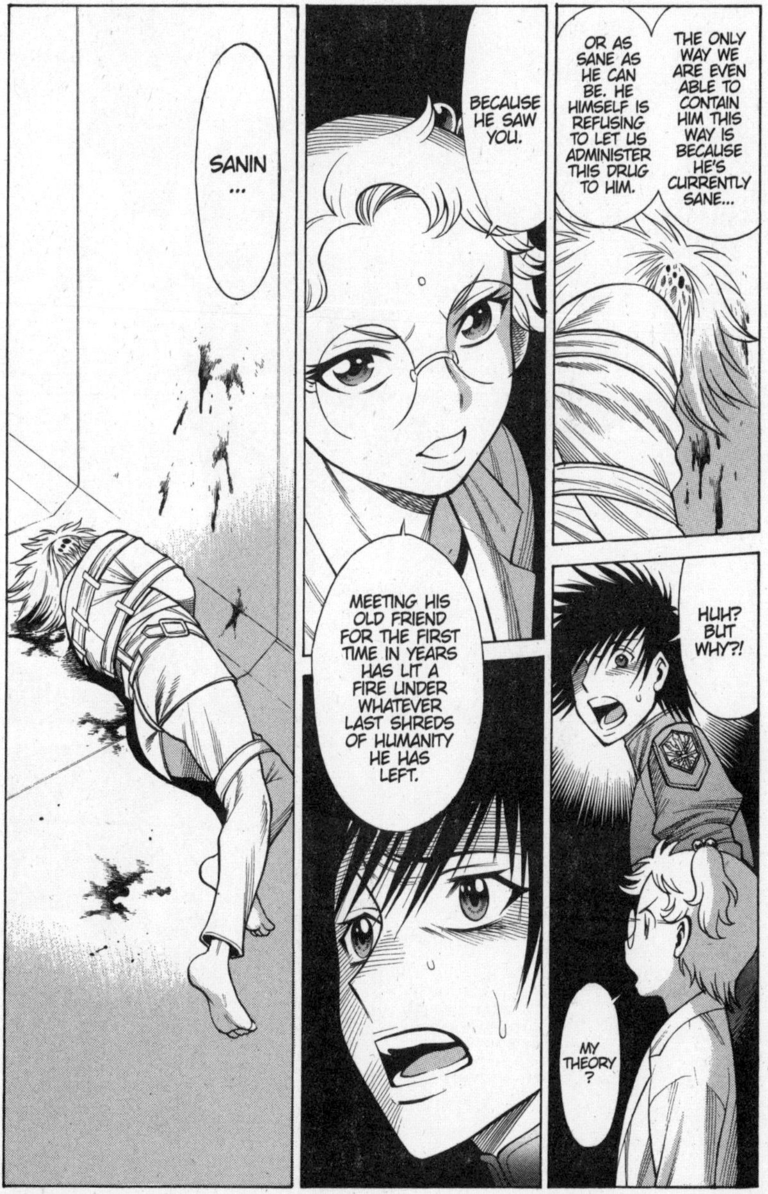
THE ONLY WAY WE ARE EVEN ABLE TO CONTAIN HIM THIS WAY IS BECAUSE HE'S CURRENTLY SANE...
OR AS SANE AS HE CAN BE. HE HIMSELF IS REFUSING TO LET US ADMINISTER THIS DRUG TO HIM.
HUH? BUT WHY?!
MY THEORY?
BECAUSE HE SAW YOU.
MEETING HIS OLD FRIEND FOR THE FIRST TIME IN YEARS HAS LIT A FIRE UNDER WHATEVER LAST SHREDS OF HUMANITY HE HAS LEFT.
SANIN ...

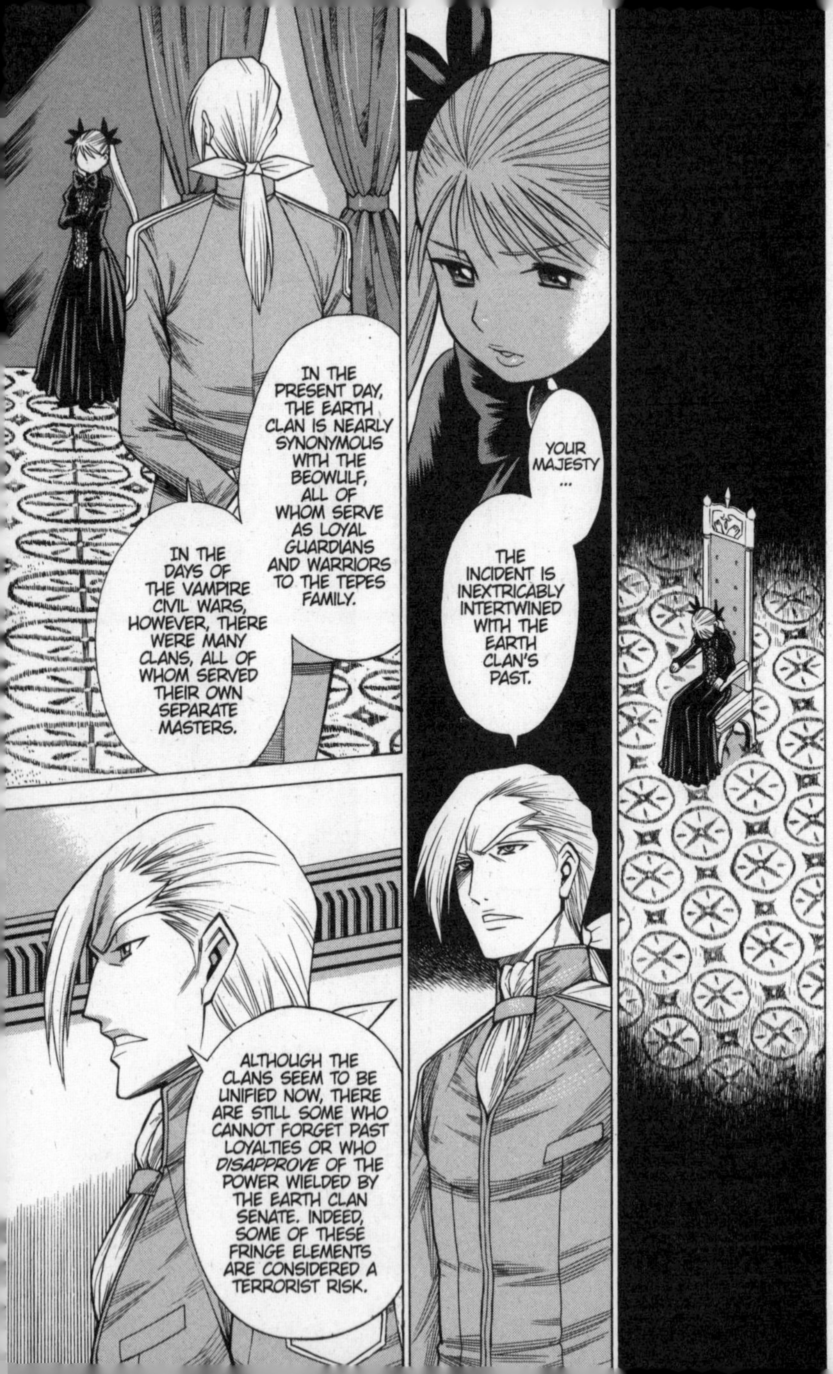
YOUR MAJESTY ...
THE INCIDENT IS INEXTRICABLY INTERTWINED WITH THE EARTH CLAN'S PAST.
IN THE PRESENT DAY, THE EARTH CLAN IS NEARLY SYNONYMOUS WITH THE BEOWULF, ALL OF WHOM SERVE AS LOYAL GUARDIANS AND WARRIORS TO THE TEPES FAMILY.
IN THE DAYS OF THE VAMPIRE CIVIL WARS, HOWEVER, THERE WERE MANY CLANS, ALL OF WHOM SERVED THEIR OWN SEPARATE MASTERS.
ALTHOUGH THE CLANS SEEM TO BE UNIFIED NOW, THERE ARE STILL SOME WHO CANNOT FORGET PAST LOYALTIES OR WHO *DISAPPROVE* OF THE POWER WIELDED BY THE EARTH CLAN SENATE. INDEED, SOME OF THESE FRINGE ELEMENTS ARE CONSIDERED A TERRORIST RISK.

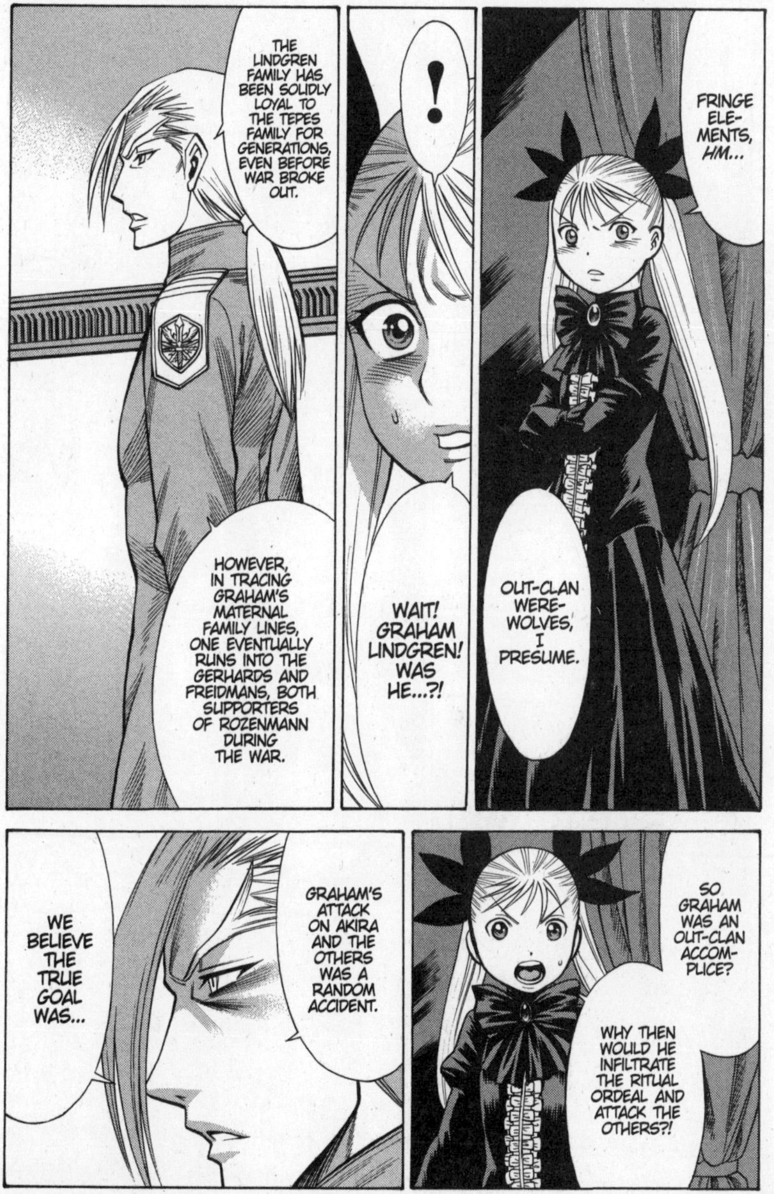
FRINGE ELEMENTS, *HM*...
OUT-CLAN WEREWOLVES, I PRESUME.
!
WAIT! GRAHAM LINDGREN! WAS HE...?!
THE LINDGREN FAMILY HAS BEEN SOLIDLY LOYAL TO THE TEPES FAMILY FOR GENERATIONS, EVEN BEFORE WAR BROKE OUT.
HOWEVER, IN TRACING GRAHAM'S MATERNAL FAMILY LINES, ONE EVENTUALLY RUNS INTO THE GERHARDS AND FREIDMANS, BOTH SUPPORTERS OF ROZENMANN DURING THE WAR.
SO GRAHAM WAS AN OUT-CLAN ACCOMPLICE?
WHY THEN WOULD HE INFILTRATE THE RITUAL ORDEAL AND ATTACK THE OTHERS?!
GRAHAM'S ATTACK ON AKIRA AND THE OTHERS WAS A RANDOM ACCIDENT.
WE BELIEVE THE TRUE GOAL WAS...

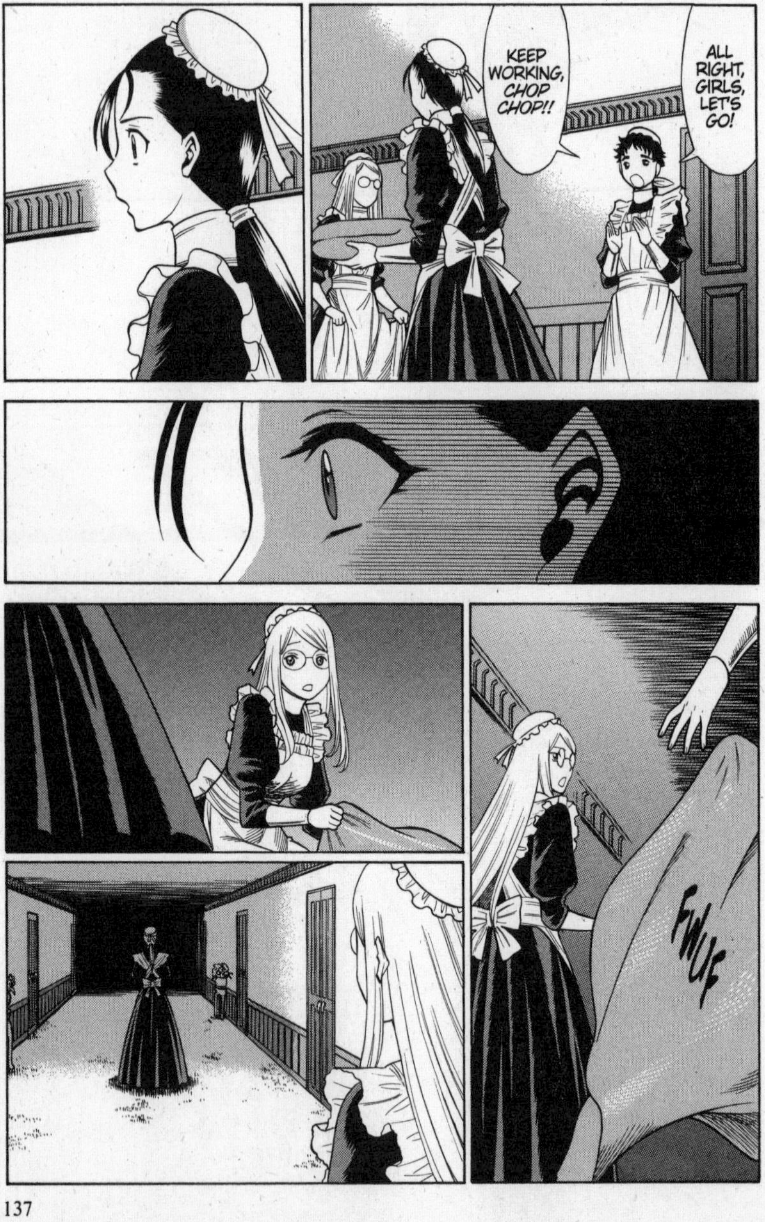
ALL RIGHT, GIRLS, LET'S GO!
KEEP WORKING, CHOP CHOP!!
FWUF

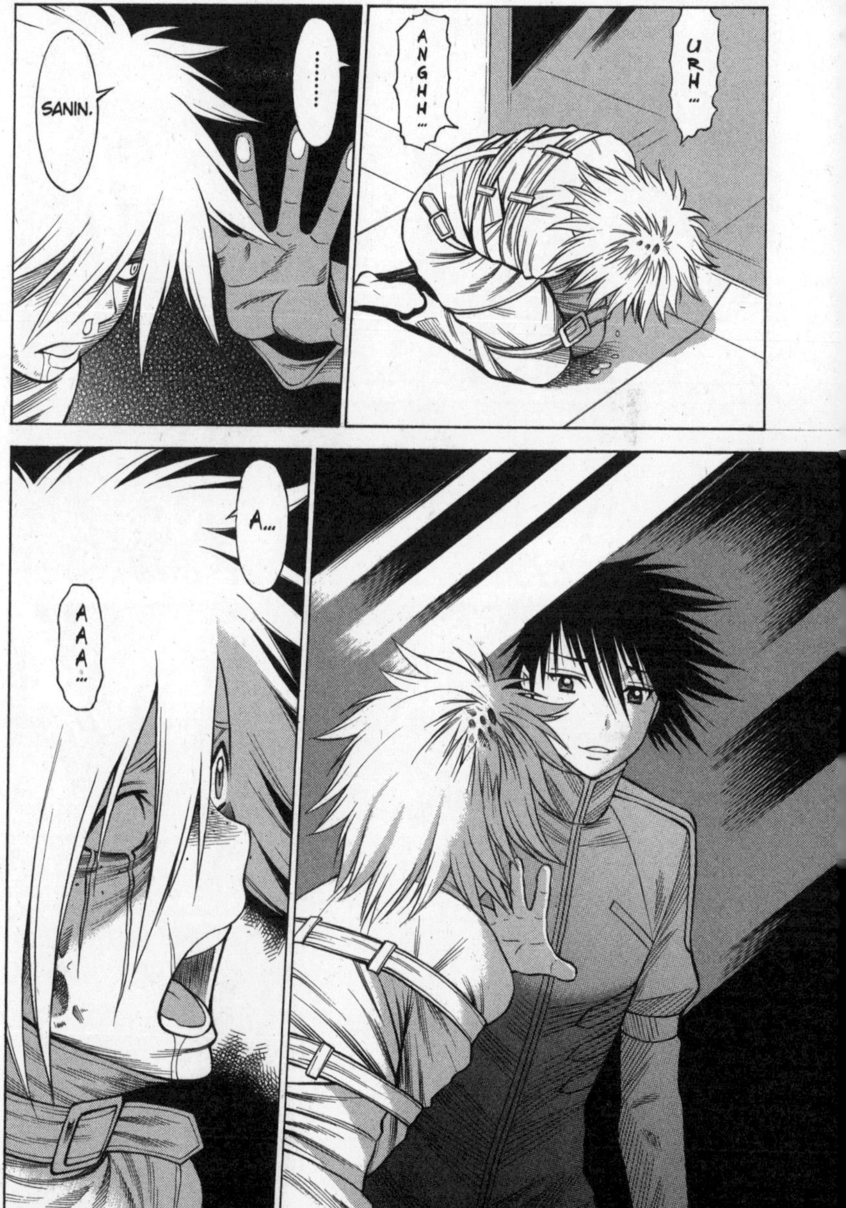
URH...
ANGHH...
....
SANIN.
A...
AAA...

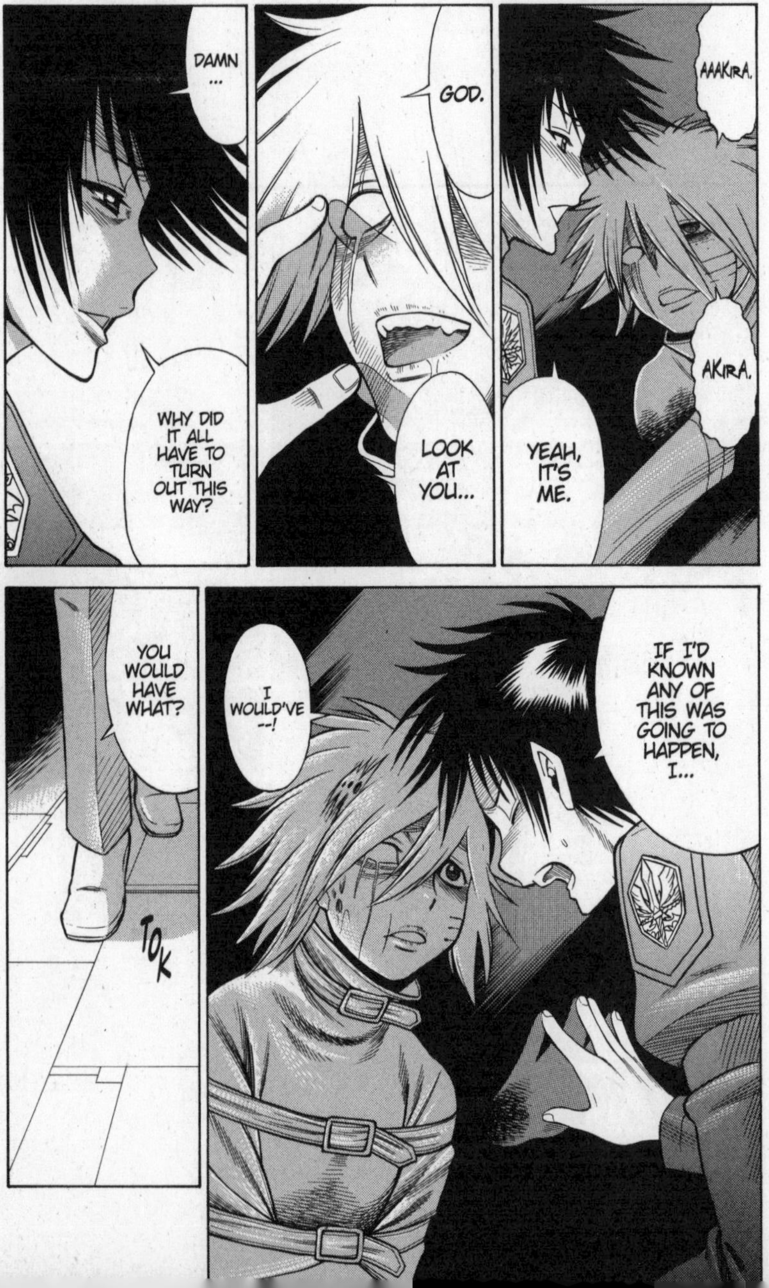
AAAKIRA.
AKIRA.
YEAH, IT'S ME.
GOD.
LOOK AT YOU...
DAMN ...
WHY DID IT ALL HAVE TO TURN OUT THIS WAY?
IF I'D KNOWN ANY OF THIS WAS GOING TO HAPPEN, I...
I WOULD'VE --!
YOU WOULD HAVE WHAT?
TOK

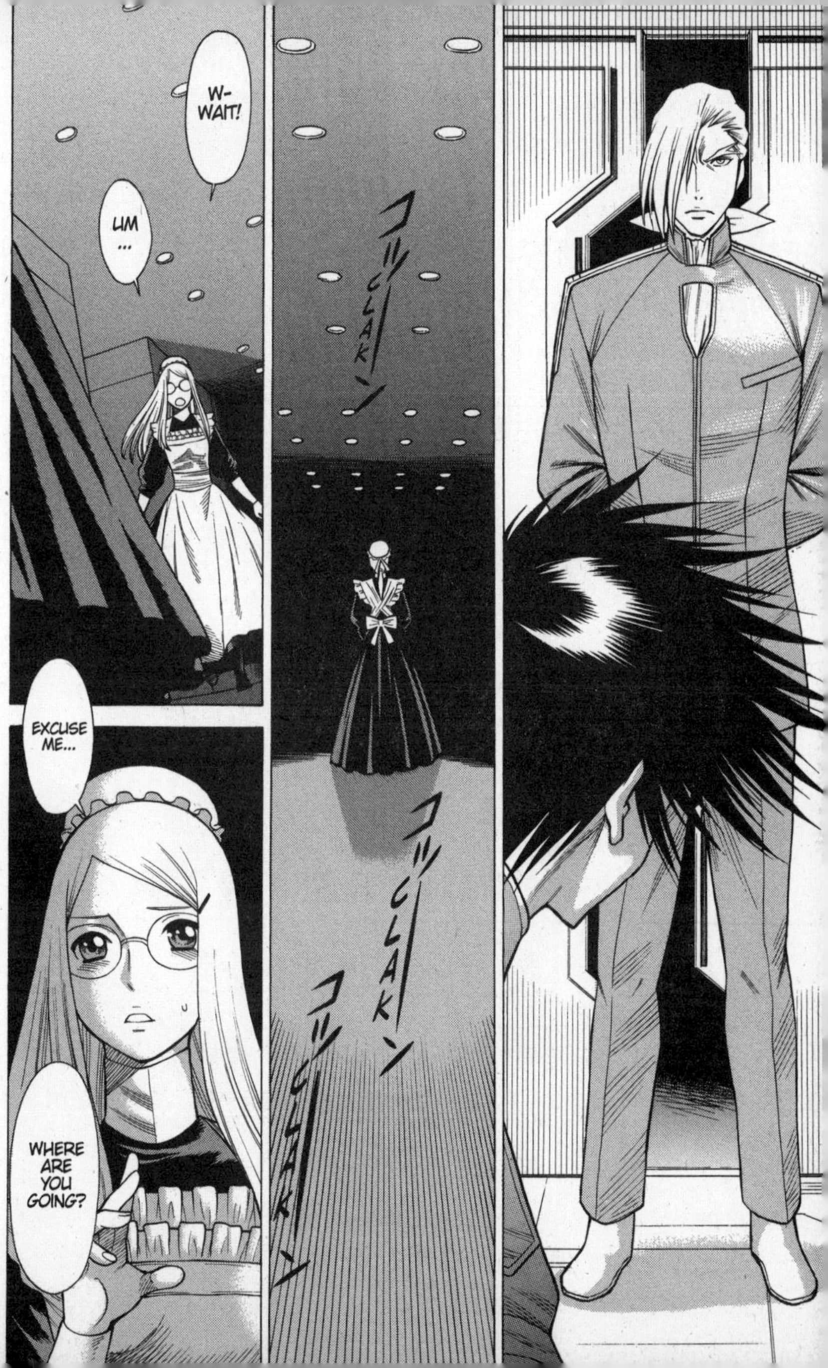
コツーン
CLAK
コツーン
CLAK
コツーン
CLAK
W-WAIT!
UM...
EXCUSE ME...
WHERE ARE YOU GOING?

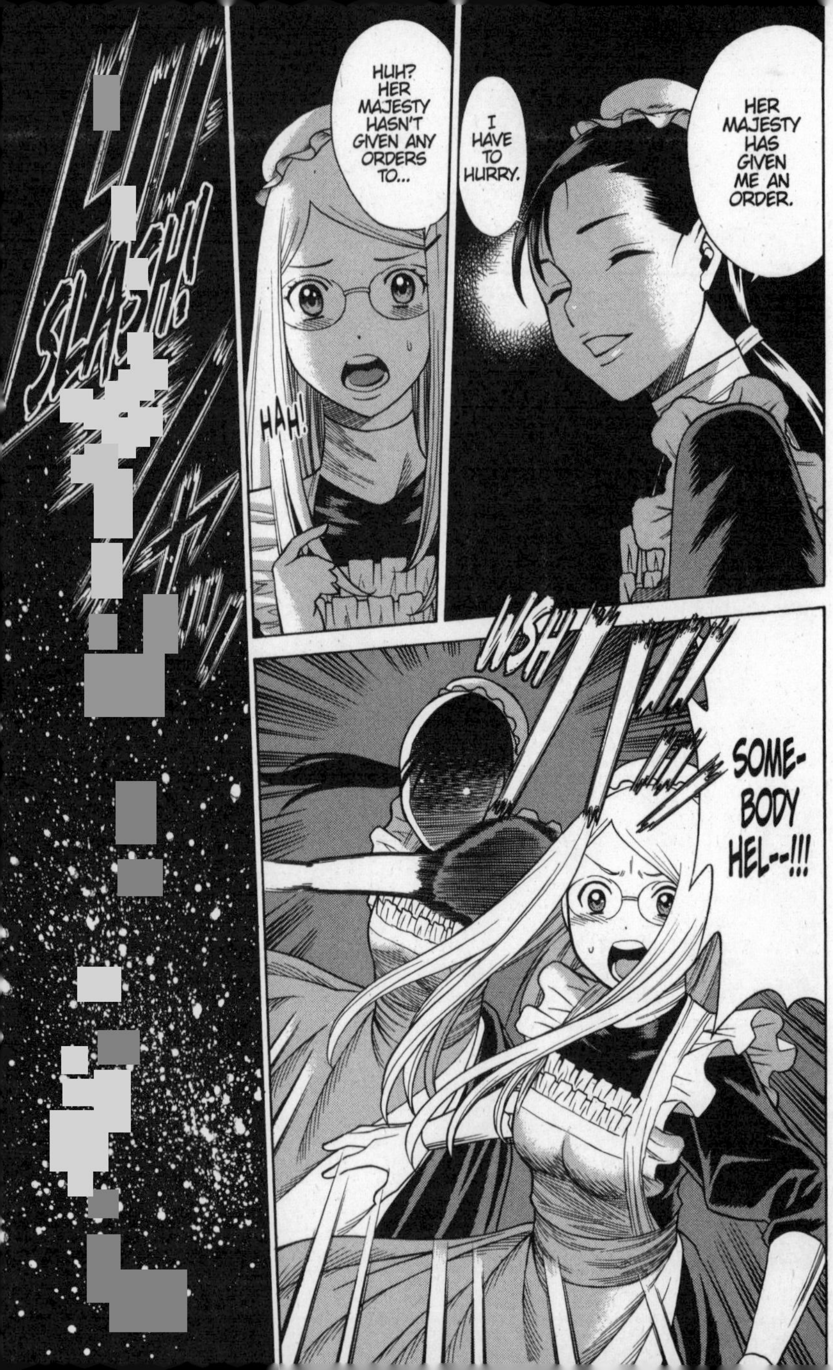
HER MAJESTY HAS GIVEN ME AN ORDER.
I HAVE TO HURRY.
HUH? HER MAJESTY HASN'T GIVEN ANY ORDERS TO...
HAH!
WSHT
SOME-BODY HEL--!!!
SLASH!

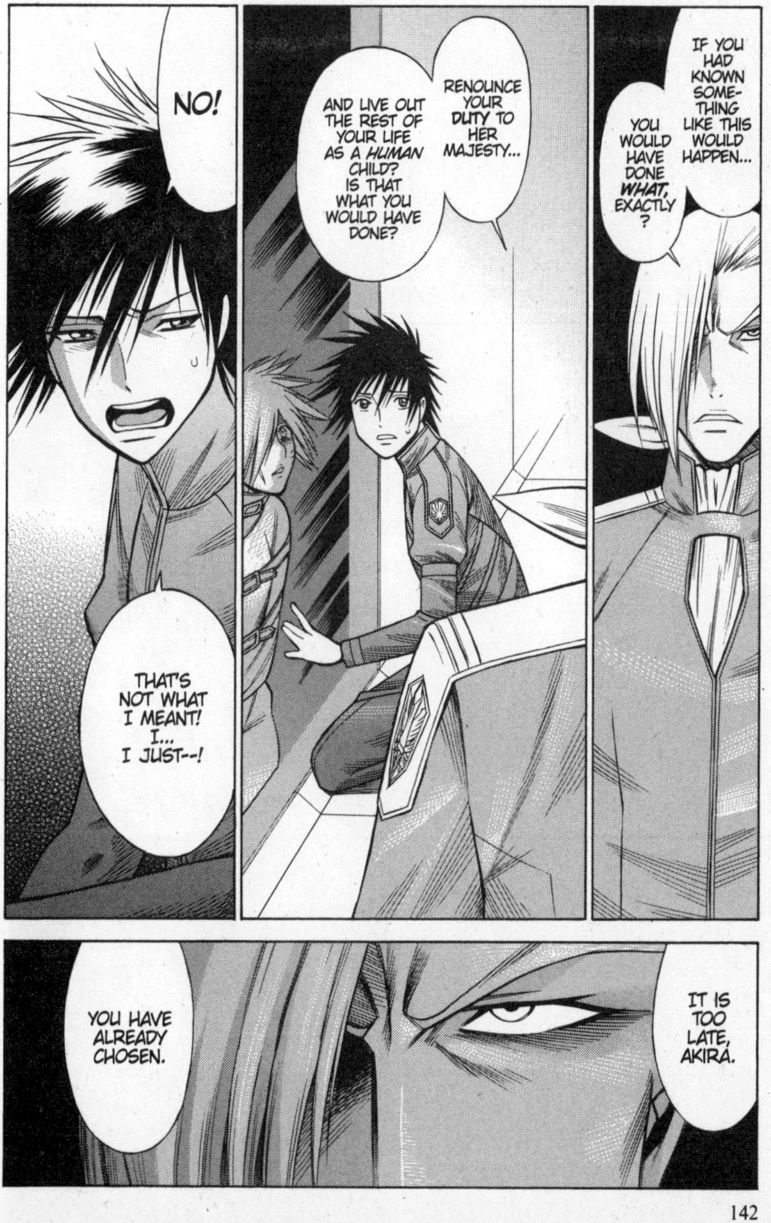
IF YOU HAD KNOWN SOMETHING LIKE THIS WOULD HAPPEN...
YOU WOULD HAVE DONE WHAT, EXACTLY?
RENOUNCE YOUR DUTY TO HER MAJESTY...
AND LIVE OUT THE REST OF YOUR LIFE AS A HUMAN CHILD? IS THAT WHAT YOU WOULD HAVE DONE?
NO!
THAT'S NOT WHAT I MEANT! I... I JUST--!
IT IS TOO LATE, AKIRA.
YOU HAVE ALREADY CHOSEN.

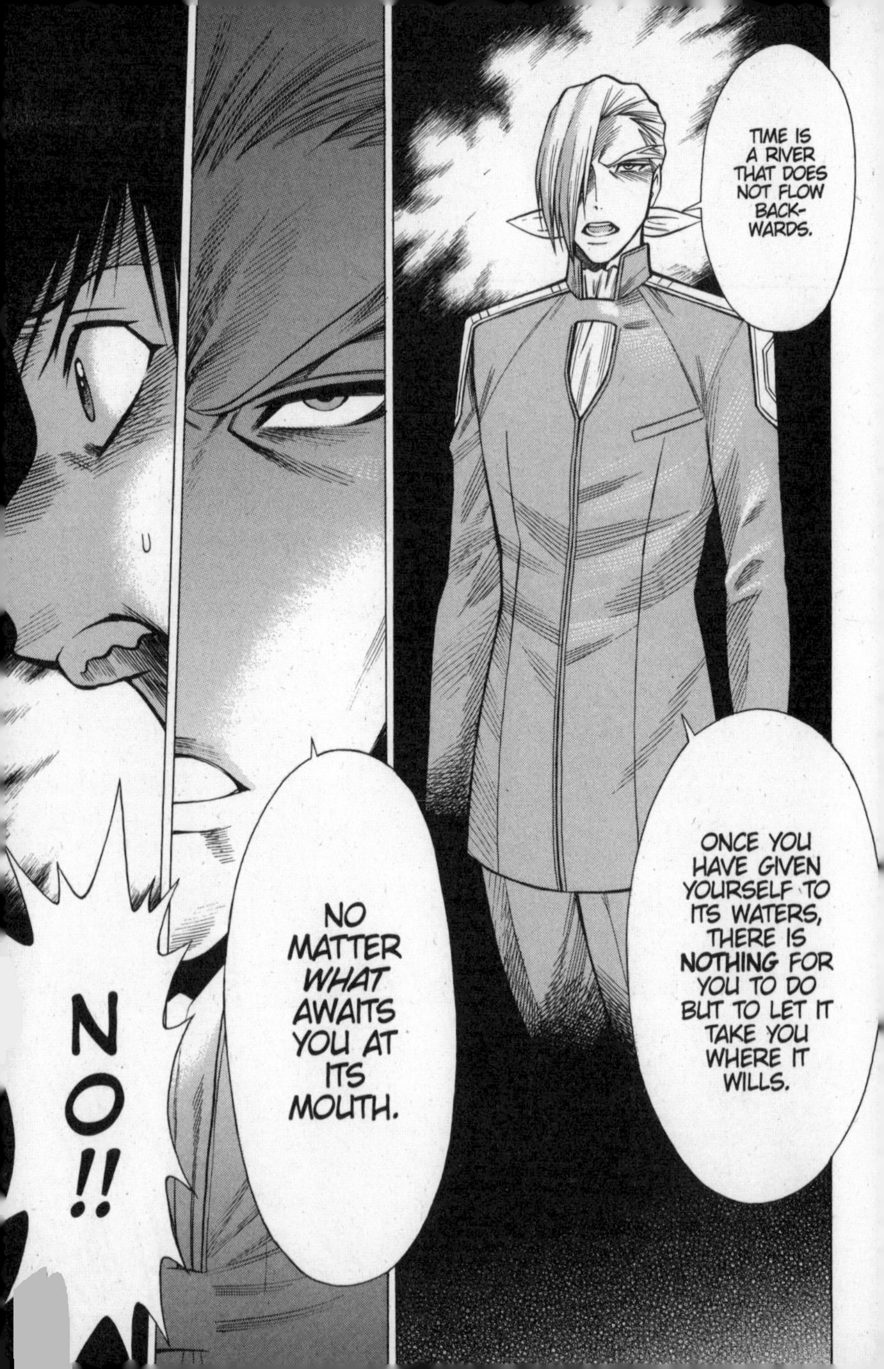
TIME IS A RIVER THAT DOES NOT FLOW BACK-WARDS.
ONCE YOU HAVE GIVEN YOURSELF TO ITS WATERS, THERE IS NOTHING FOR YOU TO DO BUT TO LET IT TAKE YOU WHERE IT WILLS.
NO MATTER *WHAT* AWAITS YOU AT ITS MOUTH.
NO!!

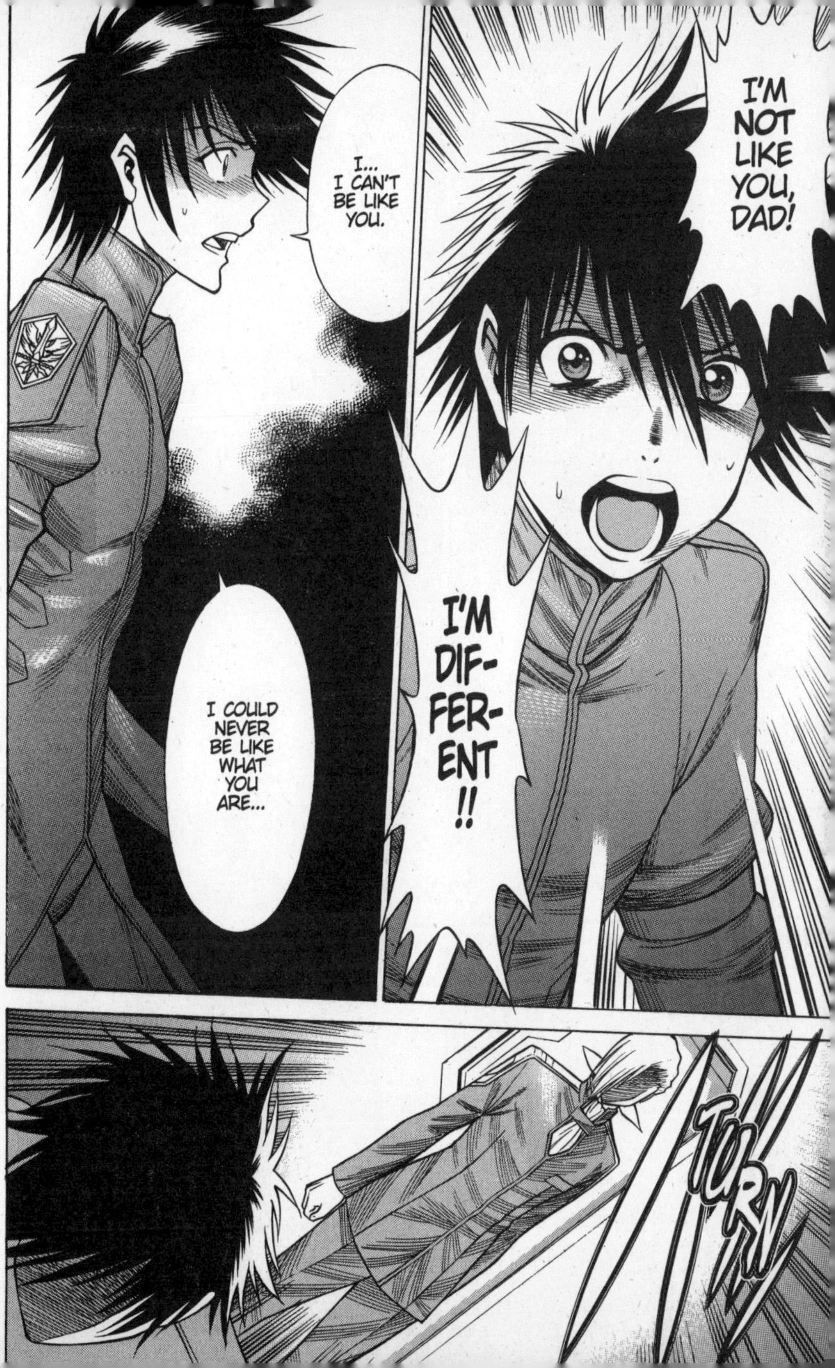
I'M NOT LIKE YOU, DAD!
I'M DIF-FER-ENT!!
I... I CAN'T BE LIKE YOU.
I COULD NEVER BE LIKE WHAT YOU ARE...
TURN

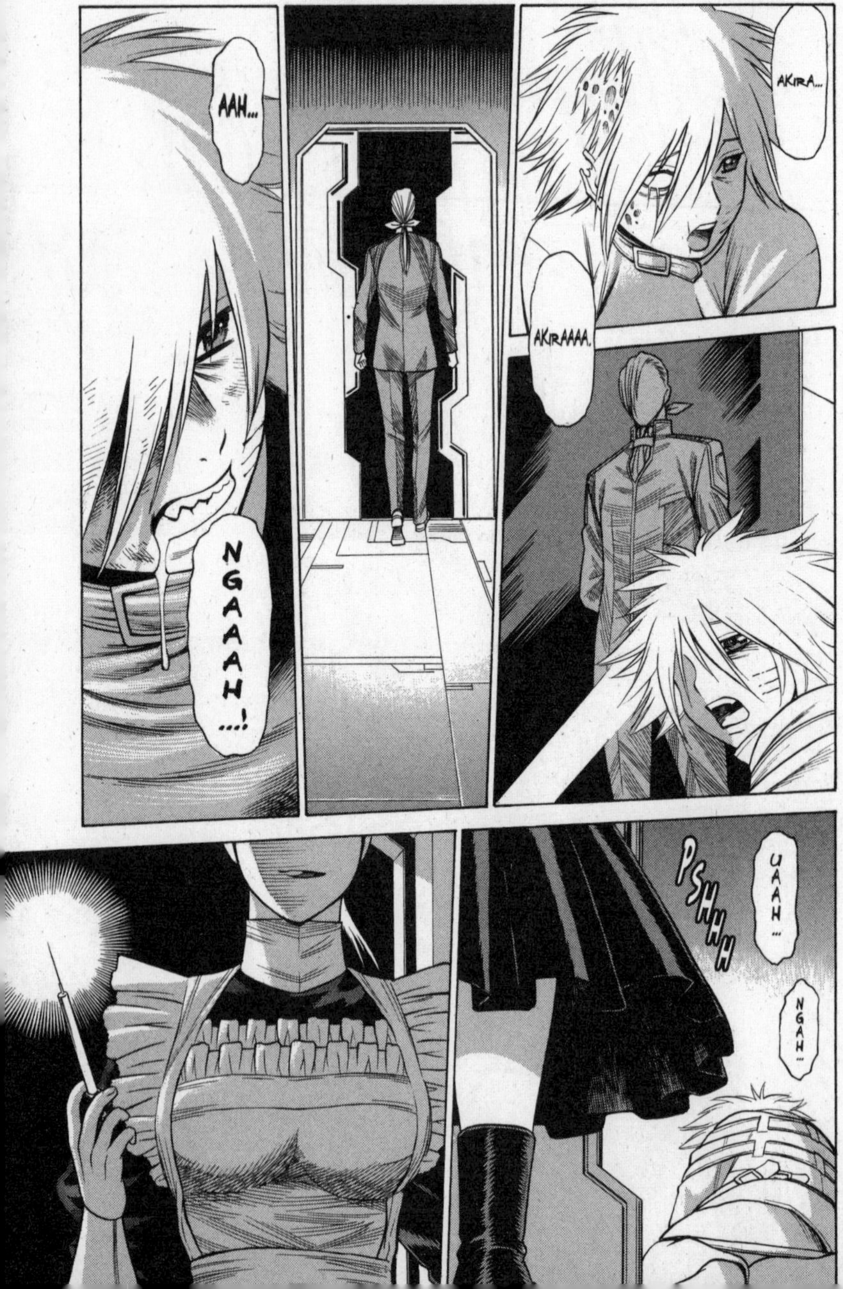
AKIRA...
AKIRAAAA.
AAH...
NGAAAAH...!
PSHHHH
UAAH...
NGAH...

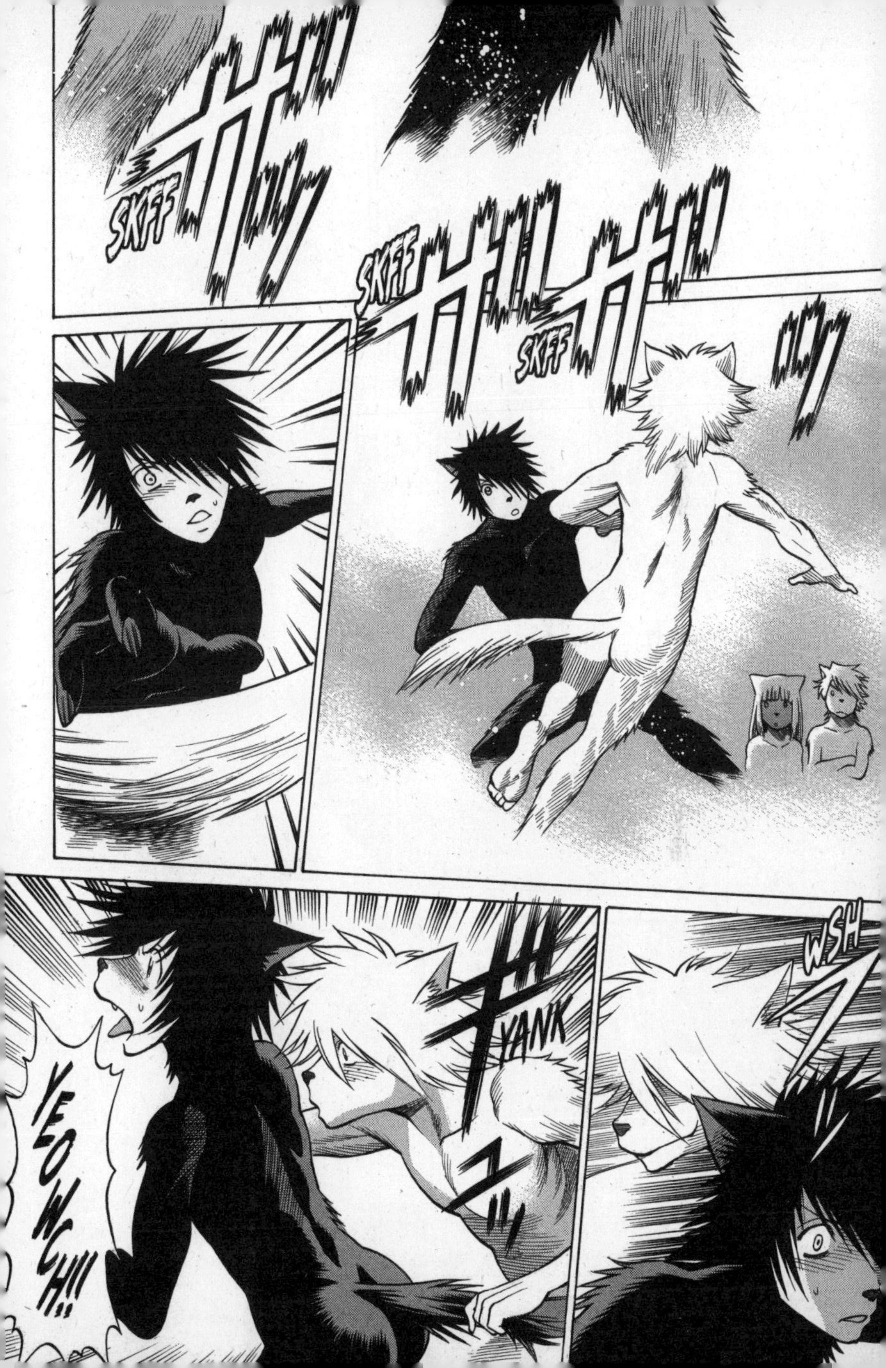
SKFF
SKFF
SKFF
WSH
YANK
YEOWCH!!!

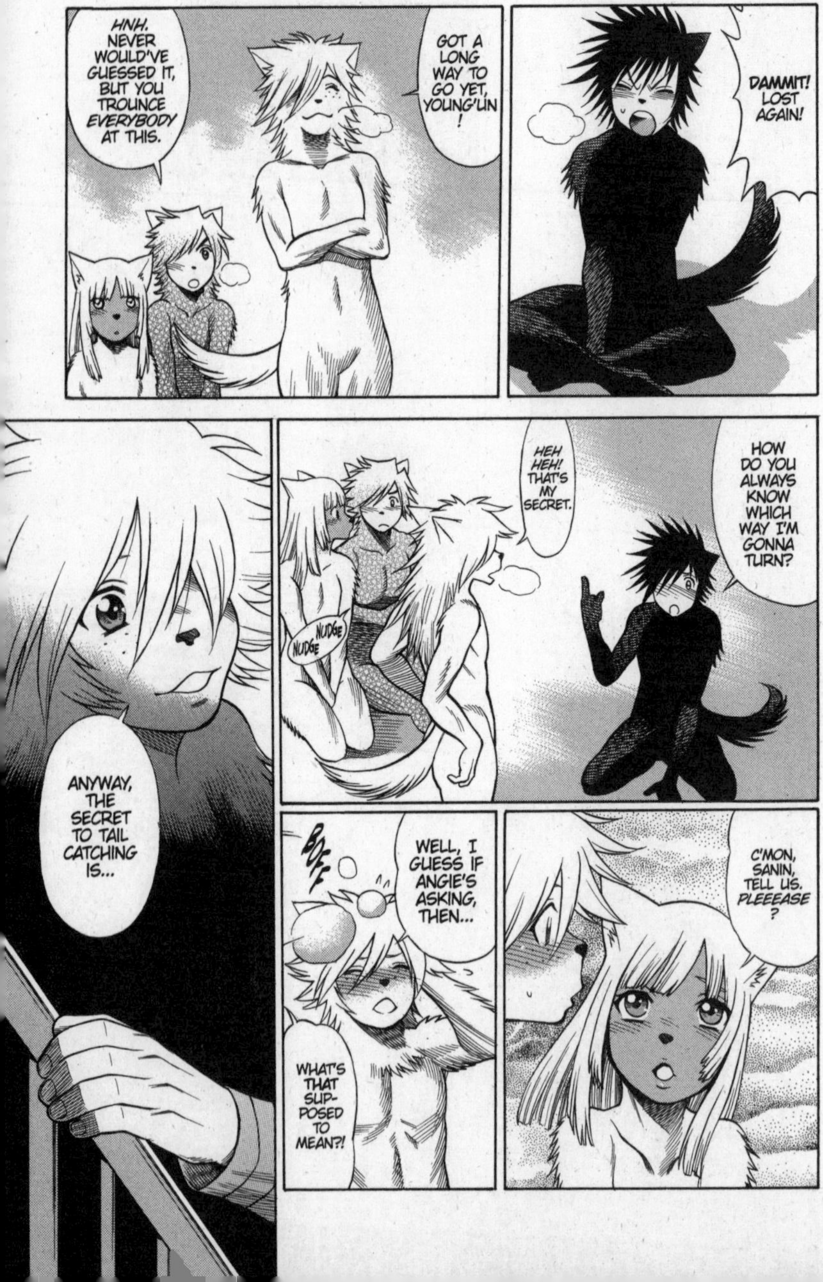
DAMMIT! LOST AGAIN!
GOT A LONG WAY TO GO YET, YOUNG'UN!
HNH. NEVER WOULD'VE GUESSED IT, BUT YOU TROUNCE *EVERYBODY* AT THIS.
HOW DO YOU ALWAYS KNOW WHICH WAY I'M GONNA TURN?
HEH HEH! THAT'S MY SECRET.
NUDGE
NUDGE
C'MON, SANIN, TELL US. *PLEEEASE*?
BOFF
WELL, I GUESS IF ANGIE'S ASKING, THEN...
WHAT'S THAT SUP-POSED TO MEAN?!
ANYWAY, THE SECRET TO TAIL CATCHING IS...

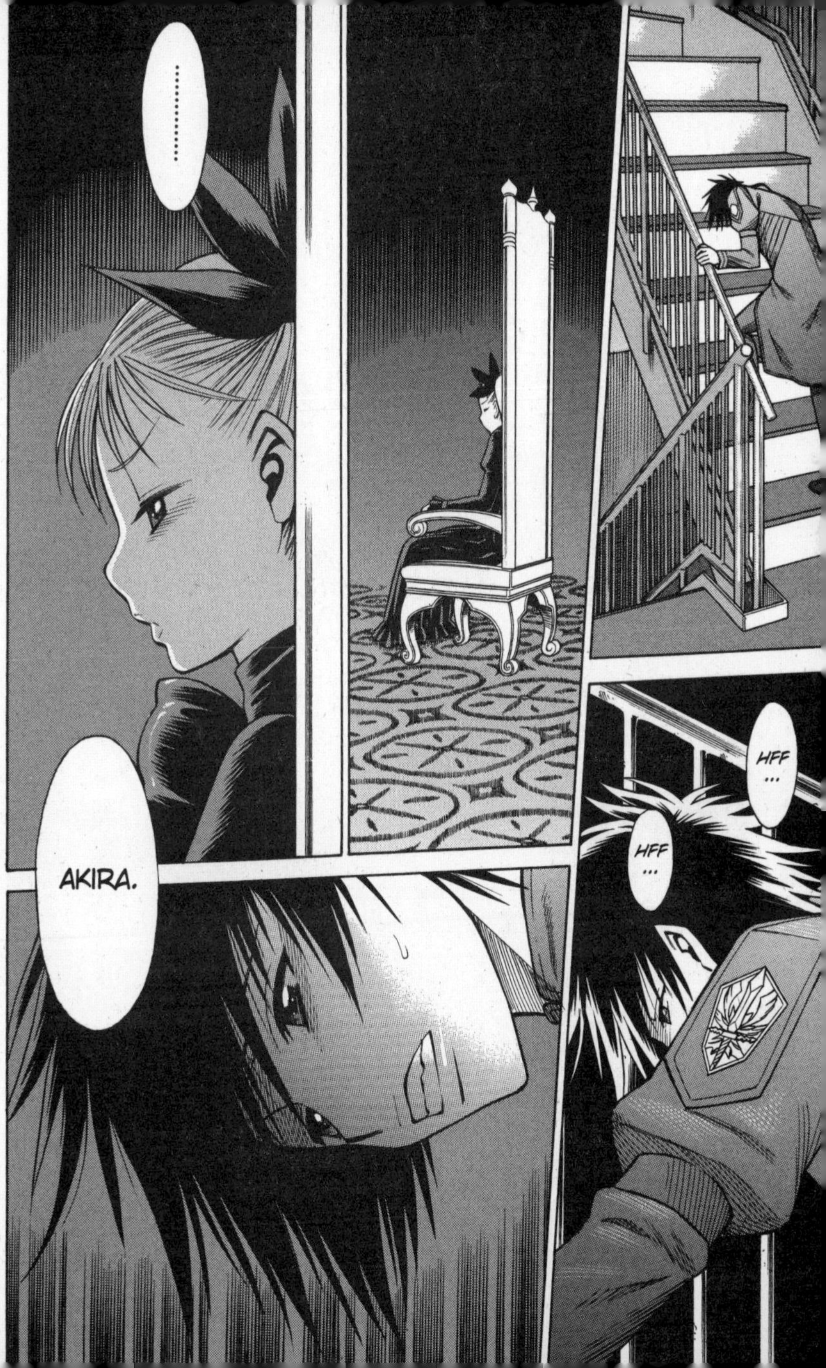

......
AKIRA.
HFF ...
HFF ...

AKIRA ...
CRUNCH
AAA...
AKIRAAA...

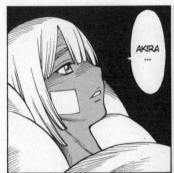

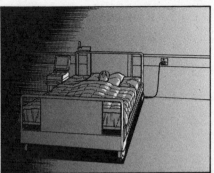

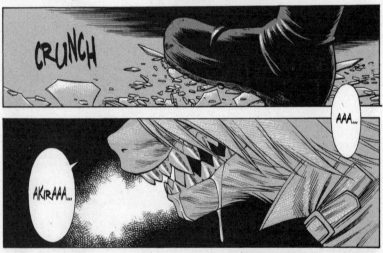

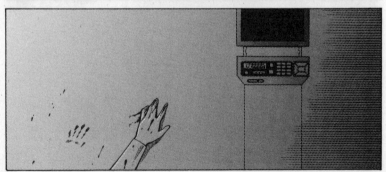

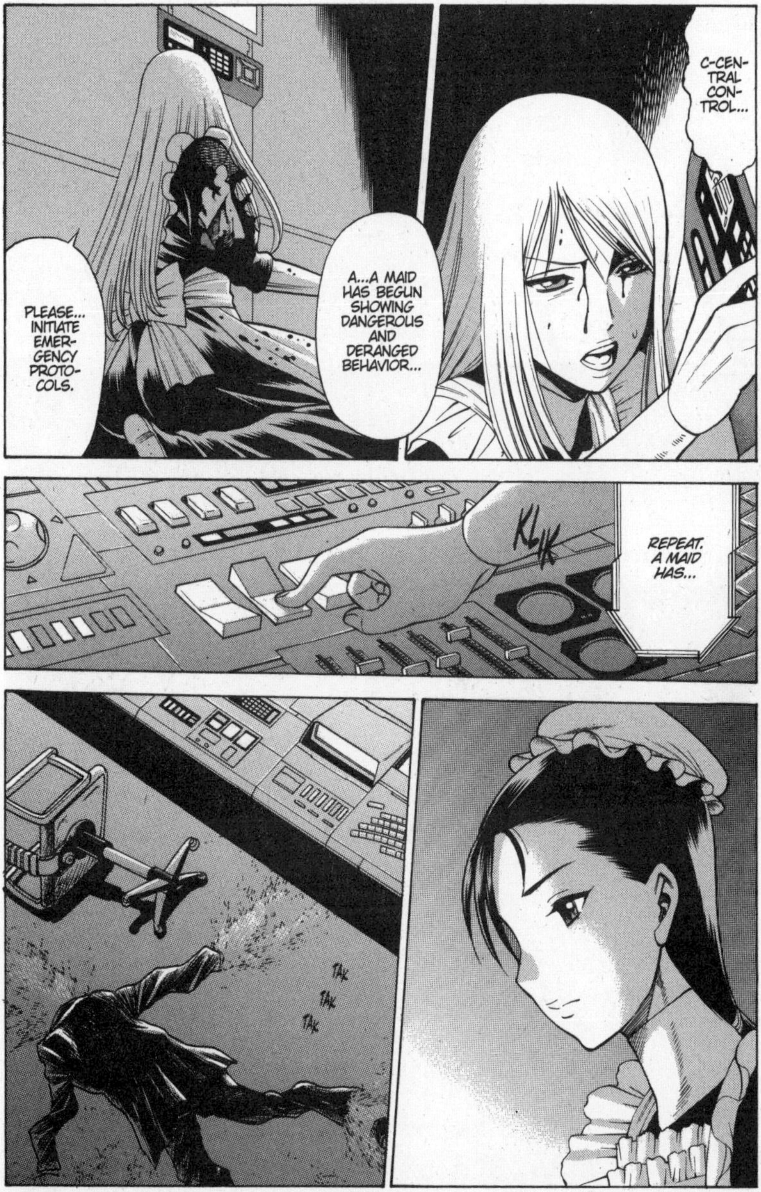
C-CEN-TRAL CON-TROL...
A...A MAID HAS BEGUN SHOWING DANGEROUS AND DERANGED BEHAVIOR...
PLEASE... INITIATE EMER-GENCY PROTO-COLS.
REPEAT. A MAID HAS...
KLIK
TAK
TAK
TAK

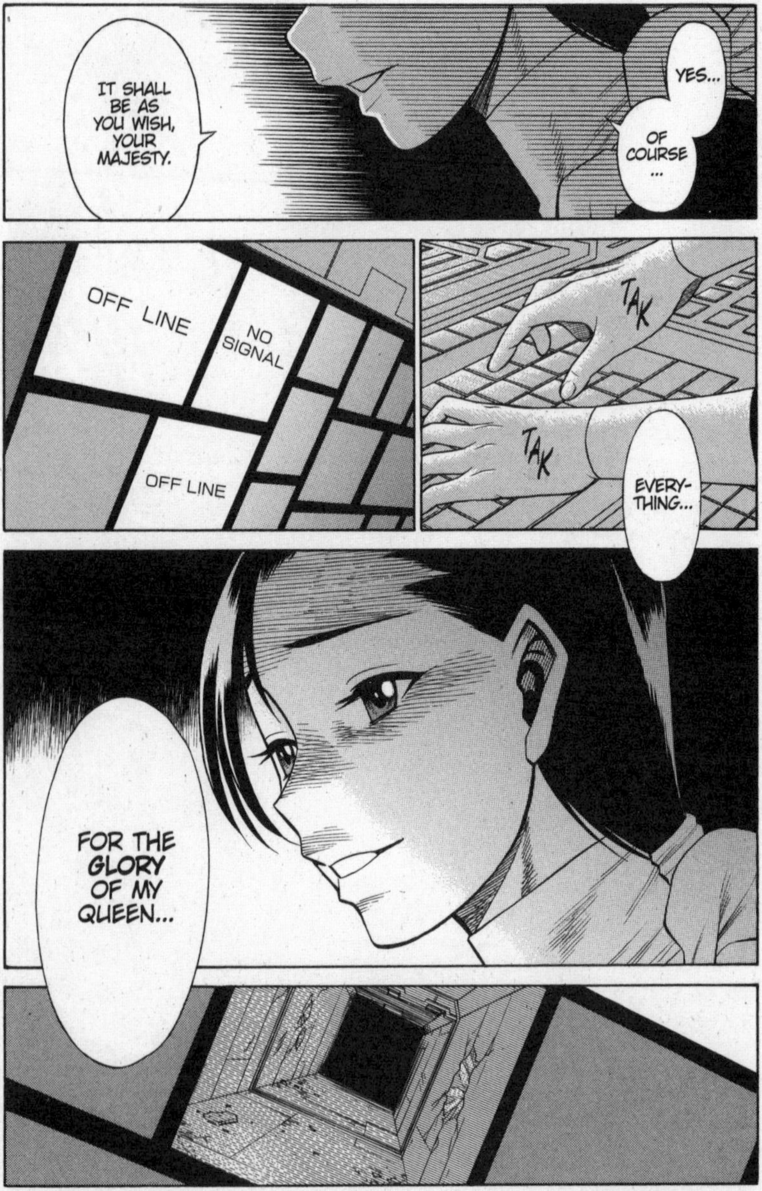
YES...
OF COURSE ...
IT SHALL BE AS YOU WISH, YOUR MAJESTY.
TAK
TAK
EVERY-THING...
OFF LINE
NO SIGNAL
OFF LINE
FOR THE GLORY OF MY QUEEN...

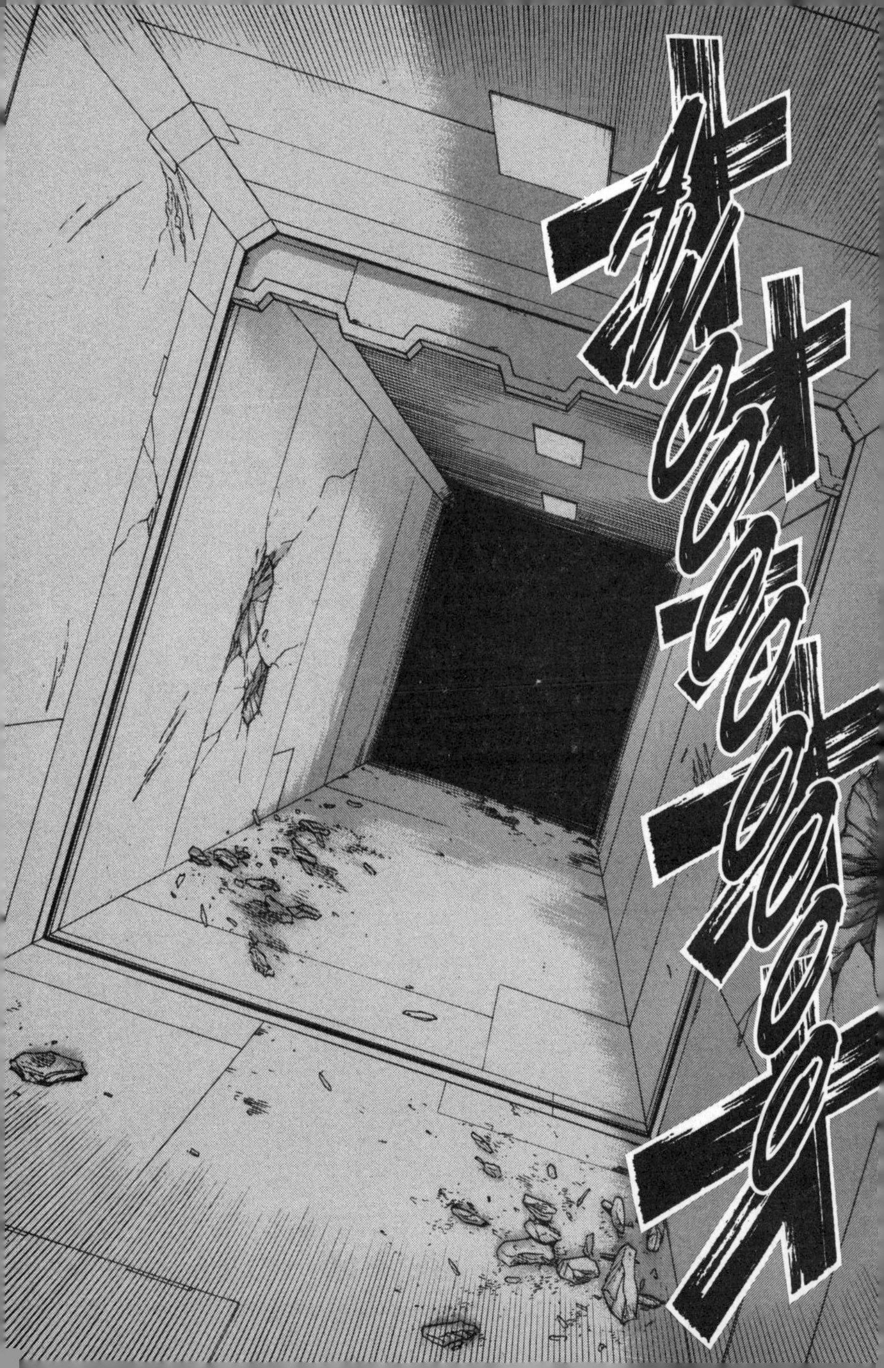

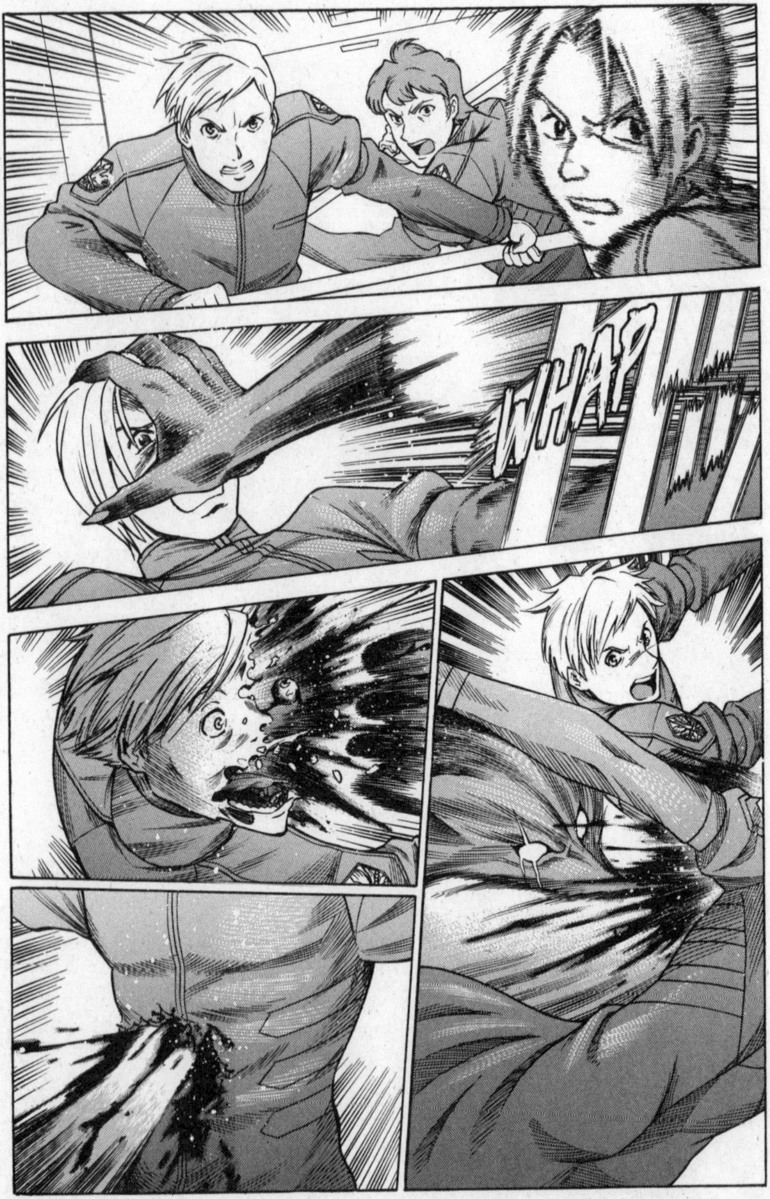
WHAP

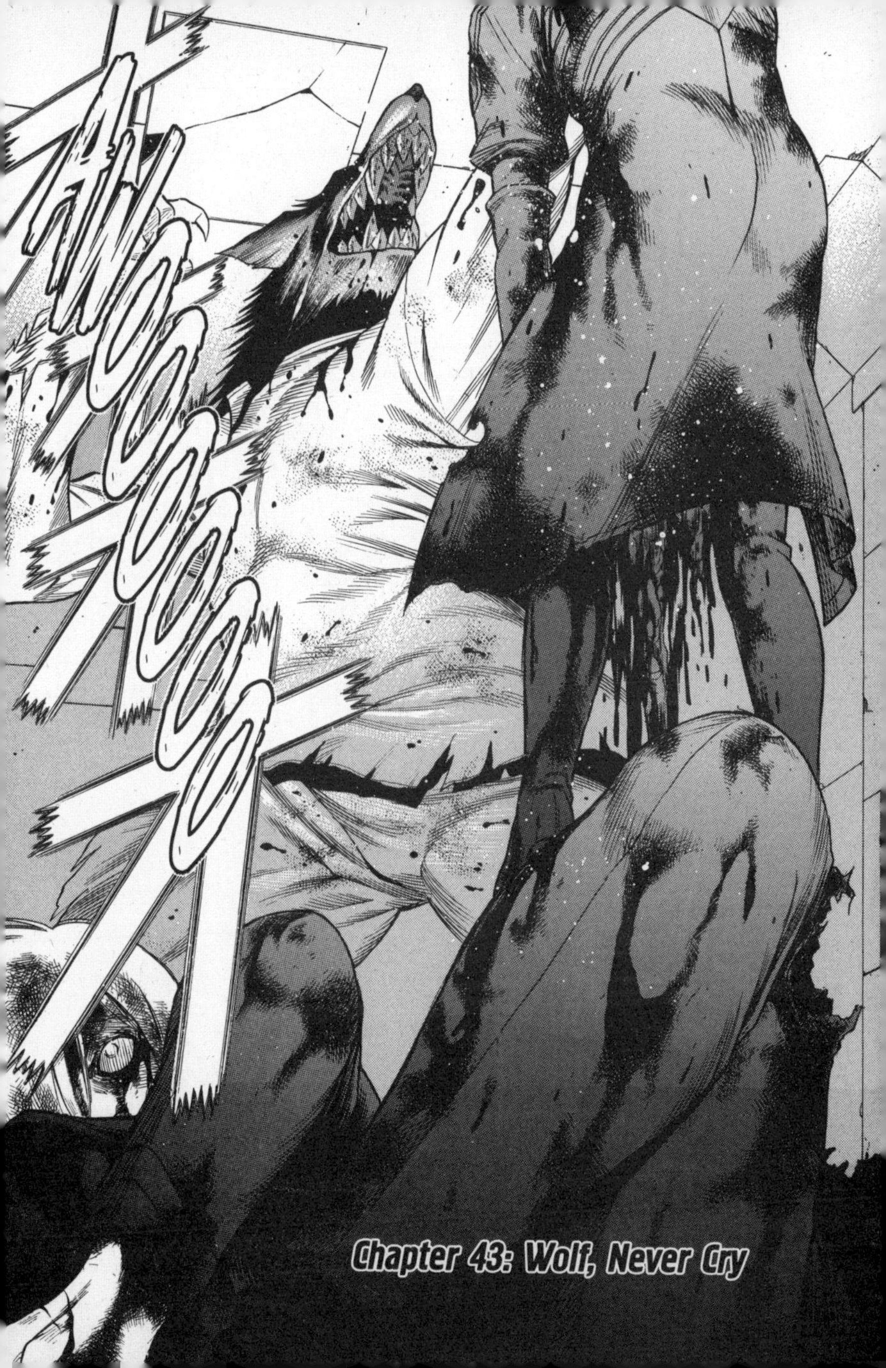
AHOOOOOO
Chapter 43: Wolf, Never Cry

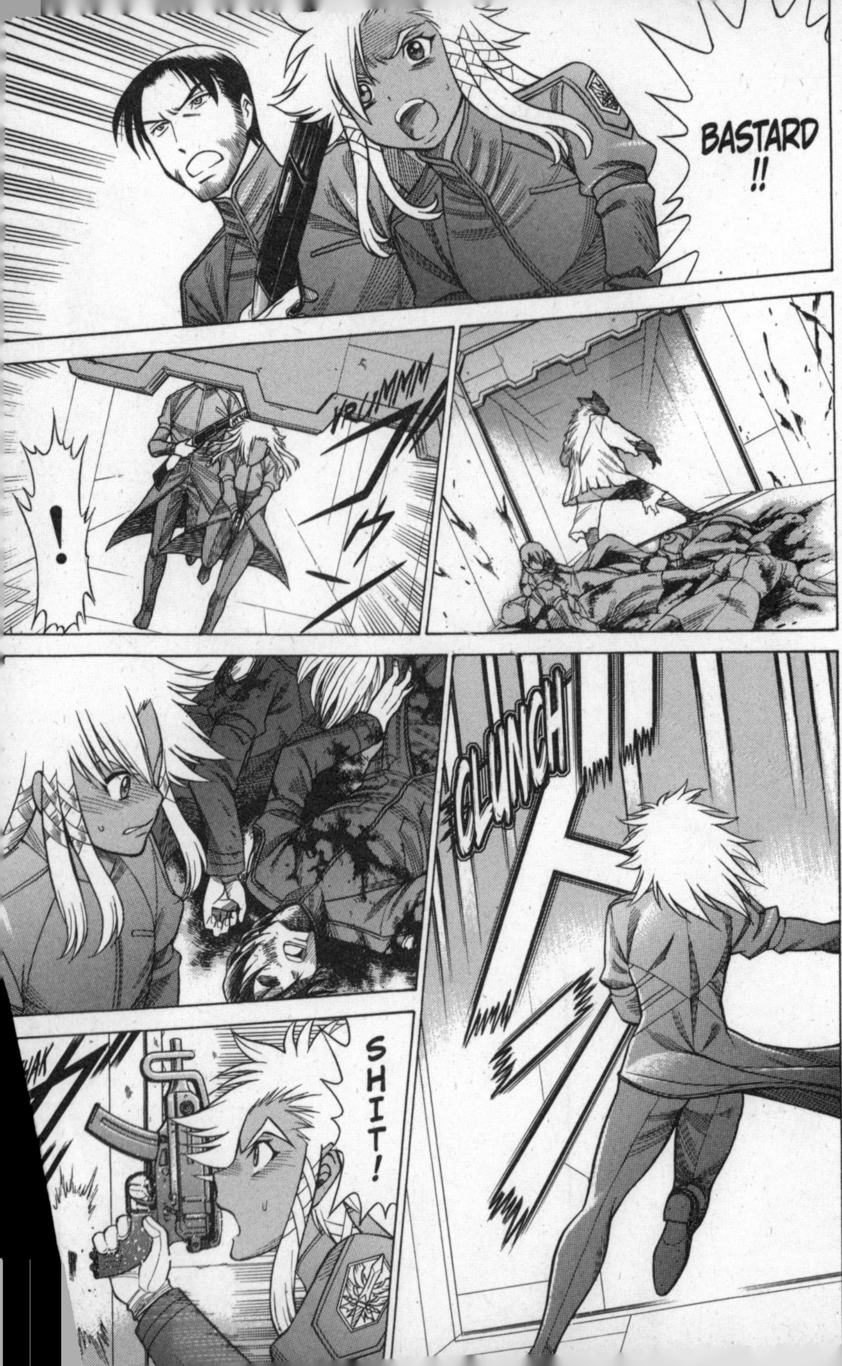
BASTARD !!
VRUMMMM
!
CLUNCH
SHIT!

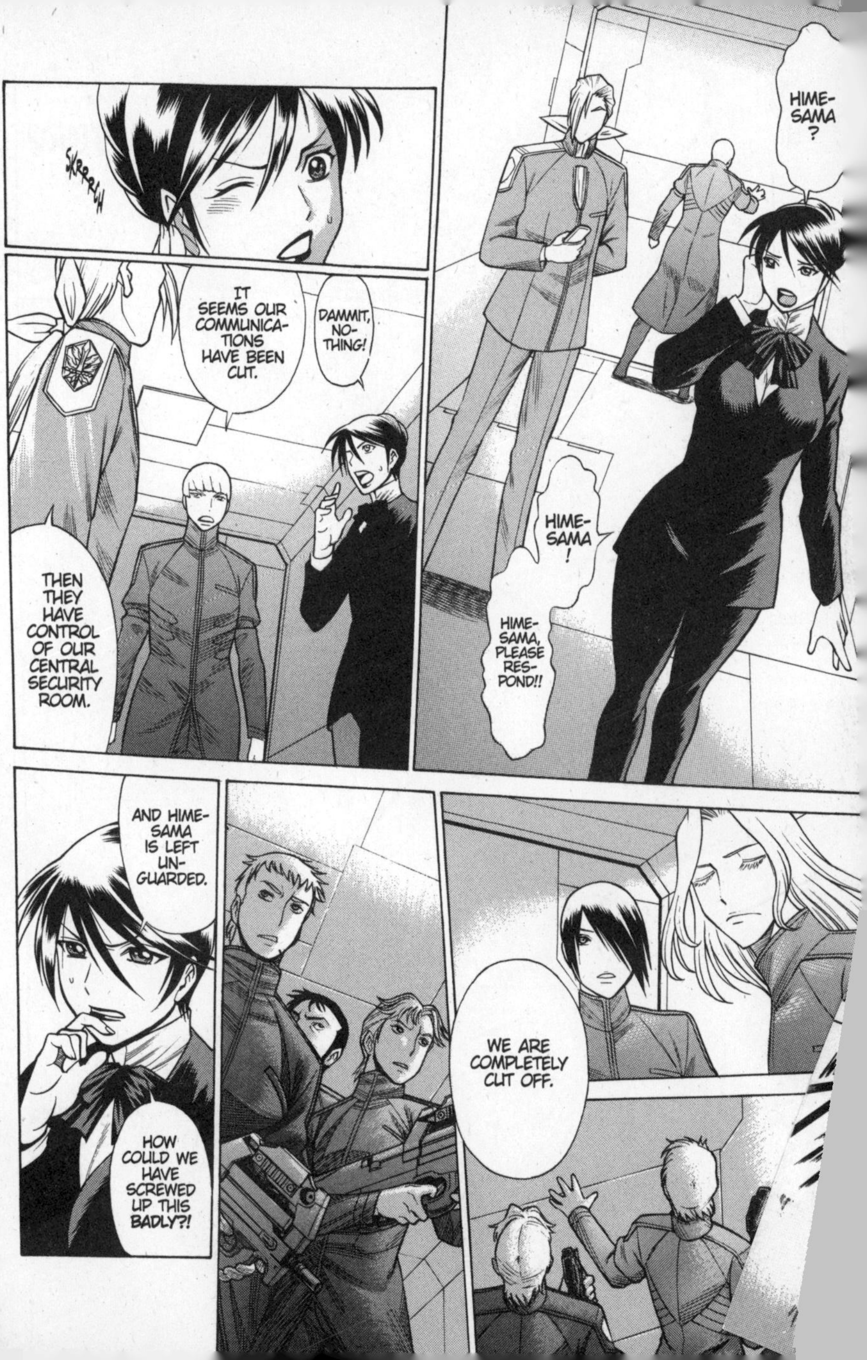
HIME-SAMA?
HIME-SAMA!
HIME-SAMA, PLEASE RESPOND!!
SKRRRRGH
DAMMIT, NOTHING!
IT SEEMS OUR COMMUNICATIONS HAVE BEEN CUT.
THEN THEY HAVE CONTROL OF OUR CENTRAL SECURITY ROOM.
WE ARE COMPLETELY CUT OFF.
AND HIME-SAMA IS LEFT UNGUARDED.
HOW COULD WE HAVE SCREWED UP THIS BADLY?!

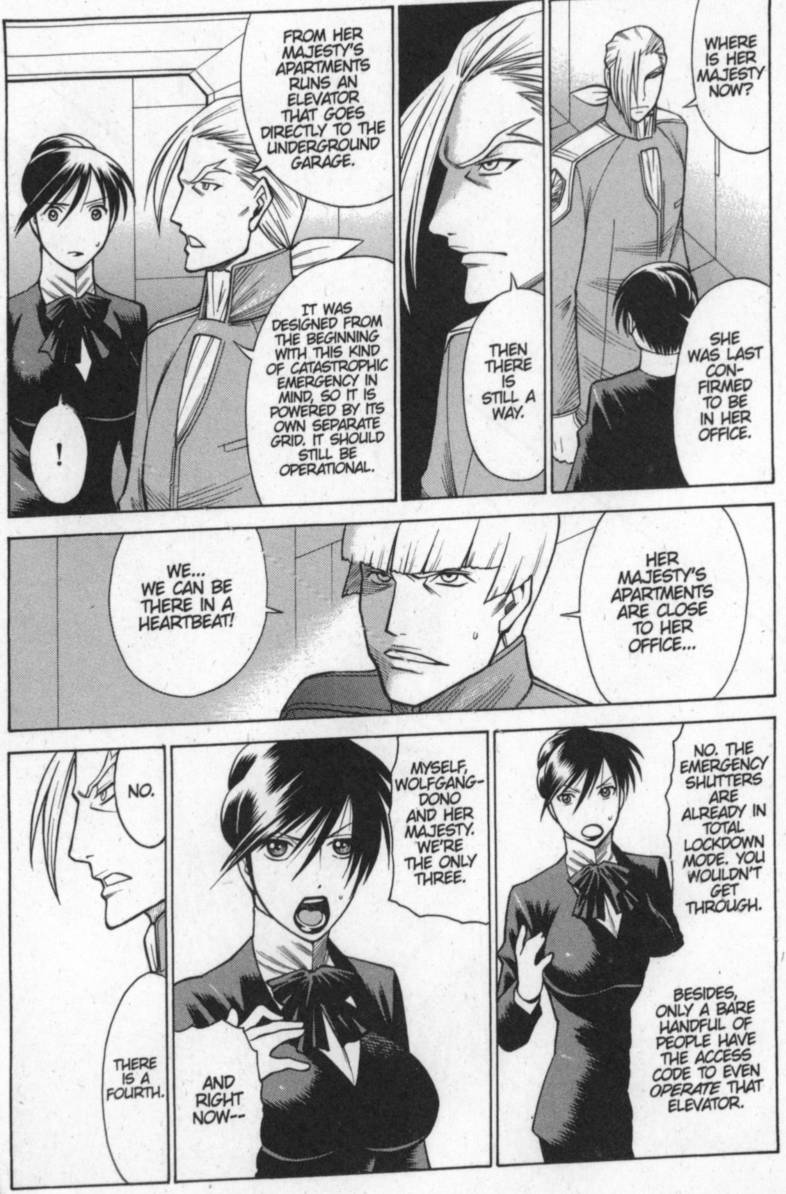
WHERE IS HER MAJESTY NOW?
SHE WAS LAST CON-FIRMED TO BE IN HER OFFICE.
THEN THERE IS STILL A WAY.
FROM HER MAJESTY'S APARTMENTS RUNS AN ELEVATOR THAT GOES DIRECTLY TO THE UNDERGROUND GARAGE.
IT WAS DESIGNED FROM THE BEGINNING WITH THIS KIND OF CATASTROPHIC EMERGENCY IN MIND, SO IT IS POWERED BY ITS OWN SEPARATE GRID. IT SHOULD STILL BE OPERATIONAL.
!
HER MAJESTY'S APARTMENTS ARE CLOSE TO HER OFFICE...
WE... WE CAN BE THERE IN A HEARTBEAT!
NO. THE EMERGENCY SHUTTERS ARE ALREADY IN TOTAL LOCKDOWN MODE. YOU WOULDN'T GET THROUGH.
BESIDES, ONLY A BARE HANDFUL OF PEOPLE HAVE THE ACCESS CODE TO EVEN *OPERATE* THAT ELEVATOR.
MYSELF, WOLFGANG-DONO AND HER MAJESTY. WE'RE THE ONLY THREE.
AND RIGHT NOW--
NO.
THERE IS A FOURTH.

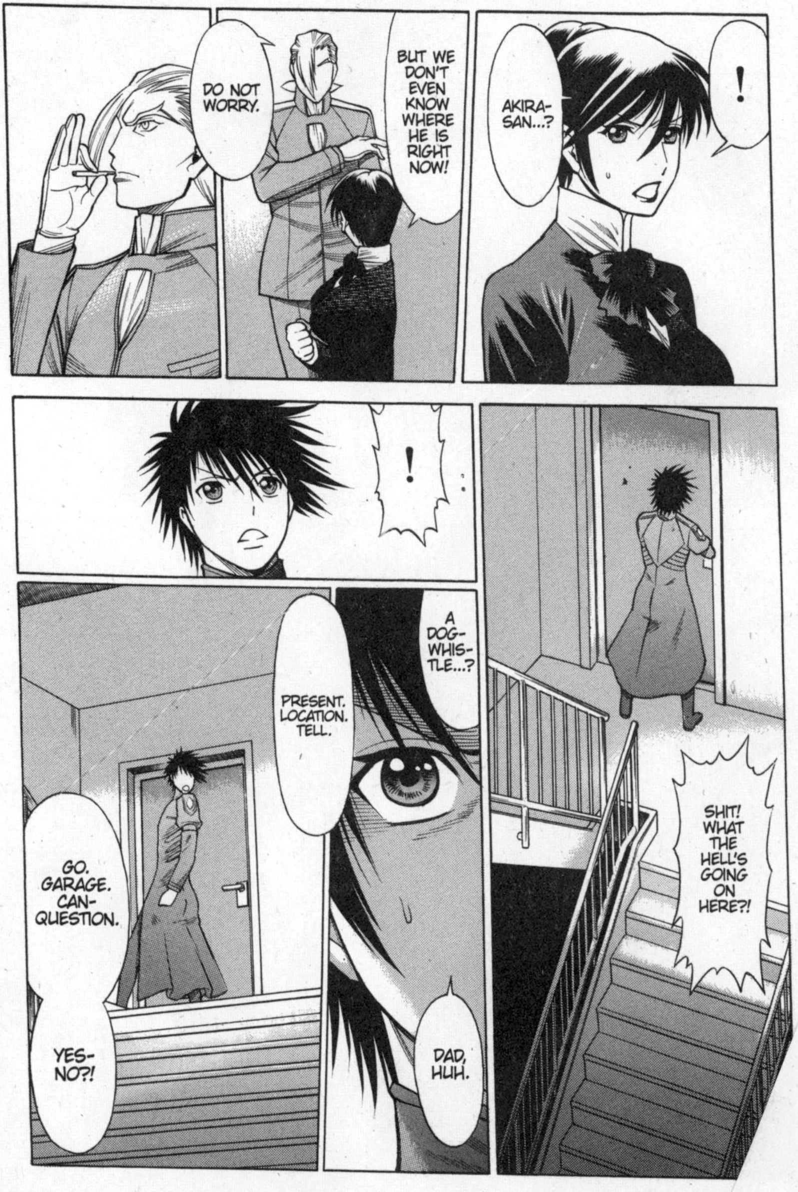
!
AKIRA-SAN...?
BUT WE DON'T EVEN KNOW WHERE HE IS RIGHT NOW!
DO NOT WORRY.
SHIT! WHAT THE HELL'S GOING ON HERE?!
!
A DOG-WHISTLE...?
PRESENT. LOCATION. TELL.
DAD, HUH.
GO. GARAGE. CAN-QUESTION.
YES-NO?!

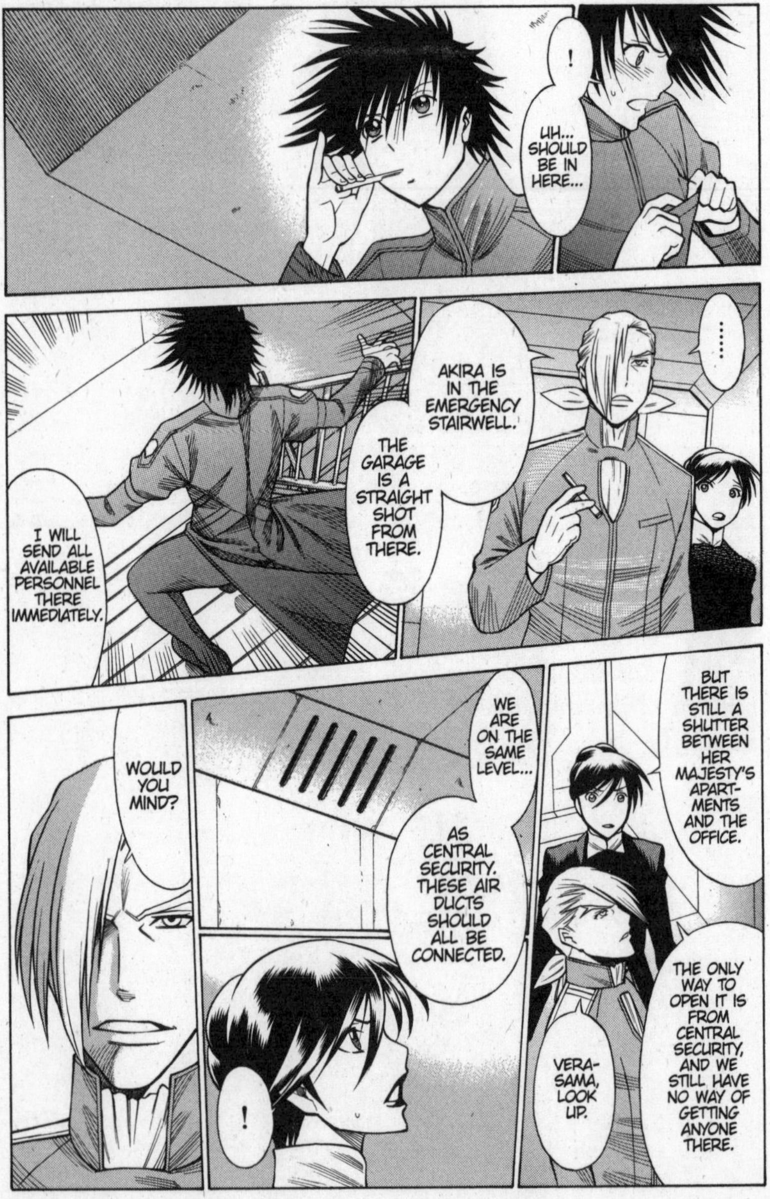
!
UH... SHOULD BE IN HERE...
......
AKIRA IS IN THE EMERGENCY STAIRWELL.
THE GARAGE IS A STRAIGHT SHOT FROM THERE.
I WILL SEND ALL AVAILABLE PERSONNEL THERE IMMEDIATELY.
BUT THERE IS STILL A SHUTTER BETWEEN HER MAJESTY'S APART-MENTS AND THE OFFICE.
THE ONLY WAY TO OPEN IT IS FROM CENTRAL SECURITY, AND WE STILL HAVE NO WAY OF GETTING ANYONE THERE.
VERA-SAMA, LOOK UP.
WE ARE ON THE SAME LEVEL...
AS CENTRAL SECURITY. THESE AIR DUCTS SHOULD ALL BE CONNECTED.
!
WOULD YOU MIND?

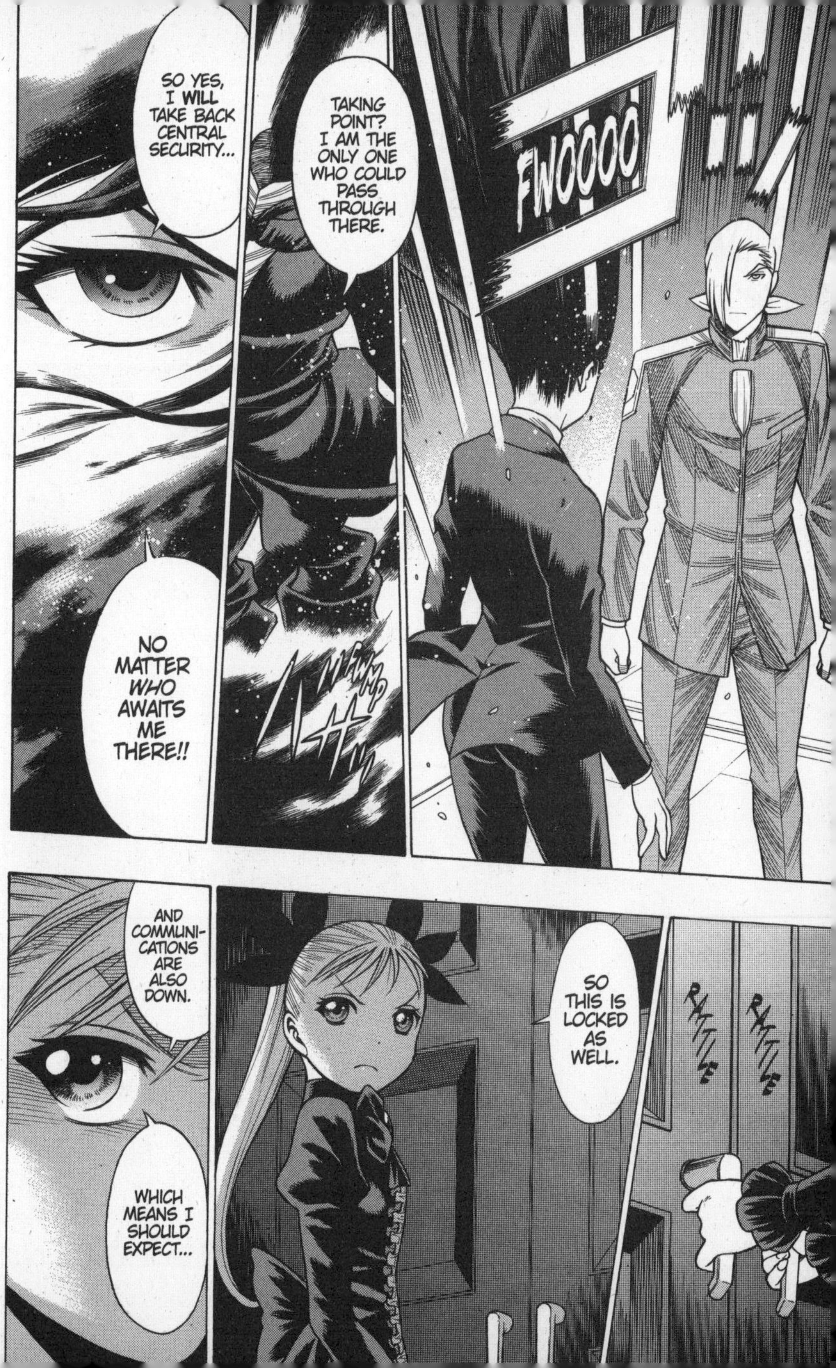
FWOOOO
TAKING POINT? I AM THE ONLY ONE WHO COULD PASS THROUGH THERE.
SO YES, I WILL TAKE BACK CENTRAL SECURITY...
NO MATTER WHO AWAITS ME THERE!!
RATTLE
RATTLE
SO THIS IS LOCKED AS WELL.
AND COMMUNICATIONS ARE ALSO DOWN.
WHICH MEANS I SHOULD EXPECT...

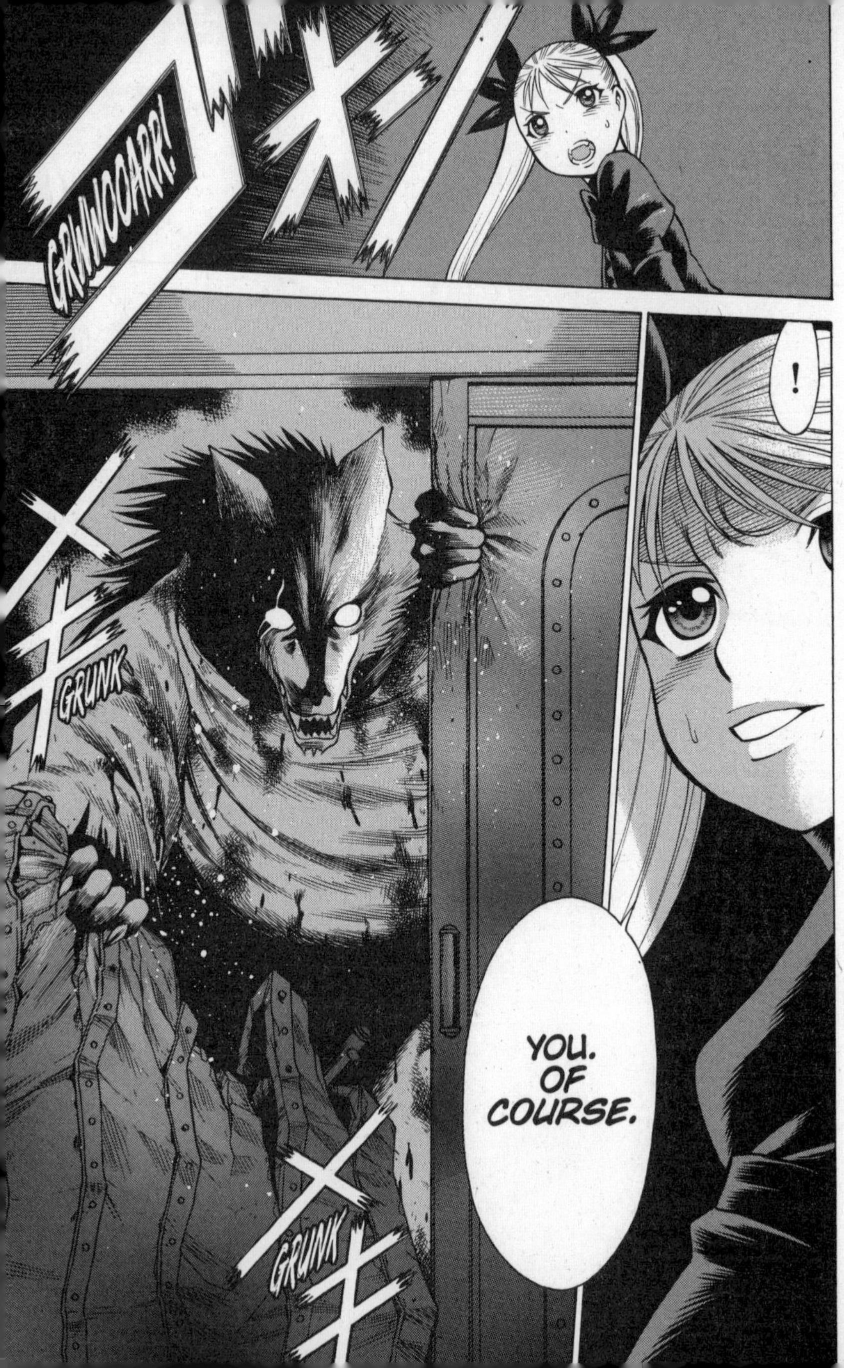
GRWWOOARR!
!
YOU. OF COURSE.
GRUNK
GRUNK

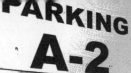

PARKING
A-2
OVER HERE, AKIRA!
WHAT, IT'S JUST US THREE?!
LOOKS LIKE IT. EVERYBODY ELSE IS STUCK SOMEPLACE OR ANOTHER!
YOU HAVE THE CODE, RIGHT?!
PALM PRINT, CONFIRMED.
RETINAL SCAN, CONFIRMED. BEOWOLF KABURAGI, AKIRA, ACKNOWLEDGED.
SHK
PSSHHH
VWMMM

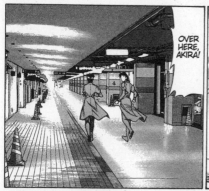

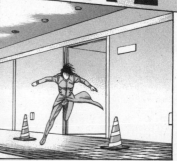

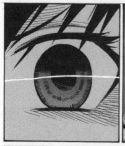

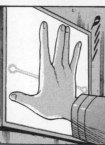

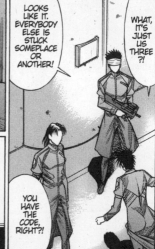

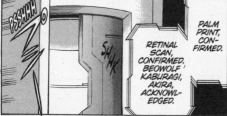

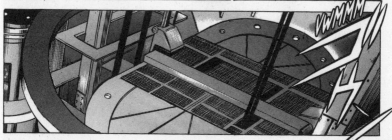

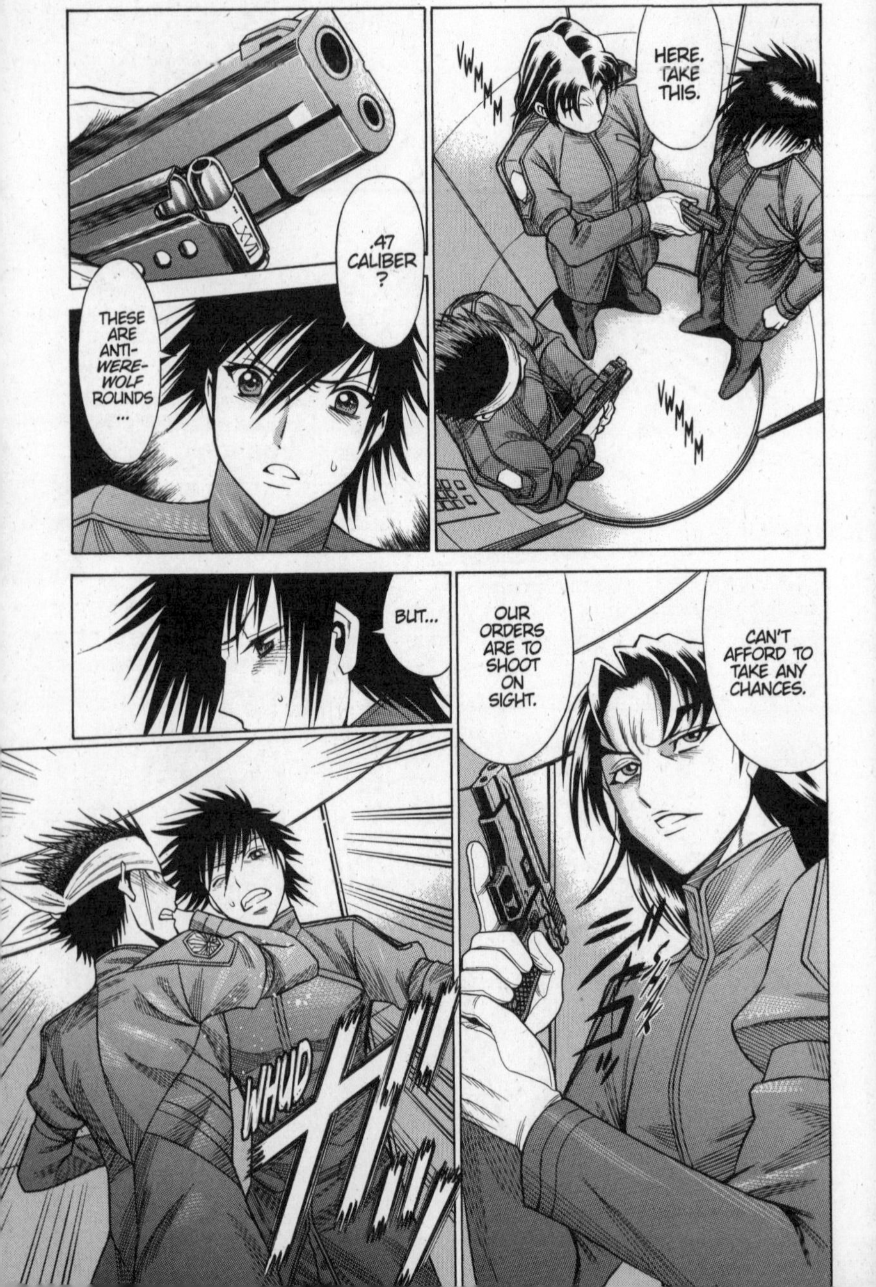
HERE. TAKE THIS.
VWMMM
VWMMM
.47 CALIBER?
THESE ARE ANTI-WERE-WOLF ROUNDS...
BUT...
OUR ORDERS ARE TO SHOOT ON SIGHT.
CAN'T AFFORD TO TAKE ANY CHANCES.
SHK
WHUD

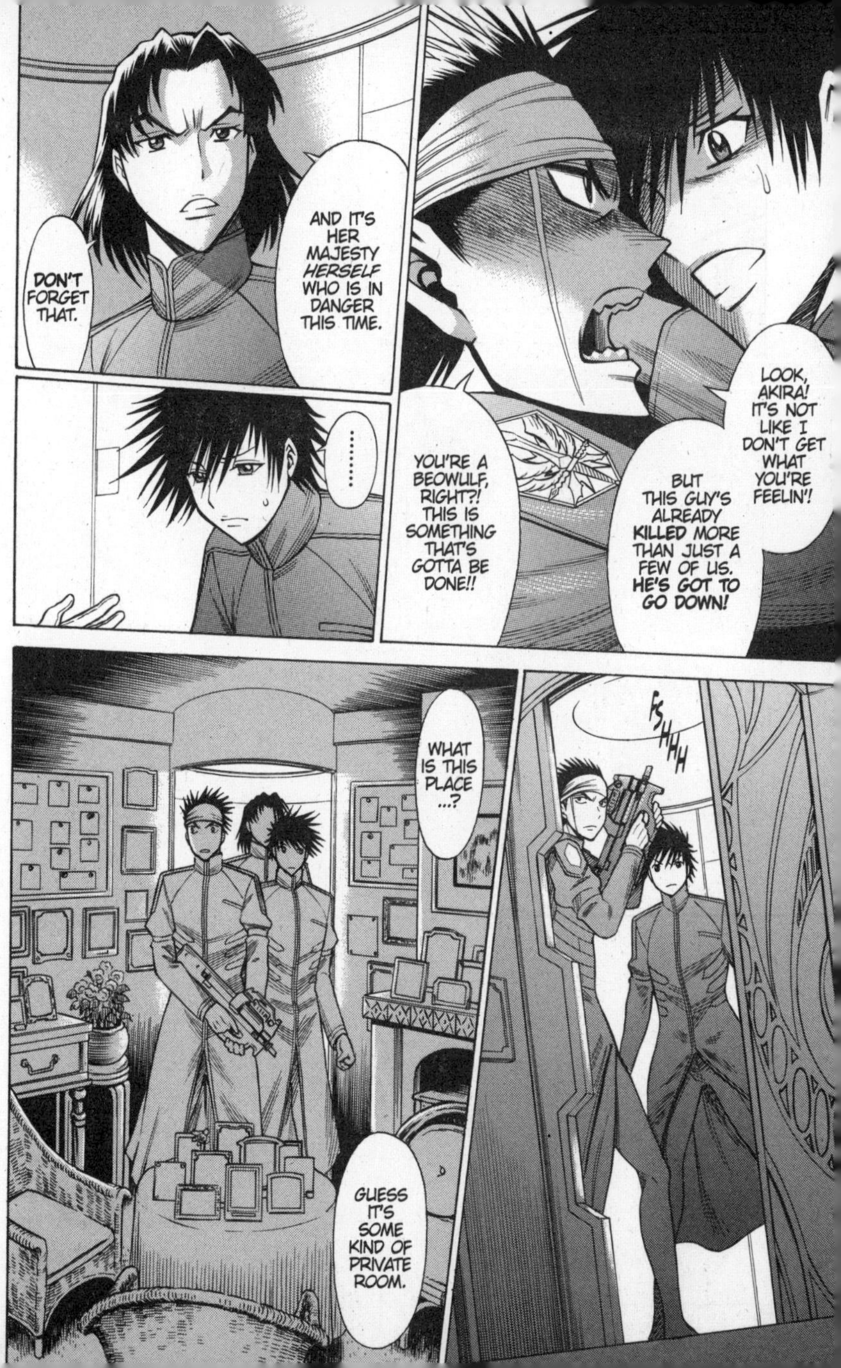
LOOK, AKIRA! IT'S NOT LIKE I DON'T GET WHAT YOU'RE FEELIN'!
BUT THIS GUY'S ALREADY **KILLED** MORE THAN JUST A FEW OF US. **HE'S GOT TO GO DOWN!**
YOU'RE A BEOWULF, RIGHT?! THIS IS SOMETHING THAT'S GOTTA BE DONE!!
AND IT'S HER MAJESTY *HERSELF* WHO IS IN DANGER THIS TIME.
DON'T FORGET THAT.
....
FSHHH
WHAT IS THIS PLACE ...?
GUESS IT'S SOME KIND OF PRIVATE ROOM.

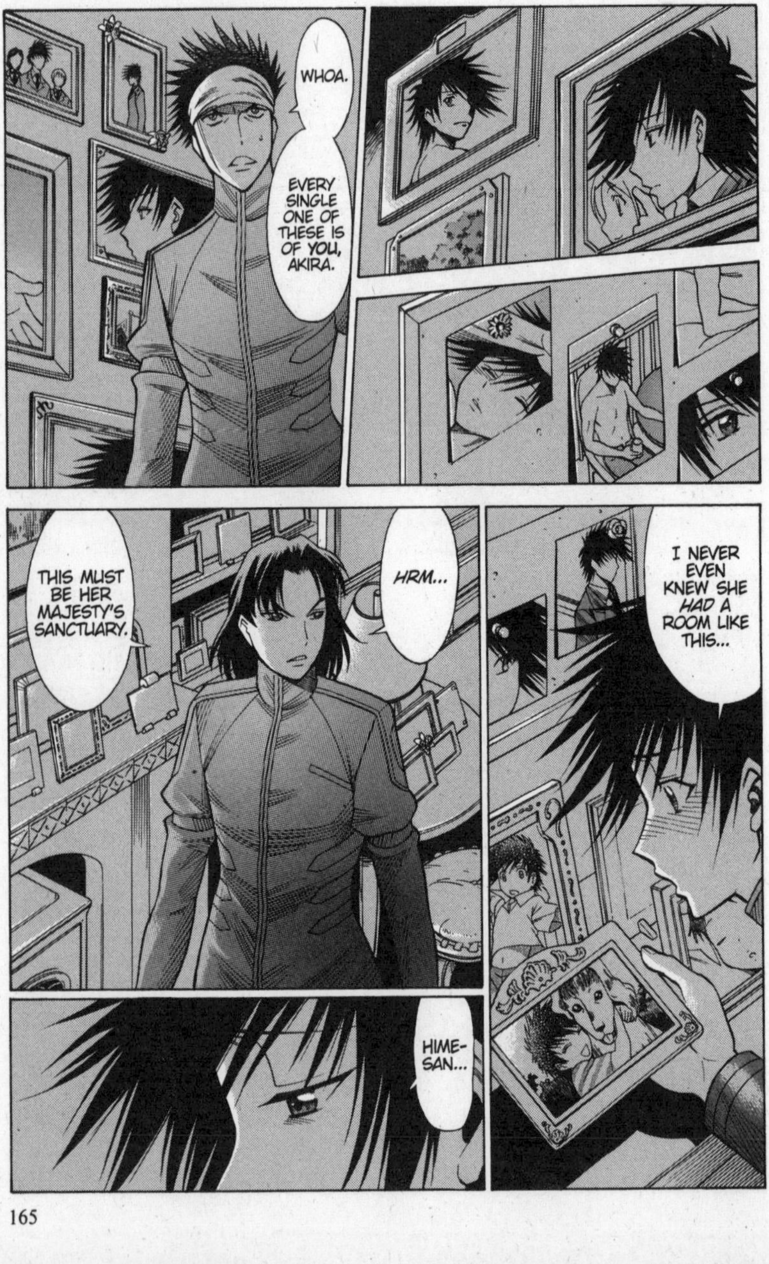
WHOA.
EVERY SINGLE ONE OF THESE IS OF YOU, AKIRA.
I NEVER EVEN KNEW SHE HAD A ROOM LIKE THIS...
HRM...
THIS MUST BE HER MAJESTY'S SANCTUARY.
HIME-SAN...

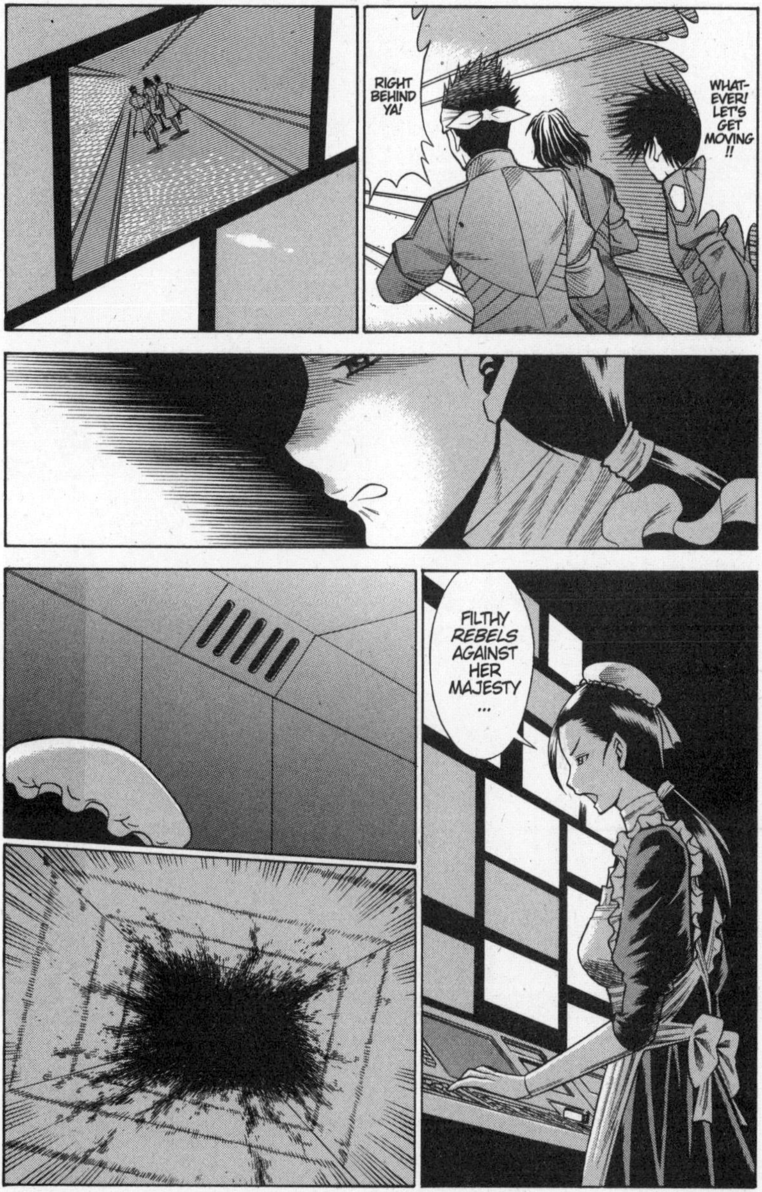
WHAT-EVER! LET'S GET MOVING!!
RIGHT BEHIND YA!
FILTHY *REBELS* AGAINST HER MAJESTY ...

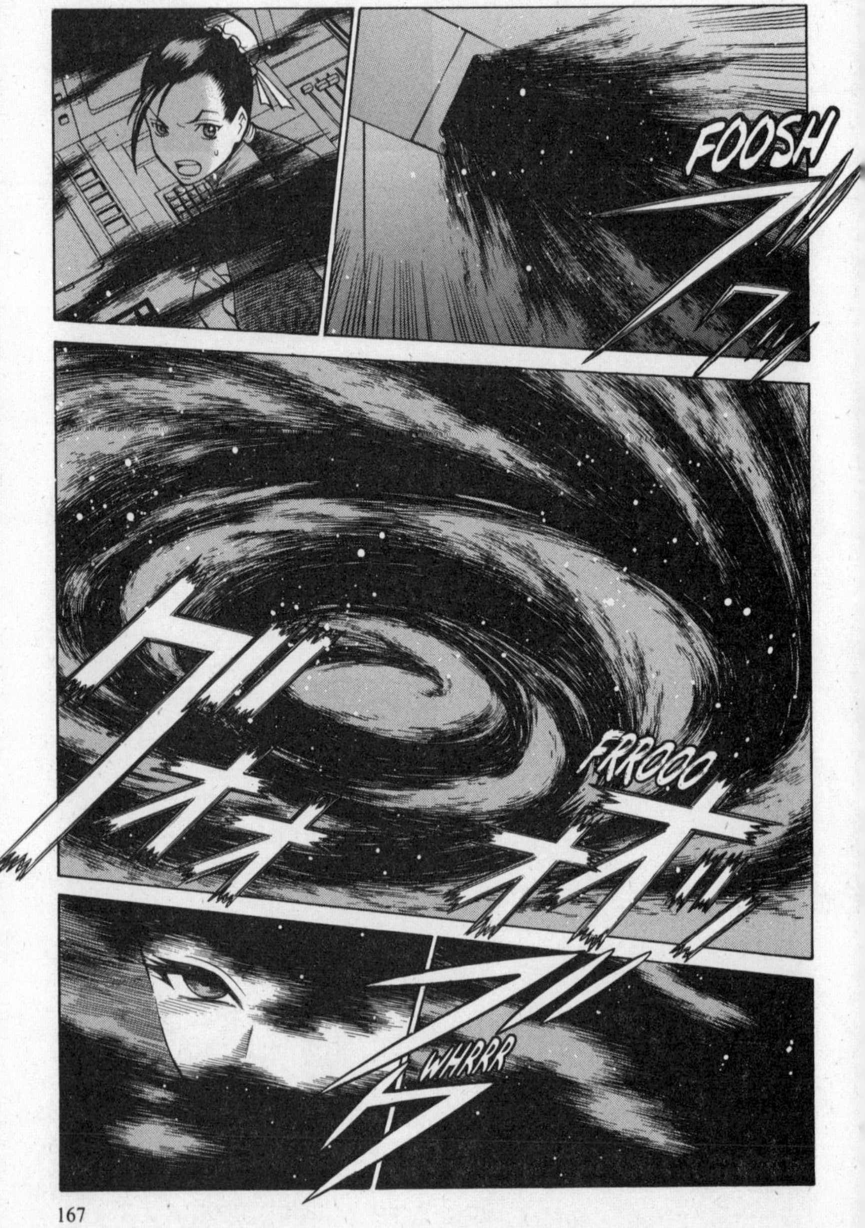
FOOSH
FRROOO
WHRRR

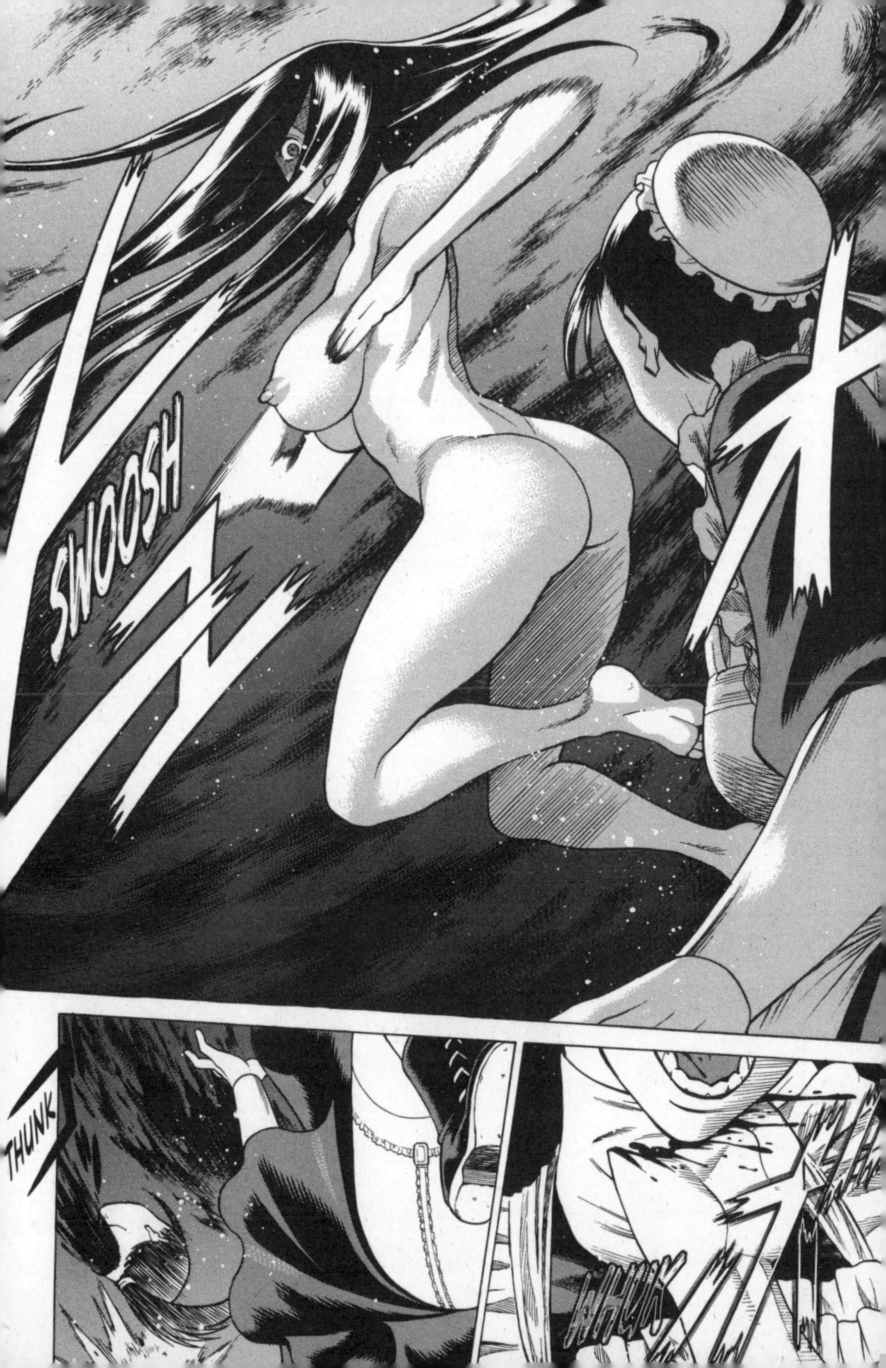
SWOOSH
THUNK

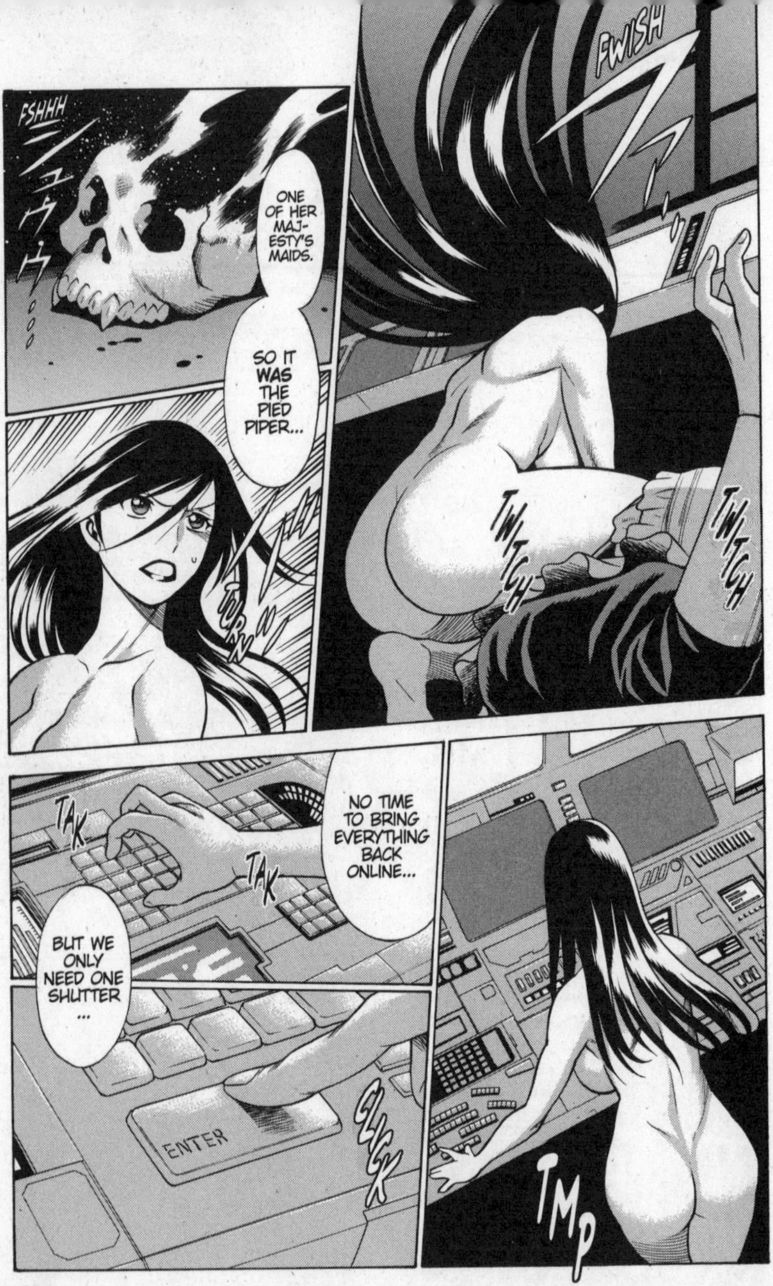
FWISH
TWITCH
TWITCH
FSHHH
ONE OF HER MAJ-ESTY'S MAIDS.
SO IT WAS THE PIED PIPER...
TURN
TMP
TAK
TAK
NO TIME TO BRING EVERYTHING BACK ONLINE...
BUT WE ONLY NEED ONE SHUTTER ...
ENTER
CLICK

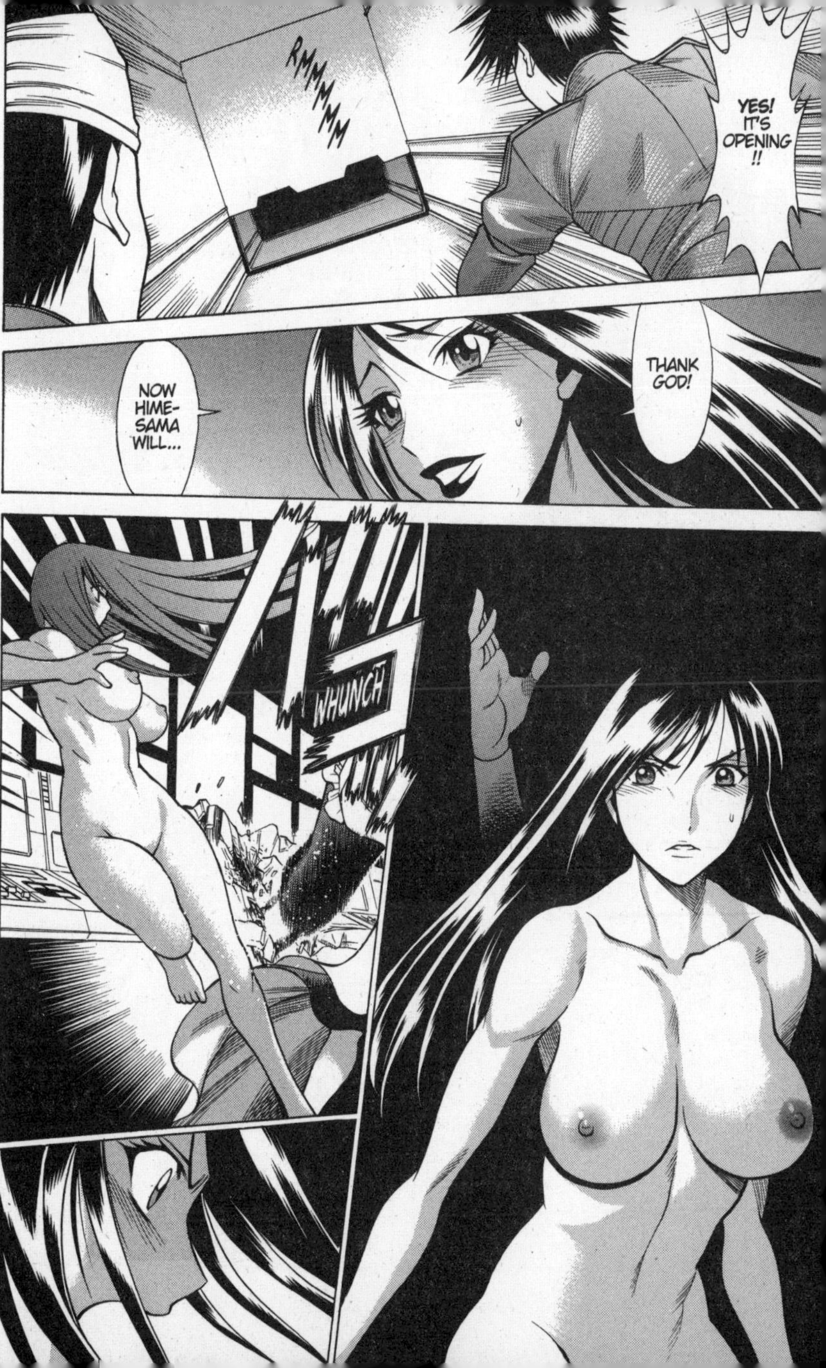
YES! IT'S OPENING !!
RMMMMMM
THANK GOD!
NOW HIME-SAMA WILL...
WHUNCH

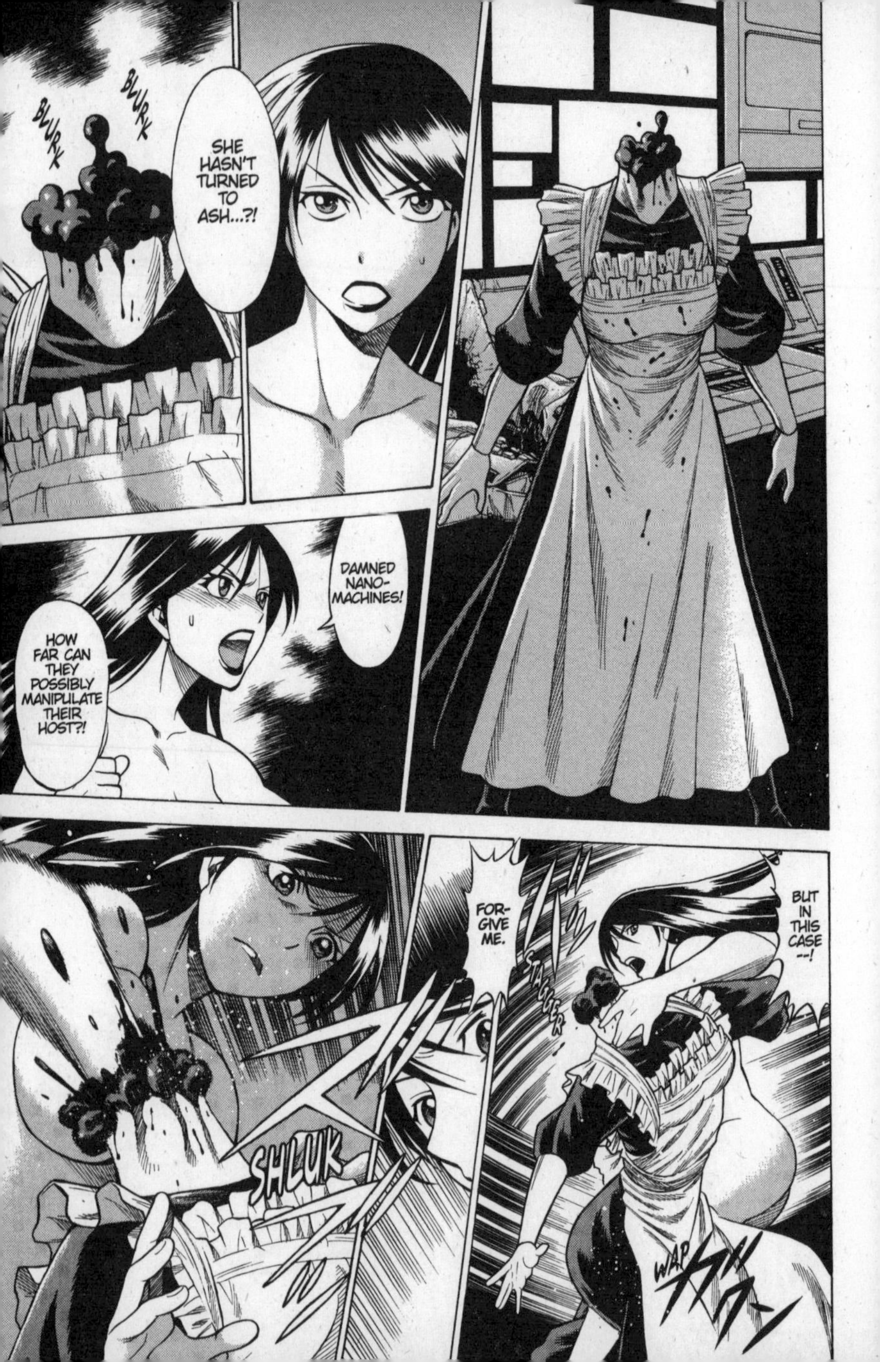
SHE HASN'T TURNED TO ASH...?!
BLURK
BLURK
DAMNED NANO-MACHINES!
HOW FAR CAN THEY POSSIBLY MANIPULATE THEIR HOST?!
BUT IN THIS CASE--!
FORGIVE ME.
STAGGER
WAP
SHLUK

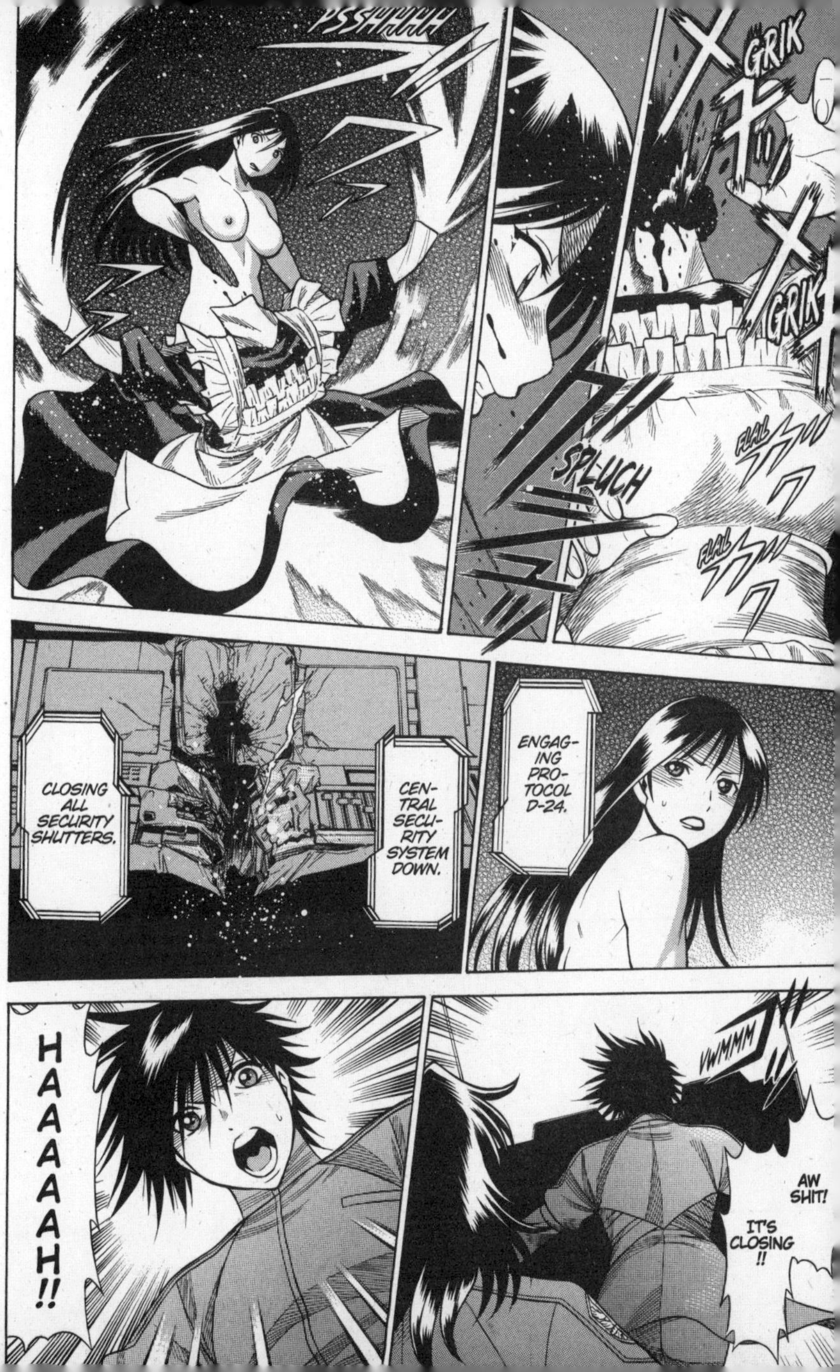
GRIK
GRIK
FLAIL
FLAIL
SPLUCH
PSSHHHH
ENGAGING PROTOCOL D-24.
CENTRAL SECURITY SYSTEM DOWN.
CLOSING ALL SECURITY SHUTTERS.
VWMMM
AW SHIT!
IT'S CLOSING !!
HAAAAAAAH!!

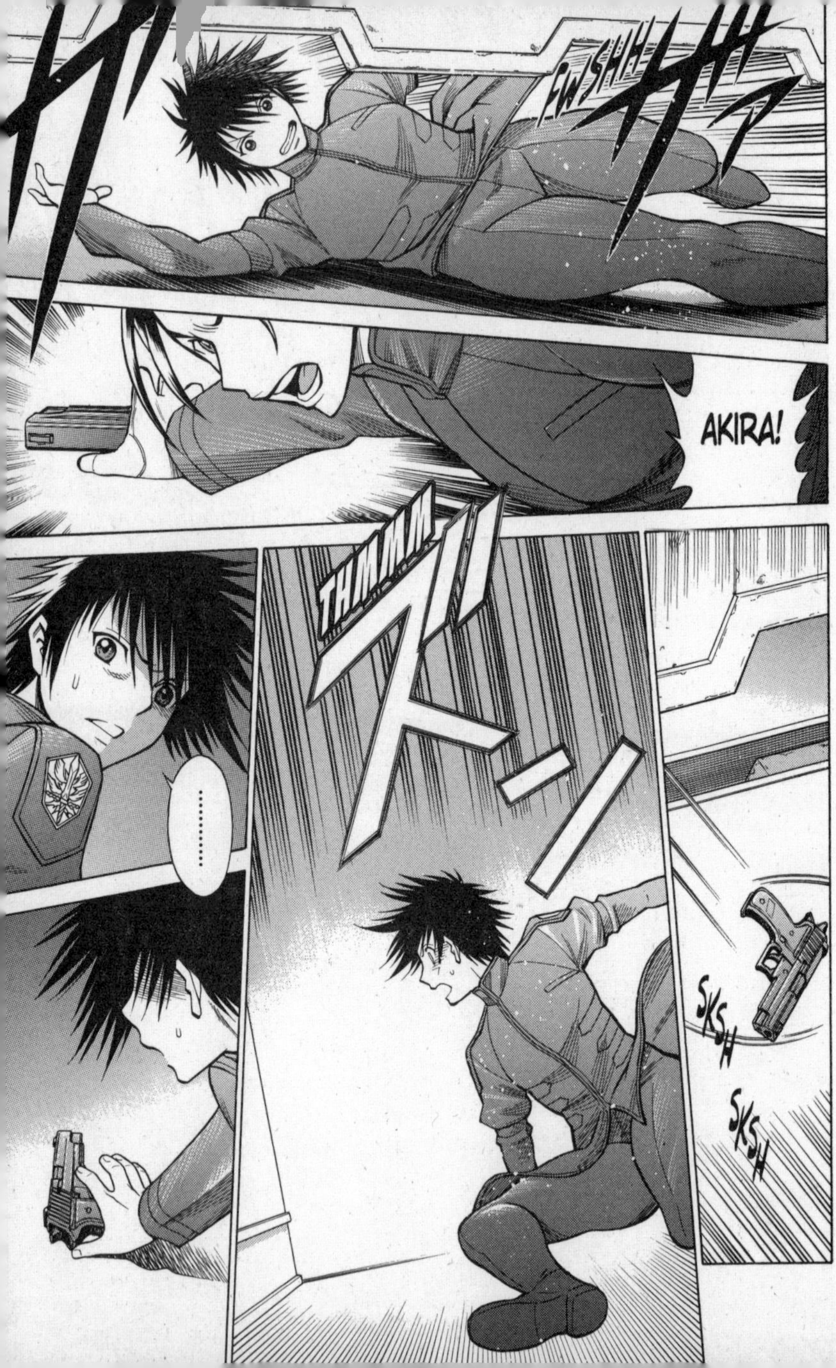
FWSHH
AKIRA!
SKSH
SKSH
THMMM
....

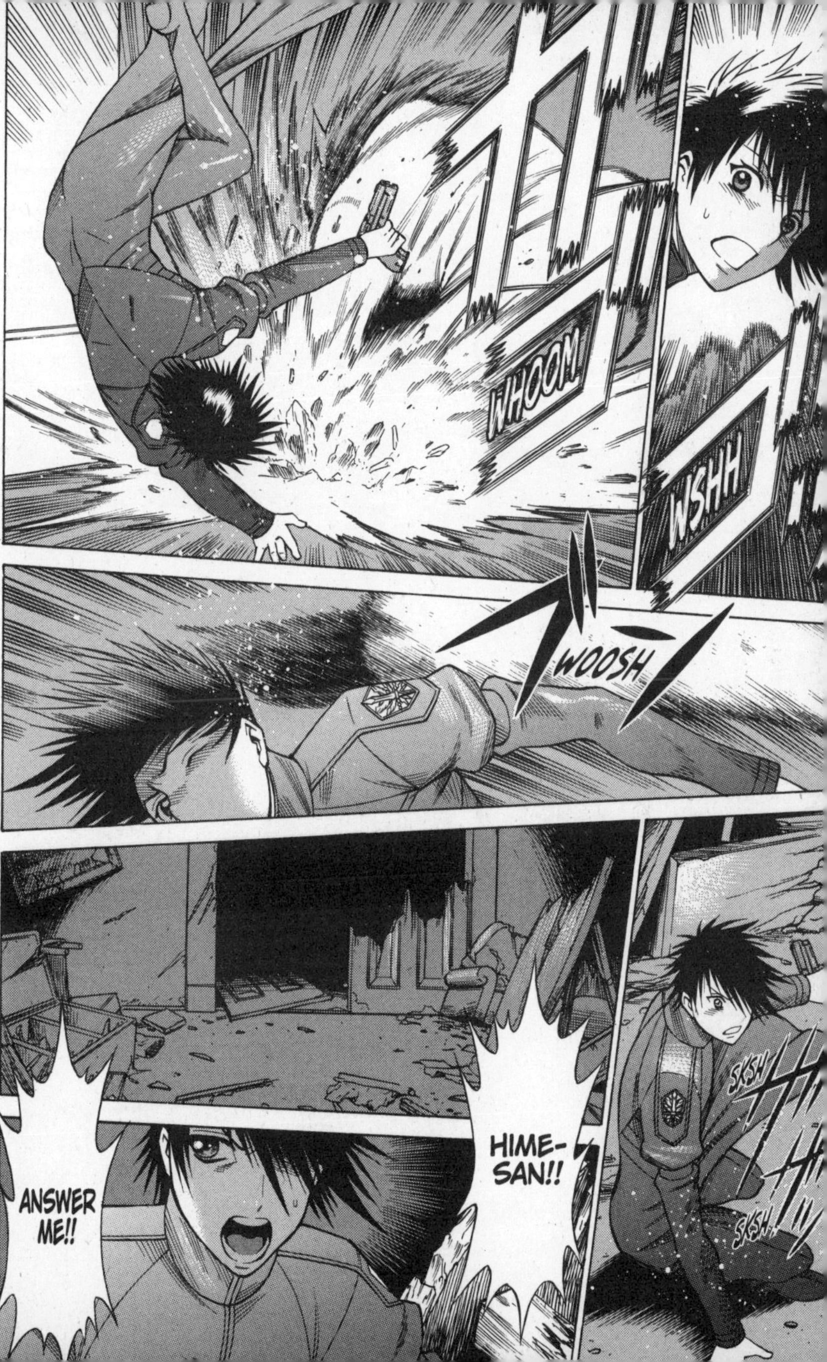
WHOOM
WSHH
WOOSH
SKSH
SKSH
HIME-SAN!!
ANSWER ME!!

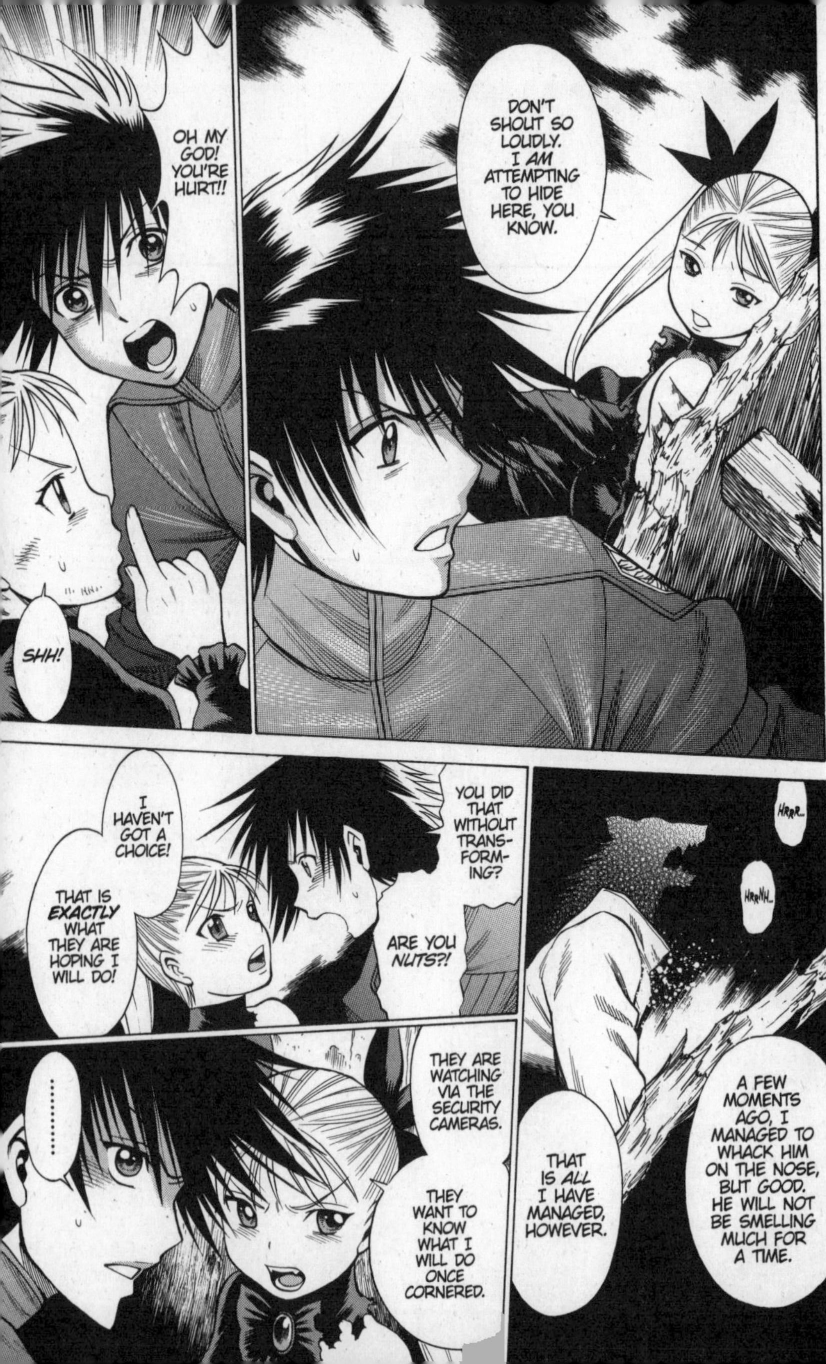
DON'T SHOUT SO LOUDLY. I *AM* ATTEMPTING TO HIDE HERE, YOU KNOW.
OH MY GOD! YOU'RE HURT!!
SHH!
HRRR...
HRRNH...
A FEW MOMENTS AGO, I MANAGED TO WHACK HIM ON THE NOSE, BUT GOOD. HE WILL NOT BE SMELLING MUCH FOR A TIME.
THAT IS *ALL* I HAVE MANAGED, HOWEVER.
YOU DID THAT WITHOUT TRANS-FORM-ING?
ARE YOU *NUTS?!*
I HAVEN'T GOT A CHOICE!
THAT IS ***EXACTLY*** WHAT THEY ARE HOPING I WILL DO!
THEY ARE WATCHING VIA THE SECURITY CAMERAS.
THEY WANT TO KNOW WHAT I WILL DO ONCE CORNERED.
......

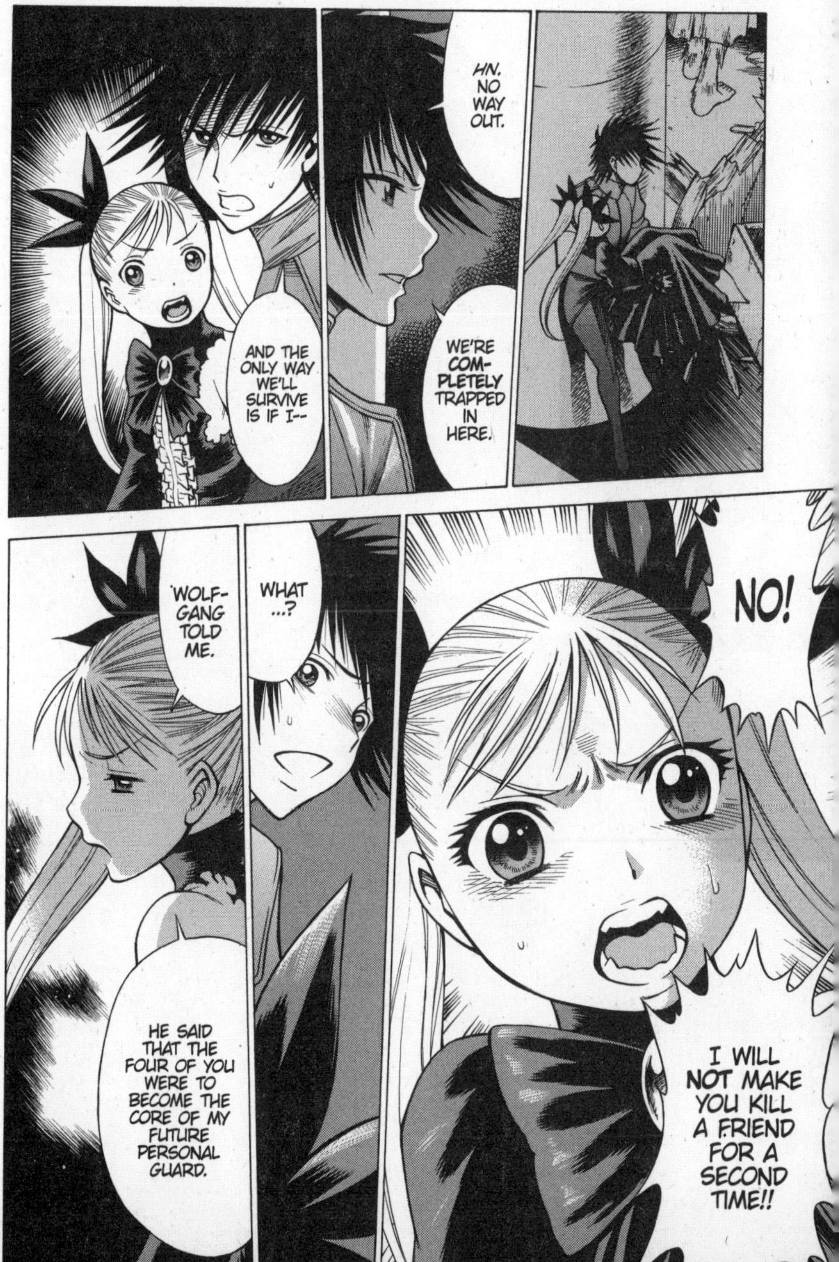
HN. NO WAY OUT.
WE'RE COMPLETELY TRAPPED IN HERE.
AND THE ONLY WAY WE'LL SURVIVE IS IF I--
NO!
I WILL NOT MAKE YOU KILL A FRIEND FOR A SECOND TIME!!
WHAT ...?
WOLFGANG TOLD ME.
HE SAID THAT THE FOUR OF YOU WERE TO BECOME THE CORE OF MY FUTURE PERSONAL GUARD.

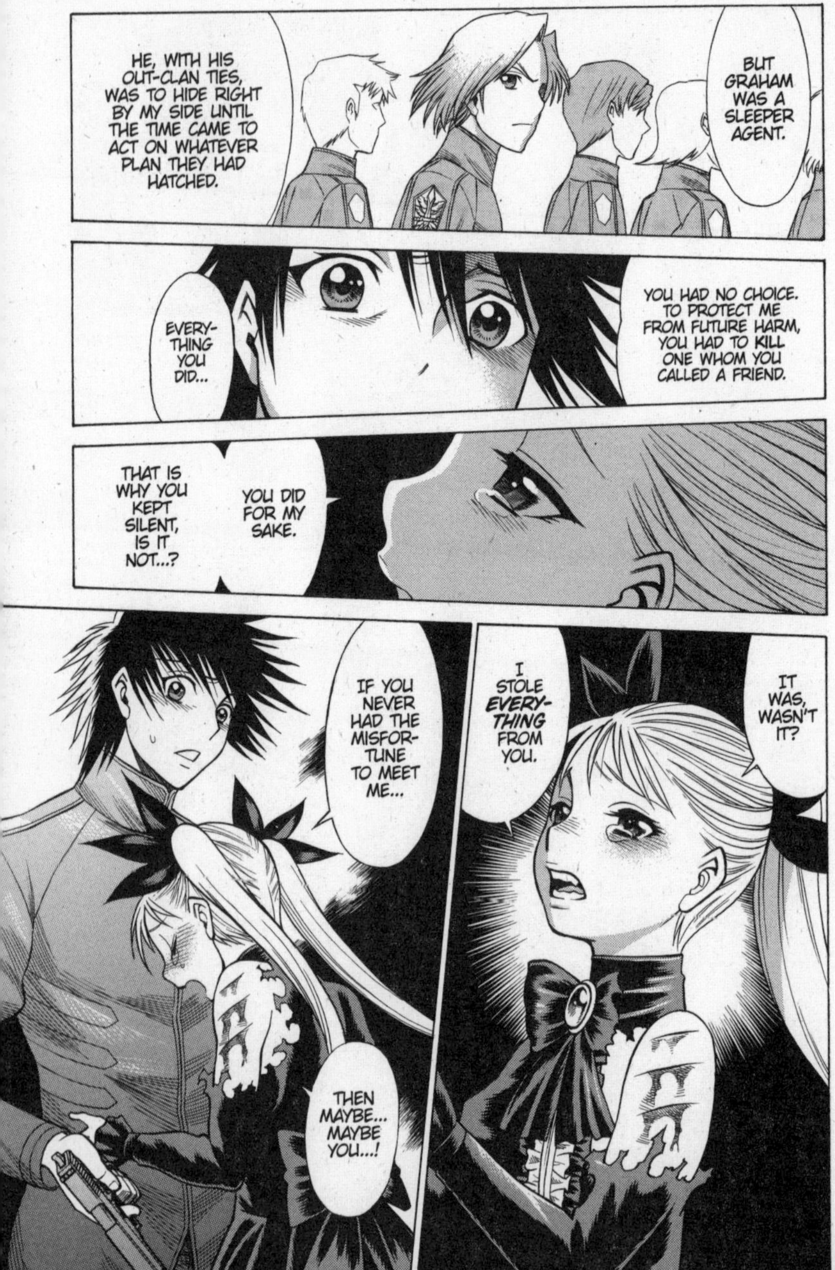
BUT GRAHAM WAS A SLEEPER AGENT.
HE, WITH HIS OUT-CLAN TIES, WAS TO HIDE RIGHT BY MY SIDE UNTIL THE TIME CAME TO ACT ON WHATEVER PLAN THEY HAD HATCHED.
YOU HAD NO CHOICE. TO PROTECT ME FROM FUTURE HARM, YOU HAD TO KILL ONE WHOM YOU CALLED A FRIEND.
EVERYTHING YOU DID...
YOU DID FOR MY SAKE.
THAT IS WHY YOU KEPT SILENT, IS IT NOT...?
IT WAS, WASN'T IT?
I STOLE *EVERYTHING* FROM YOU.
IF YOU NEVER HAD THE MISFORTUNE TO MEET ME...
THEN MAYBE... MAYBE YOU...!

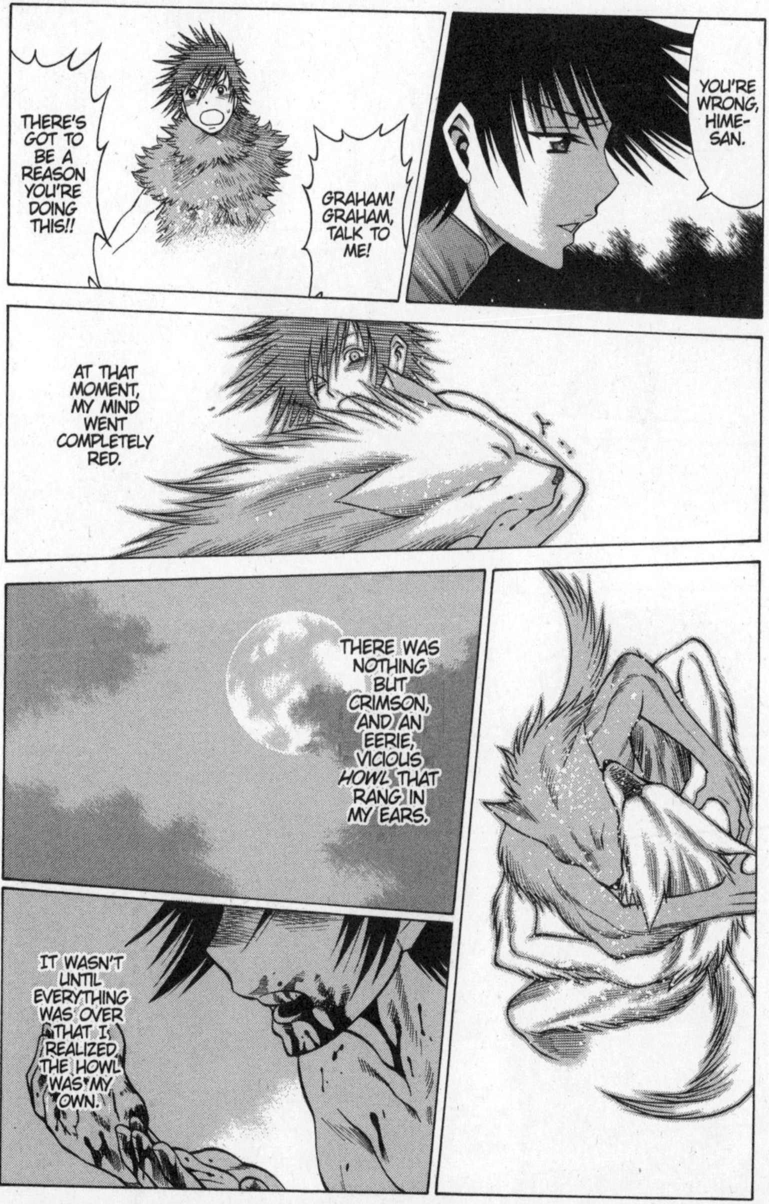
YOU'RE WRONG, HIME-SAN.
GRAHAM! GRAHAM, TALK TO ME!
THERE'S GOT TO BE A REASON YOU'RE DOING THIS!!
AT THAT MOMENT, MY MIND WENT COMPLETELY RED.
THERE WAS NOTHING BUT CRIMSON, AND AN EERIE, VICIOUS *HOWL* THAT RANG IN MY EARS.
IT WASN'T UNTIL EVERYTHING WAS OVER THAT I REALIZED THE HOWL WAS MY OWN.

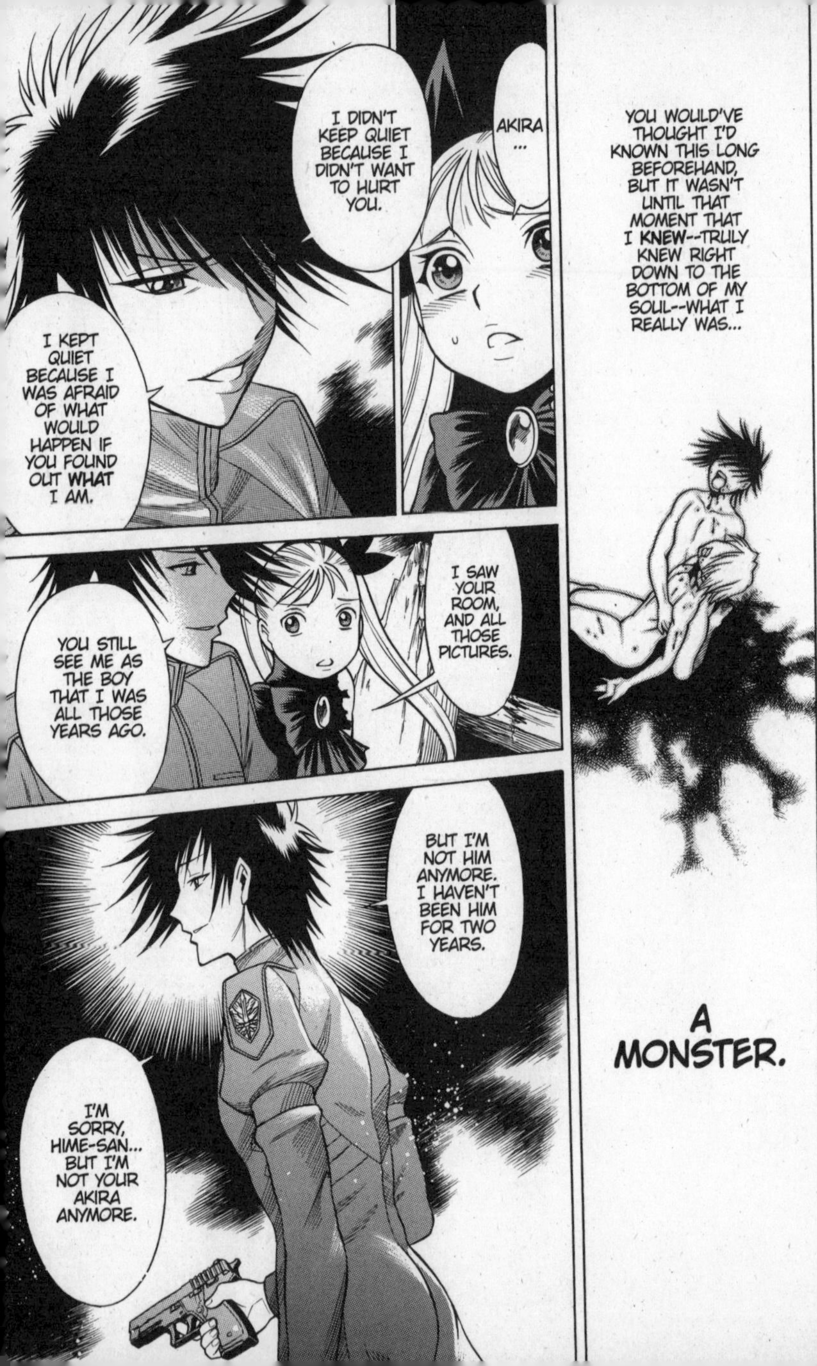
YOU WOULD'VE THOUGHT I'D KNOWN THIS LONG BEFOREHAND, BUT IT WASN'T UNTIL THAT MOMENT THAT I KNEW--TRULY KNEW RIGHT DOWN TO THE BOTTOM OF MY SOUL--WHAT I REALLY WAS...
A MONSTER.
AKIRA ...
I DIDN'T KEEP QUIET BECAUSE I DIDN'T WANT TO HURT YOU.
I KEPT QUIET BECAUSE I WAS AFRAID OF WHAT WOULD HAPPEN IF YOU FOUND OUT WHAT I AM.
I SAW YOUR ROOM, AND ALL THOSE PICTURES.
YOU STILL SEE ME AS THE BOY THAT I WAS ALL THOSE YEARS AGO.
BUT I'M NOT HIM ANYMORE. I HAVEN'T BEEN HIM FOR TWO YEARS.
I'M SORRY, HIME-SAN... BUT I'M NOT YOUR AKIRA ANYMORE.

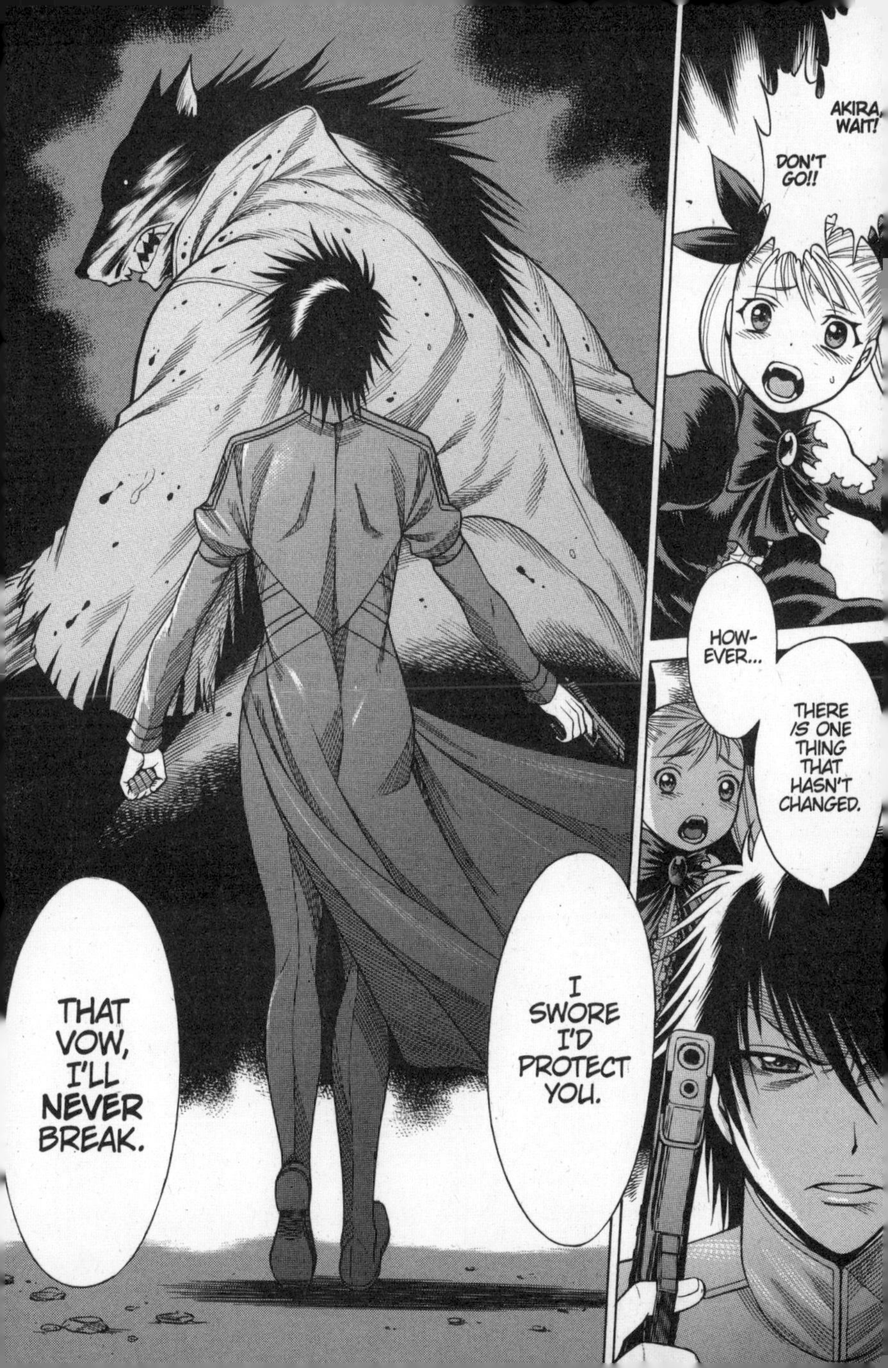
AKIRA, WAIT!
DON'T GO!!
HOW-EVER...
THERE IS ONE THING THAT HASN'T CHANGED.
I SWORE I'D PROTECT YOU.
THAT VOW, I'LL NEVER BREAK.

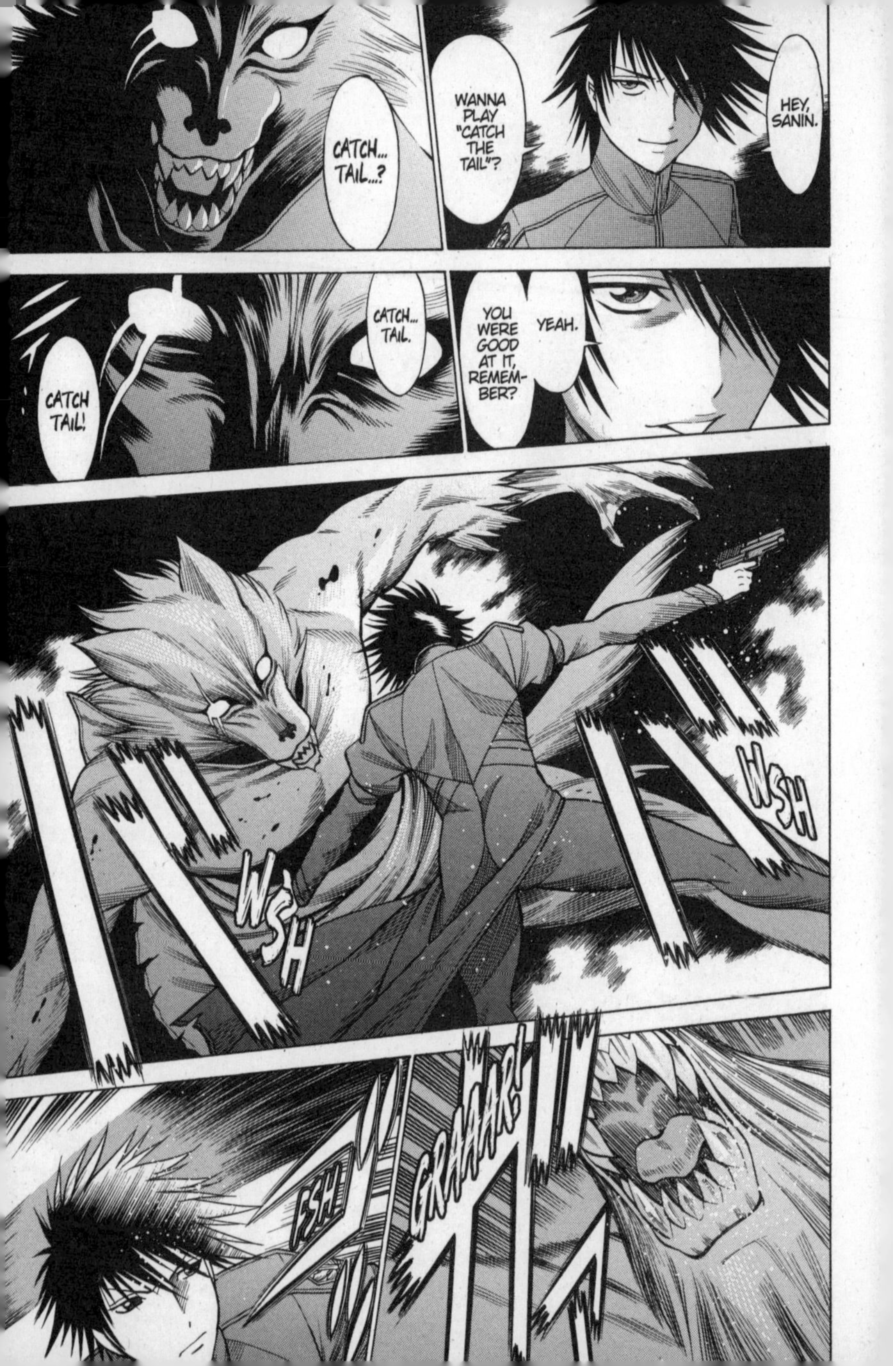
HEY, SANIN.
WANNA PLAY "CATCH THE TAIL"?
CATCH... TAIL...?
YEAH.
YOU WERE GOOD AT IT, REMEMBER?
CATCH... TAIL.
CATCH TAIL!
WSH
WSH
GRAAAR!!

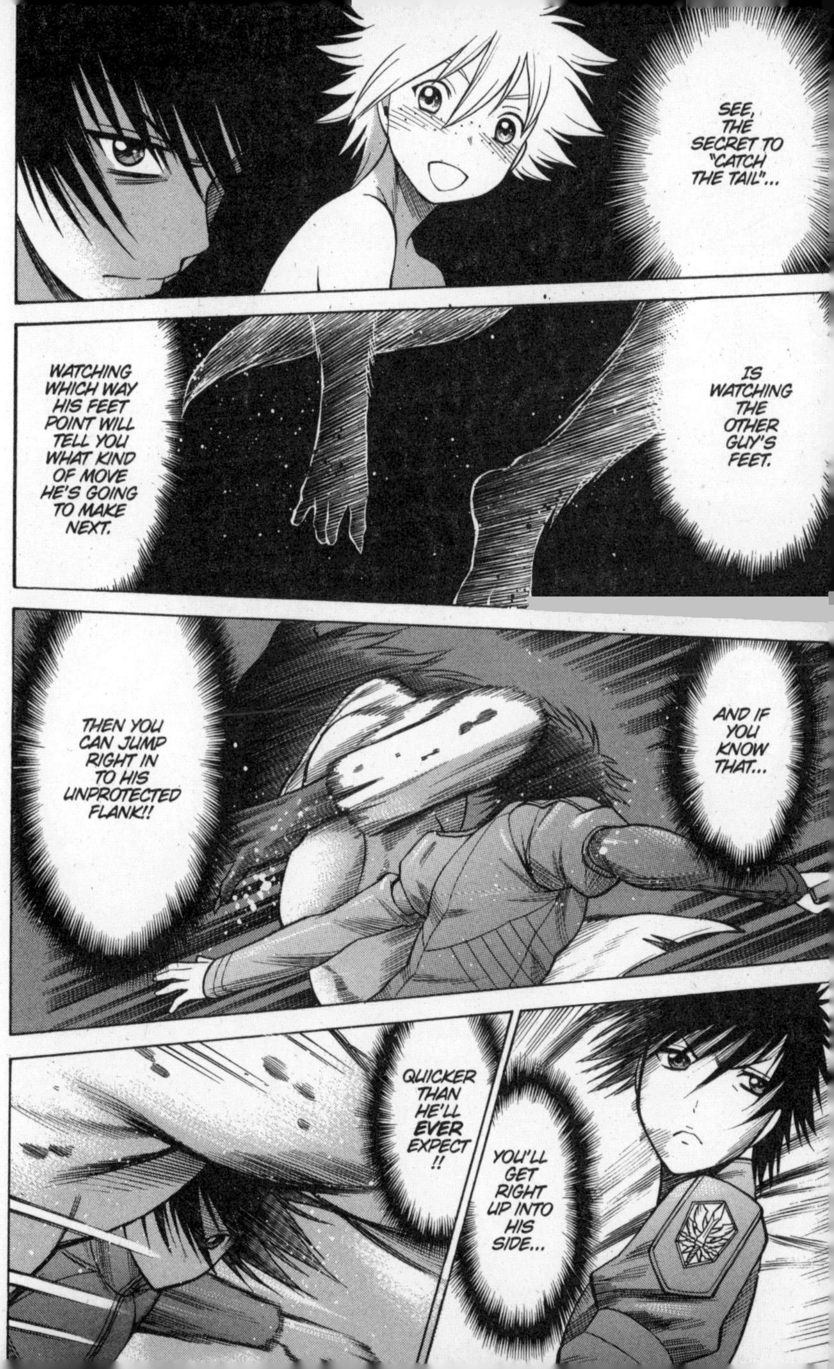
SEE, THE SECRET TO "CATCH THE TAIL"...
IS WATCHING THE OTHER GUY'S FEET.
WATCHING WHICH WAY HIS FEET POINT WILL TELL YOU WHAT KIND OF MOVE HE'S GOING TO MAKE NEXT.
AND IF YOU KNOW THAT...
THEN YOU CAN JUMP RIGHT IN TO HIS UNPROTECTED FLANK!!
YOU'LL GET RIGHT UP INTO HIS SIDE...
QUICKER THAN HE'LL EVER EXPECT!!

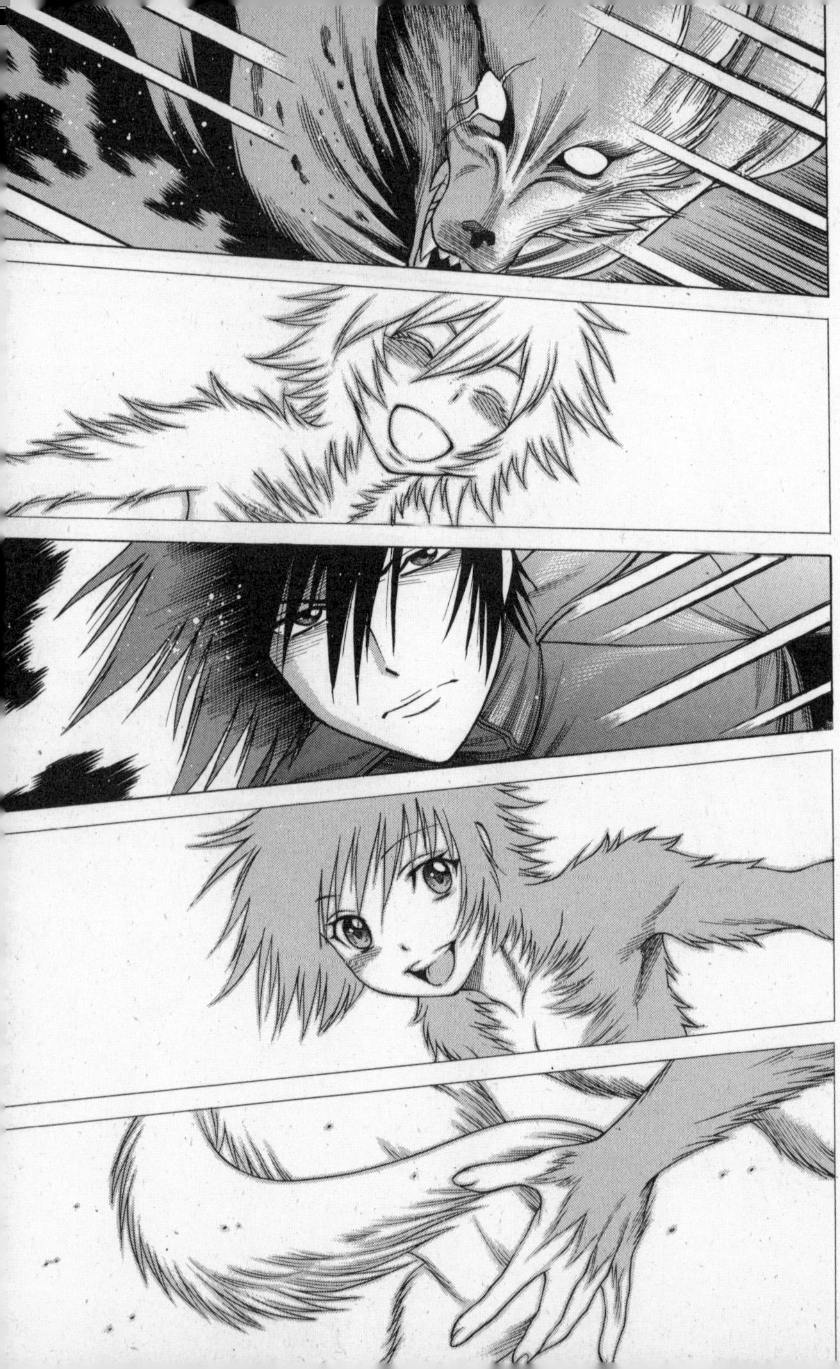

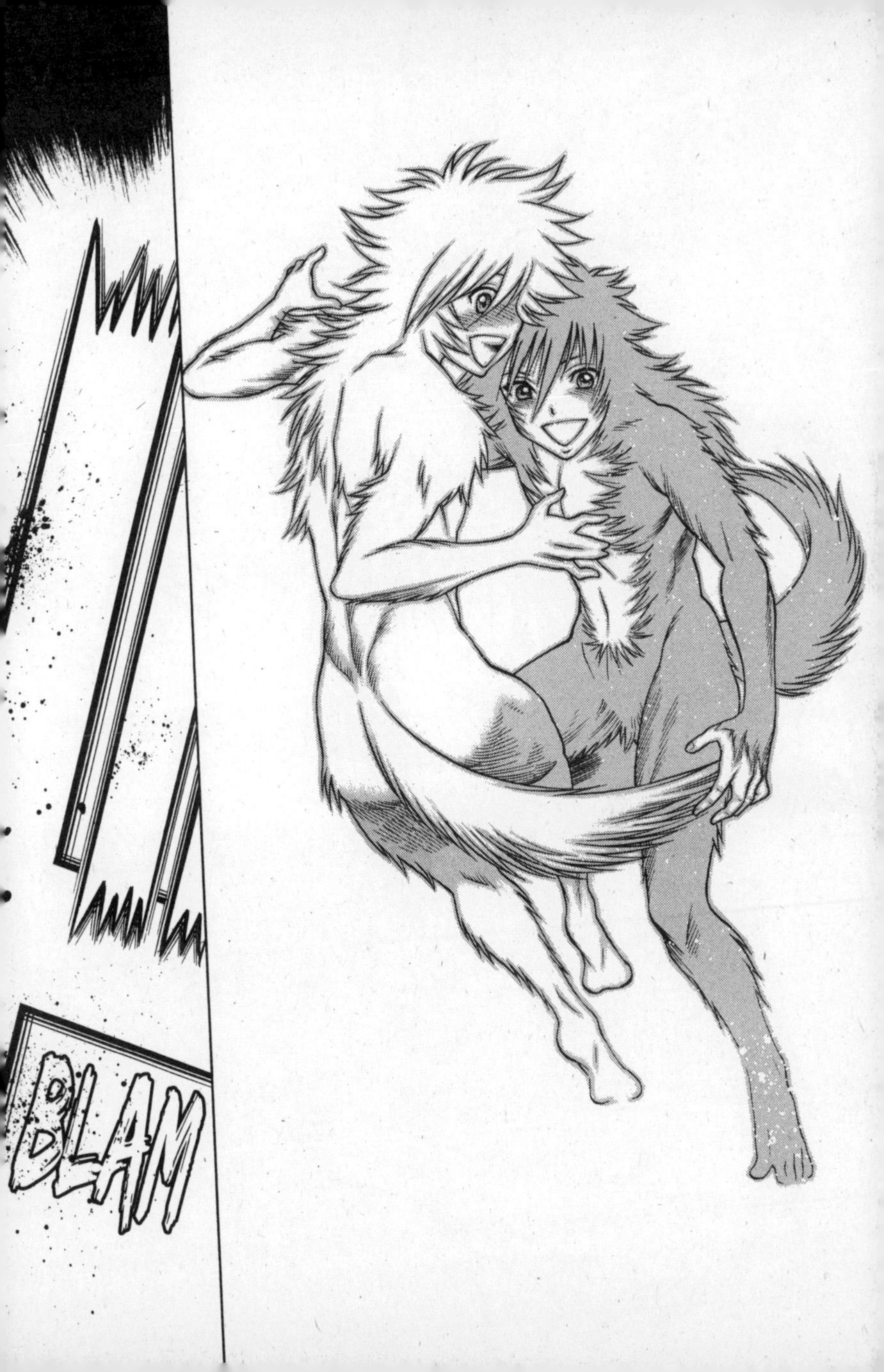
BLAM

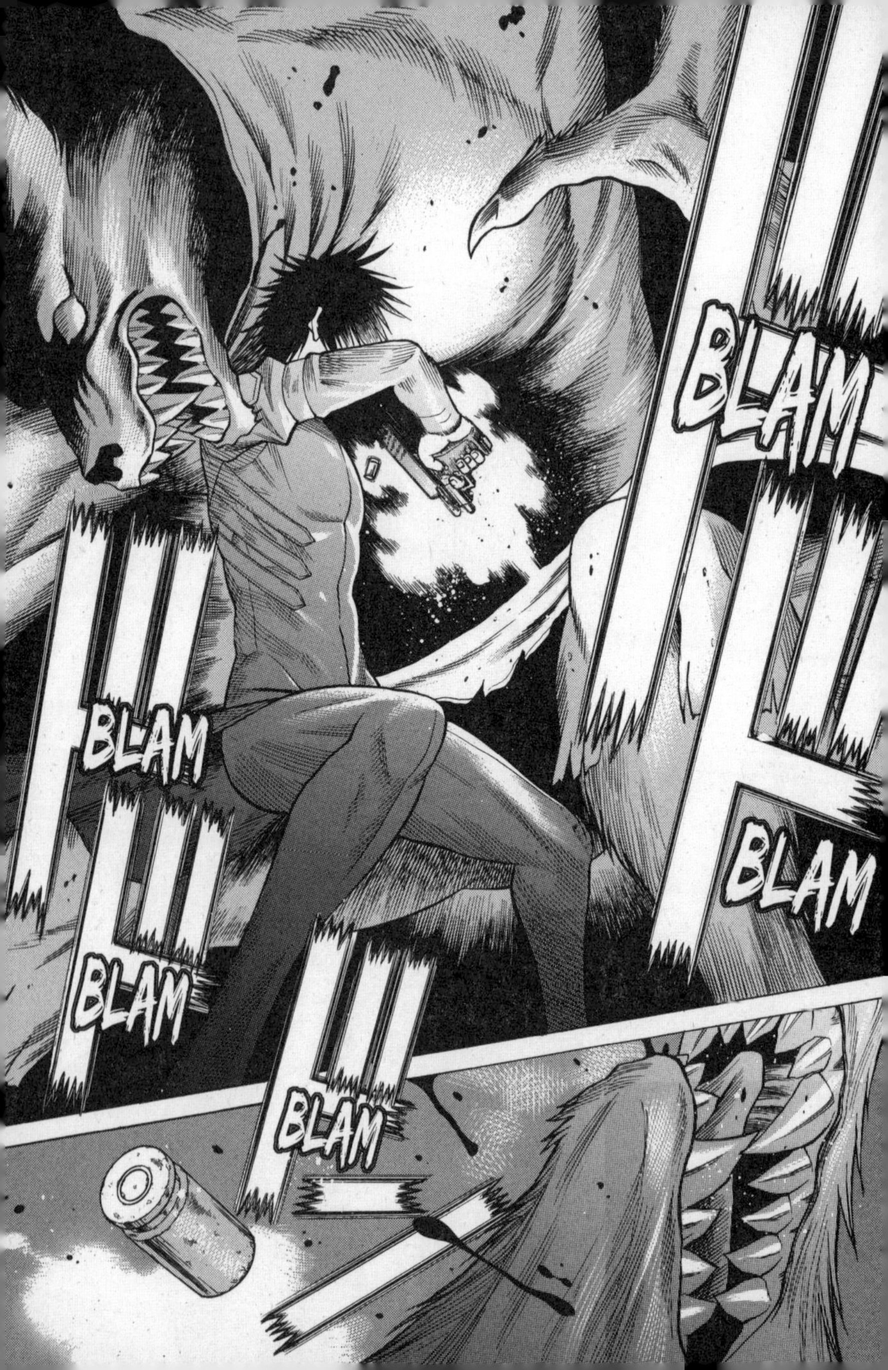
BLAM
BLAM
BLAM
BLAM
BLAM

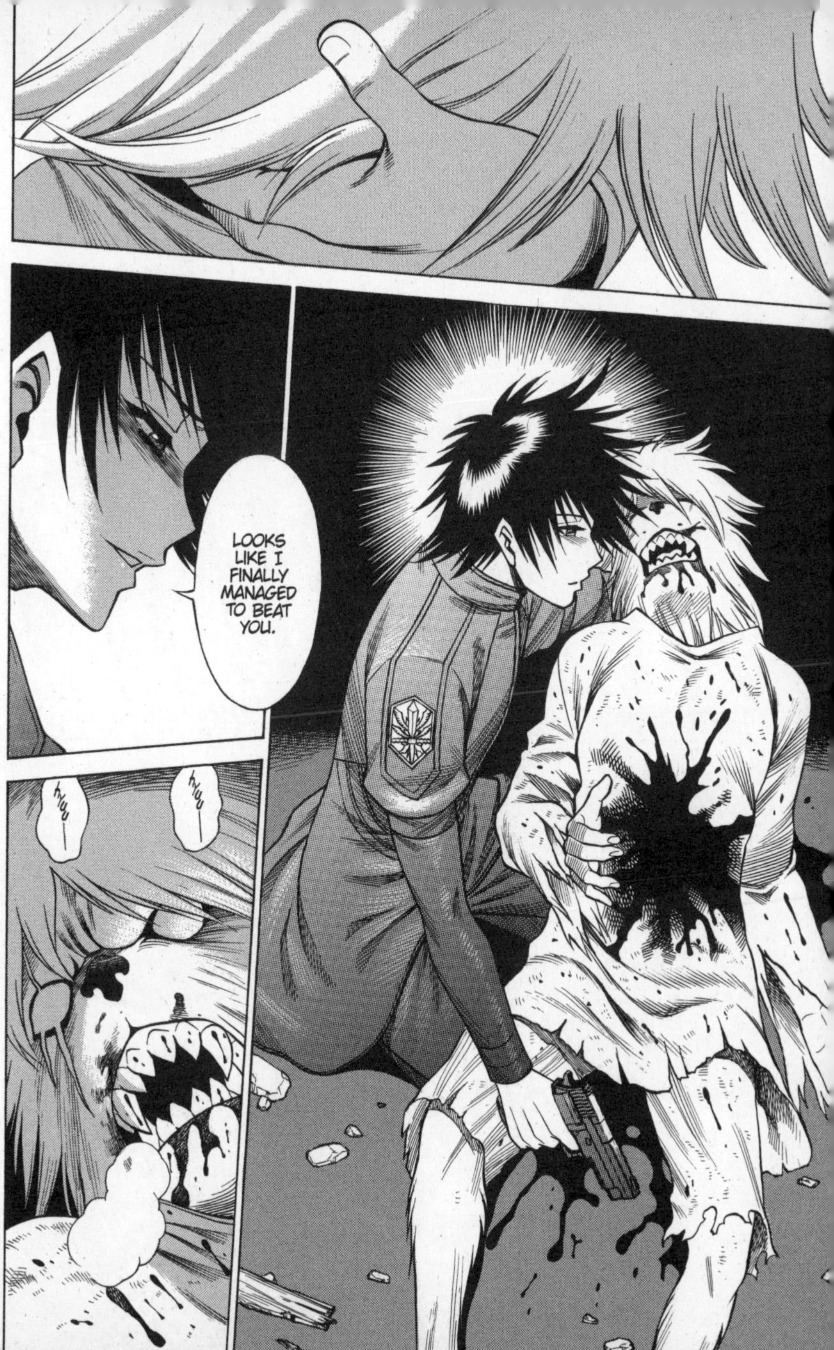
LOOKS LIKE I FINALLY MANAGED TO BEAT YOU.
hyuu—
hyuu—

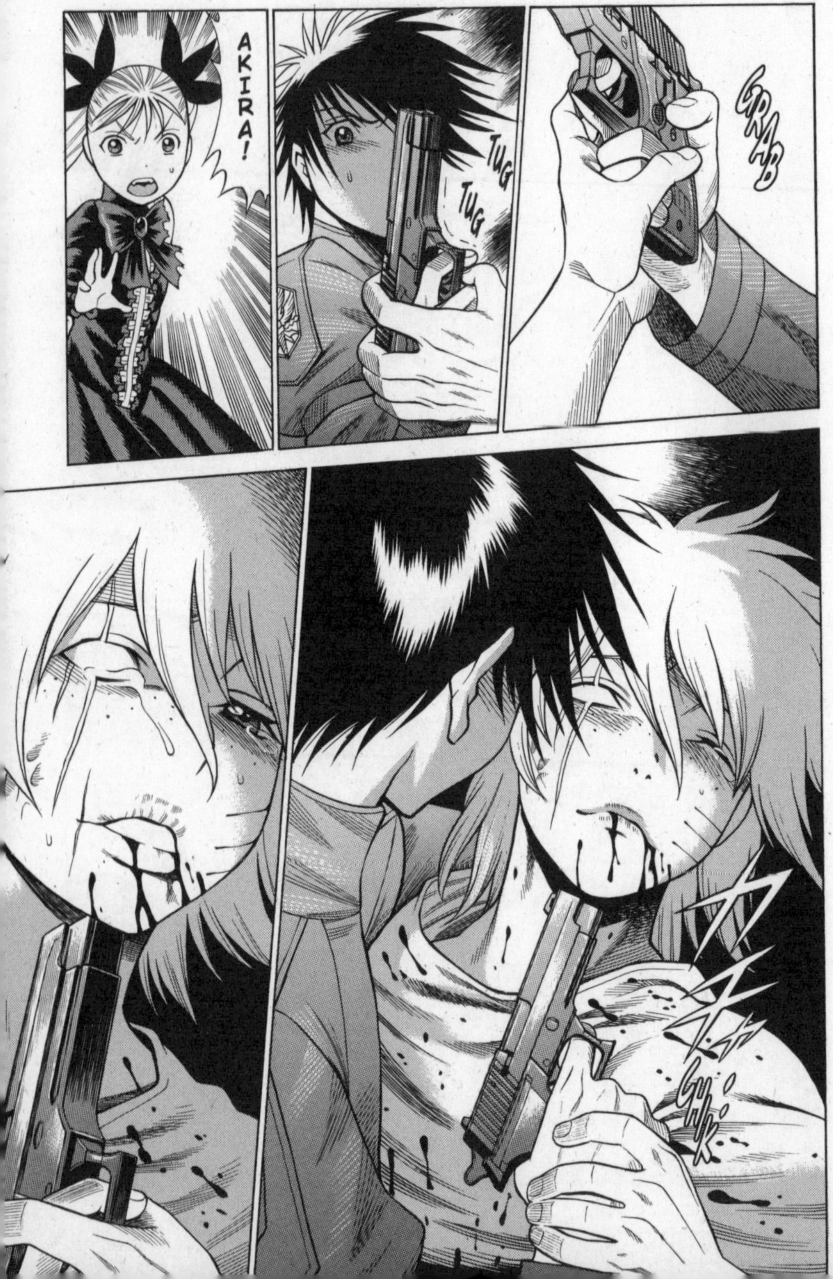
GRAB
TUG
TUG
AKIRA!
GHUK

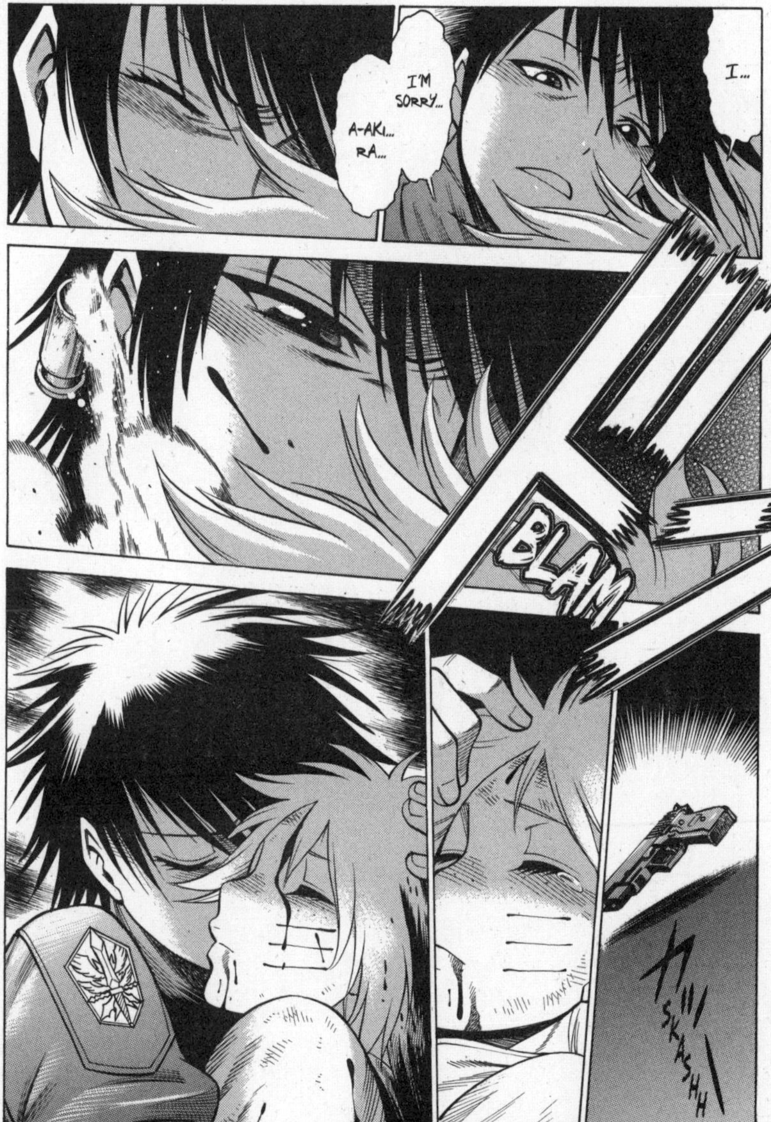
I...
I'M SORRY... A-AKI... RA...
BLAM
SKASHH

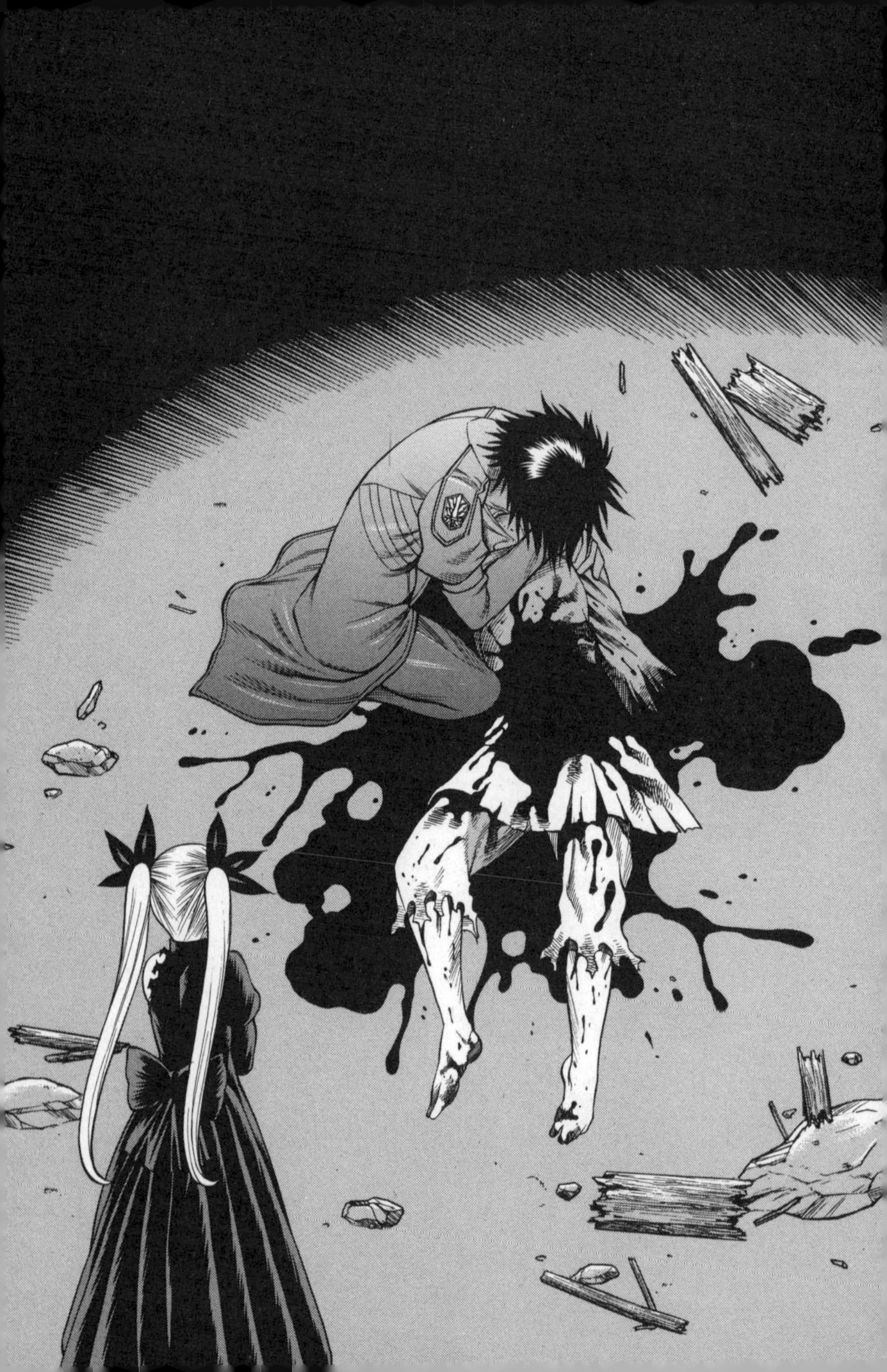

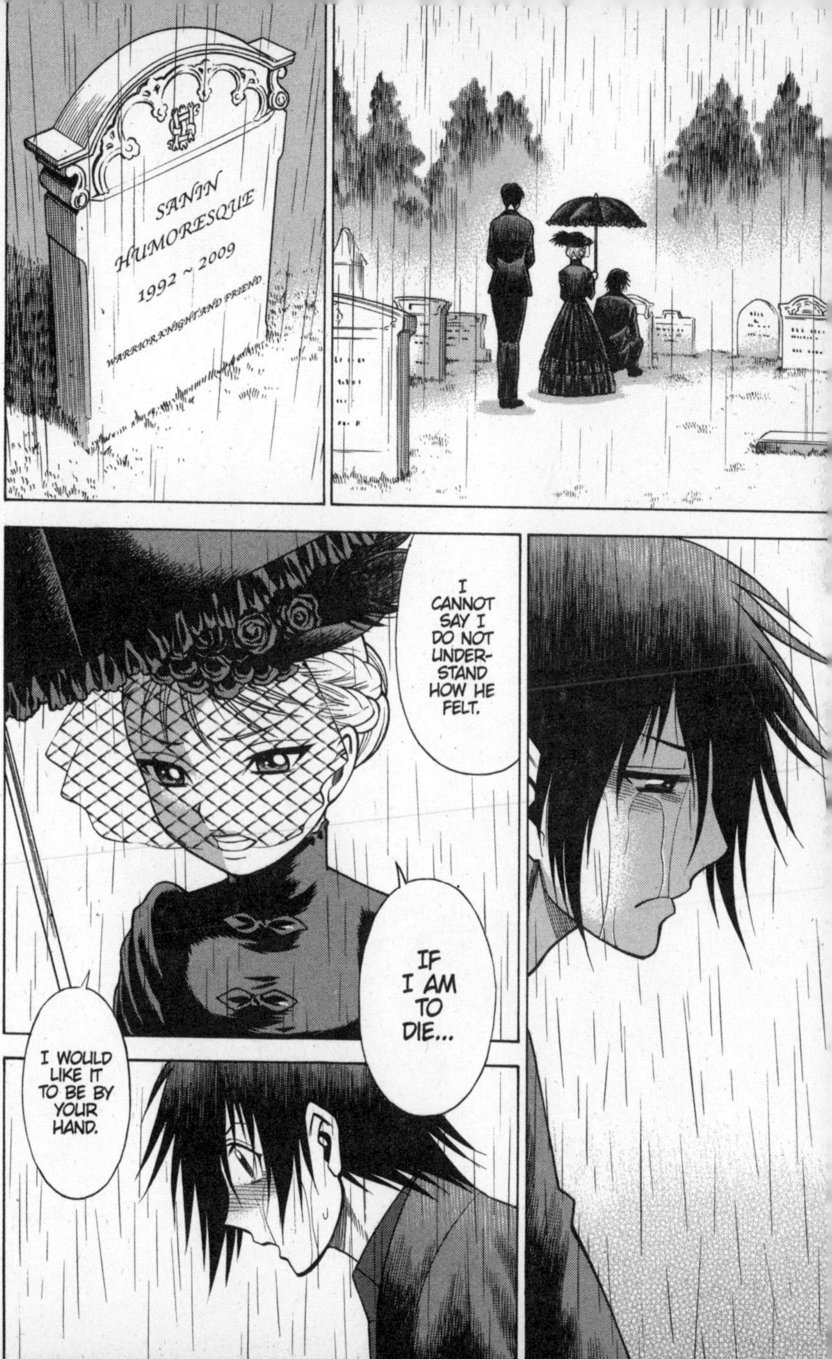
SANIN HUMORESQUE
1992 ~ 2009
WARRIOR KNIGHT AND FRIEND
I CANNOT SAY I DO NOT UNDERSTAND HOW HE FELT.
IF I AM TO DIE...
I WOULD LIKE IT TO BE BY YOUR HAND.

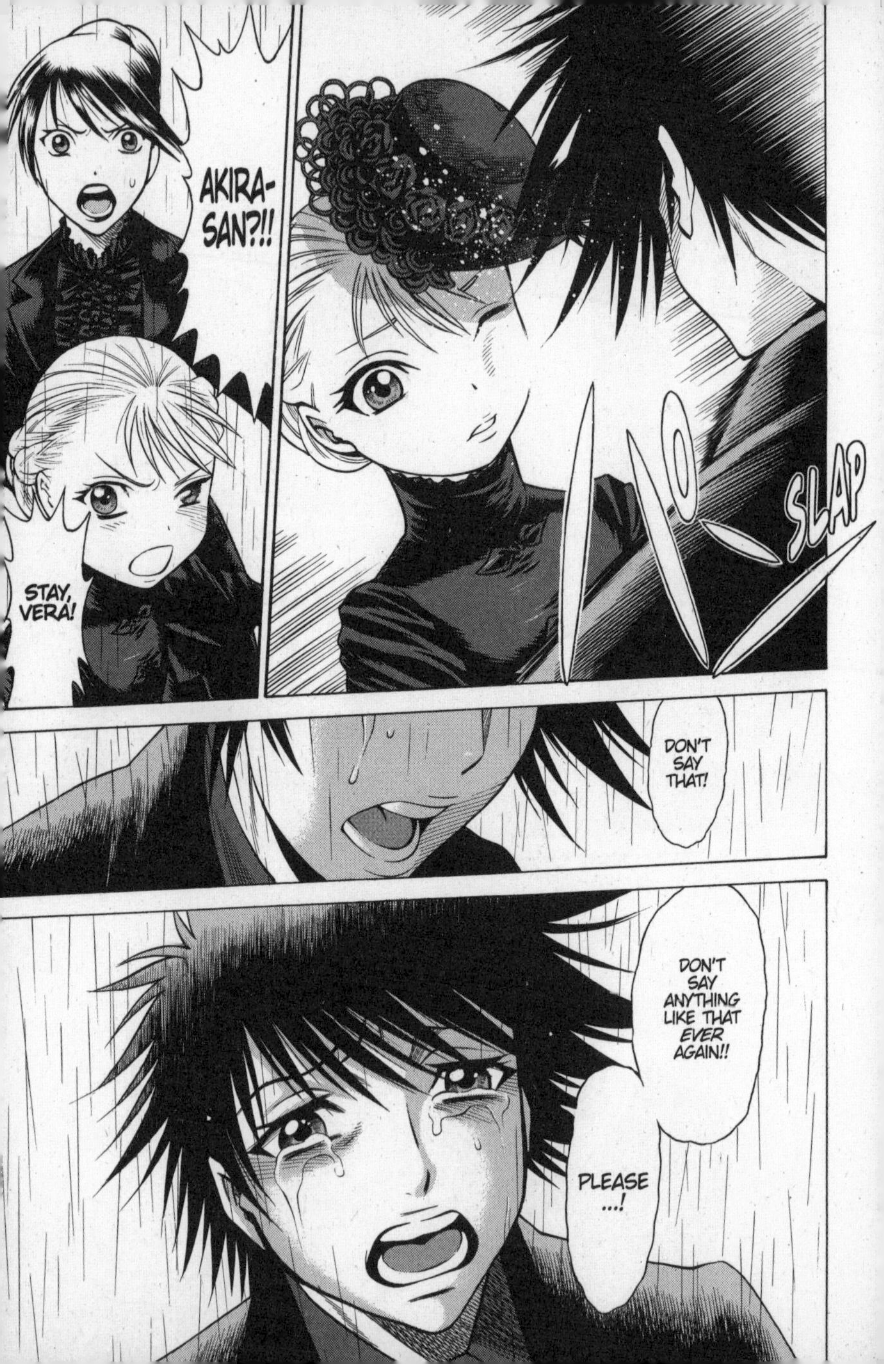
SLAP
AKIRA-SAN?!!
STAY, VERA!
DON'T SAY THAT!
DON'T SAY ANYTHING LIKE THAT EVER AGAIN!!
PLEASE ...!

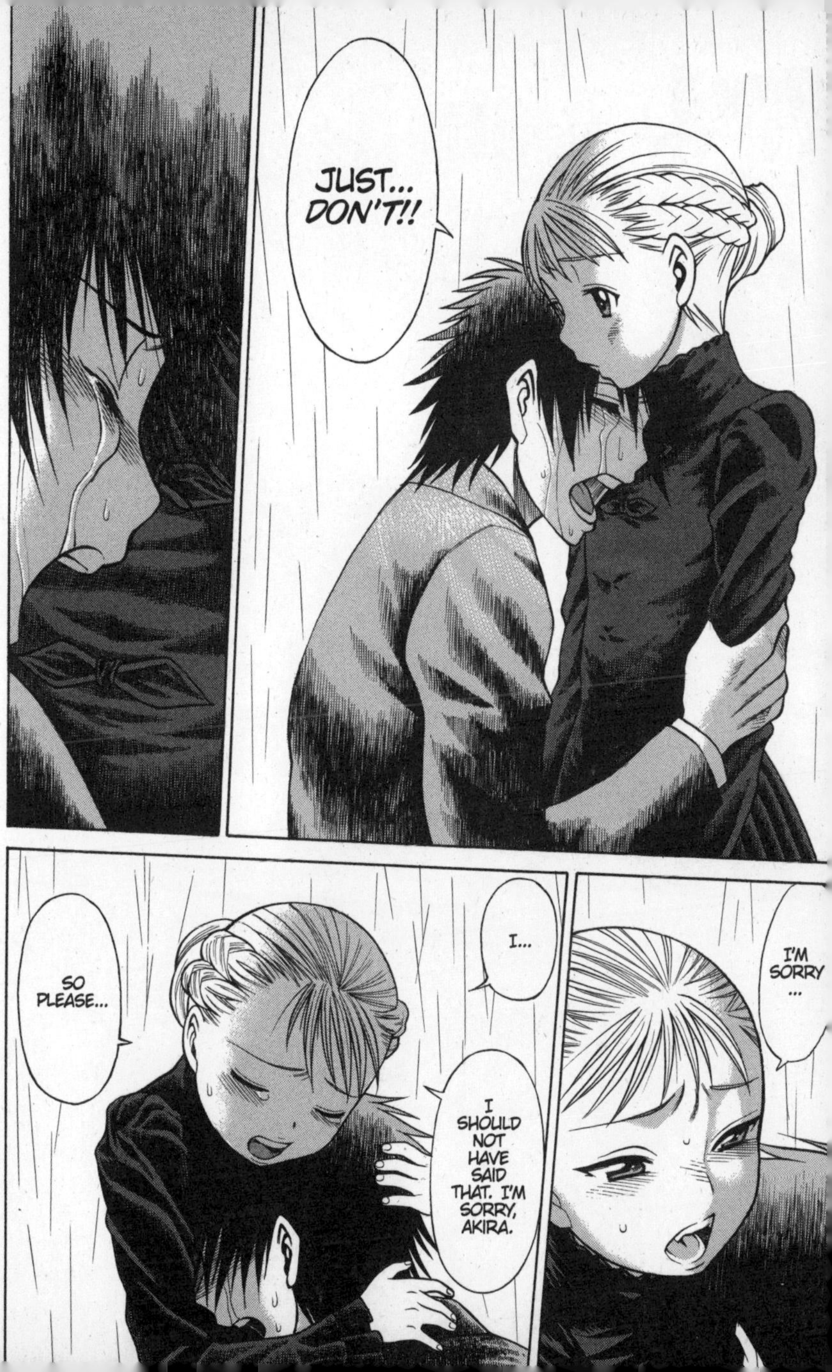
JUST... DON'T!!
I'M SORRY ...
I...
I SHOULD NOT HAVE SAID THAT. I'M SORRY, AKIRA.
SO PLEASE...

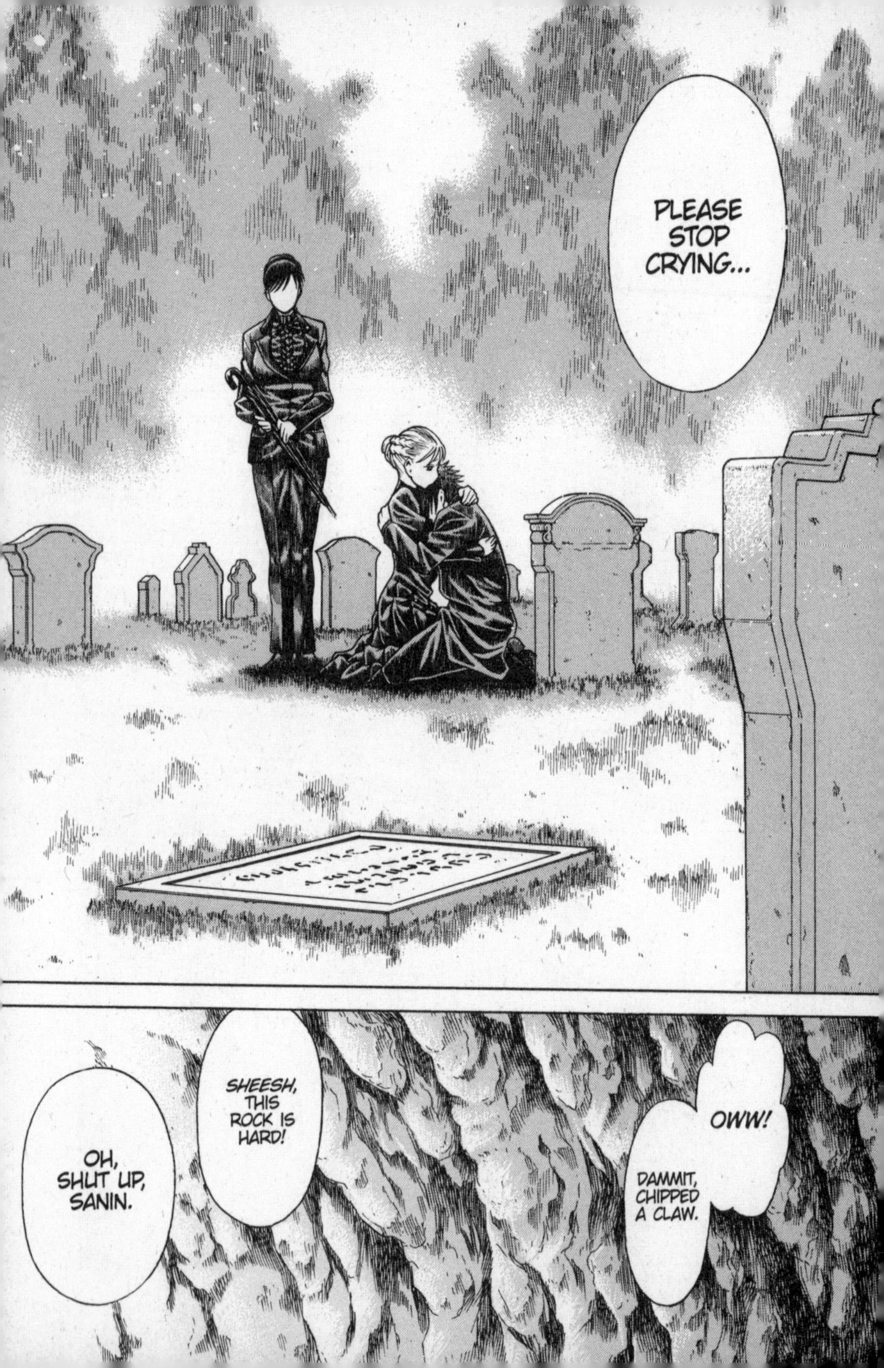
PLEASE STOP CRYING...
OWW!
DAMMIT, CHIPPED A CLAW.
SHEESH, THIS ROCK IS HARD!
OH, SHUT UP, SANIN.

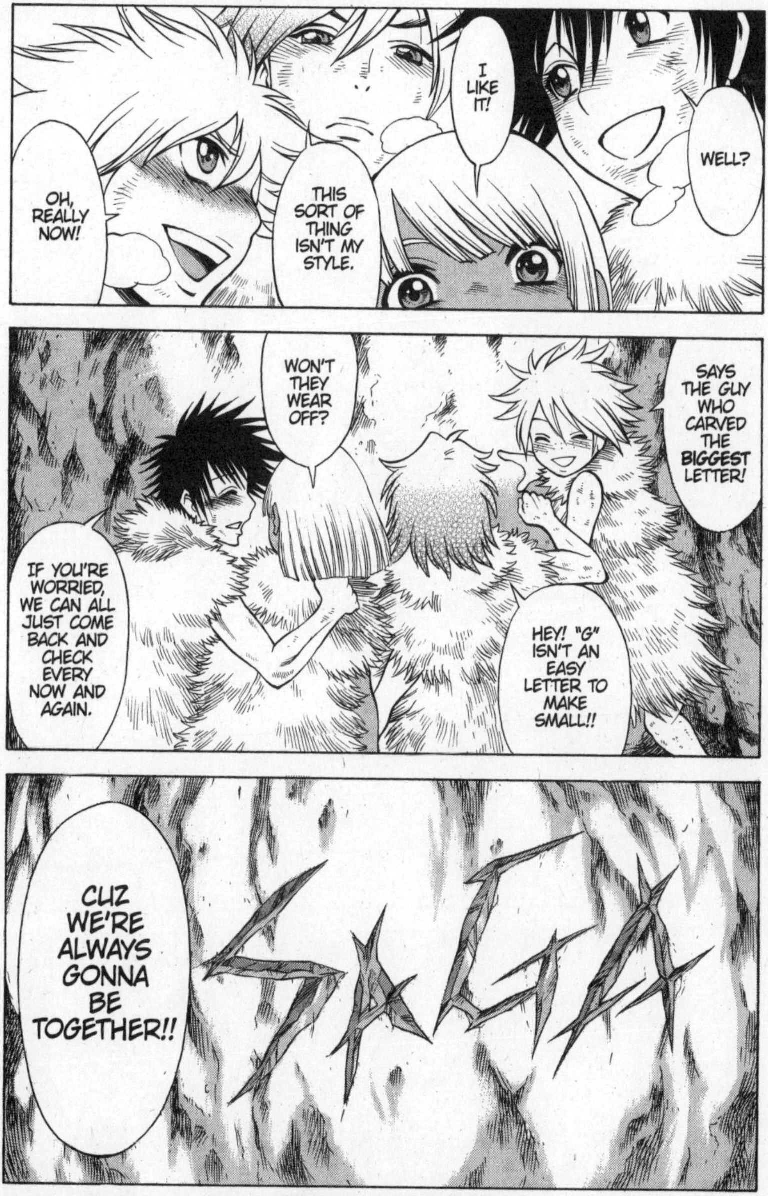
WELL?
I LIKE IT!
THIS SORT OF THING ISN'T MY STYLE.
OH, REALLY NOW!
SAYS THE GUY WHO CARVED THE BIGGEST LETTER!
HEY! "G" ISN'T AN EASY LETTER TO MAKE SMALL!!
WON'T THEY WEAR OFF?
IF YOU'RE WORRIED, WE CAN ALL JUST COME BACK AND CHECK EVERY NOW AND AGAIN.
CUZ WE'RE ALWAYS GONNA BE TOGETHER!!

TO BE CONTINUED

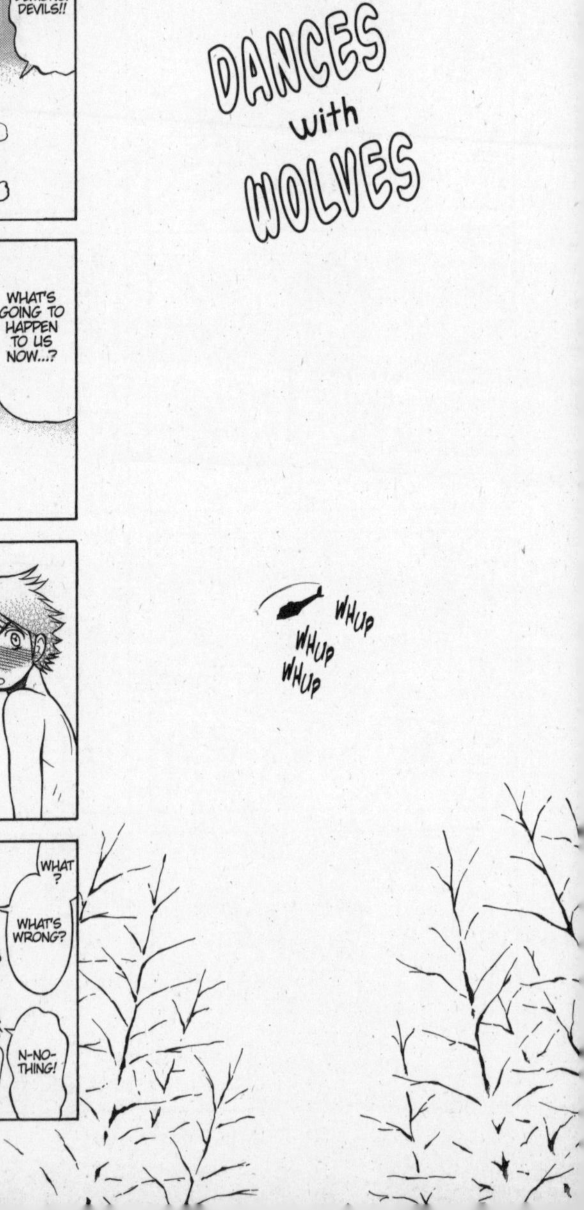
DANCES with WOLVES
WHUP
WHUP
WHUP

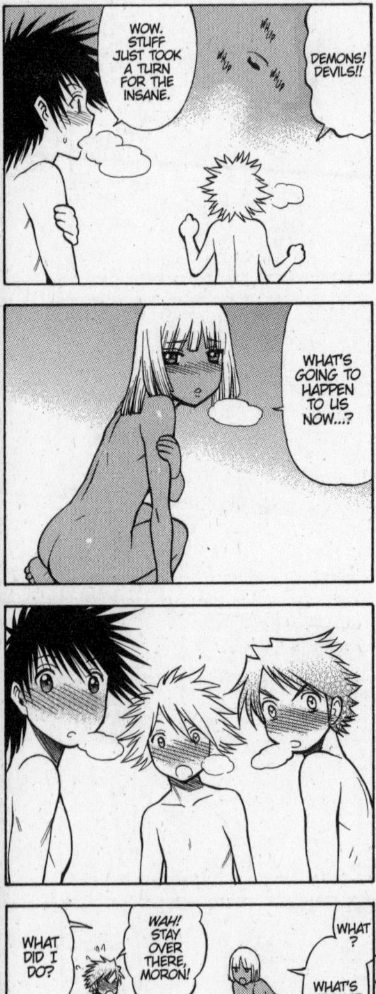
DEMONS! DEVILS!!
WHUP
WHUP
WHUP
WOW. STUFF JUST TOOK A TURN FOR THE INSANE.
WHAT'S GOING TO HAPPEN TO US NOW...?
WHAT? WHAT'S WRONG?
WAH! STAY OVER THERE, MORON!
WHAT DID I DO?
N-NO-THING!
HUH?
3.1415926535 8979323846...

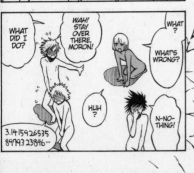

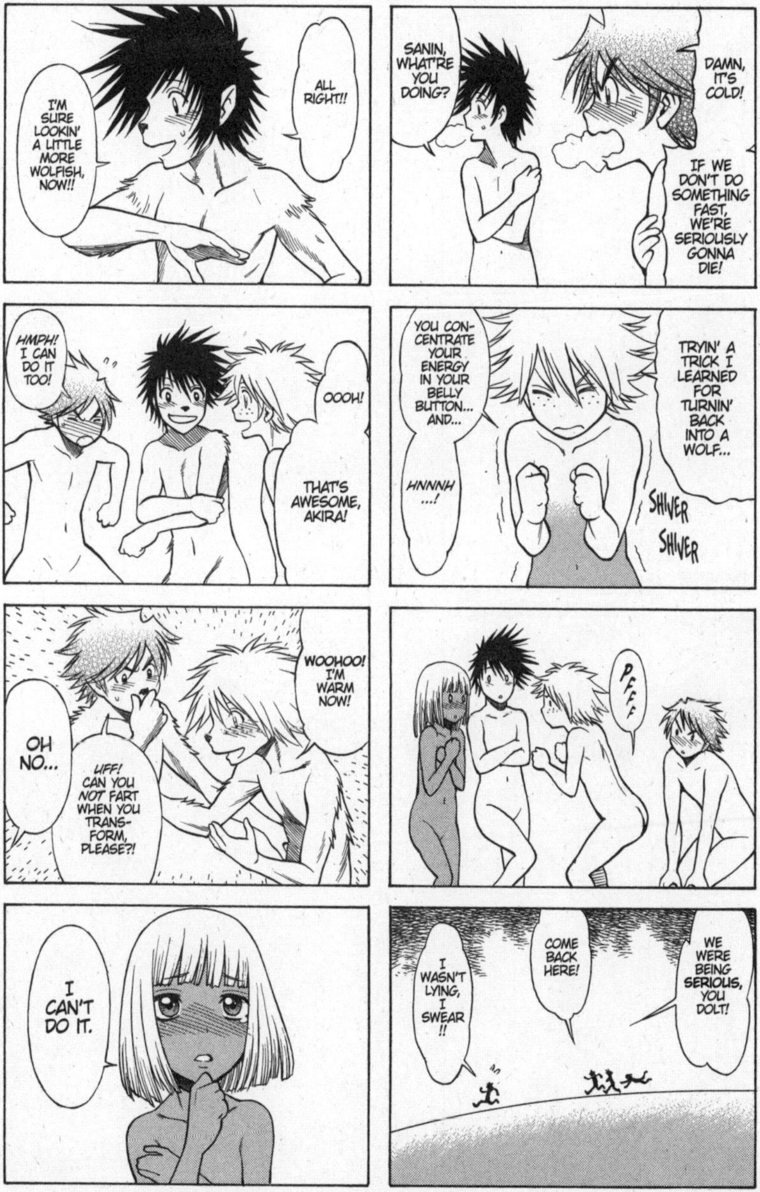
DAMN, IT'S COLD!
IF WE DON'T DO SOMETHING FAST, WE'RE SERIOUSLY GONNA DIE!
SANIN, WHAT'RE YOU DOING?
ALL RIGHT!!
I'M SURE LOOKIN' A LITTLE MORE WOLFISH, NOW!!
TRYIN' A TRICK I LEARNED FOR TURNIN' BACK INTO A WOLF...
YOU CON-CENTRATE YOUR ENERGY IN YOUR BELLY BUTTON... AND...
HNNNH ...!
SHIVER SHIVER
OOOH!
THAT'S AWESOME, AKIRA!
HMPH! I CAN DO IT TOO!
PFFF
WOOHOO! I'M WARM NOW!
UFF! CAN YOU NOT FART WHEN YOU TRANS-FORM, PLEASE?!
OH NO...
WE WERE BEING SERIOUS, YOU DOLT!
COME BACK HERE!
I WASN'T LYING, I SWEAR !!
I CAN'T DO IT.

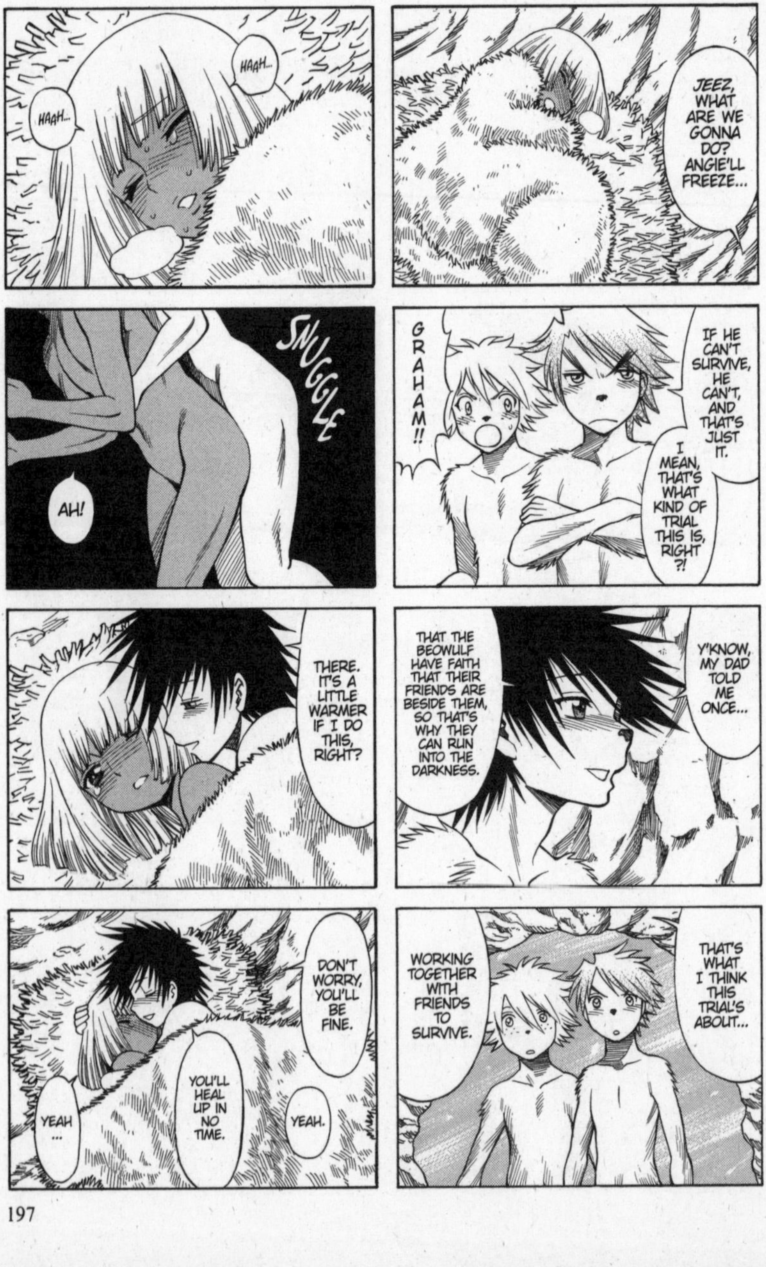
JEEZ, WHAT ARE WE GONNA DO? ANGIE'LL FREEZE...
HAAH...
HAAH...
IF HE CAN'T SURVIVE, HE CAN'T, AND THAT'S JUST IT.
I MEAN, THAT'S WHAT KIND OF TRIAL THIS IS, RIGHT?!
GRAHAM!!
SNUGGLE
AH!
Y'KNOW, MY DAD TOLD ME ONCE...
THAT THE BEOWULF HAVE FAITH THAT THEIR FRIENDS ARE BESIDE THEM, SO THAT'S WHY THEY CAN RUN INTO THE DARKNESS.
THERE. IT'S A LITTLE WARMER IF I DO THIS, RIGHT?
THAT'S WHAT I THINK THIS TRIAL'S ABOUT...
WORKING TOGETHER WITH FRIENDS TO SURVIVE.
DON'T WORRY, YOU'LL BE FINE.
YEAH.
YOU'LL HEAL UP IN NO TIME.
YEAH ...

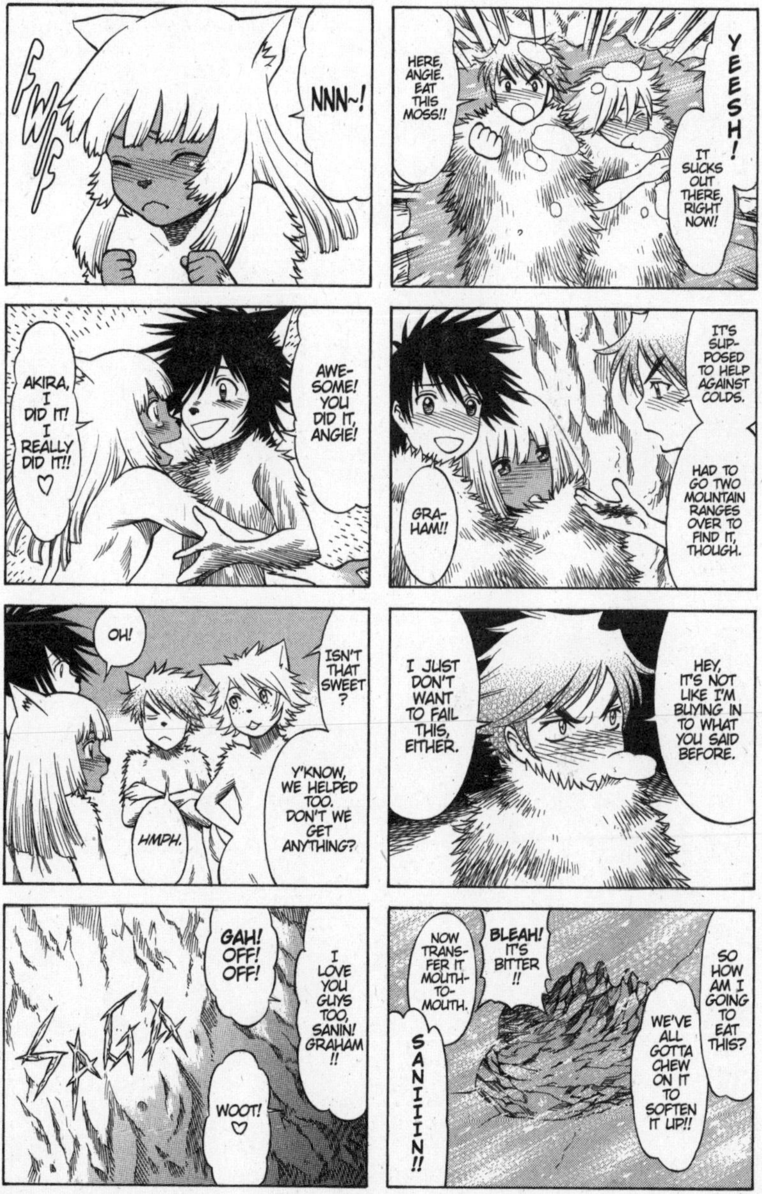
YEESH!
IT SUCKS OUT THERE, RIGHT NOW!
HERE, ANGIE. EAT THIS MOSS!!
NNN~!
FWIP
IT'S SUP-POSED TO HELP AGAINST COLDS.
HAD TO GO TWO MOUNTAIN RANGES OVER TO FIND IT, THOUGH.
GRA-HAM!!
AWE-SOME! YOU DID IT, ANGIE!
AKIRA, I DID IT! I REALLY DID IT!! ♡
HEY, IT'S NOT LIKE I'M BUYING IN TO WHAT YOU SAID BEFORE.
I JUST DON'T WANT TO FAIL THIS, EITHER.
ISN'T THAT SWEET?
OH!
Y'KNOW, WE HELPED TOO. DON'T WE GET ANYTHING?
HMPH.
SO HOW AM I GOING TO EAT THIS?
BLEAH! IT'S BITTER!!
NOW TRANS-FER IT MOUTH-TO-MOUTH.
WE'VE ALL GOTTA CHEW ON IT TO SOFTEN IT UP!!
SANIIIN!!
I LOVE YOU GUYS TOO, SANIN! GRAHAM!!
GAH! OFF! OFF!
WOOT! ♡

Dance in the Vampire Bund

NEXT VOLUME PREVIEW

THE PAST ONCE AGAIN REARS ITS UGLY HEAD... AND A NEW VISITOR APPEARS.

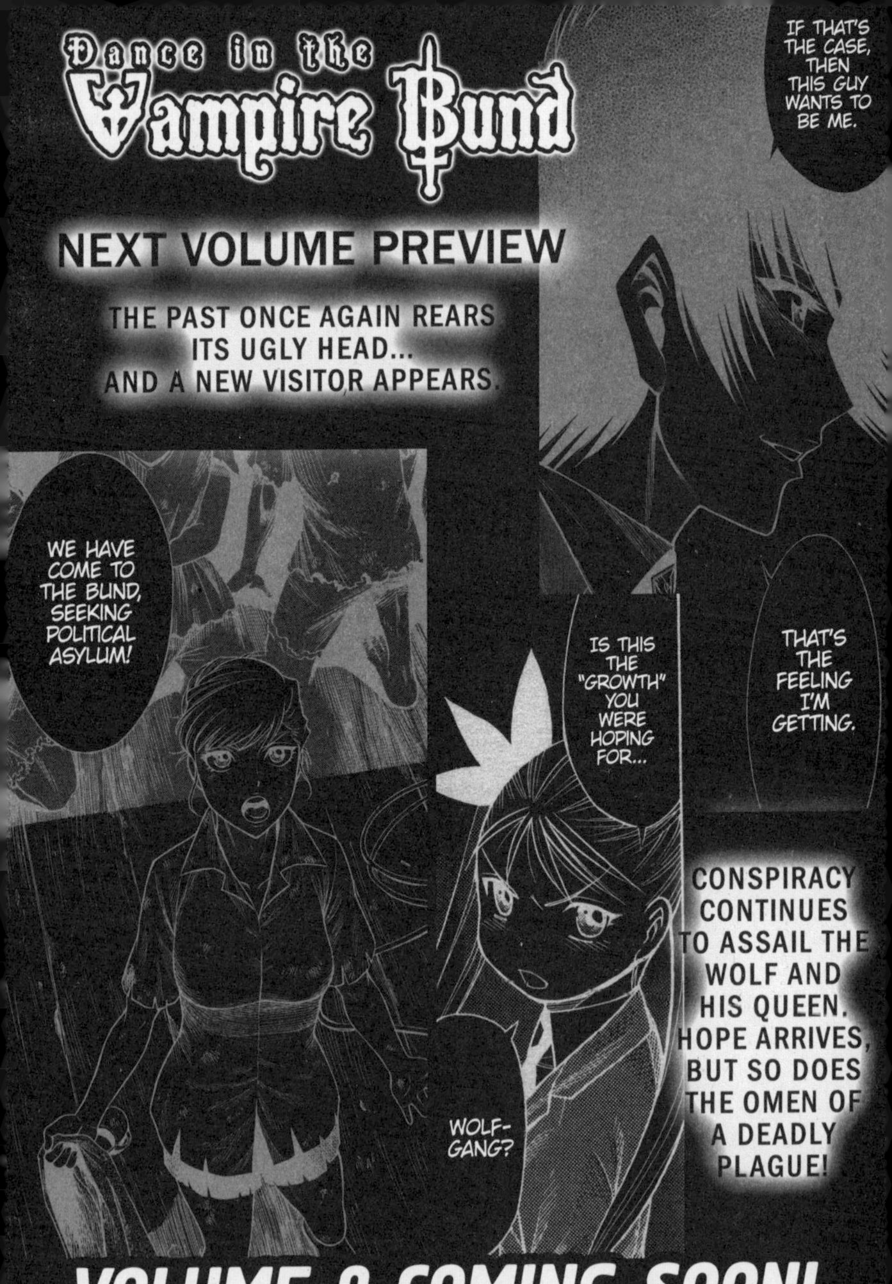
IF THAT'S THE CASE, THEN THIS GUY WANTS TO BE ME.
THAT'S THE FEELING I'M GETTING.
IS THIS THE "GROWTH" YOU WERE HOPING FOR...
WOLF-GANG?
WE HAVE COME TO THE BUND, SEEKING POLITICAL ASYLUM!

CONSPIRACY CONTINUES TO ASSAIL THE WOLF AND HIS QUEEN. HOPE ARRIVES, BUT SO DOES THE OMEN OF A DEADLY PLAGUE!

VOLUME 8 COMING SOON!

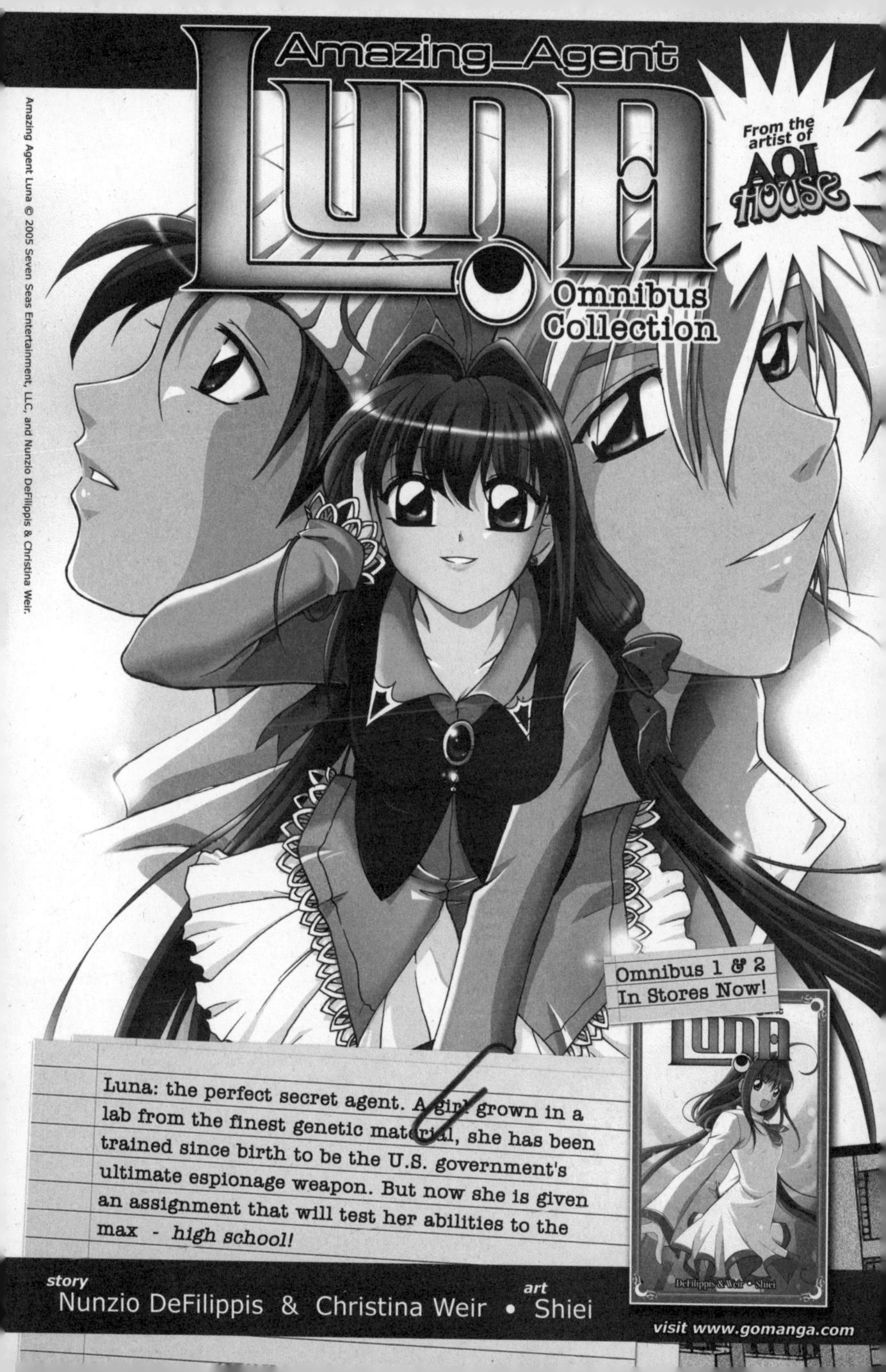
Amazing Agent
LUNA
From the artist of
AOI HOUSE
Omnibus Collection
Omnibus 1 & 2
In Stores Now!
Luna: the perfect secret agent. A girl grown in a lab from the finest genetic material, she has been trained since birth to be the U.S. government's ultimate espionage weapon. But now she is given an assignment that will test her abilities to the max - high school!
story
Nunzio DeFilippis & Christina Weir
art
Shiei
DeFilippis & Weir • Shiei
visit www.gomanga.com
Amazing Agent Luna © 2005 Seven Seas Entertainment, LLC, and Nunzio DeFilippis & Christina Weir.

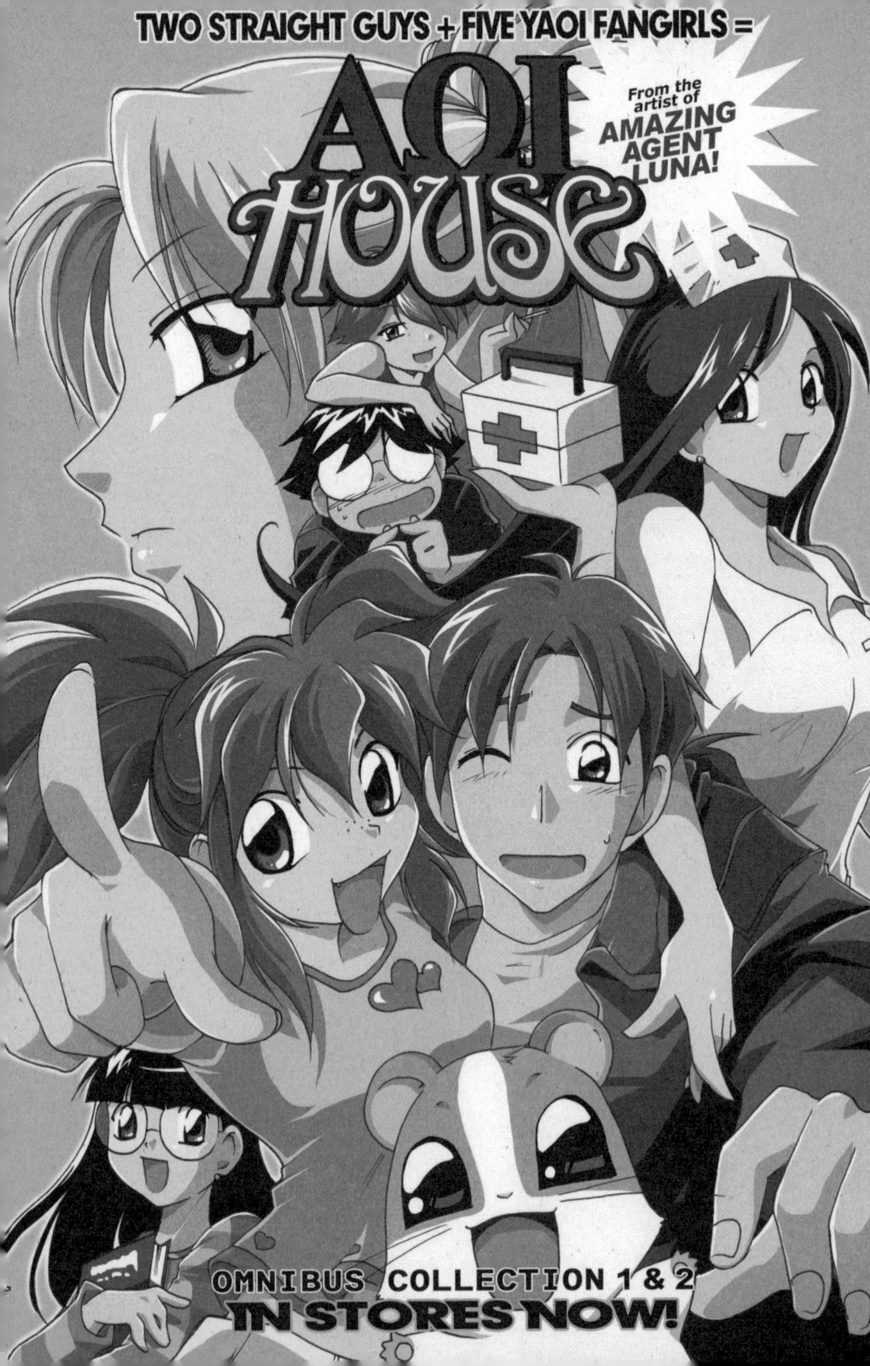
TWO STRAIGHT GUYS + FIVE YAOI FANGIRLS =
AOI HOUSE
From the artist of AMAZING AGENT LUNA!
OMNIBUS COLLECTION 1 & 2
IN STORES NOW!

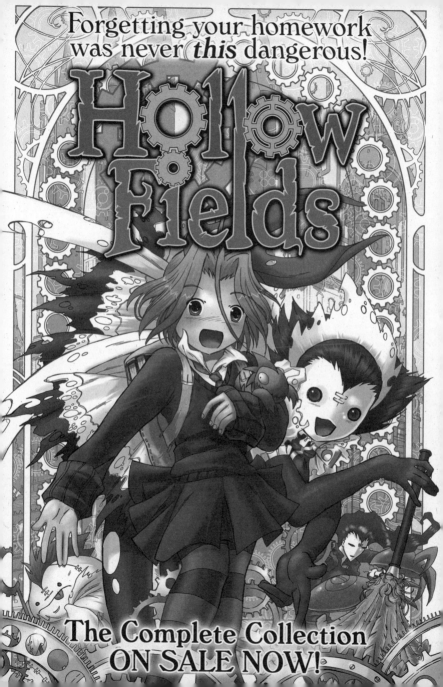

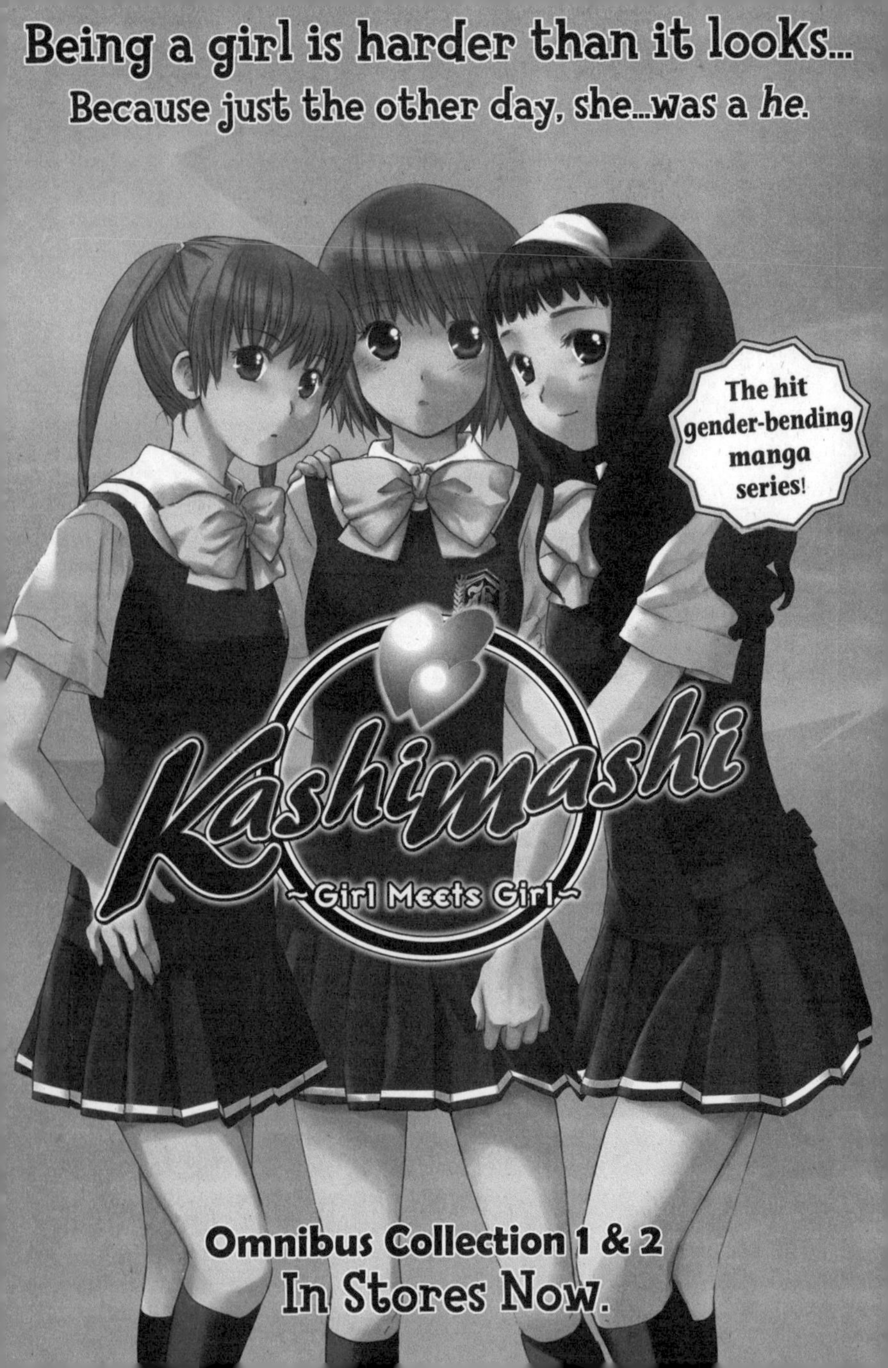
Being a girl is harder than it looks...
Because just the other day, she...was a *he*.
The hit gender-bending manga series!
Kashimashi
~Girl Meets Girl~
Omnibus Collection 1 & 2
In Stores Now.

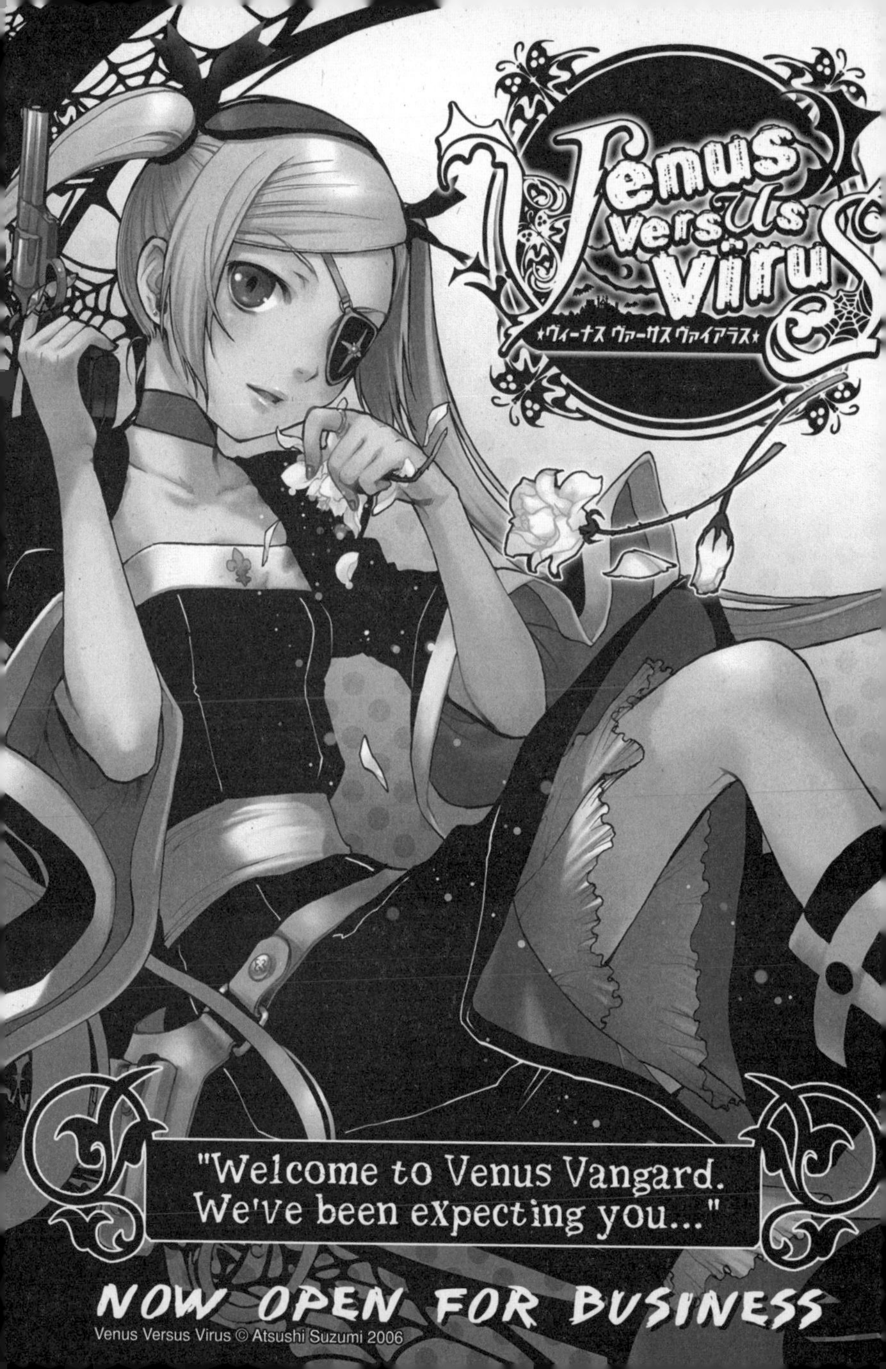
Venus versus Virus
★ヴィーナスヴァーサスヴァイアラス★
"Welcome to Venus Vangard.
We've been expecting you..."
NOW OPEN FOR BUSINESS
Venus Versus Virus © Atsushi Suzumi 2006

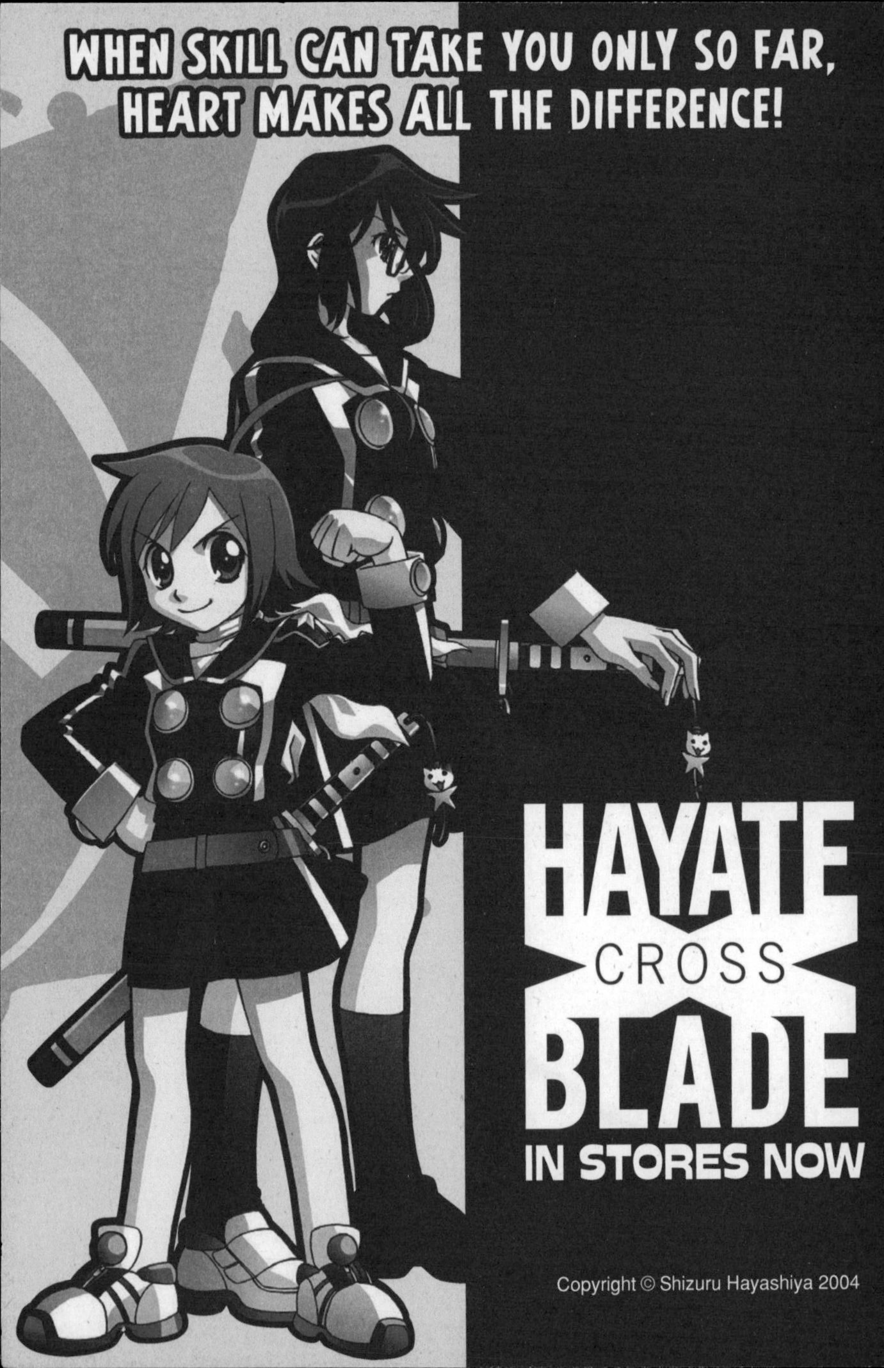

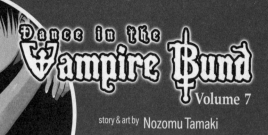

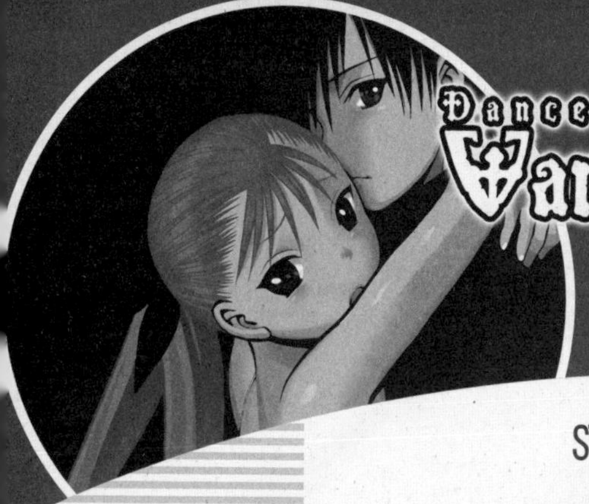

Dance in the Vampire Bund

Volume 7

story & art by Nozomu Tamaki

STAFF CREDITS

translation	Adrienne Beck
adaptation	Janet Houck
retouch & lettering	Roland Amago
cover design	Nicky Lim
layout	Bambi Eloriaga-Amago
copy editor	Shanti Whitesides
editor	Adam Arnold

publisher **Seven Seas Entertainment**

DANCE IN THE VAMPIRE BUND VOL. 7
© 2009 Nozomu Tamaki
First published in Japan in 2009 by MEDIA FACTORY, Inc.
English translation rights reserved by Seven Seas Entertainment, LLC.
Under the license from MEDIA FACTORY, Inc., Tokyo.

Visit us online at www.gomanga.com

ISBN: 978-1-934876-80-0

Printed in Canada

Second Printing: August 2010

10 9 8 7 6 5 4 3 2

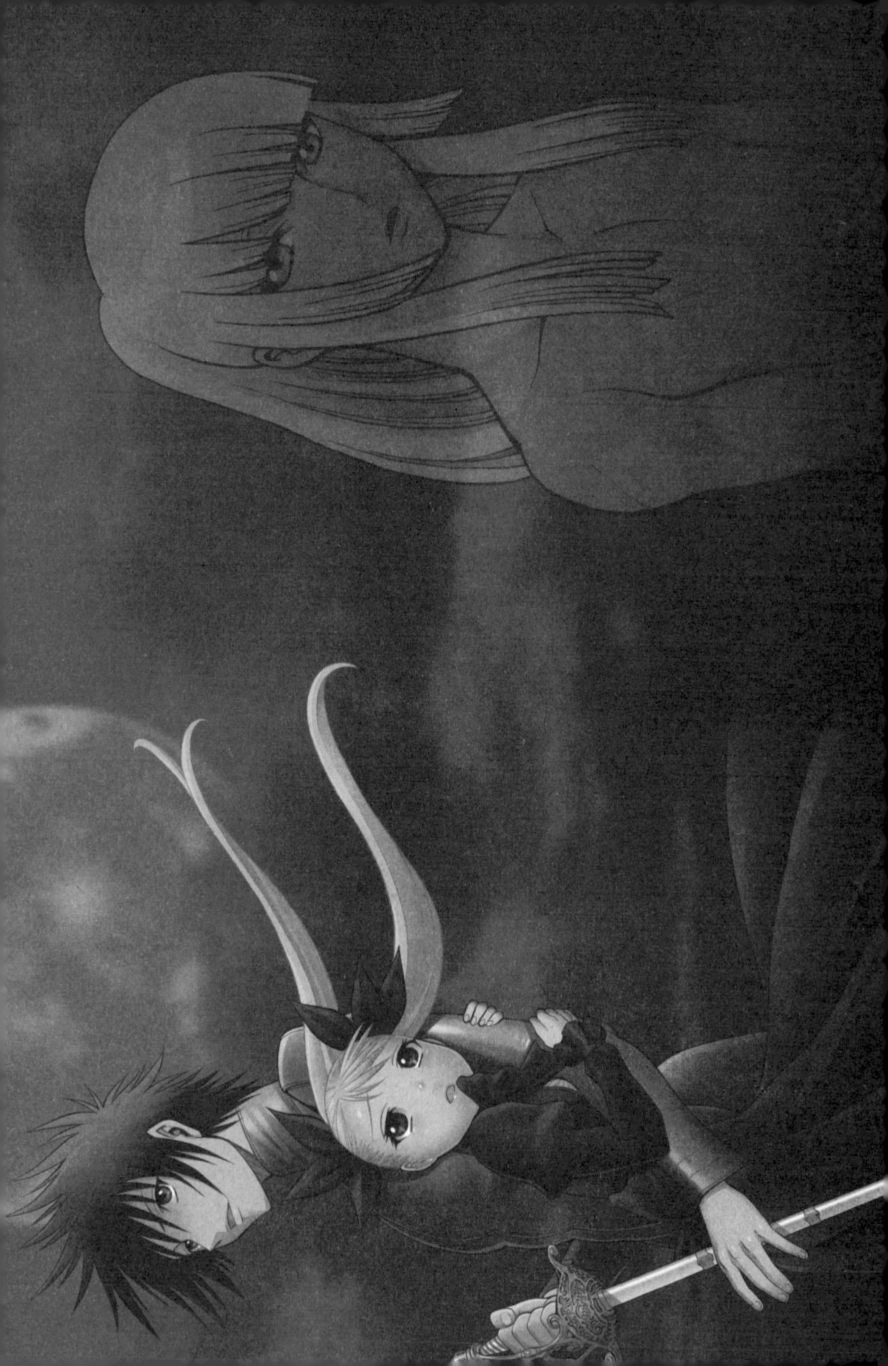

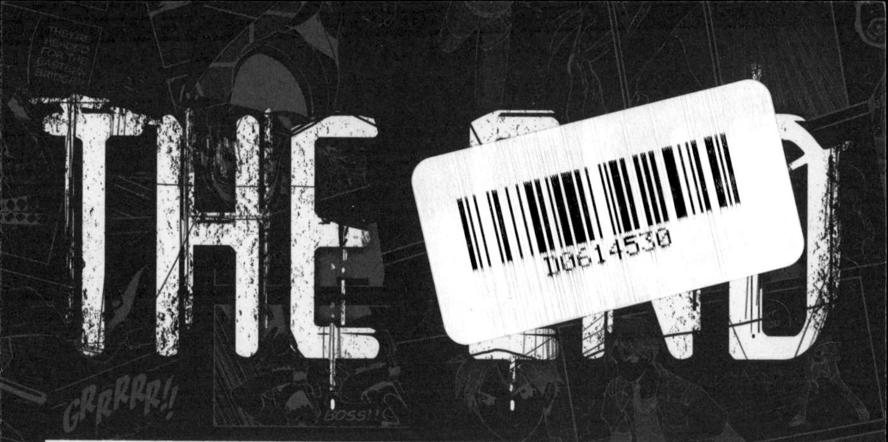
GRRRRR!!
BOSS!!

YOU'RE READING THE WRONG WAY

This is the last page of
Dance in the Vampire Bund
Volume 7

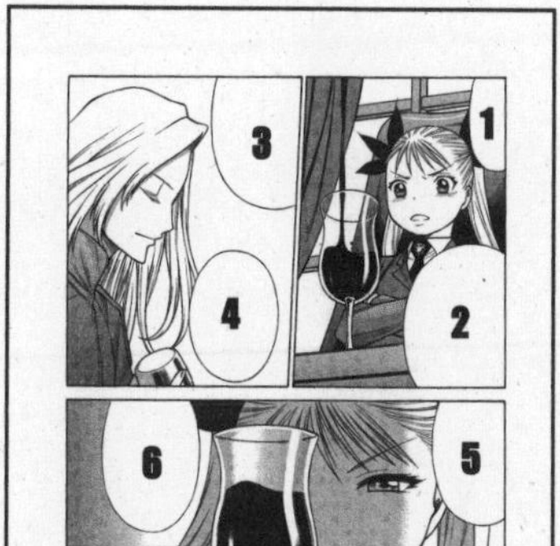
1
2
3
4
5
6
7
8
9
10

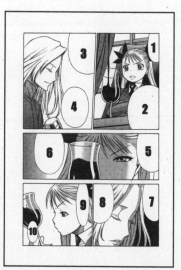

This book reads from right to left, Japanese style. To read from the beginning, flip the book over to the other side, start with the top right panel, and take it from there.

If this is your first time reading manga, just follow the diagram. It may seem backwards at first, but you'll get used to it! Have fun!